The Canton Trade

Dedicated to all Chinese who have no records or memories of their ancestors who lived, worked and died in the Pearl River Delta.

The Canton Trade

Life and Enterprise on the China Coast, 1700–1845

PAUL A. VAN DYKE

Published in conjunction with

澳門特別行政區政府文化局
INSTITUTO CULTURAL do Governo da R.A.E. de Macau

香港大學出版社
HONG KONG UNIVERSITY PRESS

Hong Kong University Press
14/F Hing Wai Centre
7 Tin Wan Praya Road
Aberdeen
Hong Kong

Hardback edition first published 2005
Paperback edition first published 2007

ISBN 978-962-209-828-2

Hong Kong University Press gratefully acknowledges the grant from the Cultural Affairs Bureau of the Macao Special Administrative Region Government which made possible the sections of colour plates.

Secure On-line Ordering
http://www.hkupress.org

British Library Cataloguing-in-Publication Data
A catalogue record for this book is available from the British Library.

Printed and bound by United League Graphic and Company Ltd., in Hong Kong, China

CONTENTS

TABLES

ABBREVIATIONS

AHU	Arquivo Histórico Ultramarino, Portugal
BC	Bancroft Library, University of California, Berkeley
BL	Baker Library, Harvard University
BML	British Map Library, in the British Library, London
BW	G.W. Blunt White Library, Mystic Seaport, Connecticut
CFI	French East India Company
CMD 1762	Van Dyke, Paul A. and Cynthia Viallé, *The Canton-Macao Dagregisters*, 1762 Macao: Cultural Institute, 2006.
CMD 1763	Van Dyke, Paul A. and Cynthia Viallé, *The Canton-Macao Dagregisters*, 1763 Macao: Cultural Institute, forthcoming.
DAC	Danish Asiatic Company
DOOZA	Department of Western Manuscripts, Leiden University Library
EIC	English East India Company
GIC	Ostend General India Company, Belgium
GUB	Gothenburg Universitetsbibliotek (University Library)
HL	Houghton Library, Harvard University
JCB	John Carter Brown Library, Brown University, Providence
JFB	James Ford Bell Library, University of Minnesota
KBC	Kungelige Bibliotek (Royal Library), Copenhagen
KBS	Kungliga Biblioteket (Royal Library), Stockholm
KITLV	Royal Institute for Linguistics and Anthropology, Leiden University
KSB	Stadsbibliotek (City Library), Kalmar
KVB	Kungliga Vetenskaps-akedemiens Bibliotek (Library of the Royal Academy of Sciences), Stockholm

LAG	Landsarkivet (Provincial Archive), Gothenburg
MHS	Massachusetts Historical Society, Boston
MMR	Maritime Museum, Rotterdam
NAH	National Archives, The Hague
NM	Nordic Museum Archive, Stockholm (Godegårdsarkivet F17)
OIO	Oriental and India Office Library, London (now in the British Library)
PEM	Peabody Essex Museum, Salem
PL	Phillips Library, Peabody Essex Museum, Salem
PMA	Plantin-Maretus Museum, Antwerp
RAC	Rigsarkivet (National Archives), Copenhagen
RAS	Riksarkivet (National Archives), Stockholm
RIHS	Rhode Island Historical Society, Providence
SAA	Stadsarchief (City Archive), Antwerp
SFG	Sjöfartsmuseet (Maritime Museum), Gothenburg
SHM	Sjöhistoriska Museet (Sea History Museum), Gothenburg
SMG	Stadsmuseet (City Museum), Gothenburg
SOIC	Swedish East India Company
UBG	Universiteits Bibliotheek (University Library), Ghent, Belgium
UBL	Universiteitsbibliotek (University Library), Lund
UPL	University of Pennsylvania Library, Philadelphia
UUB	Uppsala Universitetsbibliotek (University Library), Sweden
VOC	Dutch East India Company

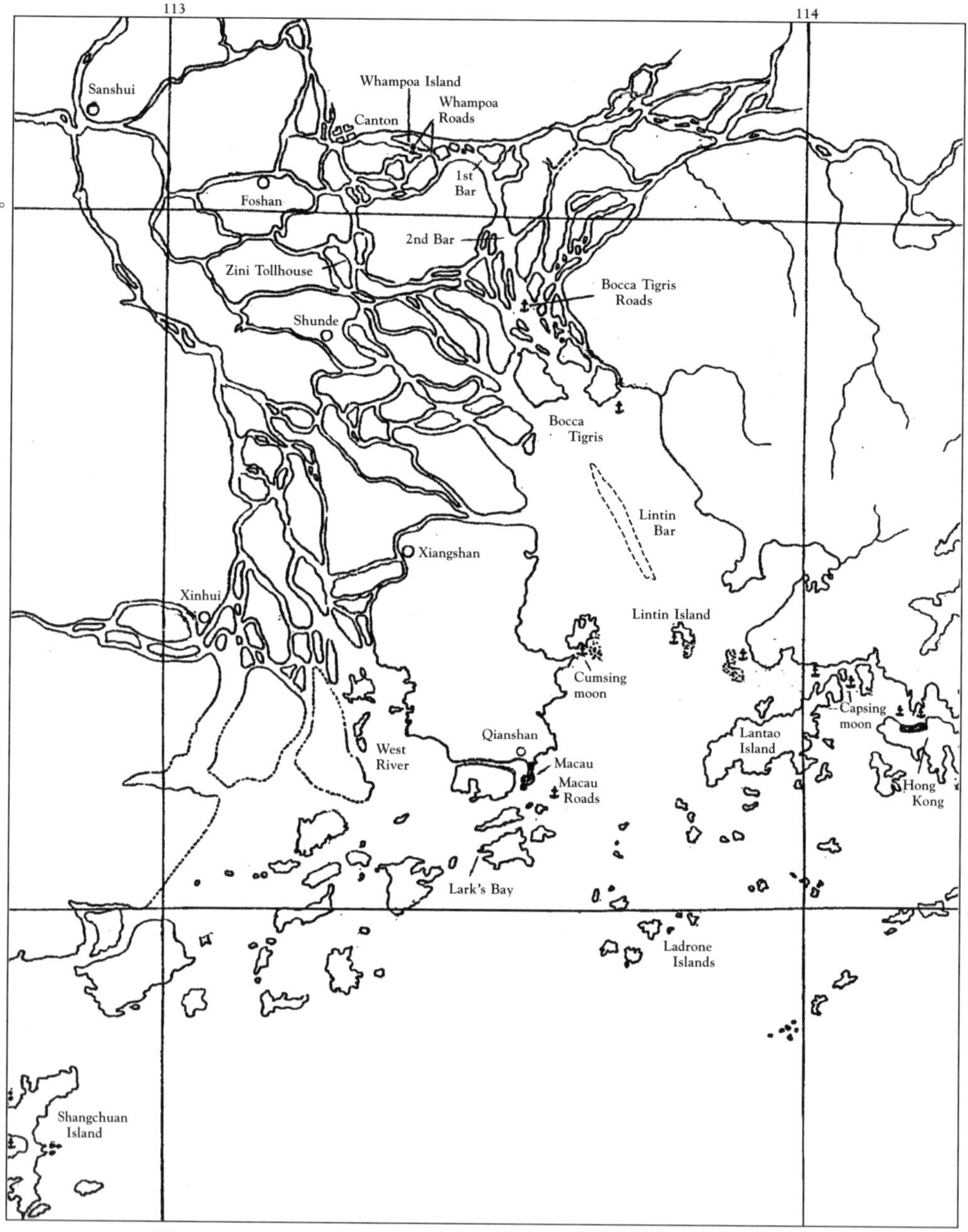

The Pearl River Delta

PREFACE

ONE OF THE GREAT DELIGHTS of studying the 'China Trade' is the enormous body of literature available to the researcher. Hundreds of foreign ships sailed to China from 1690 to 1845, and most of the captains and merchants aboard those vessels kept records, journals and logs, not only of their voyages but also of their dealings with the Chinese. Many of these records have survived and are available in archives throughout Europe and the United States.

The foreign companies trading in China also produced letters, reports, requests, expense and account books, sales catalogues and numerous other documents that provide much detail about the trade. Researchers are doubly fortunate that many official Chinese documents concerning the administration of Macao and the trade at Canton are now available in print. This rich collection of primary sources has attracted numerous scholars to the study of the China trade, which, in turn, has resulted in a huge body of secondary literature.

In the past 150 years, many books and articles have been written on aspects of the Canton trade in many languages. These histories are diverse in their areas of concern, but they can be divided into four categories: those that focus on one company or ethnic group, such as the English, Americans, or the Chinese; those that focus on one artefact or commodity, such as tea, porcelain, lacquerware, or export paintings; those that focus on the social, literary and cultural contributions of the merchants; and those that focus on one geographical area, such as Macao or Canton. Of course, some works overlap all four categories.

One of the main reasons there are numerous histories with an ethnic or artefact/commodity focus is that the enormous body of documents available requires researchers to narrow their approach. It would take decades, for example, to explore thoroughly the records from just one of the East India companies, English, Danish or Dutch. American China trade documents are equally numerous, with the added inconvenience of being scattered in libraries, archives and museums throughout the United States. French, Belgian and Swedish records are not as extensive as the others but are nonetheless important, and they too are spread out in many cities.

The enormous volume of primary sources means we in the study of the China trade are all deeply indebted to the work of scholars before us. It has taken more than 150 years for the sources to be properly researched, cited, indexed, catalogued, described, summarised, filed and compiled in libraries, museums and archives throughout the world. This enormous task was performed by an army of independent scholars, curators, archivists, librarians and amateur enthusiasts who probably had no idea they were mapping out the course so this present project could be considered. If the field had not gone through this long evolutionary process of organising the documents, this study would not have been written.

Now we turn to a summary of authors and works that pointed to the need for this book. Many studies have been written on each of the East India companies and the Americans trading with China. A number of articles and books have also been written on Chinese *Hong* merchants and Armenians, Muslims and Parsees.[1] All these secondary works focus on one group, and mention other characters only when they interact with that group.

For example, in the histories of the English East India Company, the Chinese who traded with, worked for, or serviced other foreigners are mentioned only if they interacted in some way with the English. Regardless of whether the individual authors focus on the English, Dutch, Parsees, Americans or Chinese, they discuss only those people directly connected with their subject. All other individuals involved in the trade are left out of the discourse.

This means we cannot classify any previous work as 'a history of Canton'. Just because the English contracted for tea at a specific price or in a specific way does not mean the other traders did the same. The English, French and Americans, for example, used an exchange rate of 0.72 taels per Spanish dollar, while the Dutch and the Swedes used 0.74 taels. These different exchange rates obviously affected the prices they paid, which needs to be taken into consideration when making any comparison of those transactions.

The prices the Dutch agreed to in the 1760s were also affected by the special arrangement they had with their *Hong* merchants to supply separate chop boats, while the Swedish and Danish tea contracts were affected by the preferential loans they had provided to and taken out with their Chinese merchants. Officers of each of these companies were also involved in the private smuggling of opium and other contraband, which influenced the final prices paid, the nature of the contracts signed and the amount of the tolls charged. To understand this great diversity, and to get to the bottom of the internal administrative structures within the Canton System, it was necessary to examine all aspects at the same time.

Cordier (1902) was one of the earliest scholars to write about the *Hong* merchants. He tried to match the merchants' romanised names with their Chinese names (in Chinese characters), so we could find them in both the foreign and Chinese sources. Liang Jiabin (1932) expanded the research, and his book remains a classic on the merchants and their businesses. White (1967) and Ch'en (1990) advanced the work.

Ch'en's research is especially important because it is based on extensive use of both Chinese- and English-language sources. He also refocuses the study on the family unit rather than the *hongs*, which was Liang's approach. The families were the economic and decision-making nuclei, so by focusing on them Ch'en begins to show us the complexity and interconnectedness of those households.

Cheong (1997) then continued the study, which is also based on extensive archival research, but is primarily limited to English sources. His work expands that of Ch'en, bringing out many previously unknown aspects of individual families, such as their relationships with the *hongs* through inter-marriage. However, because Cheong did not consult Ch'en's work, there is much retracing of old ground.

Huang and Pang (2001) expanded this focus on the family unit by going beyond the era of the Canton trade. They utilised Chinese sources more extensively to bring out other aspects of the merchants' lives apart from trade. This broadening of the outlook in both time and space has become a trend with a number of new collections of articles being published and new studies being conducted that focus on the social and cultural aspects of the Canton merchants.[2]

All these studies helped to expand our understanding of and broaden our outlook on the merchant families. As far as trade in the Canton era is concerned, however, there was still much more to be done. The *hong* houses were usually involved with many different foreign companies and traders at the same time, as well as with the junk trade to Southeast Asia. Much of that information is available only in other languages.

Other authors have focussed on export commodities, such as tea, porcelain, silk and paintings. These histories not only tell us the stories of the thousands of Chinese artefacts now found in museums throughout the world, but they also give us a glimpse of the economies of each of those products and the structure of their trade.[3] Some of these works developed out of extensive archival research; others are mere summaries of the China trade combined with descriptions of the items and artefacts on display in various exhibitions; and some are a mixture of both.

The extensive work undertaken on the tea trade (see, in particular, Gardella, 1994) has developed this field to a high degree but, again, there is still much more that can be done. In the Belgian, Dutch, Danish, Swedish and American archives there are extensive and detailed documents not yet used. Those archives contain more than 100 tea contracts written in both Chinese and western languages; detailed reports of the tea handled and amounts each merchant traded; and exact accounts of each merchant's dealings so that one can trace precisely when the tea was ordered as well as when it was packed, delivered and paid for.

Authors of the opium trade have generally focused on the reasons for the collapse of the Canton System in 1842, and the rise of the unequal treaties and Treaty Ports.[4] For this part of the history, English and Chinese records are probably the best sources available. For the earlier years of the opium trade, however — from 1750 to 1820 — significant data in the Dutch, Danish, Portuguese and Swedish archives had not been used so more work was needed here as well.

Louis Dermigny was among the first scholars to attempt a more generic geographical approach to the history. His *Le Commerce à Canton* (1964) was the result of decades of research in English and French archives, but he relied heavily on Morse's *Chronicles of the East India Company* (1926). With this focus on the port, Dermigny gives us a first glimpse of the enormous expansion of the trade from 1700 to the 1830s. While many of Dermigny's numbers are simple estimates he constructed himself and were not taken directly from the records, they nonetheless give us a rough idea of the large number of ships and huge volumes of items involved. It is primarily owing to Dermigny's extensive compilation of data that historians could begin to show Canton's huge influence in the early modern world.

Dilip Basu (1975) continued this focus on the port in his comparison of Canton and Calcutta for the years 1800 to 1840. In addition to the British records, which Morse and Dermigny had already explored extensively, Basu also used American and Chinese sources, which helped to broaden the work. Although focussed primarily on Macao, George Bryan Souza expanded the use of sources and the discussion with his monumental work on the Portuguese trade in Asia (1986). From Souza's research, we could begin to see that Macao was an intricate part of the Canton trade that needed to be included in any discussion of the port. Do Vale (1997) and Guimarães (2000) have continued the discussion of Macao's trade to cover most of the Canton era.

Chen Bojian and Huang Qichen (1995) then put together a three-volume history of the trade, which begins in ancient times and continues to the 1990s. While this work depends heavily on Chinese sources and secondary English-language literature such as that of Morse, it is a thorough survey of those sources.

Because the Chinese records lack the detail necessary to recreate the daily activities in Canton, Chen and Huang could provide only a broad survey of the history.

Together, all these works pointed clearly to the need for a multi-archival research so an overall picture of the daily activities of the port could emerge. The many people involved in, and all aspects of, the trade needed to be analysed at the same time so that the complexity of the port's internal mechanisms and structures could come into full view. The long process of making the documents in the many archives and institutions more accessible to researchers ran parallel to the writing of these many histories and the consequential maturing of the field. But the traditional means of collecting information physically was still too slow and clumsy to accommodate a study like this.

With the mid-1990s arrival of notebook computers that could be carried into the archives, and accompanying software that could handle, organise and make all data instantly available, the researcher was finally equipped to take on a project of this magnitude. As for a road map of where to begin and what information to include, I am deeply indebted to one book, Arthur Pierce Middleton's *Tobacco Coast* (1953), which, ironically, has nothing to do with China.

ACKNOWLEDGEMENTS

I AM VERY GRATEFUL AND much indebted to countless individuals who guided me through the many collections: Jack Wills, Ed Perkins and Harrison Cheng for their endless advice and support; the late Mr Oyevaar and Mr Plantinga at the National Archives in The Hague; Jack Parker, Carol Urness and others at the James Ford Bell Library; fellow researchers and veterans of the Dutch archives, Cynthia Viallé and Natalie Everts; Leonard Blussé, Femme Gaastra and the staff at the Centre for the History of European Expansion; Erik Gøbel at the Rigsarkivet in Copenhagen; Anders Larson, Ulf Andersson and Kristina Söderpalm in Gothenburg; Chang Pin-tsun and Ch'en Kuo-tung at Academia Sinica in Taiwan; Eddy Stols and Bart de Prins at Leuven University in Belgium; and Carl Feddersen in Kristiansand, Norway, for his endless encouragement and hospitality between research trips. There are many others, too numerous to mention here, in Leiden, Rotterdam, Amsterdam, Antwerp, Ghent, Brussels, London, Stockholm, Uppsala, Lund, Bergen, Oslo, Beijing, Macao, Hong Kong, Taipei, Boston, Salem, Providence, Mystic Seaport, Canberra and other places whom I must thank in general for their kind assistance.

Without the unwavering support of family, this project would have derailed early in the process. They endured much for its sake, for which I shall never be able to repay them. My only hope is that the final product is worthy of the many sacrifices they endured on my behalf.

Finally, I am very grateful to the following societies, agencies and institutions for their generous support in funding this project: Institute for International Education Dissertation Fellowship (Fulbright 1996–97); Chiang Ching-kuo Foundation Dissertation Fellowship (1996–97); American Scandinavian

Foundation Dissertation Fellowship (Los Angeles Chapter: Summer 1997, and New York Headquarters: 1998–99); McVicar Foundation of the University of Southern California (1996–97 and 1999); National Resource Dissertation Fellowship (1998–99); Massachusetts Historical Society Research Fellowship (Summer 1999); Peabody Essex Museum Research Fellowship (Summer 1999), Australian National University Visiting Fellowship (2005), and Macao Cultural Institute.

There are several institutions in Macao that have been instrumental in advancing this study. Special thanks to friends and colleagues at the Macao Sino-Latin Foundation, University of Macao, Macao Historical Archives, Macao Cultural Institute and Macao Inter-University Institute for their support.

INTRODUCTION

CHINA OPENS ITS DOORS TO THE WORLD

THE GREAT CANTON TRADE ERA is a phenomenon that has fascinated historians and enthusiasts for 150 years. From its beginnings in the late seventeenth century, the trade grew steadily until it was forced to end in 1842. Many reasons have been given for its collapse, such as its heavy dependence on silver, widespread opium smuggling, internal corruption in Chinese administrative structures and a lack of interest on the part of the Chinese in encouraging international trade. While there is a kernel of truth in all these reasons, none can explain why the trade grew to the extent it did, for so long, despite all those negative factors.

The increasing numbers of foreigners going to Canton and the constant expansion of the overall volume of goods being handled in the port are testimony that the trade's heavy dependence on silver, and widespread corruption, did not, as might have been expected, hinder its growth. If Chinese regulators in Canton were indeed only interested in discouraging and restricting the trade, as is so often the hypothesis of modern histories, how is it that the opposite happened? Because this issue of constant growth has never been fully addressed, my aim is to identify both the strengths and weaknesses of the structure of the trade so we can begin to explain this phenomenon of growth. After we gain a deeper understanding of how the Canton System operated, we can determine better why it failed.

The strength of the Canton System was its flexibility in addressing the concerns of the Beijing court, both in controlling foreigners and trade while at the same time serving their needs. Many mechanisms were built into the port's administrative structure that allowed Customs Superintendents (more commonly known as 'Hoppos' 戶部) and governors-general simultaneously to control and foster trade. These checks and balances kept prices competitive, gave preferential treatment to large ships and large volumes of goods, and allowed the entire system to operate on credit.

The system's major weaknesses included its inability to change policies and practices to accommodate and address the long-term viability of commerce. Funds and power were siphoned away from the central administration in the effort to accommodate local administrative substructures. This reconciliation led to inefficient management, increased corruption and rampant smuggling.

As these control mechanisms began to weaken, the coastal defence administration was also not recognizing, analyzing or responding to social and economic changes taking place in Europe, North America and Asia. As the number of foreigners entering China increased, so did smuggling. The control mechanisms and coastal defence networks became more strained and less efficient. This combination of ever more threatening inner decay and outside forces gradually led to the system being unable to sustain itself.

In the long-term, the system's strengths overshadowed its weaknesses. The increase in the volume of trade brought an increase in revenues sent to Beijing. The expansion of imperial funds camouflaged a corresponding expansion of structural weaknesses spreading throughout the lower echelons. Smuggling complemented the growth of the legitimate trade in tea, so there was a tendency for Hoppos to tolerate it rather than stop it. They preferred to leave port at the end of their three-year appointments with a well-oiled machine in place that put money into their pockets and state coffers. Because the quashing of contraband and connivances could lead to a corresponding reduction in court revenues, no effective measures were initiated to stop smuggling or to curb corruption.

Structural changes that were needed had to come from Beijing, but a lack of knowledge of the extent of the problems, and perhaps an unwillingness to upset state revenues, prevented that happening. The final blow came when two innovations were introduced to Canton: the press and the steamship. The former educated the foreign community in China and worked to unify and unite their intentions and the latter effectively shifted the balance of power away from the Hoppos into the hands of foreigners. The fact that the Chinese defence systems did not adequately monitor events in the outside world meant that they had no effective means of dealing with the new technology.

At the same time, large East India companies were losing their hold on trade in Canton. By 1834, all monopolistic companies had ceased sending ships to China, and the interests of private traders emerged as the dominant voice. With the press uniting their minds and the steamship encouraging their wills, private traders gained power and resolve to force the changes they had long wanted to make. Once foreigners undermined the foundation of the system by overcoming the natural constraints of the Pearl River with the steamship, the system collapsed. It could not respond effectively to change because it did not have an administrative body with the initiative, will, power and information necessary to analyze its weaknesses; review the effectiveness of its trade policies and procedures; and make the changes needed to survive. Without a detailed account of all the particulars of trade and changes in the environment, there was no way to arrive at an accurate or comprehensive understanding of the problems. Without a monitoring device with which to correct and counter the weaknesses in administrative networks, policies and procedures, it did not matter that the critical information was not being collected because there was no one to make the changes anyway.

Because of these failings in administrative control, government regulators were forever treating the symptoms rather than curing the disease. Unfortunately, the regulators did not understand the depth of the problems they faced, so the corrective measures taken before 1835 were always too little, too late, and often ill-matched to the situation. This crisis-type management allowed contraband and corruption to put down deep roots within the government, which, in turn, continued to undermine its effectiveness. The lack of any adequate countermeasures allowed trade and the consumption of, and addiction to, opium to grow until it became a real threat to Chinese society. This internal disintegration, which spanned about 100 years, eventually led to foreigners being able to overcome the system.

We begin our analysis in chapter 1 by retracing the establishment of trade at Canton in the early eighteenth century. After laying down the basic foundations of the structure on which the trade could grow, we then go deeper into the administration of the trade in chapter 2. The day-to-day operations are brought to light so we can see more clearly why foreigners gained trust in the system, resulting in a dramatic increase in the numbers of ships going to China.

Chapters 3 through 5 give detailed accounts of three groups of professionals servicing the trade: pilots, compradors and linguists. Chapter 3 examines the process of piloting large ships up and down the shallow Pearl River, so we can see better how Chinese officials controlled their comings and goings. Chapter 4 turns to the maintenance of the foreigners while they were in China by retracing the structure of the provisions trade and the way in which they obtained materials and labourers to accommodate their needs. Chapter 5 looks at the bureaucratic procedures carried out by linguists that enabled customs to control and keep track of the trade so all duties and fees could be collected.

After laying the foundation upon which the trade grew, we then look at some of the changes that were made in the structures and shortcomings that developed. In chapter 6 we retrace some important initiatives introduced in the administration in an effort to shore up the weaknesses and make the system operate more effectively. Chapter 7 wraps up the examination of the internal mechanisms by looking at the connections between silver, contraband and rice. We retrace the establishment of extensive smuggling networks in the delta, and show the inability of the system to curb the spread of the contraband trade.

Chapter 8 then turns to other factors shaping and influencing the commerce that were not part of the internal mechanisms, namely the Macao trade, junk trade, capital market and commission merchants. After identifying, describing and explaining the major components and factors controlling, influencing and affecting the commerce, we then turn to an analysis in chapter 9 of how all the elements interacted with each other to move the trade forward and define the course it was to take. The conclusion then zeroes in on the reasons why the system could no longer sustain itself and collapsed.

CHAPTER ONE

FORGING THE CANTON SYSTEM

THE DUTCH AND ENGLISH HAD been interested in establishing trade with China since the early seventeenth century, when they first arrived in Asia. Both nations tried without success to set up a base on the South China coast, such as the Portuguese had done in Macao.[1] The Dutch managed to conduct trade with China via Taiwan after 1624, but then lost that base when the Ming loyalist Zheng Chenggong and his fleet were forced to leave China and take control of Taiwan in 1662. In the next two decades the Dutch tried to open direct trade with China, but in the end decided to let the Chinese bring the goods to them in Batavia aboard Chinese junks.[2] The English carried on a short and limited trade with China via Taiwan and Xiamen (Amoy) in the 1670s and 1680s, but without much regularity or permanence.

Qing attitudes towards contact with foreigners changed for the better after Taiwan came under China's control in 1683. With the island now under its wing, the Imperial Court was more interested in opening up direct commerce with foreigners. In the late 1680s and early 1690s foreign merchant ships began arriving at China's ports to try their luck at establishing trade.

Gradually both parties worked out an arrangement that each could accept (or at least tolerate), which attracted more foreigners to China. These outside contacts continued to increase in conjunction with an expansion of the Chinese junk trade to Southeast Asia.[3] Foreigners had to renegotiate the terms of trade with the arrival of each ship, but, by the late 1690s, some regularity began to emerge in the way business was conducted. In the early years of the eighteenth century, Canton quickly emerged as one of the most flexible places to negotiate business. While it was not what one would consider 'free' or 'open', and not always consistent from one year to the next, the terms that could be agreed upon in Canton were almost always more beneficial than any that foreigners could find in other Chinese ports.

Chinese officials had to consider several factors when wooing foreign traders to China. Regulators had, above all, to accommodate Beijing's concerns about the maintenance of peace, security and harmony in the region. The Imperial Court needed to be assured that foreigners would be properly controlled; once those fears were assuaged, trade could be considered. Commerce, however, also had to take place in a fair and orderly manner so that all the proper taxes, duties and fees were collected and distributed to the appropriate administrative bodies — especially those funds due to Beijing. The Imperial Court had to be satisfied on all of these issues before it would permit foreign trade. Canton quickly proved to be one of the best places to accommodate those concerns.

Once Beijing was satisfied, the Hoppos had to focus on the interests and concerns of the Chinese merchants. To what degree would foreigners be allowed access to the Chinese market? Would prices be controlled and/or regulated? The Hoppos also had to establish port fees that would be charged to each ship and the import and export duties on all goods. These concerns had to be worked out in advance so that transactions were properly monitored. All these factors could affect the profits of Chinese merchants, so a compromise had to be reached before trade could commence. And of course, the stipulations had to be in line with Beijing's commercial policies.

The final concern was the foreigners themselves. If competitive prices were not maintained, if fees, duties and taxes were too high, and if mechanisms used to control trade were too restrictive, then foreigners would not return to China, and that would be the end of trade. It took many years to forge an arrangement that satisfied, or at least addressed, the interests of all parties. The Hoppos in Canton were better at accommodating all these concerns and forging compromises among all parties than those at any other Chinese port, and there were good reasons for this.

Canton had the unique experience of 150 years of controlling trade in Macao. Authorities drew heavily on knowledge gained from dealing with the Portuguese. The governors-general and Hoppos knew commerce could be continued effectively and the concerns of Beijing met if foreigners were not allowed to roam freely, but restricted to a specific area. If all the Chinese doing business with the foreign traders were likewise closely monitored and controlled, then the Hoppos could keep a tight rein on the exchanges. Stopping the flow of daily provisions to foreigners and preventing them coming and going as they wished were powerful tools of persuasion that could be employed to settle disputes that arose. The need for daily rations, and the fear of having to lie over for a season owing to insufficient time to load merchandise and depart before monsoons changed, put great pressure on foreign traders to solve disputes quickly. These factors and control mechanisms had efficiently regulated the Portuguese trade in Macao and, in the early years of the eighteenth century, they were also employed to good effect in Canton.[4]

When foreigners first arrived in China in the late seventeenth century, they stopped in Macao to try to initiate trade negotiations. Because Macao was under Canton's control, traders had to obtain permission from Canton officials. All the merchandise came from markets in Canton, so that was where the merchant warehouses (known as 'factories') were built.

At various times, some Chinese officials considered making Macao the centre of foreign trade, but the impracticality of transhipping merchandise up and down the river via lighters (sampans), together with the many reservations of the Macao Senate about a huge influx of foreigners (who were often non-Catholics), ensured that such proposals were never realised. As late as 1733, there was still talk about making Macao the centre of the foreign trade, but it never happened.[5]

Keeping the ships in Macao would have required a much more extensive and costly network of river patrols. Customs checkpoints would have had to be established to tax and monitor the many sampans required to accommodate a foreign trade centred in the delta. The great increase in the numbers of vessels travelling from Canton to Macao would have made it much more difficult for customs to control smuggling activities. It was not a viable option at the time to establish a new base such as that which later emerged in Hong Kong. The Chinese government had no desire to allow other foreigners to stay in China permanently, so it was better to set up a system whereby they could visit to trade, but then had to leave after they received their cargos.

In the harbours near Macao, the Chinese authorities had less control over the foreign traders because there was nothing preventing them leaving. The large foreign ships with their deep draughts could not enter the shallow waters west of Macao so they anchored southeast of the city in a mooring known as 'Macao Roads'.[6] This place was situated east of Cabrite Point on Taipa Island, and gave foreigners easy access to the open sea. They could leave Macao Roads whenever they pleased — even if the duties on their cargos had not been paid — so the place did not accommodate the concerns of Beijing well.

The only physical means of keeping foreign ships in Macao was to maintain a fleet of junks on constant patrol, which was an enormous expense. The Qing authorities could have held the foreigners to ransom by retaining some of their property, their sails or their persons until permission was granted to leave, but that was not conducive to friendly commerce. Further, there was still the problem of finding shelter during storms. The harbours in the region that could provide safety to large ships were quite a distance from Macao, either upriver or across the delta. Thus, even if the Portuguese had been open to trade development on the peninsula, its geography ruled it out as the centre of commerce. In the end, all these factors led to trade being centred at Canton.

In the early years of this new commerce the initial negotiations between foreigners and Chinese took place in Macao Roads. It usually took a few weeks for the two parties to hammer out all the particulars. The stipulations that were finally agreed on, however, pertained only to particular ships. When new ships arrived, the supercargoes and captains of those vessels had to engage in the same hard bargaining as their predecessors.

The fact that foreigners could leave Macao whenever they pleased gave them the leverage needed to reach a compromise with Chinese administrators. In Chinese harbours where foreigners needed to hire Chinese pilots to guide them out to sea again, local authorities could pressure them to conduct some trade even if they did not agree to all the terms. In fact, officials could also press them to pay fees and administrative costs even if no trade was done.

In Macao no fees were paid until agreements had been reached on all particulars, and only then were foreigners given permission to take their ships upriver. The ships could not go all the way to Canton, but had to anchor twenty kilometers downriver on the south side of Whampoa Island (黃埔島). This mooring was called Whampoa Roads.

Sometimes the Hoppos in Canton tried to tack on additional charges or apply additional restrictions on foreigners after their ships arrived upriver, but those issues would then become part of the negotiations in the next season. Each year, when the foreigners returned, they insisted on having the freedoms they had been granted previously. With time, the two parties became more aware of the terms that each would accept, or at least tolerate, which established precedence. With precedence came regularity.

As duties collected from the trade became more uniform from one year to the next, so did the revenues sent to Beijing, which also established precedence. To protect their reputations the Hoppos needed to match the revenues of previous years, but surpassing them was, of course, even better. It was very much in the personal interests of the Hoppos and governors-general not to make drastic changes in the way that trade was conducted from one year to the next so there was no disruption in these imperial funds. This meant that, in practice, Beijing was the only authority that could make fundamental changes to the conduct of trade.

Precedence held strong sway in trade throughout the Canton era. Port procedures became regularised very quickly, which gave it stability and nurtured trust. Foreigners continued to test the Canton authorities by trying their luck in other Chinese ports such as Xiamen and Ningbo, but they invariably returned to Canton because of better and more consistent terms obtainable there.

Unlike many other Chinese seaports, Canton was also a major inland river port, which gave it access to inland supplies of provisions, naval stores, and packaging materials. There was a good source of lumber upriver for the manufacture of chests needed to pack the goods, and the Canton hinterland afforded many of the raw materials necessary for the repair of ships and stowage of cargo. There was also a huge artisan community in Canton to service trade and make all necessary repairs to factories and foreign ships. All these goods and services were essential to a smooth, regular and timely commerce. Other Chinese ports had some of these advantages, but Canton had them all.

Its being an inland seaport also helped the Hoppos to monitor trade and to assuage Beijing's fears better than they could at any other port. After the ships went upriver, foreigners depended on the Chinese for all their daily provisions, for pilots to guide their ships and for linguists to negotiate the daily transactions. In the early years of trade, many of these lower-level Chinese came from Macao, where they had learned enough Portuguese to communicate with foreigners. Officials in other Chinese ports could request that Chinese with language skills be sent to them from Macao, but they had to go through the authorities in Canton. The Hoppos in Canton, however, could simply request Chinese in Macao to come upriver whenever they needed them, which was a great advantage in the advancement of commerce.[7]

The Hoppos could also find Chinese who had learned a little of a foreign language in Southeast Asia, in such ports as Xiamen and Quanzhou, but whether they spoke the same language as the foreign persons who arrived was an issue that changed from one ship to the next (e.g., Malay, Siamese, Dutch, English, Portuguese, French, etc.). The Chinese in Macao, on the other hand, often worked their entire lives there and, if they learned any foreign language at all, it was Portuguese. Thus, when going to Canton to trade, all foreigners needed to do was to make sure they had a Portuguese speaker aboard, which was not a difficult requirement to meet for early traders like the English, Dutch and French.

By controlling all Chinese who were in contact with foreigners, the Hoppos in Canton had a stranglehold on the trade, which helped to pacify Beijing. No foreigner could eat, drink or leave China without the Hoppos' permission. And, if all else failed, the Hoppos could ask the Portuguese in Macao to step in and mediate the disputes. All these negotiating and controlling mechanisms, combined with its special relationship with and proximity to Macao, gave Canton a unique trading environment.

Consequently, there is much justification for calling the entire period from about 1700 to 1842 the 'Canton System'. This broad usage of the term is different from the way scholars have used it in the past, but for the purposes of this study it makes more sense.[8] Because the Canton System was so heavily dependent on the special geographical, topographical and hydrographical qualities of the Pearl River Delta, and on the special relationship with Macao, it was a system that could not be duplicated in any other port. All these factors will be explained in the chapters that follow.

From meagre beginnings the Canton trade grew steadily each decade. From 1699 to 1714, the French East India Company (CFI) and English East India Company (EIC) sent one or two ships each year. Armenian and Muslim traders were already active in the trade by 1700, and other 'Country' (private) traders such as English merchants in India began sending ships annually to Canton as well.[9] References from 1703 and 1704 show that Canton authorities were patronising and encouraging trade by offering presents to each ship that arrived, by eagerly going down to Macao to negotiate terms with foreigners, and by being fairly regular and consistent with each ship, regardless of its origin or nationality.

Specifics, such as the exact amounts of the port fees and other expenses, took several decades to become standardised, but the way in which those fees were determined was already established by 1704. The methods that customs officers used to monitor foreigners, the mechanisms used to control the flow of goods between Whampoa and Canton, and the formula used to calculate duties on all merchandise were firmly in place by that year.[10]

During the entire Canton era, port fees were always based on two measurements: the length and width of ships.[11] In the 1720s another charge was added to fees, which became known as the 'emperor's present'. In earlier years a similar charge had been applied to some ships, so this addition was probably a restructuring and formalisation of a previous practice rather than an entirely new expense.[12] In the 1720s the emperor's present became a separate and fixed amount applied to every ship. By 1830 the present had been reduced but the way it was applied and calculated remained the same. From 1830 to 1842 the amount of the present did not change and, in 1843, it was eliminated. The emperor's present and the way that port fees were calculated had no connection to the value of the cargos so they did not fluctuate with inflation. This meant that their basic structure remained the same for 140 years.[13]

The emperor's duties on imports and exports were determined by charging a fixed sum to each unit of measurement, such as a picul, a piece, or a unit of volume or length. Like port fees, duties were not directly connected to the value of merchandise. The Hoppo's portion of the import and export duties and the fees of all his officers and servants were calculated as a percentage of the emperor's duties. Calculating the fees and duties as a fraction of those due to the emperor ensured that all parties were given appropriate remuneration — no more and no less and always in the same proportion. Besides maintaining the hierarchies of rank and file, this practice gave officials, on all levels, strong incentives to conduct their affairs in such a way that trade was not hindered, but encouraged to grow.[14]

After calculations were made, the emperors, Hoppos and servants' charges were added to give the total port fees due for each ship. The normal practice in Canton was for the Chinese merchants to be responsible for all duties owed. In the early years of trade, foreigners sometimes paid port fees directly to the Hoppos, but in later years those charges were passed to the Chinese merchants for collection.

Except for a few cases in the early decades, where merchants tried to use their Beijing connections to conduct business in the delta, freedom to trade with a foreign ship required the approval of either the Hoppo or governor-general in Canton.[15] Permission usually required hefty payments to the authorities. Merchants were usually held responsible for foreigners with whom they traded. In later years this practice became formalised into a system in which one specific merchant or merchant house (which could be a consortium of merchants) was assigned to each ship.

In return for taking responsibility for the ship and the crew, the assigned person or consortium usually insisted on first options to the trade of that vessel, which included first rights to both imports and exports. Merchants were not allowed to monopolise the trade of the ships to which they were assigned, but they usually handled a good share of the cargos. Those appointed 'guardians' were later called 'security merchants' or '*fiadors*' (*baoshangren* 保商人). The basic structure of the security merchant system was in place by the early 1720s.

As early as 1703 the English dealt with one primary merchant house for the majority of their company trade: Linqua, Anqua and Hemshaw.[16] The EIC continued their contracts with Linqua and Anqua into the 1710s, but in the 1720s, Suqua (Chen Shouguan 陳壽官) emerged as the primary supplier to EIC ships.[17] Suqua and Cudgen of the Ye (葉) family were the primary suppliers of the Ostend General India Company (GIC) from at least 1720 to 1726.[18]

In 1726, Robert Hewer, supercargo for the GIC, gave the following report, which shows clearly what was expected of these merchant-guardians:

> Wee … made Cudgin & Suqua undertake to be our Protectors and Guardians, for it is always necessary at this Port, in cases of any Disputes or Quarrel with the Government, or any other People, occassion'd by your trade, Sailors or other ways, to have a Principal Merchant or Merchants, who undertakes to be

answerable for all your actions, and is always ready to be called upon for that purpose.[19]

As major suppliers of export goods, Chinese merchants were held responsible for the payment of port fees of each ship they serviced. In 1722, for example, the English mentioned that Suqua was responsible for payment of the port fees for that year.[20] In 1724 Suqua was again appointed to stand 'security' for the measurement of the EIC ships, and in 1727 Ton Hunqua stood security.[21]

In the early 1730s the Dutch East India Company (VOC) also depended primarily on one merchant for each ship, Tan Tinqua (Chen Tengguan 陳騰官) or Beau Quiqua (Li Kaiguan 黎開觀).[22] In 1732 the first Swedish East India Company (SOIC) ship in Canton also appointed one specific merchant to be responsible for and supply most of their cargo.[23] In 1734 the Danish Asiatic Company (DAC) was also dealing with one primary merchant or trading house for the cargo of each ship.[24] Thus, by the early 1730s, the practice of making one person responsible for each ship had emerged as the dominant way in which companies conducted business in Canton.

This policy appears to have developed out of private preference rather than being forced upon the traders by the Hoppos. Chinese merchants could be persuaded to offer better terms if they were granted exclusive privileges to a large share of the ships' imports and exports, but in some cases the Chinese did not want the entire import cargos. If that happened, then foreigners might insist on taking imports in exchange for the privilege of supplying a good share of the exports. In other cases, the Chinese insisted on first rights to the imports, so the practice varied from year to year and from ship to ship.

The granting of special privileges to the cargos of each ship was a common tool used by both the foreign supercargoes and the Chinese merchants to negotiate the best terms. By the late 1730s the customs administration had incorporated the practice into its own policies by insisting on a 'security merchant' for each ship. This requirement remained in force until the end of the system in 1842.

This policy was also in agreement with other practices in the administration. Merchants, linguists, compradors (provision purveyors) and pilots were all expected to monitor the foreigners during their stay in China and report any troubles that arose. Their specific responsibilities will be explained in the chapters that follow, but it is important to mention here that this personal responsibility-management structure was a fundamental aspect of the control of trade from the beginning.

The 1730s saw a good deal of restructuring within the customs network. In 1731 the vice-magistrate from the Xiangshan County (香山縣) seat was moved to a military garrison (Junminfu 軍民府) at Qianshan (前山). The new location gave customs a better watch over the trade and foreigners in Macao so that, if any trouble arose, they could quickly move in and take control. This was also the year linguists and compradors were officially licensed and brought more clearly under their respective administrative units.[25]

By the 1740s Customs had tightened the collection of many of the transaction fees, so that almost all costs connected to trade had become regularised. In February 1741 all foreigners were required to move to Macao in the off-season, which further helped to minimise conflicts (see Plate 2).[26] Because the documentation from the 1740s and 1750s is incomplete, there has been considerable confusion about when the foreigners were ordered to leave Canton. The regular flow of Portuguese going to Canton and *Hong* merchants going to Macao has also been much underrepresented in the historical literature.

One of the possible reasons for foreign residents not showing up in the Macao records in these decades is because it was illegal for citizens to rent houses to outsiders before 1757.[27] No applications would have been sent to the Macao Senate asking for permission, and therefore no records would have been generated. It is also possible that the records simply did not survive, because many of the early Macao documents are missing.[28] Because of these uncertainties and confusion, we will point out a few references below (there are others) that help clarify these issues.

In 1737 several Dutch officers remained in Canton year-round, and the French supercargoes spent the off-season from May to July in Macao. In this year, two Manila ships arrived at Macao, and the captains and supercargoes went to Canton and stayed there from February to May (which means their crews were in Macao during that time).[29] The Danish, Dutch, English and French supercargoes spent the off-season in Macao in 1741, after they were ordered to leave Canton in February.[30] In 1744, the French, Danish and Swedish supercargoes moved to Macao in the off-season and returned to Canton when their ships arrived.[31] In 1748, Macao resident Miguel Pedro Heytor rented a room to Armenian Gregorio, who was probably in China to trade.[32]

In 1755, the French and English supercargoes were in Macao from April to July, but the Swedish officers remained in Canton year-round. Portuguese supercargoes from Goa, who had arrived at Macao on July 12, were in Canton from July 22 to November 9 purchasing their cargo.[33] In the same year, governor-general Li Shiyao reiterated the requirement to leave Canton in the off-season, which suggests that some foreigners (like the Swedes) were ignoring it.[34] In 1757, Armenian Antonio Baptista rented a house in Macao, and Armenians continued to stay in Macao each year to the end of the century.[35]

Despite the many years missing from the data, the examples suggest that foreigners were probably staying in Macao fairly regularly, perhaps every year. As long as it was a temporary stay, they were allowed (unofficially) to reside in the city before 1757 even though it was illegal to rent houses. But there were concerns among Macao merchants that these outsiders would bring more damage to the trade, and, of course, many of them were non-Catholics so there was opposition to allowing them to stay there.[36] In early-1759 after the James Flint affair the emperor again reiterated strict compliance with the requirement to leave Canton, but some foreigners continued to procrastinate.[37] It was not until 1765, that the move to Macao became routine.[38]

As far as the Portuguese traders in Macao were concerned, they were, of course, going to Canton each year to purchase their cargos. Spanish traders from Manila (some of whom were consigned by Manila Chinese) were allowed to bring their ships to Macao and they went to Canton as well. The Portuguese supercargoes stayed in apartments provided by the *Hong* merchants with whom they did business, and did not rent out separate factories like the other foreigners. For much of the eighteenth century, the Spanish appear to have had a similar arrangement, but in 1785, they also began renting a factory in Canton.[39]

When the *Hong* merchants went to Macao to examine the imports that had arrived, they either stayed in apartments provided by the Portuguese and Spanish or in the residences of their agents and relatives living there. They would typically stay a week or two negotiating that business. These were private arrangements, which is why they do not show up in the Macao records.[40]

As we can see, besides foreign ships and Asian junks going up and down the river, there was a steady flow of officers, merchants and cargo sampans making the trip each year. All foreign movements between the two cities were closely monitored by the Yuehaiguan (粵海關) so Hoppos knew where everyone was at all times. Even though the Portuguese and Spanish merchants paid their port fees and duties in Macao, Canton kept track of ships arriving there, because the Yuehaiguan had to give permission for the Macao merchants to come upriver and for the *Hong* merchants to ship their goods between the two cities. All other foreigners paid their port fees and duties in Canton.

Because import and export duties were not connected to the value of the merchandise, the only way they could be adjusted to accommodate a rise in prices was to change the fixed rates. Hoppos, however, were reluctant to introduce new pricing structures because if such a move led to a reduction in the volume of goods being traded, they would be criticised by Beijing. Beijing was also reluctant to interfere with pricing structures for the same reason. As a consequence many of the fees, duties and charges levied on foreigners remained constant for long periods, and even when some were raised it was done infrequently. This regularity helped to create uniformity, which nurtured trust.

The tolls and fees for linguists, compradors and river pilots were all fairly uniform in these early decades. The river tolls between Whampoa and Canton were charged according to the number of visits to each tollhouse; linguists' fees were charged at one percent of the ship's cargo plus additional fixed fees for other services; compradors' prices for provisions were always set according to their unit of measure in the local market, which was usually calculated by weight, but could also be tabulated by the piece or the length; and Macao pilots' fees were charged according to the size of the ships and how long it took to guide them upriver (two or three days).

If pilots hired additional boats or helpers to assist them, or if foreigners wanted to employ pilots to transport passengers from ship to shore or deliver messages, then those expenses were listed separately. All these fees were well established by the time the Europeans began trading in Canton because Asian junks were already using their services.[41] Tollhouse keepers, linguists and compradors had long been servicing the Portuguese and Spanish trade in Canton, Macao and Manila, so it is not surprising that those fees were consistent.

Specific freedoms afforded to foreigners during their stay in Canton were renegotiated each year, but their basic parameters were already established by 1704. Foreigners insisted on the freedom to choose their merchants, linguists, compradors, pilots and the factories they rented for the season. They requested that prices be allowed to float according to the forces of supply and demand, and they asked that their silver be allowed to land on shore free of duties. While foreigners were never granted any of these freedoms to the extent that they desired, the Canton authorities did partially accommodate their demands.

Just like the Portuguese in Macao, there was never a time when the foreigners in Canton could associate with whomever they desired, but they were allowed a choice within a select group of individuals. There were always several linguists, compradors and pilots to choose from. There were also several factories that foreigners could choose to rent in Canton, but they were all situated within a specific area outside the city walls. Access to Chinese markets was always restricted to a few select merchants, but, for the most part, the Hoppos and/or the governors-general ensured that there were several of them to choose from who competed with each other for the privilege of that trade.

The competition that prevailed within each select group of merchants, linguists, compradors, pilots and landlords helped lower the prices and costs of their goods, services and rents. Thus, even though it was not an entirely 'open' or 'free' market, there were measures built into the structure to accommodate the foreigners' demands. On the whole, prices fluctuated according to the pressures of supply and demand. There were times when Chinese merchants attempted to monopolise the trade of one company or form a cartel to set prices, but such efforts were always short-lived.

If monopolising and price-setting had been allowed to continue in Canton, then the foreigners might have been reluctant to return. If the foreigners did not return, then the Hoppos and governors-general might be summoned to Beijing to give an account of their actions, so it was not in their interests to encourage cartels that could control access to markets or set prices. The fee structures gave Chinese officials on all levels incentives to encourage the trade to grow, so there were several reasons why they would not want prices to be fixed.

Because of the advantages that Canton offered to foreigners, from 1700 to 1842, traders rarely refused to return to Canton because they were unable to negotiate 'acceptable' terms. There were many foreigners who thought the terms were barely 'tolerable', but they rarely reached a point where they were considered 'intolerable'. This accommodating spirit was a prominent characteristic of the trade in Canton — much more so than other Chinese ports. Sometimes the negotiations took several weeks or months to iron out, but Canton administrators were sufficiently flexible and knowledgeable to come up with terms that both the foreigners and Beijing could accept.

It was not until 1757, when the English tried to establish trade at Chusan, that another Chinese port formed any kind of threat to the dominance of Canton. Once the emperor caught wind of this development, however, he quickly intervened by restricting all foreign trade (except Russian and Japanese) to Canton. Because of this move we will never know if Chusan could have competed with Canton at balancing the concerns of the Imperial Court, while at the same time accommodating and encouraging trade to grow. The emperor's harsh and rapid response to the intrusion suggests that Chusan could never have pacified Beijing as well as Canton did.

From 1757 to 1842 Canton was officially designated China's centre of foreign trade.[42] In reality, however, the decree only put into writing what was already fact. The expertise of the Canton merchants and officials in negotiating and conducting trade, coupled with the other advantages enjoyed by Canton, compared with other Chinese harbours, meant that the port had already become the centre for foreign trade by the early eighteenth century.

As far as the control and administration of foreigners were concerned, there were other reasons why the Chinese government preferred to keep trade centred in Canton. The restricted access of a long shallow river that deep-draughted foreign ships could only navigate with the flow and ebb of the tides gave administrators the assurance they would always be in control of their guests. The Hoppos had a say over who would be allowed up the river and when they would be allowed to leave. Even if a small foreign vessel with a shallow draught tried to enter or leave Canton illegally, it could still only move with the ebb and flow of the tides. This allowed the Hoppos time to learn of their illegal manoeuvres and to dispatch patrols to block their passage.

Whampoa was a good, safe anchorage that provided protection against the typhoons in the South China Sea. The harbour had nothing of significance that the foreigners could damage or threaten, and it was out of sight and out of gun-range of Canton. As long as foreign ships were restricted to Whampoa, they were at a safe distance from both the local provincial centre of government and the central political administration in Beijing. All these factors combined to make Canton the obvious centre of China's foreign trade.

From 1717 to 1732 the GIC sent ships to Canton, and in 1727 the Dutch dispatched a small sloop to try out the trade.[43] In 1729 the first VOC ship arrived; in 1731 the first Danish ship went upriver; and in 1732 the first SOIC ship anchored in Whampoa. By this time private English, French, Indian, Armenian, Muslim and other traders were visiting Canton on a regular basis.[44] Portuguese and Spanish ships were, of course, still trading with Canton via Macao, so the overall volume of trade expanded dramatically in its first 30 years.

By the mid-1730s, enough regularity had been built into the procedures that foreign supercargoes and captains no longer waited in Macao to negotiate the terms, but sent their ships directly upriver as soon as their permits were obtained. They had gained enough confidence in the system that they did not feel the need to negotiate the terms in advance. Of course, they still complained unceasingly about some of the restrictive measures and the 'high fees' charged, but those prejudices can be found in business regardless of where or when it is conducted.

When we analyse the Canton trade from the records of foreign supercargoes, we need to look past all these complaints about how expensive and restrictive the trade was and consider the wider historical evidence. Businessmen and women are always battling with those in charge of regulating commerce in order to have restrictions removed so that trade will expand. It does not necessarily matter whether their complaints are justified or whether the way trade is being conducted is fair and mutually advantageous. All that matters is that in some way constant pressure to remove or modify existing restrictions is placed on regulators.

Constant downward pressure also needs to be maintained on the costs of services and prices of commodities so they do not rise. Again, it also does not matter whether or not the costs or prices are already at a fair rate. The primary responsibility of all supercargoes trading at Canton was to negotiate the figures down to the point at which they maximised profits. For this reason alone, we need to look at the wider historical evidence.

In Canton's case, we can see that the authorities experimented with many different policies and practices until they found something that worked. By the mid-1730s, the foreigners had gained sufficient trust in the system, and with trust came growth. The fact that traders continued to return year after year and that more ships arrived with each passing decade is testimony that they were content with the way trade was being conducted in China, despite their endless complaints.[45]

Chapter 2 goes into greater detail on the specific nature of the daily transactions of the trade so we can see more clearly why foreigners gained trust in the system.

CHAPTER TWO

CANTON CUSTOMS PROCEDURES

CHINA'S MARITIME CUSTOMS (Yuehaiguan) in Canton were responsible for all ships in the Pearl River Delta. Only trading vessels were allowed to travel up the river, and they had to follow a series of procedures to clear customs. When they first anchored in Macao Roads, each ship had to apply for a pilot to guide them to the customhouse at the mouth of the river, known by foreigners as Bocca Tigris (Humen 虎門). There was a small group of individuals licensed by Chinese customs to guide ships upriver, and they were called 'Macao pilots' (*Aomen yinshuiren* 澳門引水人).

Macao pilots had to report to the Pilot Bureau on the Praia Grande (Nanwan Yinshuiguan 南彎引水館) to apply for a permit from the Xiangshan County seat — the administrative body in charge of Macao. The Junminfu was housed in a large white fortress on top of a hill just north of Macao at Qianshan. Because the building was white, the garrison came to be called 'Casa Branca' ('White House') by the Portuguese and others.

The most important administrative divisions within the customs network for foreign trade were the Portuguese governor in Macao who was the official spokesperson for the city and received the foreigners when they arrived, the ouvidor who enforced the laws of the Macao Senate and oversaw the city's administration, and the procurator who handled all official correspondences with the Chinese authorities including any problems that arose between foreigners and Chinese. There was a Chinese customhouse in Macao, and by 1744, there was also a vice magistrate positioned just outside the city walls in the Chinese village of Mongha (望厦).[1]

These Portuguese and Chinese officials were responsible for watching over the foreigners and their trade in the lower delta, with the aid of the Junminfu at Qianshan, the Xiangshan County magistrate and the customs post at Bocca Tigris. There was also a vast network of forts and tollhouses between Macao and Canton on the many channels of the Pearl River. All these posts were either directly or indirectly under the authority of the Yuehaiguan in Canton. They worked more or less together as a single unit to regulate shipping in the delta and to monitor the movement of foreigners.[2]

In the first half of the eighteenth century, foreign traders requested a personal audience with the Hoppo at his residence in Canton. Here they formally established the stipulations of trade, which had already been worked out prior to the audience. In many cases, the audiences were held before the ships went upriver because the foreign wanted to be assured of 'a free and liberal trade'. The linguists would be apprised of all the foreigners' demands before the audience so the Hoppo had time to consider them. A stipulation that was almost always included in the list was the freedom to choose the merchants with whom they traded. This was vital to foreigners because competition between the Chinese ensured that prices would fluctuate according to supply and demand.

For the most part Hoppos and governors-general were very keen to maintain competition among the Chinese so they licensed several merchants from whom the foreigners could choose. Even in the 1760s, when the merchants successfully established a cartel called the 'Co-hong' (*gonghang* 公行), the Hoppos and governors-general monitored the situation so prices did not become discouraging to their foreign customers.[3]

In 1763 the Co-hong managed to force all its members to agree on set prices for both imports and exports. This led the Hoppos and governors-general to declare the group to be 'a monopoly of the highest degree that was contrary to the law'. To ensure competition would continue, a new policy was introduced at the beginning of the trading season in 1764. The Canton merchants were forced to cede 30 percent of their trade to the inland tea merchants, who were allowed to approach the foreigners directly, thereby openly competing with the Co-hong.[4]

The Hoppos and governors-general knew that maintaining competitive prices would increase the annual revenues sent to Beijing which, in turn, was vital for their reputations and future careers. It was, of course, not good to have too large an increase in any one season because the Hoppos would then be expected to match it in the following years. It was important, however, to see a strong and steady increase over time. Consequently, when the Hoppos held their audiences they promised the foreigners that there would be no fixing of prices.[5]

By the late 1730s audiences were becoming less frequent because foreigners had gained more trust in the system. Hoppos and governors-general had become more selective about granting these meetings because they were turning into a platform for traders to reiterate their age-old complaints. By the late 1750s audiences were granted only under special circumstances, such as negotiating the settlement of debts of failed Chinese merchants.[6]

In the absence of audiences, questions or complaints could be brought to the Hoppo's attention when he or his deputy went to Whampoa to measure the ships. A petition could also be sent to the Hoppo via the security merchants or the linguists.[7] If the matter was urgent a request could be delivered in person to the sentry at the Yaoulan city gate (油欄城門), which was near the factories on the southwest corner of the new city wall. The sentry would then deliver the petition to the Hoppo's residence. The drawback of this method, however, was that the petitioners had to wait for several hours at the gate while the document was received by the Hoppo, read and explained to him, and word sent back that he was considering their request.[8]

Once all the terms were agreed upon, word was sent to the ships to go upriver. They had to engage a Macao pilot to guide them, and the pilots were required to report the name of the foreign captain who hired them, the country he represented (not necessarily his nationality), his ship's armaments, the size of his crew and the trade goods he carried. This information was forwarded to the Canton customhouse. Foreigners had to have some trade goods aboard, even if they were only a few vats of salt pork or a few kegs of foreign wine. Having a cargo of nothing except silver coins was not acceptable, nor was coming to China to escape a storm or to make repairs. It was generally assumed that foreigners who had no merchandise to trade — regardless of their situation — were smugglers or had come to cause trouble.[9]

Once a Macao pilot was aboard, the ship could move upriver to the customs station at Bocca Tigris where its papers were inspected. The customs officers made sure the pilot's documents matched the ship he was piloting by checking the name of the captain and whether other information matched with what he had reported in Macao. They counted the cannon doors on the side of the ship to know how many cannons it had, recorded the number of persons aboard and took account of other armaments in the ship's magazine. Some of this information had already been collected by the pilot in Macao, but, at Bocca Tigris, everything was officially verified to ensure it was correct. This information was then forwarded to the Hoppo in Canton.

Two Chinese officers or 'tidewaiters' boarded the ship at Bocca Tigris to ensure no merchandise was loaded or unloaded during the passage upriver.[10] One of these officers was from the military garrison at Bocca Tigris, the other from the customhouse.[11] If the documents were in order, the foreign ship was allowed to leave Bocca Tigris when the pilot returned from having his documents checked. The records show that pilots often went ashore to do this, which suggests that his papers may have been checked against other documents received from Canton or Macao.

Unlike many other commercial rivers in the eighteenth century where tolls were charged for each leg of the passage, foreign merchant vessels paid no tolls along the 65 miles (about 100 kilometres) of the Pearl River from Macao to Whampoa.[12] After ships came to anchor at Whampoa Roads, two guard boats from the Whampoa customhouse were chained to the sterns.[13] The tidewaiters from Bocca Tigris then handed their watch to these new tidewaiters.

These tidewaiters or guards were called many different names, which sometimes make it difficult to identify them. They or their sampans were referred to as 'Jack Hoppo', 'Hoppomen', 'guards' (*vagters*), 'guard boats' (*vagt baaden*) 'Mandarins' and 'Longside Mandarins'. Because they weighed the goods aboard the foreign vessels, they were also called the ships' weighers (*skibs vejers* or *schips waagters*). The sampans they lived in were known as 'government service boats' (*yachuanting* 押船艇), but were also referred to more specifically as the 'left hatchway' (*zuocangkou* 左艙口) or the 'right hatchway' (*youcangkou* 右艙口).[14] Tidewaiters had a writer to keep the weight records and several servants who took care of such domestic duties as cooking and washing clothes. The tidewaiter's job, of course, was to watch the ship day and night to make sure nothing was smuggled on or off.

Foreigners transported all their import and export cargo on lighters that were more commonly known as 'chop boats'. These specially built sampans were required to stop at all tollhouses between Whampoa and Canton. Because foreign ships were forbidden to sail any farther upriver than Whampoa Roads, the only river tolls they paid were charged against the chop boats. Chinese merchants owned these vessels, which made them liable for the tolls if foreigners refused to pay. There were three customhouses between Whampoa and the factories in Canton. Whampoa was under the control of Panyu County seat (番禺縣), and Canton, where all trade was conducted, was under Nanhai County seat (南海縣). Regular networks of couriers, patrols and inspectors kept communication lines open among all the posts in the delta all the time.[15]

The first tollhouse on the way to Canton, the Huangpu Shuiguan (黃埔稅館), was between Whampoa Roads and the Whampoa pagoda. Whampoa Roads was at the downriver end of Whampoa Island, so all boats had to pass this tollhouse on their way to Canton. The second tollhouse was just south of the city near the military post called 'French Folly' (Dongpaotai 東炮台). The tollhouse itself was sometimes referred to as the Dongpaotai, but it was a separate building from the fort, and displayed the tollhouse flag 'Shuiguan' (税館). The third tollhouse was on the quay in Canton near the factories outside the city walls and was known as the Haiguan Shuiguan (海關税館). This was the place where import and export duties were paid along with any other customs charges, such as tolls levied on personal baggage, special express sampan charges, or fees for landing company provisions and furniture.[16]

There were other customs posts on the quay where the tidewaiters were stationed, but these were not tollhouses. The station on the quay where all the chop boats docked was called the Hanghou Guankou (行後館口), but the foreigners referred to it as 'jackass point'.[17] At the west end of the quay, next to the Danish factory, was another station that the Dutch called the 'Danes tollhouse'. On the east end of the quay next to the Dutch factory and a water canal was a station called 'Creek tollhouse'. Foreigners stopped at these two posts only when they went to Macao in the off-season via the West River route.

The chop boats had their permits and cargo checked at the three main tollhouses. The passes were chopped at each one and then surrendered at the last post (Canton or Whampoa, depending on the direction of travel). Passes surrendered at Whampoa tollhouse were sent back to the headquarters in Canton.[18]

Customs kept a tally of the number of chop boats visiting each tollhouse according to the name of the Chinese merchant who owned the boat and the name of the captain of the ship it was servicing. This information enabled customs to keep a running total of all fees owed for each ship and of the Chinese merchants who were guarantors for those charges. The exit permit, or Grand Chop (*Da Chuanpai* 大船牌, see Plate 1), would not be issued until all duties and fees were paid.

One privilege foreigners insisted on, and that Hoppos usually granted, was the freedom of foreign officers to sail to Canton in service boats flying their flag without having to stop at the tollhouses. This was not an unreasonable request because the captains and supercargoes had to go back and forth to the ships regularly to oversee the loading, and stopping at the tollhouses was a great inconvenience to them. It would have also been expensive as well because a fee was charged every time a boat was inspected. The Hoppos understood the logic behind granting them this right, but limited it to chief officers and no goods were to be carried on the boats.

When a ship arrived at Whampoa Roads, a Chinese linguist had to be engaged to take care of all formalities. In the early decades the first task of a linguist was to negotiate the terms of trade with foreigners, establish the parameters of trade with Chinese authorities, and then arrange for an audience with the Hoppo. The linguist's next task was to arrange for the ship to be measured so port fees could be determined. This measurement had to be taken before Chinese merchants were allowed to inspect import goods, and before cargoes could be unloaded.

In the early years of trade, as many as 40 or 50 junks and sampans accompanied the Hoppo to Whampoa for the measuring ceremony.[19] Chinese officials and merchants had to be properly saluted during the event, so these were very noisy occasions.[20] Neighbouring ships were also involved in the gun salutes even if they were not on the Hoppo's measuring list for the day because it was protocol to salute all dignitaries and large vessels as they passed by in the river. The Hoppo's junk responded with the appropriate number of strikes on the large gong mounted on deck, and sometimes also fired cannon salutes.

In the mid-1780s cannon salutes were suspended because of the danger they posed to the local boatpeople. In their place the foreign crews climbed up the rigging and cheered the Hoppos as they boarded and left the ships.[21] Both the Hoppos and foreign traders had musicians who played during the measuring ceremonies. These bands appear to have been part of the formality from the early years of trade. In 1724, for example, the Hoppo's band performed during the measuring of the GIC ship *St. Elisabeth*. In 1737 the Danish band played during the measuring of the ship *Sleswig*, and, afterwards, the Hoppo amused himself by blowing the Danish trumpets.[22]

Sometimes a skit or chorus was performed by members of a ship's crew (under the direction of the officers, of course). The ceremonies also involved serving traditional candied fruit and sweetmeats, toasting red wine and formal welcome speeches by the Hoppo (or his deputy).[23] These orations were followed by reciprocal speeches and greetings from the foreign traders, and an exchange of small gifts. All this activity had long established protocol: well-structured procedures in which all officers and merchants — foreign and Chinese alike — were decked out in formal costumes that gave the trade much dignity.

At some point in all the pomp and circumstance, usually before the Hoppo was treated to refreshments, his officers had to take the measurements. Ships were measured either with a cord that had the covids marked on it or with precisely cut bamboo poles.[24] The cord or poles were held up at a man's height above the deck, and the attendants called out the dimensions to the secretary, who recorded them in the Hoppo's book.[25] The linguists translated the dimensions to the foreign captains and supercargoes.

A few days after the ceremony the linguists would deliver a formal statement of the measurements and corresponding port fees, which had to be translated into Arabic numerals so the foreigners could understand them (see Plate 27 and 28).[26] Immediately after the measurements were taken, the security merchants signed a bond with the Hoppo to accept all responsibility for the ship, including the conduct of the foreigners and payment of port fees, together with all the import and export duties.[27] This formal contract between the Chinese merchants and the Hoppo seems to have been introduced sometime in the 1730s.

After the signing of the bond, the Hoppo would request to see the 'sing-songs' (mechanical gadgets such as clocks or music boxes) or mirrors and other luxury items the foreigners had brought with them. These would supply the presents the Hoppo was expected to offer to his superiors each year for the privilege of his office. After selecting the best items, the Hoppo would ask the Chinese security merchant to purchase them. The merchant was expected to offer the items to the Hoppo at a huge discount for the privilege of securing the ship.[28]

The measuring ceremonies could be very tiring, because much protocol needed to be observed. If the Hoppos were not exhausted by the sweets, red wine, formal greetings, boring speeches, blaring trumpets, beating drums, banging gongs, screeching actors, bellowing choirs, cheering crews and the shouting of measurements then the constant pounding of the cannon and gun salutes, the smoke that followed and the permeating stench of fresh gunpowder would certainly finish the job. In the early years of the trade Hoppos (or sometimes the governors-general) attended many measuring ceremonies in person. But as an increasing number of ships visited China, the measuring of them became a great distraction from the overseeing of trade, and the Hoppos delegated the task to their deputies.[29]

It was such exhausting work that Hoppos arranged the measuring of several ships on the same day so they could have them all done at once and then return to their regular duties (probably after the red wine wore off the next day). Even in the early years Hoppos would often wait for more than one ship to arrive before going out to measure them. By the 1760s it was common for a Hoppo to measure six or seven ships in one day, but there were still times when he had to make the trip to Whampoa for fewer ships.[30]

As the number of foreign ships increased, Hoppos became more selective as to which would come under their personal supervision (those with the rarest and most precious cargos, of course).[31] The EIC and private traders were the primary carriers of rarities to Canton. When those ships arrived the top Chinese officials would rush to find out what luxuries they had aboard. Companies, however, tried to avoid trading in luxuries because there was so much trouble attached to selling them.[32] Private English and French traders, Armenians, Muslims and Parsees were all active in this specialty market, but company officers might also bring items to Canton to sell them privately on their own account.[33] As long as someone brought rarities there was no need for Hoppos to force everyone to bring them. The Dutch, Danes, Belgians, Americans and Swedes seem to have traded in them infrequently and only in small quantities.

After the measuring ceremony, the Hoppo, on behalf of the emperor, sent a present to each ship to show China's concern for the well-being of their foreign guests. In the early years these gifts varied somewhat, but, by the 1740s, they consisted of two cows, eight sacks of wheat flour and eight crocks of Chinese wine (*samshoo*).[34] In the early decades of trade vessels that arrived in poor condition, owing to storms or mishaps, might receive additional gifts from the emperor as sincere tokens of remorse for their misfortunes.[35]

By the late eighteenth century arrival presents had become a mere formality, rather than a token of mutual respect and appreciation. In the early nineteenth century, for example, Dobell mentioned that the Hoppo's present to each ship consisted of 'a few jars of vile samtchoo, not drinkable, and two miserable bullocks, not eatable, which the captain generally exchanges with the comprador for a few pounds of good beef'.[36]

In earlier times the two bullocks would have been butchered aboard the ship within a couple of days or kept for the return passage. The sacks of flour were readily incorporated into the ship's stores, and the crews were allotted rations from the crocks of Chinese wine. By the late eighteenth and early nineteenth centuries, however, many ships were selling the 'presents' back to the compradors or tidewaiters (if they could).[37]

A few days after the Hoppo's present was delivered, the linguists presented the foreigners with the official translation of the ship's measurements. If the foreigners had any complaints they expressed them to the linguists, who then relayed their concerns to the Hoppo.[38] The way in which the ships were measured and the formula used to determine the rates gave large ships a significant advantage.

The length measurement was taken between the foremast and the mizzenmast (or rear-most mast). The holds of foreign ships, however, always extended beyond the fore and aft of the masts, so this method of determining the length was not an accurate representation of the cargo area. The width measurement was taken aft of the mainmast (the centre-most mast), and it was done on the main deck (uppermost full-deck) between the port and starboard taffrails. No depth measurements were taken. The product of the length times the width was then divided by ten to determine the ship's measurage (port-fee covids). These measurements were the only figures used to calculate the port fees from 1700 to the end of the Canton System in 1842.[39]

Plate 27 shows the measurements of the American brig *Canton*, in Chinese characters. These were the original figures that the linguist received from the Hoppo. The linguist would then translate the Chinese numbers into Arabic numerals and give the figures to the foreigners. Plate 29 is an extract from a DAC journal showing linguist Chauqua's report of the measurements and port-fee calculations of the DAC ship *Princesse Lowise*. Plate 28 shows the measurements and port-fee calculations of the VOC ships *Velzen* and *Ouderamstel* with the Dutch supercargoes' long-hand calculations. The Chinese version (Plate 27) does not show the calculations of the port fees because those were done with an abacus.[40]

The figures in Table 1 show the breakdown of port-fee calculations of the second VOC ship to visit China, the *Duifje*. A ship's measurage fell into one of three categories, with three different rates. The figure was multiplied by the rate to determine the measuring fee. Then there were several calculations that had to be made to arrive at the final fee.

Table 1 Port Fee Calculations of the VOC Ship *Duifje* in 1730[41]

Length 67.99 covids x width 22.70 covids = 1543.373/10 = 154.3373. The Duifje was entered as a 2nd rate, which was 7.143 taels per covid (usually 7.142 taels was the 2nd rate), which amounted to 1,102.431 taels. The following calculations had to be made to come up with the final measuring fee and the total port fee.

	Taels 1,102.431
Emperor's discount of 20 percent	220.486
Subtotal A	881.945
Hoppo's 10 percent	88.194
Subtotal B	970.139
Sycee 7 percent to compensate for difference in alloy content	67.909
Hoppo's servants' 2 percent	17.638
Final measurage fee	1,055.686
Emperor's Present	1,950.000
Total Port Fee Due	3,005.686

The first entry is the 20 percent discount from the emperor. Like the Hoppo's present, this reimbursement was another incentive built into the structure to show foreigners that the emperor was personally and genuinely interested in their business. And the remaining charges were calculated as a percentage of the discounted amount (Subtotal A), and not the total (1,102.431 taels), which was another incentive. Every ship received this 20 percent discount, which more than compensated for the other charges added to the fees below it. In this case, the final measuring fee came to 1,055.686 taels.

The emperor's present was then added to the measuring fee to arrive at the total port fee. The French paid 100 taels more for the privilege of exclusive access to French Island, and private country ships from India, such as those of the Armenians, Muslims and Parsees, paid 100 taels less.[42] In the 1720s and early 1730s the emperor's present for some GIC ships amounted to 1,800 taels, while others paid 1,950 or 2,050 taels. But on the whole there was great consistency in the way the port fees were charged.[43]

There were two ways to calculate the final port fee. All individual discounts and charges could be itemised, as in the case of the *Duifje*, or a simplified rate could be used that already made those adjustments. For example, instead of using 7.142 taels as the multiplier in *Duifje's* calculations, it was easier to adjust that rate to compensate for all the discounts and charges listed in Table 1. If 6.84 taels were used as the multiplier instead of 7.142, then the final measuring fee could be figured with one calculation, rather than four. Multiplying 154.3373 covids by 6.84 taels gives a final measuring fee of 1,055.667132 (rounded down to 1,055.667). The difference between that figure and the one above (1,055.686) was so slight (only 0.019 taels or about 2.5 cents) that the adjusted multiplier was often used rather than the longhand version. In fact, many of the private traders such as the Americans did not know how the calculations broke down and thought the simplified rates were the only figures used to calculate the measuring fees.

Both the long and simplified rates were used by the Hoppos throughout the eighteenth century. By the nineteenth century, however, the simplified rates seem to have become standard. The *Duifje* was entered as a second-rate vessel although it should have been classed as first rate. In the early years Hoppos often discounted the fees or applied a lower rate in order to encourage trade, but, by the 1740s, such examples are harder to find in the records.[44]

In 1830 the EIC was successful in negotiating a reduction in the emperor's present to 1,600.683 taels (Spanish $2,223). At about the same time, the three rates used to calculate the fees were raised (probably to compensate for the discount).[45] The way that ships were measured, however, remained the same from 1699 to 1842.[46] The three-tiered rating system of ships was in place as early as 1699 and remained in effect until 1842. The three rates charged appear to have varied a little in the beginning years but, by the early 1720s, they were firmly set and remained the same until 1830.[47]

The Hoppo's 10 percent portion of the measuring fees and the 7 percent discount for sycee silver was already in place in 1699. Because of a lack of detailed records from the first twenty years of the eighteenth century, it is difficult to know how consistently port fees were applied. We do know that in the 1720s some GIC ships were charged 8 rather than 7 percent, but, by the time the first VOC ship arrived in 1729, 7 percent was again the standard. In the 1720s the Hoppo's 10 percent portion and the discount for sycee silver were being regularly applied, which suggests that there probably had been little or no change in this part of the fee since 1699.[48] As far as we can tell these amounts were used to calculate port fees of every ship from the 1720s to 1842.

In fact, the entire structure of port fees was probably firmly in place by 1722, perhaps earlier. This structure was handed down to the Hoppos from the emperor, and could not be changed without his express order.[49] Even after the 1830 reduction, the distributions within the port fees were calculated the same way until they were abolished in early 1843. This consistency not only helped to build trust, but made it easier for foreign traders to calculate their profits.[50]

There were ways, however, in which small ships could try to obtain a lower port fee. One was by knocking out the wedges that held the masts in place, loosening the stays, and then binding the tops of the masts together. This reduced the distance between the centres of the two masts at the points where they protruded through the main deck. The amount saved, however, was only the thickness of the wedges used to hold the masts in place. For ships that had thick wedges, the effort was probably worth the reward. The VOC captains appear to have made use of this innovation regularly to minimise port fees, and the Americans also made use of this procedure.[51]

The width measurement could be 'adjusted' by moving the pigsties from their normal location at the centre of the ship to the gangways adjacent to the main mast. Mounting them on capstan's bars made them look like permanent structures of the main deck. According to Chinese policy, the width measurement had to be taken just aft of the mainmast, so some customs officers were inclined to take the narrower measurement between the pigsties, rather than the width between the taffrails. This could reduce the width measurement significantly and save a considerable amount on the port fees.[52] This practice is probably what caused the Hoppo's officers in 1736 to start taking the measurements of the ships above their heads (and presumably above the pigsties as well), rather than at deck level.[53]

Taking the length measurement between the two masts only worked, of course, with ships that had at least two masts. Some American traders and others crossed the Pacific in one-masted sloops.[54] In these cases, the length measurement was taken between the mast and the rudder head.[55]

Taking the width measurement on the main deck between the taffrails did not make for an accurate measurement of foreign vessels. Unlike Chinese junks, many European and American vessels were wider below deck, where the cargo was stowed, than they were above. This characteristic in construction was known as 'tumble home' and was a way to strengthen the hull and provide more room below deck for the larger cannons. It also helped to lower the centre of gravity.

Chinese officers in charge of the measuring tried to compensate for this irregularity by measuring the ships on the uppermost complete deck (which was closer to the widest width), rather than on the narrower upper-half decks.[56] They sometimes extended their measuring rods beyond the edge of the taffrails (when the pigsties were not in the way). Foreign officers needed to be attentive to this latter practice to keep their port fees from being artificially inflated.[57]

After port fees were calculated, they still needed to be collected. The payment of fees was not very regular in the early years of trade, and sometimes they were not paid until the ships were fully loaded and ready to depart. It was often the case that Hoppos simply requested the fees when they found themselves pressed for funds.[58] After the Dutch, Danish and Swedish companies came to China in the early 1730s the Hoppos began requesting that fees be paid earlier and with more regularity. The linguists or security merchants collected the revenues from the foreigners and delivered them to the Hoppo's office.

By the mid-1740s foreign ships usually had to pay the port fees in full before the Hoppos would issue any chops to take in export cargo. After 1800 we can find records of ships that appear to have taken in all their return cargo before paying the port fees, but these are exceptions to the rule. Those cases are perhaps more indicative of the Hoppos' inability to keep up with the increasing numbers of ships going to Canton than a contradiction in their policies. From the 1740s to 1842, the usual practice was for ships to pay the port fees before any return cargo was taken in. Import cargo, on the other hand, could usually be discharged directly after the ships were measured.[59]

It usually took several weeks to a couple of months to unload the ships. The cargo was often sold and contracted for prior to unloading it, and then shipped directly to the Chinese merchants' houses on the quay. This saved them from having to handle the goods twice. Plate 17 shows a typical contract between the VOC and Chinese merchants for Dutch imports in 1760. After the contract was made, the goods would be unloaded, sent to the foreign factory for weighing and inspection, and then immediately transhipped to the merchant houses.[60] The only import goods stored in the foreign factories were products that did not sell. Sometimes items would be placed in a warehouse for several years if there was a poor market, but foreigners generally tried to sell them in China because they would be subject to export duties if loaded back aboard the ships.

Sometimes hard-to-sell goods were traded to other foreigners at Whampoa, who then took them to India and elsewhere. In these cases, the foreigners could apply to the Hoppo for permission to transfer the goods from one ship to another. Depending on the product, the Hoppo might charge a nominal fee per picul, but this exception to the normal duties covered only goods that were at Whampoa. Import goods already landed at Canton would have to pass the three customhouses in the river again and were thus subject to export duties.[61]

After ships had unloaded their import cargos, they began to purchase and take in their return cargos. Each ship first had to clear its hold so it could receive the ballast cargo such as tutenague (zinc), and several sampan loads of ballast stones (or gravel). This gravel was scooped up from the bottom of the river in Macao, and it was preferred above any other gravel. The tiny stones were smoothened by the river and consequently formed a solid and flat surface for the porcelain chests, the first items to be loaded. If the gravel was wet when it arrived in Whampoa, then it had to be spread out along the shore to dry before loading it into the ships.

Foreigners used many different articles for ballast, but they often required a large amount of Macao stones to make up the difference. A typical VOC ship of 800 to 900 tons, for example, required about 400,000 Dutch pounds of ballast. As far as the China-bound VOC ships were concerned, about half the ballast was made up of zinc, tin, alum or other such articles, and the other half was made up of Macao stones. Each sampan from Macao could carry about 40,000 Dutch pounds of gravel so five or six were needed for each ship. It usually took a couple of weeks to a month to clear the holds and lay the ballast.[62]

When the holds were ready, chop boats began taking the porcelain to Whampoa. In late November or December tea arrived from inland, and, in mid-December, silks began arriving from Nanjing. Customs officers were usually very diligent about inspecting the permission chops at the tollhouses, and made sure that the contents in the chop boats matched the details on the documents. If a chop permitted *20 full chests* of Bohea tea to be transhipped, that did not mean *40 half chests* of Bohea tea or *20 full chests* of another kind of tea. Some traders tried to get away with such substitutions, but without much success. Different import and export duties were charged on each product so, for the sake of calculating the tariffs, it was important to make certain that shipments were true to the documents, and vice versa.

The Hoppos tried to minimise the opportunities for smuggling and other illicit activities by restricting foreigners at Whampoa to the islands immediately surrounding the anchorage. In Canton, they were restricted to the factories, which were outside the city walls. Monitoring, reporting and controlling of foreigners were introduced to minimise the potential for discord and disharmony. Disagreements or quarrels between foreigners and Chinese were usually dealt with quickly, firmly and, sometimes, harshly as a deterrent to others. On the whole Hoppos and governors-general tried to be fair and just with all parties, but there were different ideas about what was 'fair' and 'just'.

There were many times when the Hoppos called a complete halt to the trade of one ship, one party or one company, or trade by all foreigners in Canton. Hoppos used this drastic measure to settle a matter as quickly as possible. In the eyes of the foreigners, however, this was almost always viewed as an indication that the Hoppos were interested only in restricting trade, not encouraging it. While it was true that the Hoppos' policies gradually became harsher and more restrictive, their core concern was still the restoration of harmony. Stopping trade often seemed to be the best and quickest way to accomplish that objective, and, for the most part, it probably was. The pressure of time was a powerful persuader. As more foreigners went to Canton and as officials faced more problems and responsibilities, the system responded naturally by becoming more restrictive. Maintaining order was always held in much higher esteem than any notions of timeliness or liberty to trade.

The foreigners had to settle all their accounts with the linguists, compradors and merchants, and the Chinese merchants had to pay all the necessary fees and duties before the Grand Chop was issued (Plate 1). The Grand Chop was a large rectangular document, about 26 x 18 inches (66 x 46 cm), printed from a large wooden block. It was called the *yang chuanpai* (洋船牌) in the early eighteenth century or *waiyang chuanpai* (外洋船牌) in later decades, and more generically known as the *da chuanpai* (大船牌).[63]

A space was left at the top of the Grand Chop for a verification mark. A small piece of paper was laid on the face of the document just above the printed portion. The customs officer then positioned the Yuehaiguan chop so half the chop was on the paper and half on the printed document. He then inscribed a combination of words and numbers in the same manner (half on the paper and half on the Grand Chop). The slip of paper was then sent downriver to Bocca Tigris and the Grand Chop to the foreign captain. The small verification slip (known as a *kaozheng* 考證) was used to check the authenticity of the Grand Chop when the ship arrived. This procedure was highly effective against forgery and was used to check the authenticity of all kinds of documents in China, including licences, diplomas and certificates.[64] The foreign ship was allowed to proceed out to sea only after the Grand Chop had been verified.

The customs office in Canton could tell at a glance which merchants and ships were in arrears. Occasionally, foreigners had to extend an emergency loan to a struggling Chinese merchant who fell short of his obligations; sometimes Chinese merchants had to search the money market in Canton or Macao for a temporary loan to settle their accounts when funds were lacking. Withholding the Grand Chop until all accounts were settled gave the trade much security as everyone could be assured that they would be paid before the ships left, which enabled the system to operate entirely on credit during the trading season.

The factors outlined above formed the basic structure of the Canton System from the 1690s to 1842. To see how important the trade and revenues were to the state, we need only look at the changes made to the port fees after the system collapsed. In 1843 the port fees were set at a nominal rate of 0.5 taels per ton for vessels 150 tons and larger and 0.1 taels for vessels smaller than 150 tons.[65]

The total revenues collected from the port fees after 1842 amounted to a fraction of what they had been. John Robert Morrison estimated that 150 ships (120 general cargo and 30 rice ships) would have incurred about 270,000 taels in port fees under the old system, but paid only 37,500 taels under the new system.[66] Under the old system the emperor's present of 1,600 taels (after 1830) applied to every cargo ship, so the estimated total revenues from port fees of 150 ships would come to about 462,000 taels. Morrison's estimate of 37,500 taels is only 8 percent of that figure, so this was 92 percent loss of state revenues for the Chinese government.

Even in 1845, when there were 327 foreign ships in Canton with a total carrying capacity of 148,273 tons (322 ships of 150 tons or more), port fees amounted to only about 73,000 taels (145,000 tons at 0.5 taels and the rest at 0.1 taels per ton). Thus, the increase in volume and number of ships did not come close to making up the difference between the old and new rates.[67]

SUMMARY

As the examples have shown, Canton's maritime customs network was well organised. Information and orders were transferred along a vast network of posts between Macao and Canton. The Hoppos and emperor gave presents and discounts to every ship that went to Canton and, in the early years, offered other incentives to encourage foreigners to trade. The procuring of permits, inspecting and measuring of ships, unloading and loading of cargo, and the sophisticated licensing structures and monitoring devices all helped to standardise the trade and facilitate the smooth conduct of business. Foreign officers were allowed free passage on company boats flying their flag, which accommodated efficiencies of time. Not a single toll was charged to the ships between Bocca Tigris and Whampoa, and, in the early years the Hoppos were open-handed with privileges and favours to others who had suffered misfortunes. All these practices encouraged foreign commerce.

In the next chapter we take a look at how the large ships managed to sail up the shallow Pearl River despite their deep draughts, and how the Hoppos controlled their comings and goings.

CHAPTER THREE

PILOTING THE PEARL RIVER

THE VOYAGE UPRIVER FROM MACAO to Whampoa was a perilous one in the early eighteenth century. Large ships often had draughts in excess of eighteen feet, and the shallowest shoals in the main course of the river were themselves only eighteen feet.[1] Thus, the only way ships could reach Whampoa was to sail with the ebb and flow of the tide.

Strong currents, frequent storms and the many hidden perils beneath the Pearl River made it a hazardous passage for all deep-running vessels. Currents and powerful eddies could send a ship whirling around in a circle in the blink of an eye.[2] Given such hazardous conditions, it would have seemed logical to commission only shallow-bottomed vessels for the journey to Canton, but this was not the case.

From the early decades of the eighteenth century to the end of the Canton System in 1842, the capacity of many company ships grew from 400 tons to more than 1,400 tons, with their draughts increasing from 17 or 18 feet to 23 or 24 feet. This happened despite the fact that the river became shallower as time passed. New shoals and new sandbars continued to form north of Lintin Island (伶仃島) and in the waters on the western side of the delta around Macao. By 1790, the water over Lintin's bar was only 24 feet and growing shallower each decade.[3]

Even this change in the river's depth did not affect the numbers of vessels going to China. From just a few ships in the first days of trade, the annual number increased to more than 20 vessels in the 1760s, 50 in the 1790s, 70 in the 1810s, 180 in the 1830s and 300 in the 1840s.[4] Increased competition in Canton led to narrowing profit margins in the two most desirable commodities: tea and porcelain. One would expect reduced profits caused by the greater number of traders in

Canton to have slowed or even reduced the overall volume of trade, as limited supplies struggled to keep up with stronger demand. However, the volume of trade grew constantly and steadily with each decade.

A small group of professionals known as the 'Macao pilots' were largely responsible for this outcome, which led to Canton becoming a great seaport in the eighteenth and early-nineteenth centuries. By establishing a routine, organised and sophisticated method of guiding ships upriver, the pilots even managed to make the passage safer over time. A close examination of their activities will show that they were responsible for enabling larger ships to come to China, and in so doing, played a central role in the Hoppos' control mechanisms.

When foreigners began to use steamships in the 1830s, they gained the ability to traverse the river without the aid of the pilots. This freedom took away the Hoppo's power to decide who came and left China, and with that loss came an undermining of the credit structures that supported the trade. Creditors could no longer be assured that all debts would be settled before their patrons departed. When the Macao pilots' fees were restructured in 1843, one of the traditional incentives was also removed that had encouraged larger ships to trade at Canton. It is only when we look closely at the pilots' operations that these important connections to the growth, control and collapse of the trade come into full view.

The first priority of a foreign ship arriving in the delta was to engage a Chinese pilot to guide it into Macao Roads. On sighting a Chinese vessel, foreign ships would fire one or two cannons to signal for a pilot.[5] During rough weather, however, there would be very few, if any, Chinese vessels in the delta, so these signals were intended to attract a pilot from a fishing village nearby. In good weather there could be hundreds of Chinese vessels in the delta, which made it much easier to find a pilot.[6] Signal shots were repeated every few hours until a pilot arrived. Smaller ships sometimes also fired signal shots, but their manoeuvrability allowed them simply to intercept a Chinese vessel and request a pilot. Chinese junks arriving in the delta signalled for pilots by lighting three torches.[7]

Foreigners called the persons who guided their ships into Macao 'outside pilots', but the Chinese often referred to them as 'fishermen pilots' (*yuyinren* 魚引人). They were not regulated as pilots by the Chinese authorities, but they were regulated as fishermen and their piloting activities were monitored by the Junminfu in Qianshan. Their sampans were issued registration numbers by the customhouse. These numbers were written in Chinese characters on the side of the boat and on the flag flown in the third position from the top of the mizzenmast. Most foreigners, however, remained unaware that it was an easy matter to identify the outside pilots by their registration numbers.[8]

Foreigners' inability to recognise Chinese numbers meant that they usually had no idea whom their outside pilots were. In the records these individuals appear as shadowy figures and are rarely identified by name. If a foreign trader wanted to file a complaint against his outside pilot, he needed to know his name and/or the number of his vessel. The uncertainty of their identities, however, meant it was fairly easy for outside pilots to cheat their foreign patrons and then disappear into the myriad vessels in the delta. As a consequence, fees that outside pilots charged tended to vary widely from one ship to the next and often depended entirely on the negotiating skills of the foreign captains.[9]

In the eighteenth century, if the outside pilots knew any foreign words they were probably Portuguese, but the records show that many of them just used gestures to communicate.[10] In the initial negotiations of deciding his fees the pilot might lay out 'two hundred pieces of copper' to represent 200 Spanish dollars.[11] After he and the captain agreed on his fee, then the pilot guided the ship into Macao by pointing out the course it was to take. The raising and lowering of sails and other manoeuvres were left to the foreign officers to decide.

This might appear to be easy money for outside pilots, but it was serious business and extremely important for deep-draughted ships to have someone aboard who knew the waters. It was so important that in 1726 the captain of the GIC ship *Arent* resorted to capturing a Chinese from a nearby junk and forced him to guide them into Macao. This move was tragic for the unfortunate sailor because he jumped overboard and drowned before the ship arrived.

The information contained in the journals of the *Arent* leave us with no reason for this man deciding to jump overboard other than a misunderstanding of what his foreign captors intended. The most likely outcome of the incident (had the man performed his duty) would have been his release with pay after arriving at Macao Roads. The ship could not pass Bocca Tigris with this man aboard, and the foreigners could not afford to have him leave disgruntled to report the case to the authorities. If anything unfortunate happened to him it could jeopardize the voyage, which is why the Belgian officers were much afraid that the Chinese would find out about his death (they kept it secret). For the same reason any mistreatment of the sailor while he was aboard would bring condemnation down upon the responsible officers so he should have had nothing to fear from them. In 1762 officers of a Dutch ship also considered capturing a Chinese to guide them into Macao. Despite the negative effects of such aggression the extremes to which foreigners would go to get a pilot show how serious it was for them to have someone aboard who knew the channels.[12]

Outside pilots were only allowed to bring ships into the delta as far as Macao. Foreign captains were then required to hire a licensed Macao pilot to guide them upriver to Whampoa. As we saw in chapter 2, Macao pilots were granted their piloting papers by the Junminfu in Qianshan on a ship-by-ship basis. Each permit was good for only one passage, whether up or downriver. This gave Hoppos control over which ships went to Canton and when they would be allowed to leave.

Unlike outside pilots Macao pilots could often speak a few words of Portuguese or English, which was needed to give commands. The many receipts from Macao pilots that have survived in the foreign archives reveal that they were often literate in written Chinese as well. Plate 32 shows a receipt from the Macao pilot A-kou for money he received for piloting a Dutch ship.[13] Macao pilots did not have to be fluent in any foreign language, but they needed to know the names of certain sails, ropes and rigging and the commands to trim sails, tack the ship and weigh or drop anchor. We cannot say whether knowing a little Portuguese or English, or being literate in Chinese, were prerequisites for becoming a Macao pilot, but it is well documented that many had these skills.

It was common practice for both outside and Macao pilots to present new clients with letters of recommendation from captains they had previously served. These recommendations were written in the language of the ship's captain, signed and dated. The document stated the name of the ship, the name of the pilot and that he had successfully guided the vessel to its destination. Such a recommendation was a good way to assuage the fears of a suspicious captain. Over the years some pilots accumulated many recommendations in several languages.[14]

In addition to offering their services as guides, both outside pilots and Macao pilots carried provisions aboard their sampans, which they sold to the foreigners. After a long voyage captains were eager to acquire fresh fish, fruit, vegetables and meat for the benefit of the sick among their crew. Macao pilots would sometimes accompany foreigners to fishing villages to purchase cows for beef, or other fresh food. Even if a pilot failed to persuade a captain to engage him he could still make some money by selling a few provisions.[15] These transactions, however, could only be done on a small scale because the provisions trade was strictly regulated in China, as we shall see in chapter 4.

Small and large vessels engaged their Macao pilots in different ways. Small ships often had to wait 24 hours or longer in Macao.[16] Because many of the small private traders did not maintain residences or agents in China they could not send for the pilots in advance. Thus, the normal procedure was for the captain or one of the ship's officers to go ashore and engage a pilot in person.

In the early decades of the nineteenth century the Macao Tavern on the Praia Grande was the favoured haunt of these private traders. The proprietor, John Budwell, was known to be 'obliging, treats you well & not very extravagent [*sic*] in his charges'.[17] He would send for a Macao pilot when a foreign captain arrived.

While waiting, the captain would enjoy Budwell's food and drink, and catch up on the latest gossip and particulars of the trade. A day or two later he returned to his ship and the pilot either accompanied him or arrived shortly thereafter via another sampan.[18]

The only real obstacle for small vessels with shallow draughts going upriver without a Chinese pilot or towboats to assist them were the guns at Bocca Tigris. Many American vessels in China, for example, had draughts of only sixteen feet so they could navigate the river without much difficulty.[19] But if they managed to make it past the forts, they could easily be detained after anchoring in Whampoa, so there was no point in trying to avoid hiring a Macao pilot. Some captains contemplated running past Bocca Tigris on the outward passage without a pilot and before their Grand Chops had been issued, but few actually carried through with their threats.[20]

Large ships needed many sampans to tow them safely over the sandbars. Small ships, on the other hand, did not necessarily need any assistance but were nonetheless pressured to hire four or five sampans as well. Not surprisingly, captains of small vessels tended to see this mandatory requirement as blatant extortion, whereas captains of large ships saw the wisdom of the course.[21]

After a Macao pilot obtained his permit from the Junminfu, he took command of the foreign ship and gave the order to weigh anchor and set sail for Bocca Tigris. The one stipulation that held for both outside pilots and Macao pilots was that they guided only trading vessels. Warships, passenger ships and ships carrying only bullion or such restricted merchandise as saltpetre (used to make gunpowder) required special permission before they could enter the delta. Even storm-damaged vessels with half their crews missing and all their masts shattered had to convince the authorities that they had indeed come to trade before they were allowed to continue upriver or lie to and make repairs.

This requirement was not a result of the Chinese officials being unwilling to help foreigners in distress, which they were often accused of. It was rather a stipulation that was handed to them from the emperor. If the Canton authorities allowed a ship to stay for repairs or any reason other than trade, then no revenues would be sent to Beijing from that ship and that could arouse the suspicions of the ministers at the court. Many foreigners thought the Chinese were being unreasonable and cold-hearted by declining to help them unless some trade was done, but such benevolence could lead to condemnation and dismissal so the Canton authorities had little choice in the matter.[22]

After the pilot had his license and permit inspected at Bocca Tigris and the two tidewaiters came aboard, the captain needed to hire sampans to assist in the passage. These fishing boats or 'towboats' kept the ship in the deepest part of the channel so it did not twist or turn in eddies and currents. Their assistance was necessary because large ships went upriver with the tides and did not depend on the wind and sails to pull them and therefore could not steer well and stay on course by themselves.[23]

Foreign ships lying at anchor at Whampoa often sent their dinghies (service boats) downriver to assist a new arrival.[24] In addition to the towboats, several sampans were hired to act as buoys over the two sandbars that lay midway between Bocca Tigris and Whampoa. These sampans were called 'signal boats' or 'bar boats' and marked out the course that the ship was to take. All the sampans displayed lanterns at night and flags during the day to indicate they were part of a piloting procession.

In the early days of trade, foreign captains were still in control of negotiations with local fishermen and the piloting of their ships, but by the 1750s the pilots were managing everything. More tow and buoy sampans were needed as the foreign ships became larger. In the early years, vessels of more than 450 tons usually engaged five to ten Chinese sampans.[25] By the 1760s many large ships were employing 30, 40, even 50 sampans. By the early nineteenth century, some ships were using as many as 70 or 80 sampans on both the inward and outward passages.[26]

For most of the Canton era the large company ships took in their cargos at Whampoa until they reached a draught of about eighteen feet, when they moved downriver past the Second Bar. This anchorage was known by several names, including the 'Second Bar anchorage', 'Bocca Tigris Roads', 'the bogue' and 'Zout Zout Ham'.[27] Records show that this removal downriver was a characteristic of the trade as early as the 1720s.[28] But it was probably common practice much earlier, because ships with a capacity of more than 400 tons were stopping in Whampoa from the beginning.[29]

In the 1760s pilots also began employing tow sampans for the trip from Bocca Tigris Roads to Macao, placing buoy sampans over the sandbar north of Lintin Island. They also began charging the foreigners according to the depth of their ships. In 1763, Macao pilots demanded Spanish $50 from the Dutch to pilot each of the three VOC ships from Whampoa to the sea, rather than the $30 they had paid until then. The pilots argued that Dutch ships now ran deeper in the water so they would have to pay more.[30]

From at least 1738 to the 1780s, however, the VOC ships going to China did not increase in size, so this excuse was probably invalid.[31] The pilots told the Dutch supercargoes that Danish ships were also paying Spanish $50 for the outward passage because they were running even deeper than the Dutch. The VOC officers questioned the Danes and verified that they were indeed now paying $50 per ship for the passage, when they had previously paid only $40.[32]

The Swedes also confirmed they were paying their pilots more on the inward passage because their ships were running deeper in the water.[33] After much negotiation the Dutch finally persuaded their pilots to agree on Spanish $35 per ship per passage. From 1763 to the 1780s the VOC paid $35 per ship and the Danes $50. By the 1790s some Danish ships were paying as much as $60 per passage so for some companies there was an increase in the fees over time.[34]

By the 1820s some of the larger ships were loading to capacity at Whampoa and then proceeding directly to sea without stopping at Bocca Tigris. Macao pilots managed this by employing more tow and buoy sampans, and they hired numerous Chinese to help them with the lines going out to the 60 or 70 sampans. Additional labourers were needed to keep the large procession moving in unison, and the expense of these extra helpers was over and above the pilot's fees.[35]

Pilots used a long bamboo pole to take the soundings of the river. If they thought a ship was coming too close to the shoals they would signal to the tow sampans to take the necessary precautions.[36] The depth of the river over the First and Second Bars decreased over time, so it became increasingly important to employ a greater number of assistants.[37]

During the entire Canton era the going rate for tow and buoy sampan hire was Spanish $1 per day or per trip (not to exceed a day), which is why they were also known as 'dollar boats'. Tow and signal sampans were paid $1 each for the trip from Whampoa to Bocca Tigris Roads (one day's hire) and another $1 if they were used between Bocca Tigris and Lintin Island (another day's hire). The same fee was charged whether going up or down the river because the sampans did not sail with or against the current, but rather with the tides. All the sampans, under-pilots and extra assistants were paid separately, so they were not included in the standard fees charged by the Macao pilots.[38]

A pilot took on an enormous responsibility when he assumed command of a foreign ship. The smallest miscalculation, either by himself or by any person under his command, could result in disaster. Even in the least serious cases it could take several days to have a grounded ship freed, which cost the owners dearly. More complicated rescues took many weeks and might require the unloading of all cargo, ballast, sails, cannons and even the ship's superstructure to re-float the vessel.[39]

Running a ship aground could also bring irreparable damage to a pilot's reputation, and it would be unlikely that he would be hired again by the same foreigners. Aside from probably losing his pay for the passage he had to be in attendance until the ship was freed and taken to Whampoa, which meant a loss of fees he could have earned from piloting other ships.[40] He might also have to endure a humiliating session before the Hoppo and/or governor-general to explain the accident.

Considering the risks, it was in the best interests of both the Macao pilots and the captains of large ships to make sure they had sufficient sampans to assist them. If the pilots wanted 50 tow sampans and 20 buoy sampans, and a dozen or more line-keepers, it was best not to argue with them. These were minor expenses compared to what it would cost if the ship ran aground.

There was much more to the process of piloting ships in the delta than appears from foreign records or the examples mentioned. Pilots had to communicate with all the tow and buoy sampans and send out proper warnings to other ships that were approaching in the night or in fog. The piloting procession set sail at all times of the day and night with the tides, and sometimes in very poor weather conditions. There could be hundreds of small craft in the delta at any time, so, to avoid collisions, every precaution needed to be taken to warn them of the approaching fleet.

For these reasons Chinese coastal patrols developed sophisticated navigation protocols and some of these tactics would have been employed by the Macao pilots. Many different sources tell us that drums, gongs, lanterns, torches, conch shells and variously coloured and shaped flags and banners were all common tools used by Chinese craft. Chinese vessels relayed commands by striking their gongs — two gongs to weigh anchor and three to set sail.[41] Gongs, rather than cannons, were also used to salute other Chinese vessels in the river.[42]

A well-established system of signals was used by all river craft. A fleet of Chinese fishing boats might consist of 40 or 50 sampans of about 25 tons each.[43] When they assembled into formation to force fish into waiting nets they moved in unison with 'great celerity' amid much commotion of gongs, drums, shouting and sending messages with torches.[44] The precision with which the fishing fleets sailed in the delta earned them the reputation of being 'extremely well regulated'. They were known to sail 'in perfect concert' with each other, with 'no boat presuming to anchor or weigh until the *Commandore* has made the signal by *Gong* or beat of the *Tom Tom*'.[45] These fishermen were the same persons who helped guide the foreign ships up and down the river so the Macao pilots needed to know these maritime protocols.

During the day there were ways of displaying various flags and banners (i.e., top-mast or half-mast) to communicate what type of vessels they were, where they were from, or whether they were anchored or moving. Flag signals were also used to give commands. During times of limited visibility, such as a thick fog, mist or heavy rain, a steady rhythm was struck on gongs and drums to warn other ships of a vessel's presence. Conch shells were also blown to sound a warning in the darkness: three long connected notes meant that a vessel was heading out to sea; three short connected notes signified they were heading inland.[46]

At night a specific number of fire arrows were sent into the sky in an emergency, such as if a vessel ran aground or came under pirate attack. A specific number of cannon shots told a piloting fleet to tack to port or starboard. Lanterns were also hung at different positions on the decks and in the masts to relay messages to others in the piloting fleet. Macao pilots had to communicate somehow with the 50 or more vessels in the processions and warn other vessels of their approach, so they were certain to have used these methods.[47]

Not all Macao pilots had a good reputation among the foreign captains. Some pilots, in fact, obtained their licenses for a fee and did not have much knowledge of ships. These 'pseudo' pilots made up for their lack of skill by hiring experienced Chinese fishermen to do their jobs for them.[48] They also hired many Chinese assistants to help them handle all the lines going out to the tow sampans. Having all these additional persons in attendance was not necessarily a sign of incompetence, because even experienced pilots needed these people to guard against running aground. On the outward passage Chinese assistants boarded the foreign ships at Whampoa. On the inward passage they boarded after the ships cleared customs at Bocca Tigris.[49]

Macao pilots, of course, had to remain aboard the foreign ships at all times because they were the ones licensed by the Chinese government. Their names were recorded with the customs office in Qianshan, and they wore their licenses around their waists. This practice of openly displaying their license on their person made it easier for customs officers and coastal cruisers to identify them from a distance.[50]

Macao pilots usually guided foreign ships between Macao and Bocca Tigris without the aid of other pilots, so they were not all necessarily without skill or experience.[51] It did not seem to matter whether the pilots did the guiding themselves or whether they hired others to do it for them, as long as there was someone aboard to take the soundings and give navigational advice. It was perhaps more important that Macao pilots knew a few commands in a foreign language. It was also very important for them to be able to lead, organise and orchestrate the myriad assistants and sampans in the piloting procession. Over time, even pseudo pilots could become experts on the river. In the event of getting a pseudo pilot, however, foreign captains were advised to be on guard so no orders were given that put the ship in harm's way.[52]

Ships of less than 450 tons did not need to take as many extra precautions when navigating the river, nor did the Chinese junks that frequented Canton. Many Canton junks had a capacity of about 250 tons, a flat-bottom, reduced keel and a shallow, seventeen-foot draught.[53] They could, therefore, clear the First and Second bars more easily than the large foreign ships, but they still needed a couple of large, oared sampans to pull them through the channels of the river. These special sampans had at least sixteen oarsmen (eight on each side) and charged a fee of Spanish $1 per oarsman.[54]

Sometimes the junks had to hire more sampans to help them navigate around the foreign ships anchored in Whampoa Roads. Ocean-going junks moored in a channel on the north side of Whampoa Island, known by the foreigners as 'Junk River'. Many junks also anchored further upriver next to the factories in Canton, where they could be more easily loaded and unloaded. Dockyards where junks were built and repaired were situated on the south side of the river, across from the city on Henan Island (河南島) so there were always several of them lying to there as well.

The junks had to manoeuvre around the foreign ships anchored in the deepest part of the channel on the southeast side of Whampoa Island. When the winds and currents were running contrary to the direction of travel, the flat-bottomed, keel-less junks were especially vulnerable to being spun around by the wind, current and eddies, which put them at great risk either of collision with other vessels or of running aground. They needed the assistance of six or seven oared sampans to keep them on course,[55] but, even in the worst situations, they did not need nearly as many sampans as the large foreign ships.[56]

A navigational guide from 1878 states that vessels with a draught of seventeen feet or less had great leeway in traversing the Pearl River; those with draughts between 17 and 20 feet needed to stay close to the main channel of the river (known by foreigners as the 'Fan-si-ak' or 'Chuen-bi' channel); and those with draughts of more than 20 feet had to sail at high tide and in the deepest channels to avoid running aground. By that year only vessels with a draught of less than seventeen feet could traverse the river safely at low tide, but they needed to stay in the Chuen-bi channel.[57]

An increase in the risks that were involved was paralleled by an increase in the Macao pilots' fees, at least until 1809. From about 150 ships of various sizes that frequented Canton from the 1730s to the 1830s, the following amounts in Spanish dollars appear in the records as being paid to the Macao pilots: in the 1730s and 1740s, $25 to $32 per passage; the 1750s and 1760s, $30 to $55; the 1770s and 1780s, $32 to $64 (sometimes higher); and, from 1801 to 1809, $40 to $68. Beginning in 1810, fees were fixed at $60 per passage (it is not known why).[58] They generally received one-third to a half of their fee up front and the balance when they were discharged.[59]

It was customary for the East India companies to tip (called *camsia* or *cumshaw*) their Macao pilots about 10 percent more than the amounts listed above. Many small American traders, on the other hand, appear to have been able to discharge their pilots without a monetary tip. This does not mean that pilots went away without a 'gratuity'.

If a monetary tip was not forthcoming pilots would pressure the ships' officers for some other type of remuneration, such as 'a piece or two of salt beef and a bottle of rum', 'a piece of rope or matting' or perhaps some 'wine-glasses'.[60] These gifts often do not show up in the ships' expense books, but they were indeed *camsia* that took the place of a gratuity. Even after the collapse of the Canton System and the restructuring of the pilots' fees in 1842, it was still customary to tip the pilots.[61]

As more ships visited China, the Junminfu licensed more Macao pilots. In the 1760s eight Macao pilots serviced all the foreign ships; by the 1820s there were fourteen licensed pilots; and by the early 1840s there were twenty-two.[62] Pilots had to pay for their licenses up front, which in 1823 was reported to be Spanish $600.[63] Licensing fees were an important source of government revenues, but they were so expensive it probably took a long time for pilots to recover their initial outlay.[64] Nevertheless, there are references that suggest these men were fairly affluent.[65]

Although they had a licence, pilots still needed permission from the Hoppo in Canton before they could guide ships from Whampoa to Bocca Tigris Roads. After arriving at Bocca Tigris, the pilots remained on call until the holds were full, which usually took about a month. They were paid Spanish $6 a month while they were on call.[66]

In the late eighteenth and early nineteenth centuries piracy was rampant in the delta, which made the pilots' jobs much more dangerous. They had to take precautions against not only pirate attacks, but also to approach a foreign ship cautiously so foreigners did not mistake them for pirates. The threat of piracy led to a more sophisticated and better organised system of piloting: Chinese patrol boats began escorting piloting groups, and the entire piloting fleet adapted military manoeuvres.[67]

Chinese pilots were not always the good gatekeepers they were intended to be. As smuggling depots sprang up in remote locations in the delta, many outside pilots bypassed Macao and guided ships directly into those harbours. Increased costs of trading in Canton, such as inflated compradors' fees and port fees that favoured larger ships (explained later) encouraged many small private traders to find ways to avoid these fees by trading illicitly in the delta. All kinds of goods were channelled in and out of China via these smuggling depots.[68]

A brief history of Macao called the *Aomen Jilüe* (1751) and the second edition of the *Xiangshan Gazetteer* (1828), both mention some of these anchorages where smuggling was carried on in the delta so they were well known places at the time.[69] By guiding ships into these smuggling depots, outside pilots directly aided the contraband trade. The customhouse in Macao tried to keep track of the activities of outside pilots but there were no effective measures in place to prevent the piloting of ships to any place in the delta.

There is some evidence to suggest outside pilots may have been forced to pay a part of their fees to local Mandarins. In 1762, for example, the Dutch Captain Hilverduin had a disagreement with the Chinese fishermen he had hired to tow his ship into Macao and, in the end, refused to pay them the amount they demanded. These fishermen then resorted to pleading with the head Dutch supercargo in Canton for compensation. They used the argument that the Mandarins of their hometown would persecute them if they did not give the officials their share of the towing fees. These cracks in the administrative structures in the delta made it possible for the contraband trade to put down deep roots.[70]

Macao pilots were also involved in contraband. In 1799 an official investigation found that they were using their foreign connections to smuggle opium into China. An imperial edict was issued to put a stop to this practice, but to little effect.[71] Customs did not have the resources to stop the trafficking. Moreover, the delta was overrun with pirates by then, which diverted attention from the smugglers.[72]

Despite these flaws, restricting the piloting of ships to licensed Chinese pilots was an important part of the Hoppos' strategy to control both the foreigners and trade. It was only effective, however, with deep-draughted sailing ships that could not safely traverse the river without the aid of a pilot. In 1830 a new era was ushered in as the first steamship, *Forbes*, made its way up the Pearl River. The advent of steam brought immediate changes to the traditional dependence on pilots and assistant boats. Steamships had their own source of power and could turn upon command, so they were much more manoeuvrable than their wind-driven counterparts. They could also tow other ships behind them. The *Forbes*, for example, arrived in China towing the opium ship *Jamesina*.[73]

Steamships might not have been dependent on tow and buoy sampans, but Macao pilots were still desirable because of their knowledge of the currents, eddies and shoals. Of course, it was still mandatory for steamships to have Macao pilots aboard in order to clear customs at Bocca Tigris. There are examples of sailing ships leaving Whampoa without pilots or their Grand Chops in the company of other ships that had their chops and pilots; they could do this only with the movement of the tides, which gave Chinese cruisers time to intercept them.[74] The steamship, however, gave foreigners power over tides, river and winds. Their shallow bottoms allowed them to bypass forts at Bocca Tigris and go up other channels in the river.

In 1840 the steam-frigate *Nemesis* sailed up the West River without the aid of a pilot or sampans. This was how it was able to commence the first attack on Canton in the First Opium War. It was thought that large ships would not be able to pass through this back entrance because of its shallow depths (about twelve feet).[75] This was true for most sailing ships, but not for steamers. The West River was protected at Luozhou entrance (螺洲門) by the Modao Fort (磨刀炮台) on one side and the Luozhou Fort (螺洲炮台) on the other, but the *Nemesis* slipped by those fortifications without trouble.[76] On 12 and 13 March 1841, the *Nemesis* returned to the West River and destroyed 105 cannons, demolished seven forts, blew up nine war-junks and burned down the 'Tszenai' (Zini 紫泥) tollhouse. It then moved on to attack other Chinese fortifications.

The *Nemesis* was a broad-bottomed frigate, and even though it carried a burthen of 700 tons, it drew a draught of only about six feet of water. A typical sailing ship of this size would have drawn about twenty feet. The *Nemesis* did not need to balance the resistance of the wind blowing against heavy topsails with an equal drag of the hull underwater, which is why it could get by with two false keels that could be raised to go over even shallower depths of five feet.[77]

Thus, the shallow-bottomed steamer single-handedly undermined the role of the Macao pilots as the gatekeepers to trade. The Hoppos could not control the steamers the way they had sail ships, and that loss of power eventually led to foreigners taking control of the port of Canton. The 1830s saw the arrival of other steamships as well, but it was not until the *Nemesis* that the Chinese government began to realise the extent to which this radical invention had altered trade. The steamer completely changed the rules of the game.[78]

By looking at the changes made in the piloting fees after the First Opium War (which were based on the way fees were structured in many other ports), we can see that the Canton System of piloting favoured large ships. In August 1843 a notice was posted in Canton 'allowing any fisherman to act as a pilot to a foreign ship, in the same manner as the old regularly licensed pilots, provided he was furnished with a pass'. Pilot offices were set up in Canton, Macao and Hong Kong to issue the permits.[79]

The old fee of Spanish \$60 a ship (regardless of size) was thrown out and a new system introduced based on five cents per registered ton.[80] Under the new structure a 330-ton ship paid only Spanish \$16.50 per passage, and it no longer had to hire extra tow and buoy sampans if it was not thought necessary. A ship of 1,400 tons, however, paid \$70 under the new system, and it still needed all the extra sampans to guide it. The small private traders benefited from the changes, and the large ships had to pay more. Thus, in a very small way, even the structure of the piloting fees helps to show why the foreigners would have been more eager to force the end of the Canton System in the late 1830s than was the case when the large EIC ships were still operating in China (before 1834). This idea will be explained in more detail in later chapters.

SUMMARY

There is no factor more clearly connected to the increase in the size of ships going to Canton than the establishment of efficient piloting procedures. Even though the river grew more hazardous over time and its depth remained perilously shallow, larger ships continued to visit Canton and the overall volume of trade expanded. This growth can, in great part, be directly attributed to the Macao pilots. They began to gain control of the piloting process in the 1750s and continued to improve the organisation of the procedure throughout the Canton era. The annual increase in revenues that was the result of this dramatic expansion in volume, combined with the Hoppos' increased control of the deep-draughted ships that could not travel the river without their permission, camouflaged the gradual weakening of internal administrative structures and the external threat of the steamer.

By the late eighteenth century cracks were beginning to appear in the piloting process. The lack of control over the outside pilots who were bringing ships into the delta (probably with the connivance of the Mandarins), coupled with the high fees charged to small ships at Canton, enabled and encouraged the development of sophisticated smuggling networks. Both the outside pilots and Macao pilots were involved in the trafficking of contraband, and thus, were not the effective gatekeepers of trade that they were supposed to be. Opium smuggling and the contraband trade ate away at both the social fabric and the effectiveness of existing administrative structures. Additional measures were needed to address the deficiencies in the customs networks, but none were forthcoming. As a result the Canton System continued to deteriorate internally while new challenges threatened it from without.

The final blow to the traditional trade in China fell with the arrival of steamers in the 1830s. Those intrusive machines rewrote the rules of engagement and pierced the heart of the Canton System. Virtually overnight, steamers undermined the role of the Macao pilots, the effectiveness of the forts at Bocca Tigris and the power of the Hoppos over trade. Thus, the arrival of the *Forbes* in 1830 can be said to mark the beginning of the end of the Canton System. Macao pilots managed to survive the initial changes that followed the system's collapse, but the Hoppos could no longer rely on them to control foreign commerce. As shallow-bottomed steamers gradually took control of much of the commerce in the delta the Macao pilots became redundant and their glory days as the commandants of the Pearl River quietly passed into obscurity.

We now turn to the provisions trade, which was another of the control mechanisms that weakened over time and contributed to the Hoppos' gradual loss of power. Chapters 4 and 5 will both show how the dependence on the Macao pilots to guide the ships out to sea enabled the provisions trade and the linguists to operate entirely on credit, which greatly accommodated a smooth and timely conduct of trade.

CHAPTER FOUR

COMPRADORS AND THE PROVISIONS TRADE

THE PROVISIONS TRADE IN CANTON provided large quantities of supplies and victuals to an ever-increasing number of ships; it became one of the most important industries for the smooth conduct of trade and control of foreigners in China. As we will see, the weaknesses that developed within the provisions trade would affect the overall effectiveness of the Canton System.

In 1731 provision purveyors or 'compradors'[1] were officially licensed by the Junminfu at Qianshan. Like the Macao pilots, they wore a wooden license around their waist so it could be easily seen from a distance.[2] The compradors' licensing fees were passed on to the foreign traders in the form of a one-off payment.[3] These fees began to rise in the 1780s and continued to do so until the 1830s. Many foreigners, especially the private traders, were charged fees disproportionate to the size and needs of their ships. This only encouraged them to seek provisions from other foreigners in Canton rather than from the Chinese.

In the 1780s and 1790s foreigners began selling provisions privately to other foreigners, bypassing the compradors. By the early 1800s the Chinese linguists and tidewaiters stationed next to the ships had gained control of much of this illicit and lucrative trade. Sidestepping the compradors siphoned funds away from the Hoppos, and weakened their control of trade. A close examination of the activities of the compradors will show other areas in the administration that were responsible for the enormous growth of the trade while at the same time contributed to the overall weakening of the central administration and foreigners' unhappiness with the way trade was being conducted.

Control of the provisions trade by the compradors began very early in Canton. In 1704 Lockyer mentioned that 'every factory had formerly a *Compradore*', but because the Hoppos tried to extract 'liberty' money from them 'they have of late been quite discarded'. A year earlier, Captain Hamilton stated that he was required to purchase all his provisions from an 'Interpreter at *Maccao*', who assisted the Hoppo and spoke Portuguese. Captain Hamilton declared he had no choice but to purchase provisions from this person.[4]

By 1716 the English were purchasing their provisions from compradors at both Canton and Whampoa, a practice that would continue for some time.[5] The GIC captains and supercargoes acquired their provisions from compradors in the 1720s.[6] Beginning in 1729, the Dutch also entered into contracts with compradors each year to supply provisions (see Plate 13).[7]

In 1730 the Dutch submitted a petition consisting of thirteen articles to the Hoppo. Article Two requested they be allowed to choose their own linguists, compradors and servants; Article Nine requested they be allowed to procure whatever was needed for the repair and maintenance of their ships, without restriction.[8] The Dutch supercargoes received the following reply from the Hoppo.

> After the ships have been a long time sailing at sea, they are in the need of cordage, wood, and other provisions. They must make a list of what is needed. I shall issue a chop to allow for their purchase. It is forbidden to purchase items without my permission or to transport items by anyone who is not in my service.[9]

Controlling the daily flow of victuals and naval stores to the crews, captains and supercargoes was one way for Hoppos to control the foreign community. Ensuring a steady flow of provisions was prudent because a crew that was not properly fed was a crew likely to cause trouble.[10] Captains and supercargoes who did not receive their packaging materials, containers and Chinese labourers in a timely fashion in order to pack goods, tranship merchandise and prepare their ships for departure were also a potential source of trouble. If their goods did not arrive on time owing to lack of materials or insufficient help in stowing cargo, the ships faced lying over for another season. Such delays could cut deeply into company profits.

If a full stomach was a way to pacify, then it stood to reason that an empty stomach was a way to persuade. Controlling the foreign community at Canton was not an easy task for the Hoppos. Foreigners fought with the Chinese occasionally and also had disagreements among themselves. Chinese living on the river often tried to take advantage of the foreigners by selling them watered-down liquor or defective products, which gave rise to disputes; foreigners often tried to cheat the customs officers or other Chinese of their fees and payments. Although contact with foreigners was 'officially' restricted to licensed individuals such as compradors, linguists and pilots, many ordinary Chinese engaged them by washing or mending their clothes, or simply begging for handouts.[11]

If a problem arose within the foreign community or trade that could not be resolved immediately, Hoppos removed the linguists and forbade the Chinese merchants from doing any trade until the matter was settled. Word was also sent to the pilots forbidding them from piloting recalcitrant foreigners. If the stoppage of trade was not enough to bring the incident to a close, then removing the compradors and ending the daily flow of water, provisions and servants usually proved persuasive.[12]

As the numbers of foreigners increased, it became much more difficult to control the provisions going to them. In the 1760s about 20 foreign ships visited China each year, but by the 1790s there were 50; by the 1810s, 70; and by the 1830s more than 180.[13] With 100 to 150 men aboard each company ship and anywhere from a dozen to a hundred or more aboard a private ship, the number of foreigners for whom the compradors were responsible jumped from thousands to tens of thousands. The number of licensed compradors was increased but this, in turn, put greater responsibility on the Hoppo's office to supervise them all. As the numbers of foreigners increased, the traditional means of controlling and persuading them became less effective.

There were two types of compradors in Canton: those who serviced the factories ('factory compradors') and those who serviced the ships ('ship compradors'). The factory comprador supplied all the provisions and Chinese personnel for the foreign trading houses, a role similar to that of a 'dubash' in India.[14] Factory compradors often lived with the foreigners and worked for them year round. Some companies hired several factory compradors, but there was usually a head comprador in charge of the others.

The foreign companies often supplied their factory compradors (and their retinues) with meals and a sampan to transport provisions and other materials necessary for the maintenance of the household. Wages for all Chinese servants in the factory were paid monthly to the head comprador. He was responsible for obtaining the Hoppo's permission for supercargoes in Macao to return to Canton in the following season (usually July, August or September). As soon as their ships arrived, foreigners sent the head comprador to request a Macao pilot to take it to Whampoa. The Macao pilots often went out to the company ships in the comprador's boat. The head comprador would then begin organising the supercargoes' trip back to Canton. He was also responsible for obtaining the permission chop or license to return, which was usually granted about a week or two after the ship arrived.

All persons in the entourage from Macao had to be accounted for at each tollhouse in the West River. If fifteen foreigners, thirteen Chinese, six slaves and one milk cow left Macao, then fifteen foreigners, thirteen Chinese, six slaves and one milk cow had to arrive in Canton a couple of days later. If a person or animal died en route (which happened), the corpse had to complete the journey so there was an accurate account on arrival. Additional transport sampans were sometimes needed to carry livestock or the company's billiard table and other furniture or personal belongings. The West River route between Canton and Macao was about 120 miles (195 kilometres), and it could take from two to four days to complete the passage, depending on the weather, tides, delays at the tollhouses and number of times the foreigners stopped to milk the cow for their afternoon tea.[15]

During the off season, the factories in Canton, which were full of furniture and wares left over from the previous season, were left in the care of their owners.[16] A couple of Chinese house servants would act as caretakers in each one. Occasionally, a comprador would be assigned to stay with these men. The owner of each building was asked to bear the expense of any repairs and was later reimbursed by the supercargoes if the repairs were not part of the rental agreement (they were usually separate). All Chinese servants and compradors in Macao and Canton were permanent employees of foreign companies and often worked for them their entire lives, some even learning the language of their employers as well as the lingo used in Canton business: pidgin English.

Over the years some foreigners and their compradors became close and trusted friends, which also contributed to the trade's stability. One of the most amazing stories of life-long service that has surfaced from the records is that of comprador Atack (Lü Yade 呂亞德). Atack began as a comprador in the Dutch factory in 1737 at the age of fifteen.[17] He worked with some of his brothers and other compradors in caring for the Dutch household and supplying provisions for VOC ships.[18]

In the 1760s Atack was a partner in the business with two other factory compradors, Amie (亞美) and Apo (亞保). The three signed contracts with the company each year to supply all the provisions needed for the Dutch factory and the VOC ships (see Plate 13). All prices were listed in detail in these contracts and the compradors were bound to supply goods at market prices. It was often written into the agreement that they had to supply goods at the lowest prices available in Canton. The compradors could not charge more than noted in the contract, and if another foreigner was able to buy an article cheaper, the compradors would be required to match the price, which provided consistency and stability to the conduct of trade.

Compradors were responsible for spillage, and in the contract in Plate 13 the wages of the factory cooks and their servants (see *koks* and ditto *maats*) are included. In the 1760s the three compradors in the Dutch factory took care of the household and commissioned four ship compradors, Adjouw (亞伍), Allay

(亞黎), Ajet (亞日) and Attay (亞帝), to supply goods to the VOC ships. Thus, in this case, the factory compradors were in charge of the ship compradors but that was not always the case with other foreigners.[19]

Beginning in about 1774 when Atack was in his fifties, he began staying in Canton the entire year, taking care of the factory in the off-season, then servicing the Dutch household when they returned from Macao in August or September. Supercargoes often dispatched letters to Atack from Macao asking for information or requesting that he pay a visit to one of the *Hong* merchants. Even in his senior years he was still employed to watch over the factory. In 1797 he fought off an extensive flood, the result of heavy rains and storms in the month of August that threatened the premises.[20]

On 15 January 1798 the Dutch supercargoes reported that 'old Atack is very sick'.[21] He died the next day at the age of 75. The Dutch officers, who held Atack in very high esteem, genuinely mourned his passing. He had been in service for so long that even the supercargoes had lost track of the number of years he had worked for them.[22] There were other compradors who devoted their entire lives to servicing foreign companies, but Atack's story is exemplary.[23]

Some of the compradors picked up a bit of their employer's language, but, as far as their careers were concerned, it was more important for them to learn pidgin English. Compradors often had to deliver errands and messages to other foreigners, so they needed to be able to speak the language common to them all. The following excerpt from an American logbook in 1815 shows how the compradors managed to communicate with all the different nationals in Whampoa.

> The comprador[s] . . . speak a broken English mixed up with Portuguese, some Dutch, and French, the same as most of the Chinamen who come about the ship. It is rather difficult to understand them at first, but one soon gets used to hearing them.[24]

The duties and responsibilities of ship compradors were somewhat different from those of the factory. Ship compradors supplied all the provisions and labourers that foreign crews needed, but they did not remain with the ships 24 hours a day and they were employed only for the time the ships were in China. The same ship compradors might be hired year after year by the same foreigners but it was not year-round employment unless they were used in the factories in the off-season. The same was true for all servants and craftsmen the ship compradors hired to care for the foreigners at Whampoa. Thus, the most fundamental difference between the two compradors was continuity of employment.

There was usually at least one licensed comprador for each ship, but some companies hired several compradors to service all company ships together. Ship compradors had their own sampans and usually had other family members and servants helping them. In 1838 the comprador of the American ship *Logan* was reported to have six sons, four daughters and two wives.[25] Being able to support such a large family is a sign of their affluence.

Ship compradors were on the move day and night so it was necessary to live aboard their sampans. They transported the provisions they purchased at the local markets in the Canton region to the ships, regardless of where they were located in the river. They often had to service ships anchored at Whampoa Roads, Bocca Tigris Roads, Macao Roads, or some other location in the delta at the same time. Someone was always at the helm of the comprador's sampan guiding it to its next destination.

Ship compradors had a huge responsibility keeping foreign crews satisfied. As we saw earlier, company ships often had from 100 to 150 men who needed meals a couple of times a day. In 1730, for example, the GIC ship *Apollo*, with a crew of 107 men, stayed in Whampoa for five months while taking on cargo. In that time, the sailors consumed thousands of piculs of fruit and vegetables; hundreds of chickens, quails and pigeons; hundreds of piculs of pork, mutton and fish; and a whole cow every two to three days, making a total of forty-six cows in five months.[26]

These provisions were only the staple items that were consumed in China. Each ship in Whampoa also purchased enormous quantities for the return passage home. In December 1776, for example, the comprador for the SOIC ship *Adolph Friedrick* delivered 300 capons, 300 hens, 100 pomelos, 60 ducks, 50 geese, 10 calves, 6 sheep, 3 cows and many other items for the return passage. If we multiply those figures by the number of ships in Whampoa (about ten in the 1730s and 30 or more in the 1770s), we begin to have an idea of the enormous volume of provisions the compradors handled every day.[27]

The compradors' wives took care of the children and the daily domestic chores aboard the sampans. The women were responsible for the rowing or sculling on most of the small Chinese craft in the river, as well as for all the family's laundering and tailoring needs. Sampan women were often seen with children strapped to their backs.[28] Many Chinese men were adept at cooking, so the boys and men aboard the sampans may have shared that duty with the women. It was in the compradors' best interests to teach their sons to cook because it could lead to regular employment with the foreigners. Chinese women were not allowed aboard foreign ships or in factories, so all the foreigners' domestic needs were provided by the compradors' male relatives and friends.

Ship compradors greeted foreign vessels upon their arrival with fresh fruit, vegetables and meat.[29] Like the pilots, compradors showed newcomers letters of recommendation from other captains they had served. In time the compradors would usually have a collection of recommendations, which were an effective tool for persuading a reluctant captain or supercargo to hire them. Recommendations were used more by ship compradors than factory compradors because the former could service several different foreigners at the same time, whereas the latter were bound to one household.[30]

Ship compradors also sold their goods according to prices set in contracts, which were already a part of the trade by the early years of the eighteenth century.[31] Prices and wages usually covered Canton, Whampoa and Macao. A contract would sometimes stipulate a different price on a couple of items for each location, but wages and most prices were the same regardless of where the ship was in the delta. Thus, as far as labour and provisions were concerned, the entire delta operated as a single market.[32]

Contracts also guaranteed that prices would cover the entire trading season, and the quality of goods was subject to approval. If the foreigners were dissatisfied with the items they received, they could ask the compradors to replace them or simply deduct the amount in question from the comprador's next payment. Because the compradors knew what the retail price was going to be, they also knew what the wholesale price would have to be in order to make a profit. Having this information in advance enabled them to pressure suppliers to acceptable terms, which gave them some ability to protect profit margins. Thus, contracts benefited both parties and helped to make the provisions trade very stable and secure.[33]

Another innovation that greatly accommodated the overall expansion of the trade was thirty-day credit. When the ships arrived at the beginning of the season, they were supplied with everything they needed, prior to any agreement with the factory or ship compradors. Foreigners insisted on this freedom because they needed to check the local market before signing any contracts. After the going prices and wages were determined, an accord would be reached. Prices in the contracts were usually retroactive, so applied to all goods already delivered on credit. As we saw in chapter 3, the foreigners could not leave without a Macao pilot, and he could not be hired until all accounts were settled so the compradors had nothing to worry about. Revolving monthly accounts were very convenient for foreigners because they did not have to keep cash on hand to pay petty transactions.[34] Instant credit was also available to newcomers in Canton.[35]

The fierce competition for foreigners' business meant that compradors could never form any kind of mutual accord whereby they could control prices or wages in Canton or Macao. Prices of many provisions continued to rise throughout the Canton era, but this was usually because of inflation, not artificial manipulation. Foreigners tried to curb the forces of inflation as much as possible by pegging their comprador contracts to the previous year's prices. This practice, however, was successful only while the goods were still available at the lower prices.[36]

As compradors gained favour and respect among foreign traders, the demand for their services increased. There was a limit, however, to the number of foreigners and ships one comprador or company of compradors could service. They worked around this problem by assigning an agent to each ship under their charge. These agents, sometimes called 'Sanpan-Sam' by the foreigners, stayed aboard the vessels the entire time they were at anchor in Whampoa Roads.[37] They kept track of the ships' provision inventories, took daily orders from the officers and relayed them to the comprador. When the goods arrived, Sanpan-Sam checked to make sure orders had been filled properly and handled any complaints that arose. He also took private orders from the crew, such as for a set of clothes or a pair of shoes.[38]

Ship compradors provided a small shack (known as a 'bankshall') on one of the islands in Whampoa Roads where foreigners could store and repair their rigging. The ships' livestock were transferred to the bankshalls, and sick sailors were sent there to convalesce. Sailors could camp out there while their ships were being smoked for rats and mice or laid on their side for careening.[39] There were always a couple of foreign sentries on duty at each bankshall, because they were often places where liquor was purchased, quarrels started and murders committed.[40]

Foreigners fell ill and died or were killed in accidents that occurred in the loading and unloading of ships. Sailors fell overboard while working on the rigging, and invariably drowned. Plate 16 shows how common death was in China. This document is an extract from one of the GIC ship journals that was anchored at Whampoa in September 1724. Note the skull and crossbones drawn in the margin each day a sailor died. Other foreign crews faced similar problems so foreign deaths were often a daily occurrence in China.[41]

Compradors and linguists had to take care of these unfortunate incidents in addition to their normal duties. A gravesite had to be purchased and prepared for the interment on either French or Danes Islands (the usual places where foreigners were buried). The compradors ordered the coffins and gravestones and made sure everything was carried out in proper order. If the death occurred in Canton, then the linguists ordered a chop to permit the body to be transported to Whampoa.[42]

Compradors obtained their provisions from many different sources. By looking at their suppliers and some of the small vendors who were dependent on foreign income, we begin to see the enormous number of people affected by a stoppage of trade. A present-day analogy might be the arrival of naval vessels in Hong Kong each year to allow the crews shore leave. For many businesses, the money they make from the foreigners in this short period is a substantial part of their annual income, so when those ships do not come into port there is an outcry from the business community. Similarly, in the eighteenth century, when the Hoppos stopped the flow of provisions and goods, compradors and foreigners suffered along with hundreds of families who lost sales and incomes.

Wild ducks were a favourite of the compradors, and there was a unique way of catching these birds. Hunters hollowed out large gourds and pierced a couple of holes through which they could see and breathe and placed these gourds on their heads. The hunters then walked into the river up to their necks (or the bottom of the gourd) and waited for a duck to land next to them. The hunter then grabbed the legs of the duck as it swam past, pulled it under the water to prevent it from alerting the rest of the flock, wrung its neck, strapped it to his girdle and waited for the next duck to arrive.[43] If a large gourd could not be found, then earthen pots were used. Wild ducks caught in this way could also be kept alive.[44] They commonly sold for almost the same price as domestic ducks (0.075 taels per catty in 1760), and all that was needed to catch them was a gourd, a lot of determination and an abundance of patience.[45]

All types of fowl and four-legged animals, such as pigs and goats, were raised aboard the tens of thousands of sampans in the river. Thus, compradors did not necessarily have to go into the city to get what they needed. Sampans were moored in avenues on the river, forming streets of floating warehouses and markets where fruit, meat, vegetables and almost anything one desired could be purchased. Naval stores, such as pitch and timber, were floated downriver from the Chinese hinterland, so these were also available without having to go into the city. Common hardware items, such as nails, iron straps and hinges, were needed by all craft on the river, so they would have also been available in the floating city.[46]

Live buffalo and buffalo meat were also regular items of the compradors' trade. These animals were raised on the many islands in the river and on the mainland, where they were allowed to graze on the patches of grass that lay between the rice paddies. They were beasts of burden so, when they were old, they were butchered and sold to foreigners. This meat tended to be very tough, so it was often made into salt-beef. Compradors also sold young bullocks, which foreigners butchered aboard the ships and consumed straight away. They purchased young animals for the return passage so many bullocks were raised specifically for the market and not used as beasts of burden. From the example of the ship *Apollo* above, we can see that hundreds of bullocks were consumed by the foreigners each year. Goats were also raised on the many mountainous islands in the delta, such as Lintin.[47]

In the river and delta there were many fishermen from whom the compradors bought fish that they resold to foreigners. Some fishermen had fishing birds, which were large cormorants that had a cord tied to one leg. A ring was placed over the lower part of the bird's neck so they could not swallow their catch. The owners retrieved the fish from their beaks, but, at the end of the day, the rings were removed and the birds were allowed to consume the final catch as their reward.[48] Other fishermen used nets, hooks and traps to catch fish, crabs, crayfish and eels, which they sold to the compradors. Nets and cords were used to catch wild ducks, geese and other waterfowl, which were abundant in the marshes and waterways in the region.

Many boats were equipped especially to raise domestic ducks for the Canton market. One sampan, with just a couple of attendants, could raise more than a thousand ducks. Their owners operated in conjunction with the rice-paddy managers. The ducks would be let loose in the paddies every day to eat and clear them of frogs and insects. They returned every evening at the call or whistle of their owners. Any stragglers were disciplined with a switch, which made them all attentive to their masters' summons. Ducks, of course, laid eggs, which were also sold to the compradors. Foreigners consumed eggs in enormous quantities, with ships and factories often purchasing them in the hundreds or even thousands, so the duck-boat operators had a very lively market in Canton.[49]

The ships' stoves required huge quantities of fuel, which was obtained from the compradors. Many people made a living from extracting, processing and delivering coal, charcoal and firewood, all of which was available from markets in the floating city. Compradors also delivered fresh water to the ships, for which they charged 0.01 taels per picul (about 133 pounds).[50]

Foreigners placed rattan or bamboo matting between each tier of cargo to secure the goods and provide a flat floor for the next layer. Bulkheads had to be braced and cargo shored up, so compradors sold many bundles of bamboo and rattan. Every ship required large quantities of tar, varnish, paint, nails and caulk to prepare for the return passage, as well as rope, yarn, string, twine and bamboo hoops to overhaul tackling, mend sails, repair gunny sacks, bind packages and chests, and repair wooden vats and barrels. Many of these goods were taken to Canton by Chinese junks and private traders from ports in Southeast Asia and India.

Like all other loyal male citizens in China, compradors had to have their hair cut in the Qing fashion. This requirement gave rise to an army of barbers in Canton who serviced the floating population, including the compradors and their male helpers. Straddling nothing more than a couple of boards, barbers paddled their way up and down the many avenues of junks and sampans.[51] They announced their arrival with their customary hawkers' call (a type of ratchet).

Compradors could obtain all the latest news and gossip in Canton from the barbers. For Chinese who had just arrived from the countryside, the first thing to do was to have a haircut because the barbers could provide them with information about employment, places to stay and business contacts.[52] Sailors aboard foreign ships in Whampoa also regarded Chinese barbers as 'walking newspapers' who had the latest news of events in Canton and from whom they could order 'any article we wanted'.[53] In this regard, barbers actually competed, admittedly on a very small scale, with the compradors in obtaining items for the common sailors. When they were not allowed to visit the ships or factories because of the stoppage of trade, they lost their daily incomes.

Not all the river people could make a living from selling to the compradors. Some were so poor they were known as river scavengers who benefited from the by-products of the compradors' trade. Foreigners regularly discarded offal, rotten provisions, dead animals and other rubbish while at anchor in Whampoa Roads, and they would complain that the scavengers fell upon these morsels with glee. The dung sampans were also a regular sight along the river, carrying human excrement to the rice paddies. Blind beggars were always present in Canton, because they meandered through the streets arm in arm begging for a trifle from a foreign sailor or supercargo. There were also colonies of lepers in and around Canton who were occasionally seen along the river bathing at places thought to have special healing powers. They were also at the mercy of others for their sustenance.

Some of the people mentioned above benefited directly from contact with the compradors and the foreigners, whereas others benefited indirectly. Any disruption in the compradors' trade that disallowed contact with foreigners could thus have a dramatic effect on many lives in the delta, especially of those who had their means of sustenance cut off. The businesses that were affected of course include the 'flower boats' (brothels) that were stationed along the river to service the foreign community. The *Hong* merchants sometimes provided the foreigners in the factories with 'loose women' in order to gain their favour in trade, which implicated the compradors as well. It was illegal for women to enter the factories so they had to be brought in secretly.[54] The sex industry had nothing to do with provisions, but the two trades suffered and prospered together because they both depended on foreigners for all or part of their incomes.

Many of the hundreds of sex workers in Whampoa and Canton were nothing less than slaves who had been forced into that occupation so we cannot say that they received any benefits from contact with foreigners (other than perhaps a means of staying alive). Prostitutes might receive better treatment from their masters when business was good, but increased interaction also meant greater possibility of pregnancy and disease. Thus it was the owners and managers of those establishments who were financially affected from a stoppage of trade, but the workers might be sold if there was not enough business to pay for their sustenance.[55]

A halt in trade could also affect preparations for the foreigners' return passage. Besides the daily delivery of food, ship compradors helped foreigners obtain the necessary labour and products they needed to refurbish the ships while they were lying at anchor in Whampoa Roads. They were often completely stripped of their tackling and painted inside and out. This enormous task required numerous Chinese carpenters, caulkers, shipwrights, cabinetmakers, painters and couriers. Chinese bricklayers were sometimes employed to overhaul the ships' stoves. A 'cooking sampan' was anchored alongside the ship while the stove was out of commission.

Compradors organised the cooks to prepare the provisions they supplied. The ships' regular cooks were often sent to the factories, and the compradors found Chinese cooks to replace them.[56] In 1747 Noble mentioned that the Chinese cooks employed on the English ships at Whampoa had been 'long employed' and 'could speak the English language pretty well'. He said that they learned to dress the 'victuals after the English manner, as well and expeditiously' as their own cooks. Noble's example suggests that the compradors probably hired the same Chinese cooks to service the same foreigners year after year.[57]

If there was insufficient space aboard the ships for all the extra labourers, a sampan was anchored alongside to provide sleeping quarters for the Chinese crew. It was more economical for the Chinese labourers to stay with the ship at all times, rather than travel from Canton every morning and evening. Some compradors and Chinese workers lived on Whampoa Island, so it was easier for them to return home at the end of the day.[58]

Half-a-dozen to a dozen caulkers were kept busy from morning until evening pounding caulk into the cracks between the deck planks. Three or more carpenters repaired and overhauled the ships' cabins, decks and holds. They also built bulkheads, false floors and bracing for the stowage of cargo.

The rigging, tackling and sails of the ships were usually left to the care of the foreign carpenters, shipwrights and sail-makers, who would spend three or four months overhauling all the items at the bankshalls. Damaged ships, however, often required immediate repairs, so from 50 to 100 Chinese shipwrights might be added to the crew of foreign shipwrights to help raise masts, set rigging or tar new spars. If many were needed, the compradors hired a Chinese foreman or supervisor to keep the Chinese crew working in unison with the foreign crew. Repair crews could be enticed to work longer days and exert themselves more diligently with offers of daily bonuses and, of course, extra rounds of rum.

Chinese cabinetmakers built and repaired the animal cages and pens. Chinese painters went through the vessels inside and out, applying fresh coats of paint and varnish wherever needed. Chinese tradesmen could also be employed in the bankshalls, to repair or expand the buildings, build pens for the livestock, or to help in the overhaul of the rigging. Chinese workmen were waited on by a crew of Chinese boys, who acted as their couriers. In addition to delivering drinking water and meals, these young helpers — probably sons and relatives of the tradesmen — carried planks, bamboo, matting, caulk, tar, paint, varnish, buckets of nails, bricks and tools from the compradors' boats to the workers aboard the ships and in the bankshalls.

Because foreign ships were often constructed with one large, leaky hull (as opposed to many small, self-concealed compartments in Chinese junks and in many present-day ships), they needed to be pumped throughout the day and night. It was usually the duty of the ship's watch to man the pumps and record the number of strokes (to keep track of how serious the leaks were), but more Chinese caulkers might be hired to have the holes plugged as quickly as possible.[59] Many ships hired about 30 Chinese craftsmen and labourers for the three to four months they spent at Whampoa, but some hired 100 or more, depending on their needs. Their wages were paid at the end of each month when the compradors submitted their expense sheets.

Plate 31 shows one of comprador Asek's monthly payments in 1759. He turned in his expense sheet to the Danish supercargoes for the cost of supplying the DAC ship *Cron Princen af Danmarck* from 21 November to 25 December (inclusive). All the items he supplied for this period were listed in the comprador's account book, and were checked against Asek's contract with the company.

Because so many people were involved with, and benefited from, direct and indirect contact with foreigners, it was wise for the Hoppos and governors-general not to stop the compradors' trade indiscriminately for insignificant reasons. This could backfire on them by giving rise to more social unrest, crime and corruption, because the Chinese affected struggled to meet their daily needs. Many of these people were living from hand-to-mouth so any disruption in their work could mean starvation.[60]

Hundreds of foreign sailors in Whampoa become bored and anxious when the trade was stopped and they did not receive fresh food every day. Foreign captains and officers also became fearful for the safety of their return passages owing to insufficient time to finish preparations. The longer the halt the more threatening this situation became, so there were many factors to consider when using this method to pressure foreigners into compliance.

We can see from the many examples presented that there were often large numbers of foreigners and Chinese working and living together in close quarters. The compradors were held responsible for all of them, but there were surprisingly few serious disputes each year. Both the foreign officers and Chinese authorities handed out harsh punishments to instigators of maliciousness and foul play. Foreign captains and compradors instructed all men in their charge to treat each other with respect and humanity or suffer the consequences — an apparently effective threat. Foreign officers aboard the ships and at the bankshalls monitored interaction at all times, as did the Chinese linguists and tidewaiters, so the compradors had help in maintaining harmony.

Punishments such as 50 lashes on a bare back were common occurrences at Whampoa. Keelhauling and hanging were also sometimes carried out on the foreign ships while they were in China. With all of these punishments, crews of every foreign ship might be required by their captains to stand at attention on deck and witness the punishments as an example to them all. Compradors and linguists were required to report all such incidents to the Canton authorities so they were aware of what was happening in the foreign community. Sometimes Mandarins were sent to Whampoa to monitor and witness the punishments. Chinese officials also carried out punishments such as beatings and decapitation in public. These graphic warnings proved fairly effective, because on the whole order prevailed.[61]

Besides earning a profit on the items they sold, compradors also charged engagement fees to each ship, which became a source of foreign discontent when they began to rise in the late eighteenth and early nineteenth centuries. In 1724 the English reported the compradors' fees to be 120 to 150 taels.[62] In 1731 the Dutch paid 80 taels per ship for their compradors.[63] In 1732 Colin Campbell of the Swedish company reported the fees to be 100 to 150 taels per ship.[64] In 1759 the Danes clarified the difference in the charges. They mentioned that the English paid 100 taels, they paid 72 taels and the Swedes and French each paid Spanish $150 (111 taels and 108 taels respectively).[65]

It is not clear why there was such a difference in the fees paid. There is some evidence to suggest the compradors charged according to the volume of provisions they handled. However, we have fairly good data on the size of the ships and crews going to China in this early period that do not correspond with the assumption that larger ships paid less than smaller ones. For example, in the 1730s the Danish and Swedish ships and crews were larger than those of the Dutch and English.[66] Thus, it is not clear why the English were charged less than the Swedes, and the Dutch charged almost the same as the Danes.

Despite the many variations, before the 1780s the compradors' fees remained consistent for the large company ships. Individual companies paid different amounts, but the same fees appear to have been charged to the same foreigners. In the 1780s, however, the fees begin to rise dramatically. This rise paralleled the expansion of the opium trade, and probably had a connection to it.

Many of the Hoppos' staff, linguists and toll officers, on the other hand, charged the same amounts in 1830 as they had in 1730. In fact, many of their fees were regulated by customs and could not be raised without permission from Beijing.[67] The cost of living, however, rose during the same period, which left officials with the dilemma of fixed incomes and rising expenses. This phenomena probably had a connection to the rise in the compradors' fees.

Table 2 shows the rise in food prices from 1704 to 1833.

Table 2 Canton Food Prices from 1704 to 1833[68]

	Percent Increase	No. of Years	Annual Ave.
Beef rose from 0.02 taels per catty in 1704 to 0.09 taels in 1833	450	129	3.5
Capons rose from 0.05 taels per catty in 1726 to 0.15 taels in 1830	300	104	2.9
Eggs rose from 0.002 taels each in 1726 to 0.005 taels in 1833	250	107	2.3
Fish rose from 0.025 taels per catty in 1704 to 0.08 taels in 1833	320	129	2.5
Goat rose from 0.045 taels per catty in 1704 to 0.15 taels in 1833	333	102	3.3
Pork rose from 0.03 taels per catty in 1704 to 0.13 taels in 1833	433	126	3.4
Poultry (duck, chicken, geese and small fowl) rose from 0.03 taels per catty in 1704 to 0.13 in the 1830s	433	126	3.4
Totals (2,519 percent/seven items = 360 percent)	2,519	823	3.1

People in Canton whose incomes did not adjust with the price rises had to find ways to supplement their salaries to compensate. Officials were always looking for a good excuse to add surcharges to their normal fees or create new fees, and there was none better than the suspicion of smuggling opium. Ship compradors and tidewaiters (more commonly known as Hoppomen) were both known to be regular opium traffickers, as the following reference reveals: 'Very Large quantities of this article [opium] smuggled in by Ships Compradors and Hoppo men'.[69] Government officials on all levels supplemented their incomes by 'taxing' the contraband in the form of bribes and higher comprador's fees.

In 1786 the English complained that they could not hire a comprador for their ships for less than Spanish $300 (216 taels).[70] In 1802 the Frenchman Blancard reported that compradors' fees were $500 to $600.[71] In 1812 American vessels and country ships were normally charged $250, but there was an attempt in that year to increase British fees to $500.[72] Then in 1815 the Chinese Chief of Police at Whampoa Roads tried to tack on an additional $100 per ship to ensure the compradors' safe passage.[73] By 1829 English compradors' fees had risen to Spanish $848 for company ships and $672 for country ships, but were reduced in the same year to $496 and $392 respectively.[74]

In 1836, the *Canton Register* translated and published a document that listed all the fees the compradors were responsible for from a handbook that was used by them and the linguists. By this year, there were 67 different fees that compradors had to pay to various officials between Macao and Canton amounting to Spanish $970. Many petty officers received a payment as did government boats and all tollhouses along the river (including those between Whampoa and Bocca Tigris). The compradors were required to make weekly reports and receive instructions and also notify officials whenever a ship arrived or departed, and they paid a fee every time this information was exchanged. There was a charge at the tollhouses called the 'fee for *non*-examination of the ship's hold', and several payments called 'crabboat' fee. There was also a 'Sunday-warrant fee' that had to be paid each week to the Panyu County magistrate for keeping the foreigners in order, and fees to the government patrol boats.

This list, of course, does not specify that any of these charges were connected to the contraband trade. But the coincidences of the compradors' engagement fees remaining constant for fifty years, then the opium trade taking off, then these fees appearing on all levels of the administration between Macao and Canton, and then the opium trade continuing to expand without interruption, all suggest they were connected.[75]

One immediate effect of this rise in compradors' fees was a black-market trade in provisions. Private traders, whose vessels were often much smaller than any of the companies' ships and could be loaded within a couple of weeks, were reluctant to pay such high fees. They found it more economical to purchase provisions covertly from other foreigners (albeit at inflated prices) and thereby avoid the compradors' fees.

Some private traders took advantage of this situation and capitalised on the trade in provisions. In the early 1800s the American Peter Dobell began brokering provisions. He bought many items from the Americans and then resold them to whomever needed them.[76] The British firm Stanford and Marks handled a wide variety of provisions and sundry items, which they sold to foreigners in China.[77] A network of suppliers gradually emerged that catered to small ships and that was entirely in the hands of foreigners. If foreign suppliers did not have the items requested, they purchased them from their own Chinese compradors and then resold them at a profit. This practice had taken place throughout the Canton era on a limited basis, but, as more small ships went to China, it spread widely.[78]

After American ginseng and furs became popular items of trade in the 1780s and 1790s, Hawaii became a major depot for the acquisition of provisions, both for the market in Canton and for the refreshment of ships traversing the Pacific.[79] The attractive prices obtainable for provisions in Canton resulted in the provisions trade becoming a full-time occupation for some foreigners.[80] In January 1780 John Rickman commented that, in comparison to other ports he had visited, 'provisions of all kinds were here [in China] very dear'.[81] As a result many companies purchased large quantities of wine, beer, butter, dried fruit, dried vegetables and preserved meats in Europe, Cape Town, Manila and other ports with the specific intention of marketing them in Canton. The rarity of some of these luxury items meant that the Hoppos tended to tolerate the activity, but they tried to keep it limited to items not found in China.[82]

Obtaining provisions in Macao was not usually a problem (as long as the ship was a trading vessel), but, as we have seen, all ships were accompanied by two Chinese tidewaiters after they passed Bocca Tigris.[83] It was customary for foreigners to exchange gifts when they visited neighbouring ships, which could include provisions, and it was possible to disguise or hide goods in tackling or other equipage, so there were ways to take small amounts of food aboard. Ships were also allowed to transfer equipment, animals and provisions back and forth to the bankshalls, so it would have been possible to purchase items there from other foreigners and have them put aboard without the knowledge of the tidewaiters.

Rather than block these illicit exchanges, linguists and customs officers capitalized on them. The two Hoppomen stationed next to the ships had always sold vegetables and *samshoo* (liquor) to foreign sailors, but only on a small scale.[84] Towards the end of the eighteenth century they had an agreement with the linguists that saw them take control of this black-market trade.

If a small ship refused to engage a comprador, the linguists stepped in and offered (demanded) to arrange a deal with the Hoppomen. Their fees were a little less than those of the compradors, and linguists shared the revenues with the officers. This new policy meant that small traders were pressured into either engaging a comprador or paying the linguists for the 'privilege' of engaging the Hoppomen.

Table 3 shows the prices the American ship *Minerva* agreed to in 1809 with the Hoppoman Samuel Bull. Note that the prices were the same as what 'Tom Bull & Other Compradors' charged.

Table 3 Prices of Provisions Charged by Tom Bull & Other Compradors at Whampoa in 1809[85]

Memorandum of agreement with the Ships Hoppo man, in lieu of Compradore not being able to procure the latter, unless at a great deal of coaxing and a cumshaw [engagement fee] of 280 dollars.

Agreement

The undersigned Samuel Bull Hoppoman at Whampoa, hereby agrees with Thomas W. Ward, Master of the American Ship Minerva of Salem, to supply the said Ship, during the time she may stay at Whampoa, with provisions & stores of every kind whatsoever, at the us'al rate of charging by regular Ships Compradors and that every thing furnished shall be the best of its kind, and that no delay shall take place in consequence of sd. Samuel Bull not being a regular Comprador.

Sd. Ward agrees to pay sd. Bull twenty dollars wages at the end of every month and to settle all accounts over a fortnight keeping the sum one week in arrears.

Whampoa September 22, 1809
(Sd.) Sam Bull
Sd Thos. W. Ward

NB All the articles are weighed on board with the Ships Stalyards But every thing is brought in Baskets, & the Baskets are weighed with the contents and paid for at the same rate if it were a dollar an over.

Prices of articles charged by Tom Bull & other Compradors at Whampoa

Beef per catty	Tls 0.09	Pork	Tls 0.13
Fowls	.13	Ducks	.13
Capon	.15	Geese	.13
Fish	.13	Bread per loaf	.04
Jams, Potatoes, Oranges, Pumpkins, Limes, Cabages, Onions, Greens	.04	Hams	.30
		Sugar per picul, Tls 5 to 7	
		Molasses	4.00
Eggs per Doz.	.08	Milk per pot	.03
Lamp black, per basket	.50	Paints mixed, per catty	.20
Lamp oil	.10	Carpenter per day	.50
Caulker	.50	Cooley per catty [*sic*][86]	.30
Iron work per catty	.30	Matts	.04
Bamboes	.04		

In this example, the captain of the *Minerva* avoided paying the comprador's engagement fees by paying the linguist Spanish $200 to engage Sam Bull. It is not certain what portion of the $200 went to the linguist, but this was the going rate for engaging a Hoppoman in the early years of the nineteenth century. It probably had to be shared with the customs officers and the local Chief of Police in Whampoa.[87]

A comprador would have cost the *Minerva* Spanish $280, so it was cheaper to pay $200 to the linguist and the additional $20 per month to the Hoppoman for the few weeks the ship was in Whampoa.[88] By the late 1810s and 1820s the compradors' fees for many small American ships had risen to $300 or more. In 1826 the American ship *Providence* paid $300 to the linguist 'to dispense with having a Comprador for the Ship'.[89] These engagement fees had to be paid regardless of whether the ships bought provisions.

With this type of competition between Hoppomen and compradors, it was impossible for either to fix the prices of their provisions. There were many compradors in Whampoa to choose from, but foreign captains could hire only those Hoppomen assigned to them. For their part, the Hoppomen had to match the compradors' prices and terms or risk losing business.

The linguists and toll officers on the quay in Canton also gained control of 'alternative' means of providing provisions to the factories. By the early nineteenth century every ship was required to pay the hiring fees for a factory comprador, whether they needed one or not. Many small traders were in Canton for a few weeks only and rented a room, rather than an entire apartment or building. They did not need full-time compradors or servants to take care of them, and they bought their meals from the other foreign households, but they still had to pay the linguists.

In exchange for a nominal fee of Spanish $96, linguists and customs officers allowed foreigners to reside in Canton. If they refused to pay, they would be reported and would then have to engage a comprador. Eighty dollars of this fee went to the linguist and $16 to the officers. Sometimes the customs attendants received $20 rather than $16 (making a total payment of $100), which may reflect a different number of officers on duty at the time. There were usually two or three of these officers stationed at Jackass Point near the factories.[90] Supercargoes of small ships were charged the $96 (sometimes $100), regardless of whether they took provisions to their rooms.

The following letter from the private trader Captain Charles Bishop of the ship *Ruby* to the Hoppo in 1796 suggests that the Hoppos were privy to this practice and did nothing to stop it.

Bishop to Hoppo, 2 July 1796:

> I am sorry to trouble your Excellency [the Hoppo] with complaints against two of the Linguists, who refuse to undertake the business of the Ship Ruby under my command, unless I pay them 300 Spanish dollars for the House and Ships Comprodores which people never Employed, or could procure, by reason of the Smallness of the Ship and her Crew they said it was not worth their while.
>
> I am well convinced your Excellency will not suffer this imposition when it is made known to you therefore I humbly pray your Excellency to interfere therein.[91]

Bishop mentions that this petition was delivered to the Hoppo, but he does not state how. It was perhaps handed to his security merchant, Punqua (Ni Bingfa 倪秉發), who then delivered it to the Hoppo. Bishop states that the *Hong* merchants gave him the reply that it was 'Customary for all Ships to pay these fees to the Linguists' and that the Hoppo thus 'did not choose to alter it in the present Instance'.[92] Because we do not have the Chinese version of this reply, it is impossible to know if the Hoppo received the same information as Bishop sent or whether this was indeed his answer. The linguists often changed the wording of these petitions when they translated them. It is also possible that the situation was exactly as Bishop reported. It was not in the Hoppo's interests to upset the local echelons for the sake of a small trader like him, whose ship had a capacity of only 101 tons and a crew of 27 men.[93]

The linguists and Hoppomen continued this collusion with provisions until the end of the Canton System in 1842.[94] As far as the trade was concerned, it did not matter whether the goods came from the compradors or Hoppomen as long as the foreigners' needs were met and commerce was not interrupted. Both sources were structured similarly, with written contracts guaranteeing the lowest prices, with instant credit available, and with discounts offered for large volumes.

Another way for ships to obtain provisions without engaging a comprador was to procure them at Lintin Island. In 1831 the American supercargo Forbes was involved in trading rum, beef and whiskey at Lintin.[95] The smugglers' sampans servicing Lintin carried import goods upriver and export goods downriver. Some articles were indeed official 'contraband' items, such as opium and gold, but others were simply regulated goods such as tea, porcelain and silk, which were exported without paying the duties.

Such examples clearly show that the traditional system and administrative structures of the Hoppos were already being undermined long before the Opium Wars brought the Canton System to an end. The growth of the illegal provisions trade might, on one level, have sustained the Canton System by supplying an uninterrupted flow of necessary goods and supplies to the small ships, but it weakened the heart of the system by diverting income and power from the customs office.

Besides supplying provisions and labour, factory compradors had another source of income: schroffing fees. It was the factory comprador's responsibility to hire a schroff or money changer to determine the alloy content of silver coins that foreigners took to Canton. Hunter points out that the American factory compradors in the 1830s:

> . . . derived a profit from the process of *schroffing* which it underwent before being deposited in the treasury; but after the goodness of a parcel and its exact amount were ascertained, he was liable for any bad money that might afterwards be found amongst it. He paid the Shroff one-tenth of a dollar per one thousand for examining it, while the fixed charge by the Compradore was one-fifth.[96]

Hunter further explains that the comprador received 'five copper cash per dollar on all payments', and that he 'derived benefit from loans or advances made to "Outside" Chinese merchants on contracts for silks and other merchandise entered into with his employers'. He also points out that they secretly took goods for trade from Canton to Macao under the pretence that they belonged to the foreign factories and, therefore, were exempt from the normal duties.[97] Ship compradors might also derive income from loans and similar services, but schroffing perks and transferring goods free of duty were privileges enjoyed by the factory compradors only.

Both factory compradors and ship compradors received a commission on the wages of all Chinese labourers they hired for the foreigners. As far as Chinese labour was concerned, the linguists could arrange that as well, but it was more often done by the compradors. Another sign that the lower echelons were taking matters into their own hands was that compradors also had Chinese sailors manning foreign ships, which was illegal because Chinese were not supposed to go abroad or board them. By the 1780s this practice shows up fairly regularly in the foreign records. A portion of sailors' wages would be paid in advance, and a percentage of those revenues went to the comprador. When the sailors returned to China the following season, the comprador would also receive a percentage of the wages still owing. Because these were special arrangements between a captain and his comprador, the Chinese sailors hired in this manner do not always show up in the ships' muster rolls.[98]

Some compradors went abroad on the foreign ships, which was also illegal. One of the most famous was the American-employed comprador 'Boston Jack'. He had the opportunity to visit Boston aboard the ship *Cossack*, and became legendary among the Americans in Canton with his many renditions of his experiences there.[99] His name shows up many times in American China trade records from 1830 to the late 1840s, and he apparently took his experience and reputation seriously. Rather than use his Chinese name, he adopted the Americanised nickname 'Bohsan Jak' (波臣則, see Plate 36).[100]

So far, from the many examples above, we have seen that the compradors played a crucial role in the servicing and controlling of foreign trade, and that many of them became respected by their employers. But the picture of their lives is still incomplete. After the collapse of the Canton System, compradors stepped into new roles and took over new responsibilities. By looking at those changes we gain a deeper understanding of the importance of their roles beforehand, and a clearer picture of the limitations they operated under during the Canton System.

After 1842 factory compradors moved into merchant and agent roles for foreign companies. They offered products for sale to foreigners that they were previously barred from trading in, and began forming links with inland markets. They also began taking over some duties previously performed by linguists, such as mediation between foreigners and Chinese officials. Many compradors continued to take care of foreign households as they had done before, but now with many more responsibilities.[101]

The provisioning of the ships also underwent significant restructuring in this new environment. Because foreign trade was no longer restricted to Canton, ship compradors quickly emerged in all treaty ports established. In 1844 and again in 1848 Morrison and Williams mention that the compradors servicing the American vessels had formed a single company and were setting up branches in the delta to service the entire American fleet. Several compradors were still servicing the English ships, but they gradually took on the English title of 'purveyor', rather than the Portuguese title of 'comprador'.[102]

Ship compradors were no longer held responsible for the good conduct of foreigners after 1842, and the provisioning of ships was no longer connected to the administration of trade. Provision purveyors needed to concern themselves only with satisfying their customers' needs. Foreigners, of course, still insisted on the lowest prices, so the combinations that emerged were not necessarily monopolies that could set prices, but rather mergers that would organise and coordinate products and services better. Even after the collapse of the Canton System, purveyors had to compete in an open market. The removal of the previous limitations of who could sell provisions exposed the trade to more competition.

All these changes in the compradors' professions were not necessarily good for the smooth and efficient conduct of trade. In 1848 Morrison stated that 'the business of purveying for ships, is however not so regular now as it used to be and ships often defer arranging with compradors until they arrive at Whampoa'.[103] In the Canton era compradors were agents of the Hoppos, which meant they were responsible for satisfying the needs of each ship, under the threat of physical punishment. Once they were assigned to a ship they were obliged to service it, regardless of where it was in the delta, and they had to provide fair and competitive prices no matter where the ships were.

Under the new system the compradors contracted for the provisioning of ships in a specific location, such as Macao, Whampoa or Hong Kong. The provisioning of ships traversing the delta was more or less left to the fishermen and other Chinese vessels, when it had been done previously by compradors. This meant that every time foreigners changed location they had to renegotiate the purchasing of their provisions, a tedious and cumbersome process at the best of times. Thus, as far as assurance of regular deliveries and dependable and efficient service throughout the delta (including Whampoa), the old system was probably much more conducive than the new to the smooth conduct of trade.

After 1842 many dockyards were established in the treaty ports. In the Canton era foreigners had repaired their own vessels in Macao or Whampoa, obtaining all necessary tools and resources from the compradors. Under the new system permanent dockyards were built at Whampoa, Hong Kong and other ports, and those enterprises needed to be supplied on a regular basis. They needed all types and sizes of timber and hardware to repair and replace masts and rebuild hulls. There were many other naval stores needed — sails, tackle, cordage, tar, pitch and caulk. Chinese chandler shops were established in Hong Kong and Canton that catered to the needs of both dockyards and ships. Portuguese and Chinese chandlers popped up in Macao too.

Dockyards needed shipwrights, so the Chinese began to learn how to repair foreign ships. Chinese shipwrights had been building and maintaining fleets of junks for hundreds of years, but those vessels were structurally different from foreign ships. Sails, tackle, masts, spars, stays, blocking and even elementary items such as cordage, tar and nails were made, shaped and designed differently for foreign vessels.[104] This was the main reason foreigners in the Canton era had repaired their own ships. Before 1842, Chinese shipwrights and craftsmen had been hired to perform rudimentary tasks such as pounding caulk between deck planks, painting and varnishing vessels and basic carpentry. The more technical repairs to the sails and rigging had been left to the foreign shipwrights. After 1842 the Chinese took care of everything the foreigners needed.

Foreigners also needed sailors, labourers and all types of craftsmen, both aboard the ships and in their plantations abroad. After 1842 many restrictions on hiring Chinese were removed, which gave rise to 'labour brokers' or 'people traffickers' setting up shop in the delta. This trade in humans came to be called the 'coolie trade' and was considered by many to be nothing more than a cover for slavery. Many Chinese were tricked or forced into signing long-term contracts, and agents received a service charge for each 'head' they delivered.

In this respect the old comprador system was probably a more responsible one. Because the Canton compradors had to answer directly to the Hoppos, they tried to make arrangements agreeable to all parties so that there was no cause for complaint. As a result we have no records showing the compradors tricking or forcing anyone into the sort of situations that took place in the coolie trade. Many Chinese went abroad during the Canton era, and they arranged for those travels through compradors. However, those arrangements were, on the whole, made voluntarily.[105]

Thus, despite its shortcomings, there is much to be admired in the way the old system operated. Its structure was practical and efficient as far as the administration and advancement of trade were concerned, but it was most effective when large companies dominated the trade. As the linguists and Hoppomen began diverting some of the provisions trade away from the compradors, and as the private traders began to gain more control of the trade, the structure became mismatched with the trading environment. Small ships could not afford to pay the high engagement fees, as the large-company ships had done, and it was inefficient to service those small ships throughout the delta, as had been done with the companies' fleets. As we see from the system that emerged after 1842, small ships would have probably been serviced better and cheaper by local suppliers than compradors travelling about the delta.

SUMMARY

The provisions trade gives us a unique window into the strengths and weaknesses of the Canton System. It formed an important part of the Hoppos' mechanisms for pacifying foreigners on one hand and persuading them on the other. Keeping the foreigners' stomachs full was the first step to pacifying them, and allowing their stomachs to go empty was one of the last steps taken in convincing them. Having the backing of the Hoppos allowed the provisions trade to operate entirely on credit, which ensured a steady and constant flow of everything the ships needed for the crews and the conduct of trade. Raising the compradors' fees weakened the system, because traders found ways to avoid them by buying provisions from other foreigners or other Chinese, which resulted in the Hoppos losing one of their tools of control.

The monopoly of the illicit provisions trade in the early 1800s by the linguists and Hoppomen also shows how the fabric of the system was deteriorating. The lower echelons continued to divert power and funds from the central administration. However, at the same time the efficiency of the provisions trade (including the illicit activities of the Hoppomen), as well as the market and volume-orientated pricing structures, encouraged the expansion of the trade overall. But it was most effective when the large companies dominated the commerce. There is much to be admired and respected in the traditional provisioning system of Canton.

No other position required more devotion than that of the comprador. After the pilots were done guiding the ships they went home to their families in Macao; after the day's work was done the linguists, merchants, provisions suppliers and even the Hoppos and governors-general could gather with friends and relatives to have a break from their duties; after the sun went down the tidewaiters and tollhouse keepers set their obligations aside and settled in for a relaxing evening; and, in bad weather, many enjoyed a quiet day at home.

The compradors, on the other hand, were on duty twenty-four hours a day, seven days a week, timing their movements to the coming and going of the tides. Whether day or night, one could see the comprador's wife, child strapped to her back, standing at the stern of the sampan guiding it to its next destination, with baskets of fruit, vegetables, grain and sundries stacked high in the hull; with cows, pigs, sheep and goats lining the deck; and with cages of geese, ducks, chickens and quail swinging overhead in concert with the waves. As far as the maintenance of harmony and the smooth conduct of trade were concerned, the compradors were the first line of defence.

We now turn to another important group of professionals who were licensed to service the trade: the linguists.

CHAPTER FIVE

LINGUISTS

THE LINGUISTS WERE THE APPOINTED mediators between the foreigners and the Chinese officials so they were constantly confronted with the limits of what each side would accept. Hoppos and governors-general had considerable freedom to negotiate the terms of commerce, but always within parameters defined by Beijing. Any requests from traders that went beyond those limitations were forbidden and could not be negotiated. Some freedoms and restrictions were clearly laid out in edicts sent to Canton from the Imperial Court, but they were not followed with the same degree of consistency. Other limitations were not written down but just 'understood' and accepted by the Hoppos and governors-general as part of the political and commercial culture. Linguists operated on this edge between the acceptable and unacceptable so a look at their activities will bring the *actual* parameters of trade closer into view.

As we saw earlier, the first linguists came from Macao and communicated in Portuguese with the foreigners. In addition to Portuguese and their native language Cantonese, they also needed to be fluent and literate in Mandarin, the language of the officials. We know from the many linguists' receipts in the foreign archives that they could read and write Chinese, which would be a requisite for that position (see Plate 35). By the early 1730s, pidgin English had replaced Portuguese as the medium of communication with foreigners, and after that change the three most important languages for all linguists were pidgin English, Cantonese and Mandarin.

Linguists were expected to handle all matters concerning trade with foreigners, but that did not mean they were to be 'experts' in anything foreign. On the contrary, any linguist who appeared overly enthusiastic, interested or fluent in foreign languages, customs, habits or mannerisms would excite the suspicions of the authorities. Their primary task was to mediate, so being able to effectively negotiate, persuade and pacify were skills more important to the linguists' careers than being able to interpret foreigners' actions correctly or translate their intentions accurately.[1]

Because of this emphasis on mediation and compromise rather than accuracy and clarity, it is not surprising to find endless complaints in foreign records of linguists' reluctance to accommodate foreigners' requests. This led to many arguments with the linguists, and sometimes to foreigners adopting more extreme measures to accomplish their objectives. In 1747, for example, the Dutch supercargoes threatened to hold their 'old linguist Ja-qua' under house arrest until he wrote a complaint against one of the Chinese merchants for them.[2] There are also examples in the records to the foreigners marching directly to the city gates to demand an audience with the governor-general or Hoppo because they could not convince their linguists to deliver the protests for them.

In 1823 Robert Morrison wrote that not one of the five licensed linguists in Canton could 'read or write any foreign language' and were not necessarily very skilled even in their own language.[3] This was something foreigners found hard to understand and accept. Linguists were not supposed to translate anything that would offend or cause problems so pleading or feigning ignorance in the language was a way to prevent that from happening.

Just like the pilots, compradors and merchants, linguists could not quit their jobs or change professions without the Hoppos' consent. Both the terms of service and duties of the linguists were non-negotiable. If they failed to live up to expectations they were subject to the usual civil penalties, including public humiliation, physical punishment, banishment and imprisonment.

Occasionally foreign companies employed a Jesuit, or other foreigner who had learned the language, to translate or deliver a message to the Chinese authorities. But the Hoppos and governors-general did not usually look favourably on these emissaries. Teaching foreigners Chinese was, in fact, a crime punishable by death. In practice, however, very little attention was paid to these exchanges. Chinese teachers were only punished if a problem arose from the foreigners who spoke Chinese.[4] If they thought it necessary, the Hoppos would sometimes call on foreign linguists to assist in a delicate matter, but never to replace the appointed Canton linguists, regardless of how well they knew the language.[5]

Every captain had a Chinese linguist of his choice assigned to him on arrival at Whampoa. There were only three to five licensed linguists in Canton in any year so there was not a great deal of choice. Captains and supercargoes could complain about their linguists, but, rather than replace them, Hoppos would issue an official reprimand or light punishment and send them back to work. A warning and a little discussion with both parties was usually enough to fix the problem. Chinese merchants were the usual mediators if a problem arose between linguists and foreigners.

Because linguists serviced foreigners from several companies at a time, they were often called on to supply information to their patrons about other traders in Canton. There was nothing foreigners could do to prevent the linguists from passing this information. Linguists had access to all the figures in the Hoppos' import and export books, which was very important to the expansion of trade.

This open policy whereby Hoppos shared their data with anyone who wanted it helped to maintain intense competition. When negotiating with the *Hong* merchants, it was very important to know the quantities and prices other companies were contracting for. If that information was hidden, then foreigners and Chinese had less negotiating power to reach the best terms. When the crucial data could not be obtained, the competition just sat back and waited for those exchanges to be written into the Hoppo's book, and then sent the linguists to collect the information for them.

For this reason, companies and *hongs* often held out as long as they could before making a contract. The need to load the ships and leave before the monsoons changed, however, kept constant pressure on foreigners to complete their transactions quickly, which meant it was just a matter of time before someone gave in. Once information about quantities and prices began to flow, then others jumped in to negotiate a better deal, and trade moved forward quickly. In the eighteenth century when there were several East India companies in Canton each year, every season was characterized like this. After 1806, the EIC was the only large company remaining and then the situation changed where private traders were the only competition to the company.[6]

The sharing of information also revealed to everyone which products were making the most profits, which prevented anyone from secretly forming a monopoly of a single commodity. If the linguists had not been allowed access to the Hoppos' trade books, it would have been easier for companies and Chinese merchants to secretly manipulate the market resulting in higher prices. Maintaining transparency between foreigners was another mechanism that was built into the trade to keep it competitive.

After the ships arrived in Whampoa Roads, the linguists scheduled a date for the Hoppos to measure them. All upper officers and Chinese merchants were informed of the appointed day so they could make the proper preparations. Chop boats were ordered in advance so ships could begin unloading import goods as soon as measuring was completed. Bills of lading, stamped with the appropriate chops, had to accompany all merchandise and bullion shipped between

Whampoa and Canton, and it was the job of the linguists to obtain these documents.

Linguists worked closely with *Hong* merchants to plan the shipping of all goods. No chop was issued until all merchandise had been inspected by the customs officers and itemised in the Hoppo's books. Linguists kept track of export and import duties and customs fees of each ship in their care. If there was a shortfall in fees, linguists were personally responsible for making up the difference, so they were usually diligent in ensuring there were no errors.[7]

A few days after the measuring of the ships, the linguists delivered the results of the port-fee calculations. The original numbers were recorded in Chinese characters, and, therefore, unintelligible to most foreigners, so a basic skill required of all linguists was an understanding of Arabic numerals. Before being translated, port fees for large ships were calculated to the thousandth decimal (see Plates 27–29). Linguists handled any complaints or discrepancies that foreigners had with port-fee calculations.[8]

As we saw in chapter 2, in the early years of trade it was customary for Hoppos to grant an audience to the foreigners. Linguists were responsible for teaching the foreigners the correct protocol and making sure they arrived at the Great Hall on time. On entering and before being seated, they exchanged bows and initial greetings with the Hoppo. The foreigners, via the linguists, were then allowed to introduce themselves and state their reason for going to China, which was supposed to be trade. Once their desire to trade was made public, the Hoppo responded with an official welcome from the emperor and expressed his appreciation for the guests who had travelled such a long way to do business with the empire.

The foreigners then read out a list of their demands, which the linguists had already translated and forwarded to the Hoppo. The Hoppo then addressed the foreigners' concerns and laid out the stipulations of trade. Most of these matters had already been negotiated with the foreigners via the linguists before the meeting, because the Hoppos did not usually grant an audience unless they felt the foreigners would accept the terms.[9]

It is not clear when linguists in Canton began using pidgin English instead of Portuguese. In 1703 Captain Hamilton negotiated with the Hoppo via linguists 'who spake the *Portugueze* Language'.[10] In 1729 the English officers in Canton said that four linguists came from Macao and all spoke good Portuguese.[11] Morse mentions, however, that merchants in Canton were already using 'pidgin English' by about 1715.[12] The GIC records also clearly show that such merchants as Suqua and Cudgen were using 'English' as their medium in the mid-1720s. Thus the use of that language appears to have developed from the merchants' needs rather than the linguists'.[13]

In 1732 during an audience with a Hoppo, the Dutch mentioned that the linguists were translating everything into 'English' (or more correctly, pidgin English).[14] In 1733 Suqua's bookkeeper Chinqua was said to be able to speak 'English',[15] and in 1738 the Danes mentioned that linguists were using that language as well. In 1743 Lord Anson negotiated with the Chinese officials via linguists who spoke broken English.[16] Thus, by the 1730s, pidgin English appears to have gained a solid footing among both merchants and linguists, and was probably the common medium of the compradors and factory servants as well.

Pidgin English was of more benefit to foreigners and trade than to the linguists. It was just as hard for Chinese to learn pidgin English as it was to learn pidgin Portuguese, and Chinese in Macao were more accustomed to the latter pronunciation. Pidgin English, however, was easier for many foreigners to begin understanding immediately because it was an amalgam of many of their languages.[17]

If Portuguese had continued as the medium of exchange, all foreign traders would have been obliged to have had someone aboard their ships who could speak the language. This was an obvious hindrance for the Scandinavians and others, who were less likely to have Portuguese speakers among their crews. Such companies as the GIC in the 1720s and the SOIC in the 1730s hired English and/or French speaking supercargoes, and some of the GIC and DAC officers were Dutch speakers, as were those of the VOC.[18] Besides the company officers and crews, there were many private traders such as Armenians, Muslims and Parsees going to China from ports in India, where English and French (not Portuguese) were the languages of trade.[19] Thus, the emergence of pidgin English was very much created, propelled and defined by the demands of commerce. Its rapid acceptance on all levels of Chinese society is another sign of Canton's ability to accommodate foreign trade.

The number of linguists varied very little over time but the number of ships and their capacities varied a great deal. The fees linguists charged to all foreigners were also different, and their incomes came from several sources. By first establishing how many linguists and linguists' helpers there were in each decade, then comparing those numbers with the numbers of ships and their capacities, and then comparing that information with the fees they charged and the incomes they might have made, we gain a better understanding of the diversity, stability, flexibility and limitations of their positions.

In 1704, Lockyer mentioned there were five or six linguists to choose from, and that it was 'usual to have two'.[20] However, in the early eighteenth century there were only a couple of ships arriving each year so it is doubtful that so many linguists were needed. In later years when many more ships were visiting China, there were only three or four linguists to service them all. The linguists' secretaries were often called 'under linguists' so Lockyer may have included them in his numbers.

From the 1720s to the 1780s there were at least two linguists operating in Canton, but more commonly three or four names can be found in the records. From the 1790s to the early 1830s there were at least four licensed linguists servicing all foreign ships, and by the late-1830s there were five.[21] More linguists were needed as more ships visited China each decade, but the two did not increase in proportion.

Linguists were able to cope with the greater number of ships by hiring more secretaries and assistants. In the early years of trade they often had two or three assistants, but by the 1790s they are recorded as having a couple of assistants and '5 or 6 pursers'.[22] Linguists subcontracted some of the ships under their charge to their head secretaries (also called pursers), who are the ones who show up as 'under-linguists' in the foreign records.[23]

Linguists charged an engagement fee for every ship they serviced, which ranged from Spanish $67.50 (50 taels) for VOC ships to as much as $216 (155.5 taels) for small American vessels. There are several possible reasons why Americans were charged more for their linguists' fees. The overwhelming majority of American vessels were less than 500 tons burthen. Small ships required fewer chop boats and fewer chops, which meant that smaller ships were much less profitable for the linguists.

American private traders often had only a few vessels, and it was less predictable when and how many of them would arrive each season. Because they were usually small ships, they stayed in Whampoa for only a few weeks. American ships were often owned by several individuals, rather than one large enterprise, as was the case with the East India companies. All these factors made it more difficult to bargain with American ships collectively. Under these circumstances, it was much simpler for the linguists to apply a single rate to each American ship rather than negotiate with each new captain who arrived.

The linguists' engagement fees might differ between foreign companies and between the companies and the private traders, but they remained fairly static for each group. The VOC, for example, regularly paid 50 taels (Spanish $67.50) per ship to their linguists, and the SOIC paid 74 taels ($100). The DAC paid the same amount per ship from the 1730s to the 1830s — 100 taels ($136) for the linguist and 10 taels ($13.60) for his secretary. In the 1720s the GIC ships paid 130 ($180.50) to 150 taels ($208) for their linguists.[24] The French were charged 113 taels ($157) per ship,[25] and the EIC and English private traders paid 125 taels ($173.50).[26] The Americans paid the same amount, 155.5 taels ($216), from the mid-1780s to 1842.[27]

It was logical for small private ships to pay more than large company ships, but it is not clear why each company paid different rates. As was pointed out earlier, Swedish and Danish ships were generally the largest vessels in Canton and they were charged 50 and 100 percent more (respectively) than the smaller Dutch ships. The GIC ships were smaller than the VOC ships, but they paid three times as much. American ships ranged from less than 100 tons capacity to more than 1,000 tons, but all appear to have been charged the same amount (Spanish $216). The East India companies sometimes sent smaller ships to Canton, but paid their usual rate. Moreover, some of those ships were two or three times larger in the later decades as they were in the earlier, but the linguists' fees remained the same. Thus, like the compradors' fees (before the 1780s), the linguists' fees seem to have been determined when foreigners first arrived in China and stayed at that rate thereafter.[28]

In addition to engagement fees, the linguists were also allotted a small percentage for each picul of import and export merchandise they handled. In 1698 the two linguists of the French Ship *L'Amphitrite* demanded 2 percent of all imports and exports, which presumably meant each of them would receive 1 percent.[29] In 1704 Lockyer stated that the linguist received 'one *per Cent* on your Cargo, and have one *per Cent* more of the Merchants on all the Goods they provide'.[30] It is not clear what Lockyer meant by 'one *per Cent*', whether it was 1 percent of the weight, the value, or perhaps the amount of the import and export duties. In their instructions to the supercargoes in 1738, the directors of the DAC also stated that the linguists 'have a certain salary from the merchants from every picul of piece goods'.[31]

Milburn (1813) and Morrison (1834) have helped to clarify the linguists' commission on imports and exports. Milburn mentioned that the linguists received 0.0176 taels per picul, but they discounted each picul 10 percent to compensate for the weight of the packaging materials. Morrison stated that the amount they collected was 1.6 percent of the duties, which was probably just another way of calculating Milburn's figure.[32]

If we use Milburn's figure of 0.0176 taels per picul with a 10 percent discount for packaging, we can estimate the linguists' income for each ship. A typical company ship in the 1760s carried about 9,000 piculs of goods. Imports are more difficult to estimate because silver was often the largest import commodity and was duty free, so the linguists would not have received a commission on it. If we take a rough estimate, however, of one-third of the import cargo being dutiable merchandise, then we arrive at a total of about 12,000 piculs of merchandise (3,000 piculs imported and 9,000 piculs exported), from which the linguists would have received a commission. After the 10 percent discount, we arrive at a subtotal of 10,800 piculs per ship.

At 0.0176 taels per picul, the linguists' average commission for a company ship would have been about 190 taels. There were three linguists in Canton in the 1760s. With 13 to 28 foreign ships arriving each year in that decade, the three linguists would have serviced from four to nine ships each. In the busiest year, their commission for the season would have amounted to about 1,710 taels.

In the 1820s there were four linguists in Canton and 72 to 115 ships arriving each year; each linguist would have serviced from 18 to 29 ships. By now the ships were almost double the size they had been in the 1760s, so the average take per ship would have been about 380 taels. This gives us a total of from 6,840 taels to about 11,020 taels for a season. However, as we have seen, the linguists subcontracted the servicing of some ships in their charge, so they had to share the proceeds with their junior linguists. They would probably have received no more than half the total commission collected each year.

In addition to the percentage on the cargos, every ship had to pay their linguists for chops they procured and sampans they hired. A chop to ship silver from Whampoa to Canton ranged from 0.66 taels for the large companies to as much as Spanish $3 (2.16 taels) per chop for private traders. Large ships paid 10 taels for a chop to ship trade goods, but this amount went to the customhouses and was not part of the linguists' revenues. The charge for the chop boats ranged from about 3.5 taels (about $5) to 5.92 taels ($8) for each one they procured, depending on their size and the number employed each day. Plate 30 shows the charges for the chop boats the linguists supplied to unload the imports from the VOC ship *Ruyteveld* in 1764. In this list, duties and other expenses are not included. The Dutch were charged 3.5 taels for each chop boat, which was about the cheapest rate. Linguists discounted the charges when more than one sampan was ordered each day.[33]

Each chop boat had at least two Chinese labourers aboard, but some had many more. Sometimes the chop-boat fees included the tollhouse fees between Whampoa and Canton, but other times they did not. The fee to procure the chop might also be included in the total figures, or it could be paid separately. The majority of foreigners hired most of their sampans and Chinese workers aboard them directly through the linguists and/or merchants.

In the 1720s the Belgians ordered their chop boats through the linguists, but sometimes paid for those services monthly rather than at the end of the season. The Dutch used both their compradors and their linguists to arrange those services. They also paid for their sampans and labourers' wages on a monthly basis, rather than at the end of the season, so the figures do not show up in the linguists' year-end expense lists. The Danes, Swedes and Americans ordered a chop boat each time they needed one and paid all those charges to the linguists at the end of the season before their departure.

Sampans could also be hired according to a flat rate per job, which included all expenses. Most American ships and country traders were charged a simple flat rate, and they did not usually have any choice in the matter. The Spanish $23 fee that appears in the American ship records consulted for this study includes all labourers on the boats, the procuring of all chops, the use of the boats themselves and the linguists' service charges.

Plate 35 shows Linguist Heequa's receipt for a chop boat he supplied to the American ship *Empress of China*. The '38 Dollars' included all the expenses related to the hiring of the boat (usually Spanish $23) and the duties on the goods. The arrangements that Heequa made with the Americans were different to those made with the Dutch in Plate 30.

Wages and sampan rates were well established in Canton, but the companies that traded every year and ordered large numbers of sampans could negotiate better terms with their linguists. The best way to strike a bargain was to separate each expense and then deal with each part individually. As all these examples of the various linguists' fees and incomes show, there was much diversity in the ways trade took place in Canton.[34]

Other duties of the linguists that shed light on the stability of the environment were the hiring of labourers and the collecting of wages, tips, and various fees. All wages of tradesmen and labourers in Canton, both foreign and Chinese, were paid by the day or month. If they did not work a whole day or month, then they were paid for part of a day or month (i.e., 1/4, 1/2, 3/4 or 1). Hourly or weekly wages do not appear in the records. Foreigners were charged for the meals of all full-time workers, but they could either compensate the workers for their meals at a set rate per day, or they could supply the meals by ordering provisions from the compradors and hiring a Chinese cook. If there were many workers involved, the latter option might be more cost effective.

In addition to wages, all full-time workers expected a tip at the end of the season. This yearly 'gratuity' (*guiyin* 規銀) was given to the weighers, guards, customs officers, Hoppos' secretaries and all Chinese labourers aboard the sampans. The linguists determined the proper tip to pay each worker (including themselves), which was often 50 to 100 percent of a month's salary and varied according to a formula the linguists never revealed.

Some of these charges were, in fact, 'service charges' rather than 'gratuities'. The fees for the three tollhouses between Whampoa and Canton, for example, were calculated according to the number of visits made by the chop boats of each particular ship. Just like the linguists' engagement fees, the gratuities were applied at the same rates to the same traders year after year.

By the mid-eighteenth century, all these fees and other charges had become so well established and uniform that foreigners began lumping them together into one grand total. In 1765 the Swedes calculated the composite linguists' fees to be 265 taels per ship. The Danes calculated the linguists' fees to be 212 taels per ship beginning in 1772, which was later adjusted to 259 taels in 1789 and 260 taels in 1826. From 1772 to 1794 the VOC also used composite linguist figures and applied them to all four ships each year. The fact that the foreigners could calculate all these expenses in advance helps to show the level of transparency in the costs of trade, which in turn, is a reflection on its stability.[35]

Other linguists' fees, however, tell us that in some respects the trade was becoming less stable. As was pointed out in chapter 4, in the late-eighteenth century, the linguists joined together with the Hoppomen in Whampoa to gain control of the black-market trade in provisions. Linguists also began charging a fee to dispense with having a factory comprador. The foreigners received no services or benefits from the latter payment, so the practice is difficult to describe in any other terms than extortion. Most fees and charges in Canton had services or benefits attached to them to justify their existence, but this charge to dispense with having a comprador did not. This subversion of the compradors' businesses in both the factories and aboard the ships shows that the ability of the Hoppos to control the lower echelons in the trade was decreasing.[36]

There were other tasks linguists had to perform from time to time in addition to their 'normal' weekly activities, which show us the diversity of their responsibilities and the flexibility of the Hoppos in accommodating trade. Ships sometimes ran aground in the delta, which required the linguists' attention. They had to work closely with the security merchants to obtain all the necessary chops for the hiring of junks and sampans so the merchandise could be unloaded and ships re-floated. Customs officers oversaw these special rescue missions, and they needed to be informed regularly of the foreigners' actions. Sometimes anchors were lost and had to be retrieved. A few foreign ships sank in the South China Sea, and foreigners then hired Chinese divers to salvage what they could.

As far as these emergencies are concerned, there is no evidence to suggest that Hoppos or governors-general interfered in the normal negotiation processes. As long as all necessary chops were obtained, customs fees paid, appropriate officials assigned to monitor operations, and regulations properly observed, negotiating these special services with Chinese merchants and labourers was left to the individual parties.

It could take from a few hours to several weeks to free a ship that ran aground in the river, and everyone had to stay at their posts until the job was done. In addition to the regular wages, a healthy tip was expected by all workers at the end of these rescue operations, regardless of whether they were foreigners or

Chinese. While ships were being rescued, the vessel in peril supplied daily victuals for all officers and workers involved. Extra meals and extra rounds of rum could keep crews working longer and exerting themselves more diligently, but would not reduce their expectation of a tip at the end of the job.

Linguists and their secretaries kept track of all these expenses. They made sure all parties (including themselves) were properly compensated so there was no cause for complaint from any of the Chinese officers, soldiers, sailors, divers or sampan men. The Hoppo and supercargoes in Canton needed to be constantly updated on the progress of the rescue operations, so the linguists and compradors' boats were kept busy delivering 'express letters', miscellaneous messages and general information to and from Canton. Contrary to the picture often presented in histories of the Canton trade, government officials were very accommodating in these situations.

On 1 August 1772, for example, the Dutch supercargoes learned that their ship *Rynsburgh* from Batavia had been lost off the South China coast a couple of weeks earlier. With the aid of the *Hong* merchant Pan Qiguan (潘啟官), the Dutch were able to put together a salvage team to recover some of the cargo. This operation required approval from the Chinese authorities and the services of the linguists in procuring the necessary permits.

Rather than pay all fees individually, the Dutch made a special arrangement with the Chinese officials to salvage their ship: the Chinese Mandarins agreed to accept 30 percent of the salvaged goods as payment for their duties and services; the thirty Chinese divers split 20 percent among themselves; the owners and operators of the Chinese sampans and junks agreed to take another 20 percent; and the remaining 30 percent of the recovered cargo went to the VOC.[37]

By making this special arrangement, the Dutch avoided the heavy costs often incurred in such operations. There was no guarantee enough merchandise would be salvaged to cover any of the costs, so subcontracting the rescue on a commission basis meant that the VOC had nothing to lose and 30 percent to gain. The Dutch sent the Chinese salvage team to the site of the *Rynsburgh* several times after 1772, so this was not the end of the affair for either Pan Qiguan or the linguists. A few years later, the ship had broken up, the remaining goods had been badly damaged by seawater and 'Oesters' (oysters), and the waters had become increasingly infested with sharks, which cost the lives of some divers. This led the Dutch to give up the salvage operation in January 1778.

The entire operation, which lasted about five years, had the backing of the Hoppos in Canton, so they probably received a commission on the recovered goods as well.[38] The example of the *Rynsburgh* shows how flexible the Chinese authorities could be in arranging these projects. Any reasonable offer that did not sacrifice or threaten the political and social harmony in Canton, or arouse the suspicions of superiors in Beijing, could be discussed, negotiated and arranged.

There were other situations that required such coordinating efforts from the linguists, which also reflect on the Hoppos' many responsibilities. Fires were frequent in Canton and the moment that one broke out the linguists were called on to assist.[39] Fires threatened everyone, so foreigners often rushed to the scene to offer assistance. They kept water pumps (called 'fire engines') in their factories, and Chinese merchants also purchased pumps from the foreigners and kept them in their *hongs*. When a fire broke out in the vicinity of the factories (foreigners were not allowed in the inner city), everyone rushed to the scene with their pumps and all able-bodied men offered assistance.

On 7 February 1773, for example, a fire broke out at about 6PM near the factories. Everyone worked throughout the night to fight the flames, but it was not until 5:30 the next morning that the fire was extinguished. Three hundred to 450 houses were consumed by the flames, and many foreign factories and Chinese *hongs* suffered considerable damage.[40] Another fire broke out on 8 February 1777 at 3AM, destroying 300 to 340 houses and again badly damaging a number of factories and *hongs*.[41] On 18 December 1778, a fire broke out at 4AM and 40 to 50 houses were reduced to ashes.[42] In all three incidents, foreigners and Chinese worked together to put out the flames and linguists were on hand to monitor developments and help police keep order.

Sometimes, however, linguists were called to keep foreigners from lending a hand. On 22 December 1778, a fire broke out at 3:30AM and consumed 80 houses. This time foreigners did not come to the rescue because the Hoppo had closed trade and restricted them to their factories, owing to an incident a few days earlier.[43] In this case, the linguists had to be on the spot to ensure the foreigners stayed indoors.

These emergencies were especially stressful because tensions ran high, tempers and tolerance were strained by hard work and a lack of sleep, and foreign and Chinese officers were anxious to control matters quickly. Property, profits, reputations and lives were all at risk, and one mistake by the linguists, such as misunderstanding an instruction, could make a bad situation worse. There could be much shouting, name-calling and apportioning of blame between parties when things were not going well. Linguists had to run back and forth, interpret the angry words (correctly) and, at the same time, send encouraging reports back to the Hoppo and supercargoes in Canton. In all emergencies that involved foreigners, the linguists were on the front line doing what they could to prevent things from spiralling out of control.

In addition to crises, there were normal gatherings with both foreign and Chinese officials in attendance that the linguists had to handle, which also help to show the many concerns of the Hoppos and governors-general. Officials from Beijing sometimes went to Canton for a visit; new Hoppos and governors-general arrived and departed at the beginning and end of their terms; and officials from neighbouring provinces passed through on their way to new assignments. All these dignitaries had to be honoured with the appropriate welcome and farewell ceremonies, which were linguists' responsibilities.

On 3 December 1738, for example, the linguists informed all the supercargoes that two commissioners from Beijing, the viceroy and tsontock (governor-general), would arrive the following day and that ships were to be made ready for a reception. The foreign captains were notified, and, when the viceroy's entourage passed the ships in Whampoa, all ships were instructed to fire the customary cannon salutes.[44]

A few days later, the linguists went round again informing all the supercargoes and captains their presence was requested (required) at a special farewell banquet for the viceroy.[45] The event was to take place in a 'large square before the audience hall' in Canton (probably near the Hoppo's or governor's residence). Besides the important Chinese officials and merchants, there were 29 Europeans in attendance.[46]

The viceroy made his entrance into the square on horseback with the customary retinue of officials and servants following on foot. After he and his entourage had entered the Great Hall, the foreigners were invited in. The viceroy exchanged greetings with them then everyone was seated in their proper places. A tragicomedy was performed for the amusement of the guests. The viceroy then 'made a long speech in his own language' and the linguists translated everything into 'English'.[47] Drinks, toasts and greetings were exchanged before the viceroy made a short farewell speech, in which he expressed how 'very lucky he was' to have had such an experience, that he knew the foreigners 'were all good people' and that he wished them all a 'speedy voyage' home. He then 'sprang on his horse' and departed, with exuberant expressions of gratitude, and the supercargoes, in turn, wished him a long and 'prosperous life'. The linguists, of course, translated all the exchanges on the spot.[48]

Events such as these had to be very stressful for the linguists as well as the local officials. Linguists had basic language skills at best, so they were constantly being put to the test to translate everything correctly. Important people attended these events so there was no room for blunders. The ceremonies were also stressful for the foreigners: they had to pay close attention to proper Chinese protocol, which could seem strange to them. Foreign supercargoes were, of course, also anxious to satisfy local officials in Canton and impress the honoured dignitaries. Good performances would help them build goodwill with the Hoppo and governor-general, which might stand them in good stead in time of need or difficulty.

Even the junior officers and common sailors experienced stress because of pressure placed on them to do everything right or suffer the consequences. The various ceremonies held in 1738 seem to have been especially difficult for some of the foreign musicians. After they had practised and performed on several of these occasions, the Danes reported that one of their trumpeters was missing. The next day they learned that, a week earlier, he had deserted with Swedish trumpeters for Macau.[49]

Foreigners often tried to take advantage of these occasions to present special requests or complaints. The linguists were sometimes asked to deliver these petitions, which put them in a precarious position. On 2 February 1739, for example, the Dutch, via their Chinese linguist, sent a request to the new tsontock asking him to intercede in the procuring of their Grand Chop. (The Hoppo had withheld their Grand Chop because they had not yet paid the duties owing on their goods.)[50] This attempt by the Dutch to sidestep the Hoppo and apply directly to the tsontock put the linguist's relationship with the Hoppo at risk.

These were 'no-win' situations for the linguists. On the one hand they were responsible for taking care of all the foreigners' needs and for delivering their petitions as requested; on the other hand, they also needed to maintain a good working relationship with both the Hoppo and the governor-general. If the linguists refused to deliver a message there was the possibility that foreigners would seek other means of delivery, such as forcing their way past the sentries at the city gates and marching directly up to the governor-general's residence. This would cause much embarrassment to the linguists, merchants and city officials who would be blamed for not settling the matter before it reached that point. Linguists and merchants were sometimes successful at balancing all these concerns; other times they were not. These were situations that put many local officials at risk, and help us to understand better the role of the Hoppos and governors-general.

In addition to being mediators between the Chinese government and foreigners, linguists were also used as examples of public humiliation to pressure foreigners into compliance. On 7 May 1763, the Dutch mentioned that 'one of the three head linguists [Sinqua] was put in chains', to pressure the Europeans to remove quickly to Macao. The foreigners continued to procrastinate, and, as a result, the other two linguists were then put in chains.

In some cases, linguists, compradors and others would be paraded past the factories in chains to show the foreigners what would happen to them if they did not comply. These seemingly harsh measures, however, were actually rather mild tactics the Hoppos and governors-general experimented with to persuade foreigners to comply with their edicts. In almost all of these situations, the use of visual threats was much preferred to the use of force. These events caused the linguists and merchants a great deal of trouble, discomfort and embarrassment.[51]

By looking at the roles of the linguists after the collapse of the trade in 1842, we gain a better understanding of their contributions during the Canton System. As we saw in the previous chapter, compradors took over some of their responsibilities as mediators between foreigners and Chinese officials and merchants. Linguists were still more knowledgeable about customs regulations, but, as many of those procedures changed under the new Treaty Port System, the compradors and foreign linguists (who could speak Chinese) soon learned how to take care of those matters themselves.

Immediately after the collapse of the system, the five Canton linguists were employed by the Canton customs offices to help negotiate new terms. They helped draft new forms and documents and initiate new procedures. Linguists still secured chops and interpreted when needed, but because they could not read, write, or speak any foreign language fluently, the duties they could perform in this new trading environment were limited. Their traditional dependence on pidgin English was now becoming more of a liability than an asset. By the 1840s, there were several Christian missionaries and other foreigners in Canton, Macao and Hong Kong who had learned to read, write and speak Chinese. Now that they were no longer barred from performing the linguists' duties, they quickly took over many of their tasks.

Some of the compradors became merchants in their own right, and because they could usually speak a foreign language, or at least some pidgin English, and they could usually read and write Chinese (see Plates 34 and 36), they did not need the linguists either. In 1863 Wells Williams mentioned that the Canton linguists

> . . . have all been broken up by the changes recently introduced, and their members have mostly found employment in other branches of the general trade, with which their intimate acquaintance rendered them useful aids.[52]

For the most part the former Canton linguists were hired either by an establishment (foreign or Chinese) or by a government office, such as the Canton customhouse, to help with internal affairs. They ceased being the general mediators of trade between foreigners and Chinese.[53]

All these changes were not necessarily improvements on the way that trade had been conducted previously. During the Canton System, the linguists performed without payment all their duties during the three or four months the ships were at Whampoa. Some wages were paid to the linguists on a monthly basis, but linguists' personal fees were usually not collected until the ships were all loaded and ready to leave, which greatly facilitated a smooth and steady commerce. After 1842, however, this was done away with, and foreign ships had to pay the petty charges and fees as they were incurred, which was a great inconvenience to them. In 1863 Williams mentions that

> Previous to the present system coming into operation, it was the usage at Canton for the duties of all kinds to be paid when the ship was loaded and ready for sea, the linguists managing its business and making out the accounts. That plan was certainly less encumbered with petty details which the foreigner has now to attend to, but the imperial revenue suffered in proportion, and no one ought to complain of measures taken for its protection.[54]

SUMMARY

We have shown some of the day-to-day responsibilities of the linguists during the Canton era, which help define the parameters of trade. Linguists used Portuguese to communicate with foreigners in the early decades, but by the 1730s they had adapted to the language of the merchants, pidgin English. The fact that everyone in Canton switched to this language, which was an amalgam of several tongues, shows how flexible and focused the environment was in accommodating trade. But it also meant the linguists did not have the ability to translate anything accurately because pidgin English was crude at best. This factor nonetheless served administrators well, because they wanted only as much contact with and understanding of foreigners as was needed to carry on commerce.

The exchanges were never supposed to go beyond being anything but strictly commercial, which was one of the unwritten rules of the trade. Knowing a foreign language well enough to translate specific and detailed complaints from the foreigners was dangerous. It was a capital offence to teach a foreigner Chinese, and in the same light it could just as easily be a capital offence for a Chinese to become fluent in a foreign language if it resulted in problems for the officials. As a result, there was no formal school established in Canton to learn foreign languages, despite the many opportunities available to do so. Social and political interests kept pressure on Chinese to only learn pidgin English, nothing more. The dependence on pidgin English disadvantaged the Canton linguists in the Treaty Port era when new demands required higher language skills.[55]

By comparing the numbers of the ships with the numbers of linguists in Canton, we can see that the administration did not let the two expand in unison. Linguists were allowed to subcontract ships to junior linguists to handle the expansion so that each one of them could take care of more ships. This increased their incomes but also transferred power downward. It was, however, an effective way of keeping the upper ranks from having to expand in unison as well, which would have made Hoppos and governors-general look good in Beijing. But as a result, the Hoppos had to allow the linguists great leeway in carrying out their duties.

All these factors helped to build transparency in trade costs, which led to composite linguists' figures being compiled. The linguists, in turn, operated the entire season on their own funds, and were not paid until the ships were ready to leave. But operating on credit was a good way to facilitate trade, so it was also in the interests of the Hoppos to continue this practice. Commerce gained stability, but at the expense of the linguists diverting some revenues such as the compradors' engagement fees into their own pockets. These examples help to explain the increase in collusions in the lower echelons.

Finally, the role of the linguists went through a dramatic change after the collapse of the Canton System, which sheds light on the earlier period. From those changes we learn there were others, such as the factory compradors, who could have performed some of the linguists' duties in the Canton System but were not allowed to do so. By restructuring and redistributing the responsibilities of the linguists and others involved in the trade from time to time, the Hoppos could probably have adjusted to the expansion more effectively to avoid losing power. But they did not have the freedom to make those decisions, which points to another limitation of the commerce.

Now that we have laid out the administrative structures, the next chapter turns to some of the problems that arose and changes that were introduced to make the system operate more effectively.

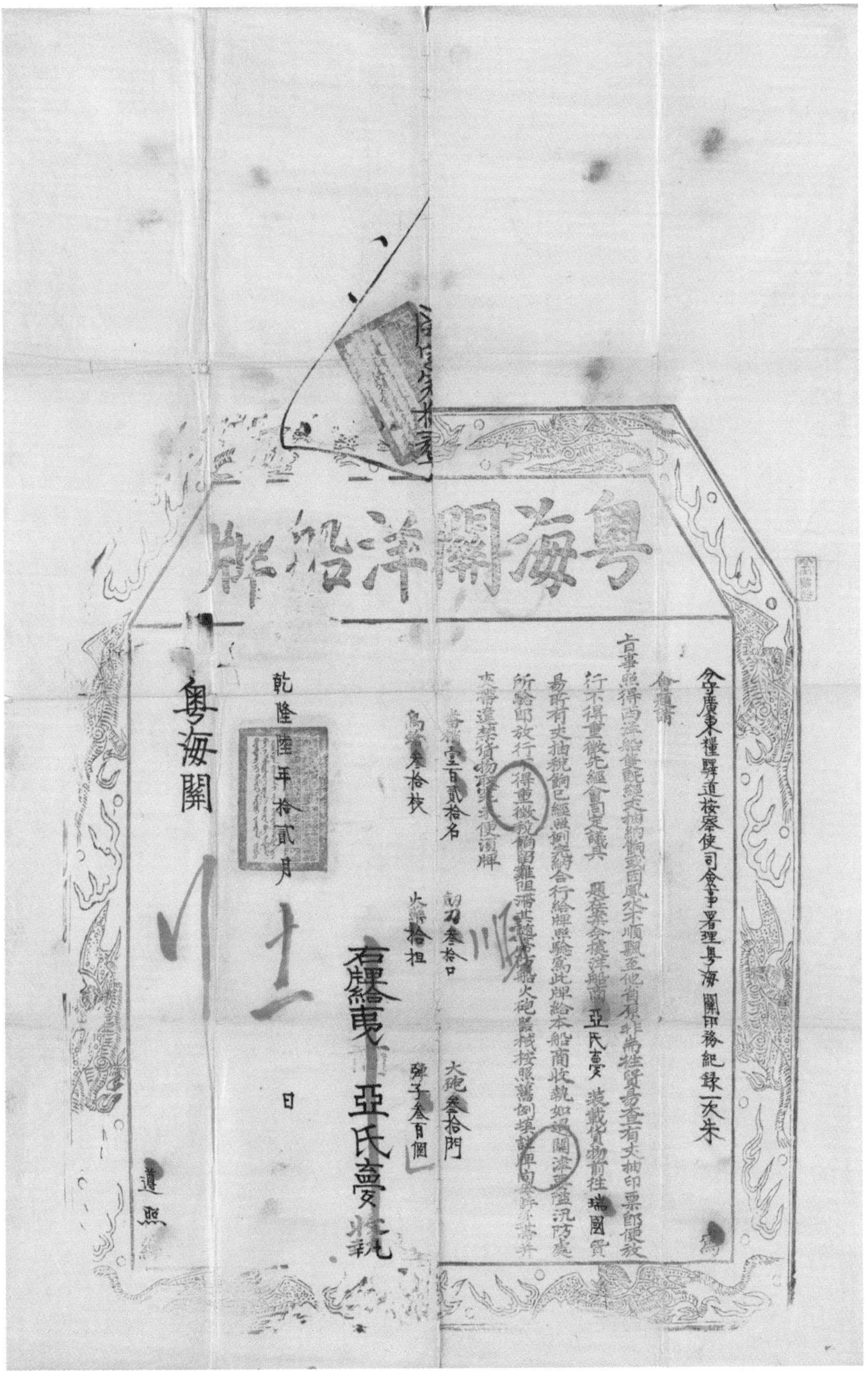
粵海關洋船牌

番梢壹百貳拾名
鳥鎗叁拾枝
腰刀叁拾口
火藥拾担
大砲叁拾門
弾子叁百個

乾隆陸年拾貳月 日

粵海關

Plate 1 Grand Chop issued to the SOIC ship *Götheborg* on 17 January 1742 granting permission to leave China. Courtesy of Kungliga Biblioteket (Royal Library), Stockholm (KBS: Kine, Ms 14).

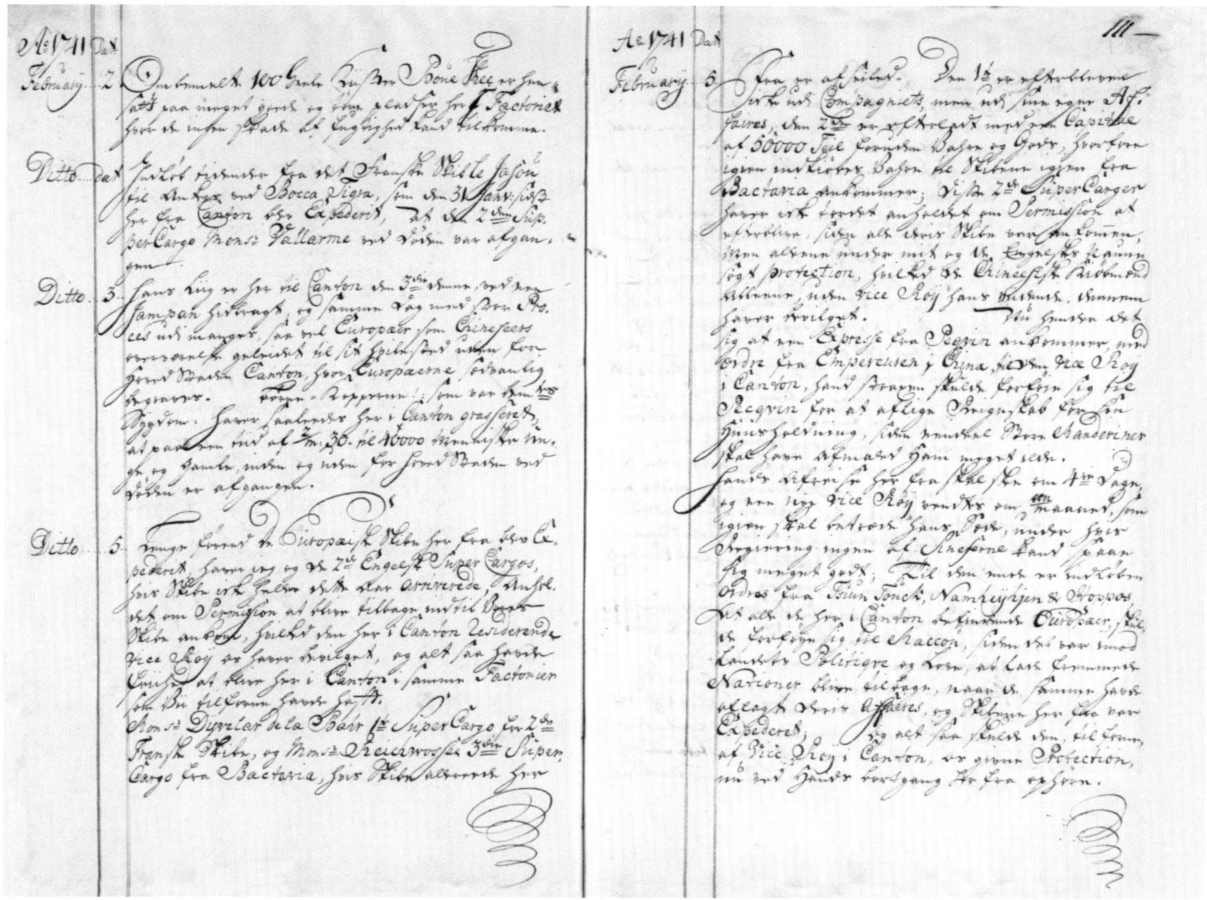

Plate 2 Extract (in Danish) from a DAC journal dated 5 February 1741 ordering all foreigners to leave Canton and go to Macao by order of the emperor. Courtesy of Rigsarkivet (National Archives), Copenhagen (RAC: Ask 1120).

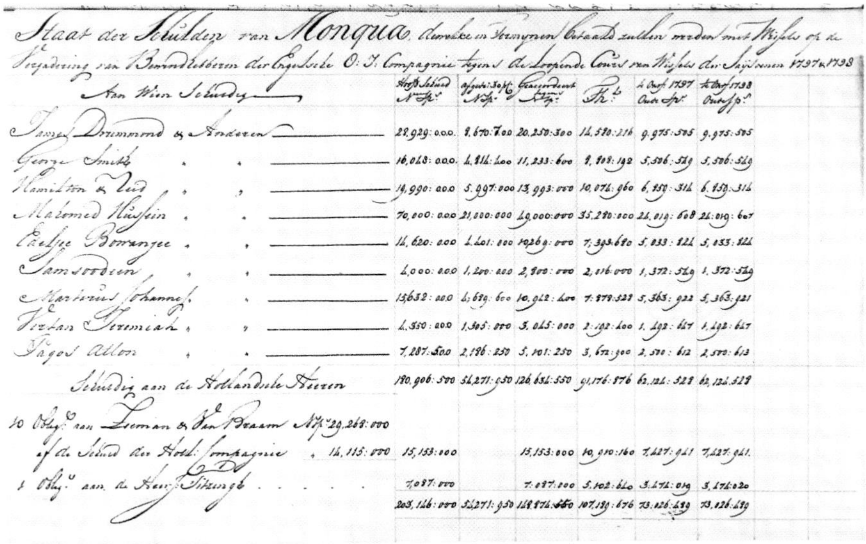

Staat der Schulden van Monqua, dewelke in termijnen betaald zullen worden met Wissels op de Vergadering van Bewindhebberen der Engelsche O: I: Compagnie tegens de loopende Cours van Wissels der Jaarsaisoenen 1797 & 1798

Aan Wien Schuldig	Hoofdschuld Nsp.	afgetrokken 30 pct Nsp.	Geaccordeert Nsp.	Th.	1797 Oude Sp.	1798 Oude Sp.
James Drummond & Anderen	28,929:000	8,670:700	20,250:300	14,580:216	9,975:585	9,975:585
George Smith	16,048:000	4,814:400	11,233:600	8,088:192	5,506:549	5,506:549
Hamilton & Reid	18,990:000	5,997:000	13,993:000	10,074:960	6,859:314	6,859:314
Mahomed Hussein	70,000:000	21,000:000	49,000:000	35,280:000	24,019:608	24,019:607
Cawsjee Bomanjee	14,620:000	4,401:000	10269:000	7,393:680	5,033:824	5,033:824
Samsoodeen	4,000:000	1,200:000	2,800:000	2,016:000	1,372:549	1,372:549
Martinus Johannes	15,632:000	4,689:600	10,942:400	7:878:528	5,363:922	5,363:921
Vertan Jeremiah	4,350:000	1,305:000	3,045:000	2:192:400	1,492:647	1,492:647
Fagos Allon	7,287:500	2,186:250	5,101:250	3,672:900	2,500:612	2,500:613
Schuldig aan de Hollandsche Heeren	180,906:500	54,271:950	126,634:550	91,176:876	62,124:528	62,124:528
10 Oblig.n van Lieman & Van Braam Nsp.s 29,268:000 af de Schuld der Holl: Compagnie 14,115:000	15,153:000		15,153:000	10,910:160	7,427:941	7,427:941
1 Oblig.e aan de Heer Titsingh	7,087:000		7:087:000	5,102:640	3,474:019	3,474:020
	203,146:000	54,271:950	148,874:550	107,189:676	73,026:489	73,026:489

Plate 3 Declaration (in Dutch) of the failed merchant Monqua (Cai Wenguan 蔡文官) in 1797 and 1798 showing debts held by English, Parsees, Muslims, Armenians, Dutch and others. Courtesy of National Archives, The Hague. (NAH: OIC 197).

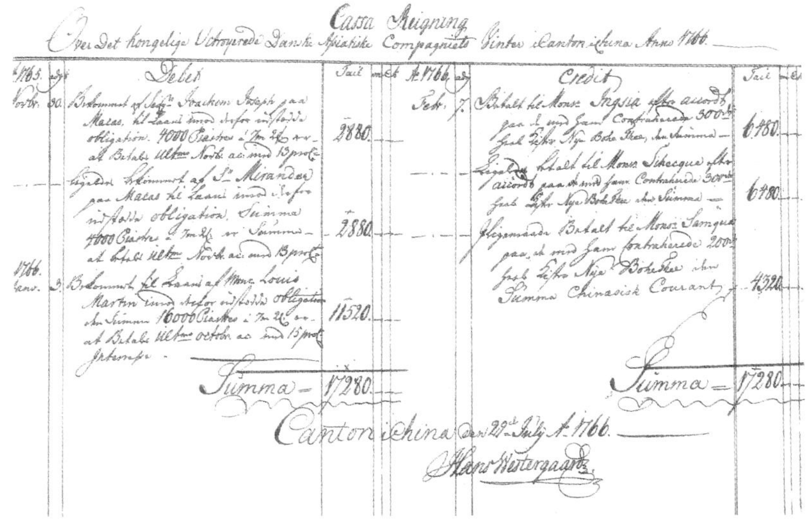

Cassa Regning
Over det kongelige Uctroyerede Danske Asiatiske Compagnies Vinter i Canton i China Anno 1766.

1765.		Debet	Tail	1766		Credit	Tail
Novbr.	30.	Bekommet af Sign.r Joachim Joseph paa Macao, til Laans imod derfor udstedde obligation. 4000 Piastres à 7m 2 f er at Betale Ultimo Novbr. a.c. med 13 pro Cento	2880	Febr.	7.	Betalt til Monsr. Ingsia efter accord paa de med Ham Contraherede 300 Kist Nye Bohe Thee, den Summa	6480
		Bekommet af Sr. Miranda paa Macao til Laans imod derfor udstedde obligation, Summa 4000 Piastre à 7m 2 f er Summa at betale Ultimo Novbr. a.c. med 13 pro Cto	2880			Betalt til Monsr. Sikequa efter accord paa de med Ham Contraherede 300 Kist Nye Bohe Thee den Summa	6480
1766. Janv.	3.	Bekommet til Laans af Monr. Louis Martin imod derfor udstedde obligation den Summa 16000 Piastres à 7m 2 f er at Betale Ultimo October a.c. med 15 pro Cto Interesse	11520			Ligeledes Betalt til Monsr. Samqua paa de med Ham Contraherede 200 Kist Nye Bohe Thee den Summa Chinasisk Courant	4320
		Summa	17280			Summa	17280

Canton i China den 29 July A. 1766.
Hans Westergaard

Plate 4 Balance sheet (in Danish) from the DAC in 1765/66 showing money borrowed from Portuguese in Macao and paid to Chinese merchants in Canton for the purchase of Bohea tea. Courtesy of Rigsarkivet (National Archives), Copenhagen (RAC: Ask 1156b).

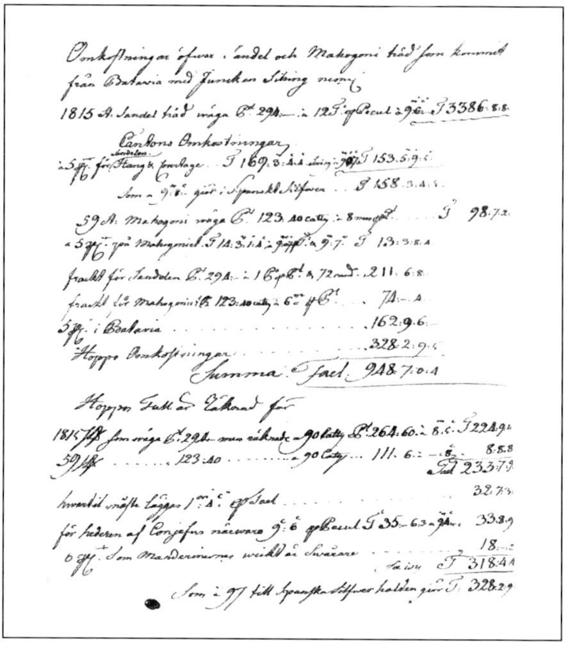
Omkostningar öfwer Sandel och Makogoni träd som kommit från Batavia med Junken Sihing neml.

1815 St. Sandel träd wäga Pc. 294.

Cantons Omkostningar

Summa Tael 948.7.0.4

Plate 5 Calculations (in Swedish) from the private trade of SOIC supercargo Jean Abraham Grill showing his costs for shipping sandalwood and mahogany from Batavia to Canton aboard the junk *Sihing* in the mid-1760s. Courtesy of Nordic Museum Archive, Stockholm (NM: Godegårdsarkivet F17).

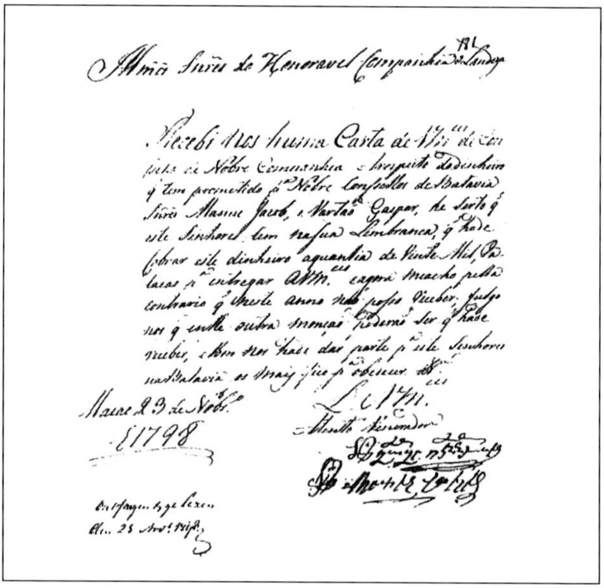
Illmos Snres de Honoravel Companhia de Olanda

Macao 23 de Novbro 1798

L. e M.

Plate 6 Letter written in Portuguese dated 23 November 1798 from Armenians Lazaro Johannes and Macartes Basilio (also spelled Macatish Vasilio) in Macao concerning a loan to the Dutch arranged through Armenians Manuc Jacob and Vartao Gaspar in Batavia. It is signed by Johannes and Basilio in Armenian. Courtesy of National Archives, The Hague (NAH: Canton 60).

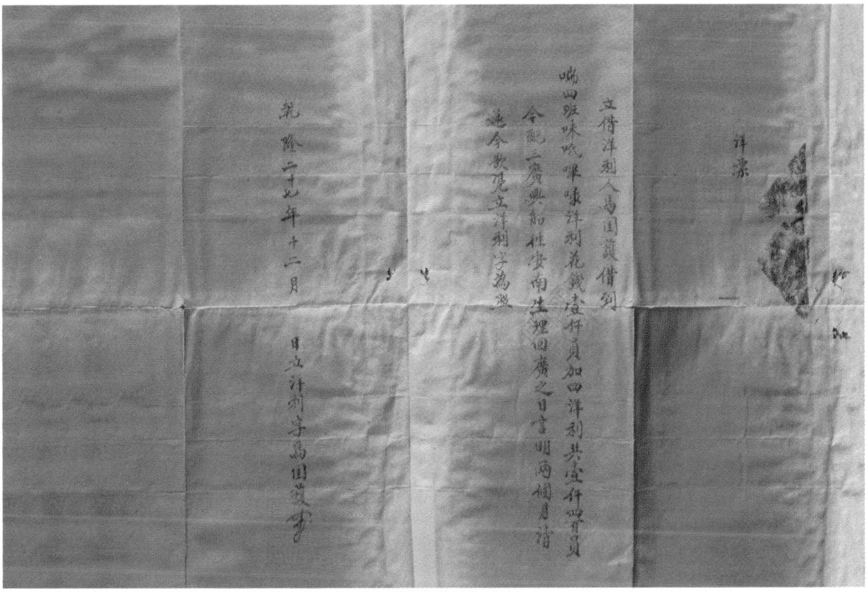

Plate 7 Bottomry contract without a co-signer given to Ma Guohu (馬國護) for junk *Samkonghing* (Sanguangxing 三廣興) sailing to Cochin China (Vietnam) from a SOIC supercargo dated 3 February 1763. Courtesy of Nordic Museum Archive, Stockholm (NM: Godegårdsarkivet F17).

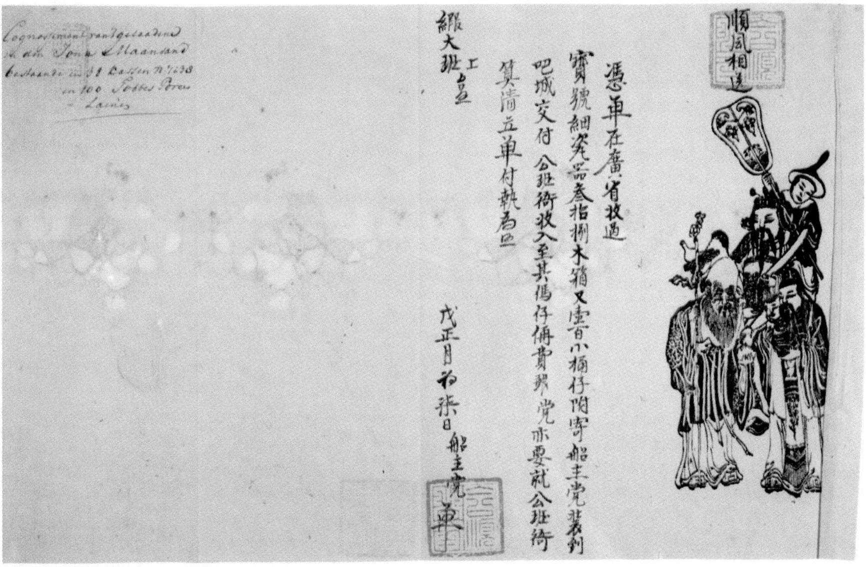

Plate 8 Bill of lading for porcelain shipped for the Dutch from Canton to Batavia aboard junk *Maansand* (in 1788?). Courtesy of National Archives, The Hague (NAH: Canton 296).

Plate 9 Drawing in a Swedish journal from 1747/48 of two Chinese vessels, one being an ocean-going junk flying a Dutch flag. Courtesy of Kungliga Biblioteket (Royal Library), Stockholm (KBS: M 280).

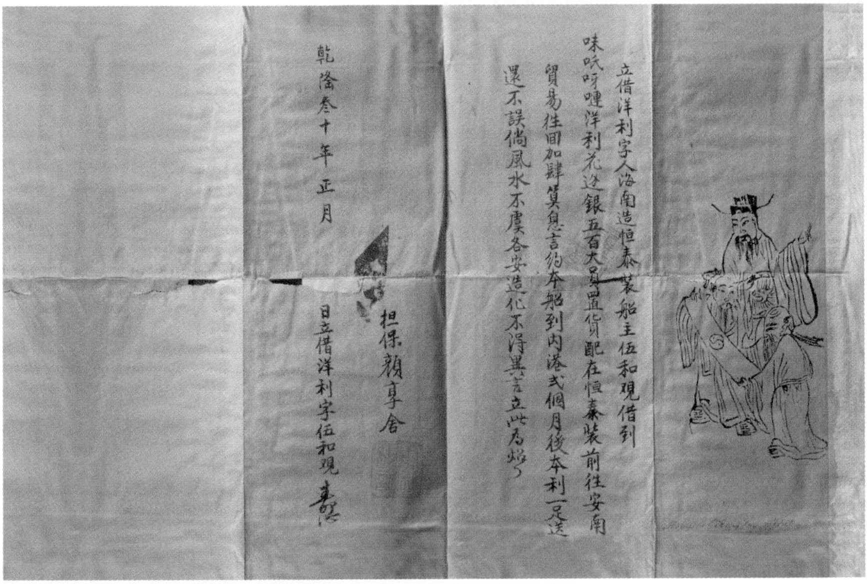
立借洋利字人海南造恒泰裝船主伍和觀借到
味呧吁嗹洋利花边銀五百大員置貨配在恒泰裝前往安南
貿易往回加肆算息言約本船到內港弍個月後本利一足送
還不誤倘風水不虞各安造化不得異言立此為炤
乾隆叁十年正月
担保顏享舍
日立借洋利字伍和觀

Plate 10 Bottomry contract given to Wu Heguan (伍和觀) for junk *Hingtay* (Hengtai 恒泰) sailing to Cochin China (Vietnam) from a SOIC supercargo for 500 piastres with co-signer Hongsia (Yan Xiangshe 顏享舍) dated January/February 1765. Courtesy of Nordic Museum Archive, Stockholm (NM: Godegårdsarkivet F17).

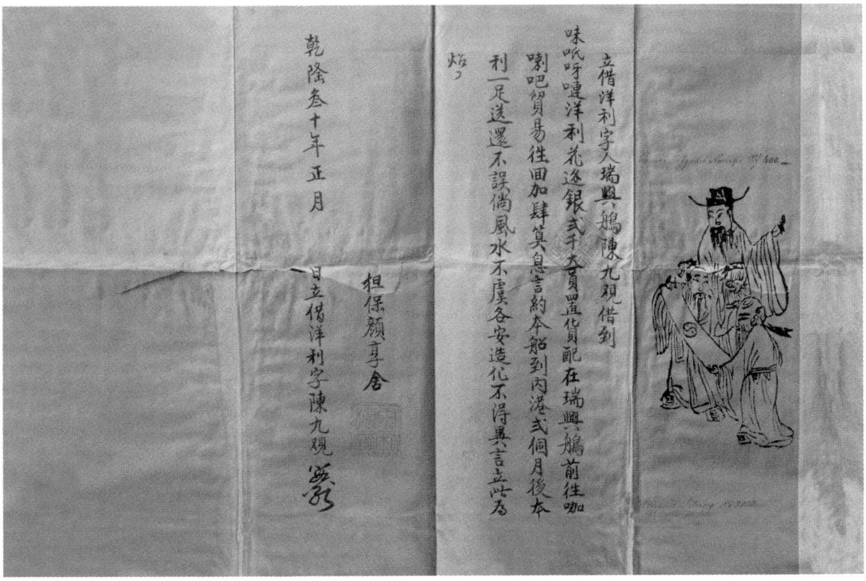
立借洋利字人瑞興艚陳九觀借到
味呧吁嗹洋利花边銀弍千大員置貨配在瑞興艚前往咖
喇吧貿易往回加肆算息言約本船到內港弍個月後本
利一足送還不誤倘風水不虞各安造化不得異言立此為
炤
乾隆叁十年正月
担保顏享舍
日立借洋利字陳九觀

Plate 11 Bottomry contract given to Chen Jiuguan (陳九觀) for junk *Sihing* (Ruixing 瑞興艚) sailing to Java from a SOIC supercargo, with co-signer Hongsia (Yan Xiangshe 顏享舍) dated January/February 1765 and showing 400 of the 2,000 piastres coming from Armenian Ignace Narcipe in Macao. Courtesy of Nordic Museum Archive, Stockholm (NM: Godegårdsarkivet F17).

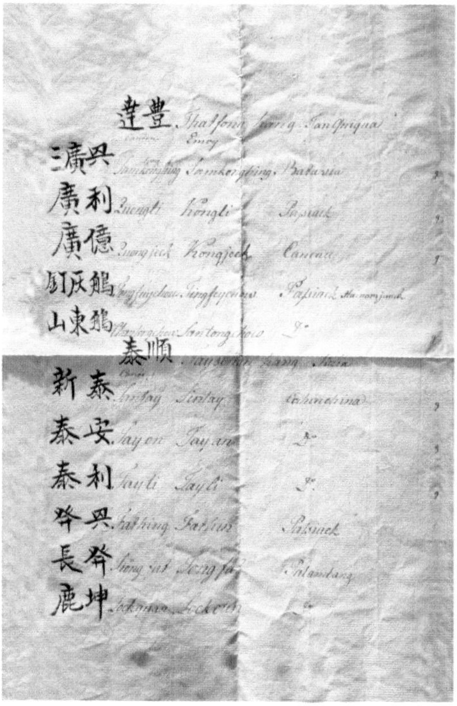

達豐
三廣興
廣利
廣德
釘灰船
山東船
泰順
新泰
泰安
泰利
發興
長發
鹿坤

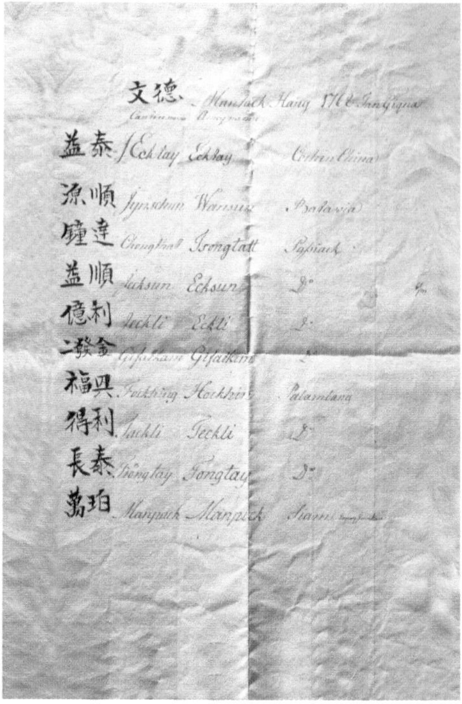

文德
益泰
源順
鐘達
益順
億利
二發金
福興
得利
長泰
萬珀

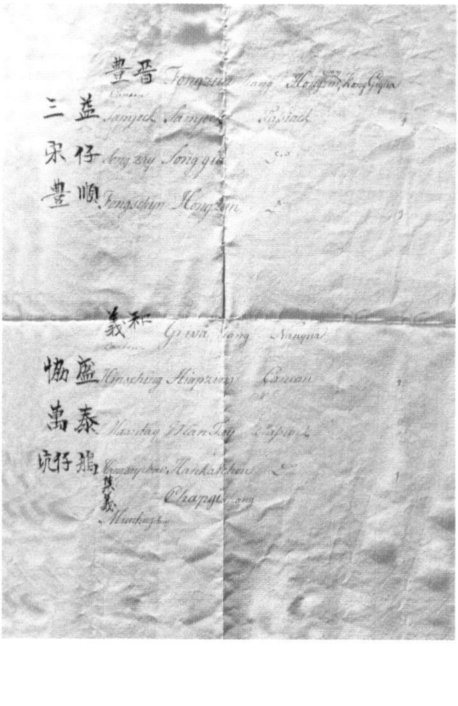

豐晉
三益
宋仔
豐順
義和
協盛
萬泰
坑仔船

Plate 12 List of 28 Canton junks and their managers and factories in 1768, with names in Chinese characters and their Cantonese and Fujianese pronunciations. Courtesy of Nordic Museum Archive, Stockholm (NM: Godegårdsarkivet F17).

(13.1)

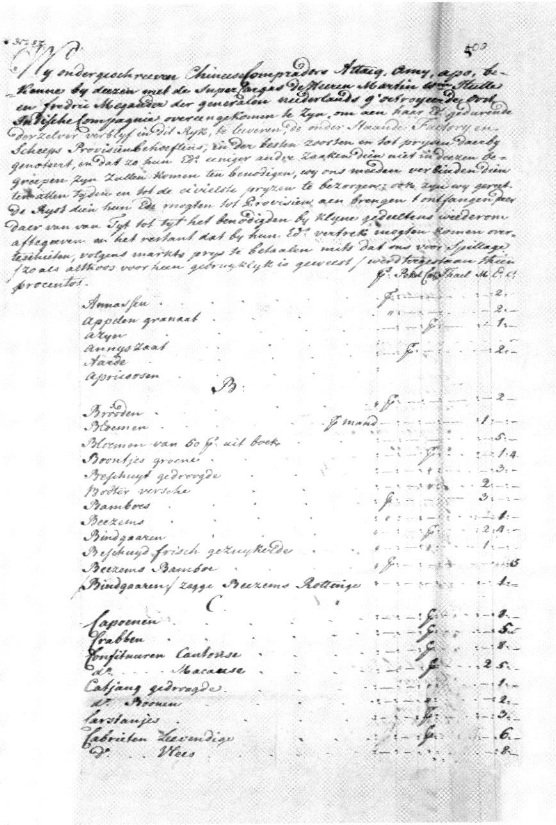

(13.2)

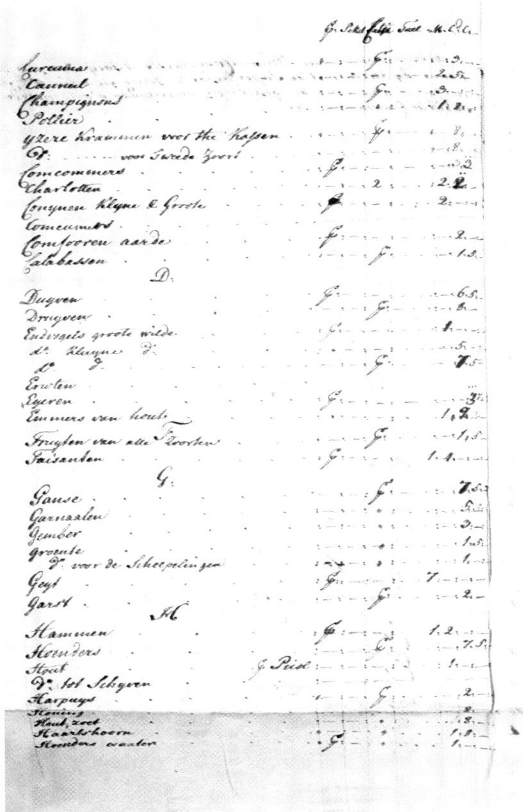

Plate 13 (1–6) Contract (in Dutch) between the VOC and compradors Attacq (Atack), Amy and Apo to supply provisions and labour for the Dutch factory and the Dutch ships at the prices stipulated, dated 7 August 1760 and signed by all three compradors. Courtesy of National Archives, The Hague (NAH: VOC 4384).

(13.3)

K.

	Unit	Price
Kaarsen van wax	p° Catje	3.
d° d° Smeer		6.5
Karin bollen		3.
Kool		3.
Kik vorsen		8.
Kalveren	p°	3.5.
Knofflook	p° Catje	2.
Koolen van hout	p° P. — p° Pekol	3.2.
Kalk		8.
Kruyd nagelen	p° Catje	1.6.
Koks	p° maand — p°	1.8.
d° maats	d°	1.4.8.
Kuykens	p° Catje	7.5.
Kayjangs matten	p°	2.5.
Kruyt	p° Catje	2

L.

	Unit	Price
Lamp oly	p° Catje	5.5.
Lamppitten		1.5.
Glasen groote	p°	4.
D° kleene		2.5.
Linkings gedroogde	p° Catje	5.
D° verse		2.
Lemmetjes		1.
gezoute d°		5.
Limoen Sop	p° Bootle	5
Lantarens in de Factory	p°	1.2.
Laxa		4
Linnen Groff	p° Cobit	1.
d° fyn	d°	2.5.

M.

	Unit	Price
Meel	p° Catje	24
Melk		1.4.
Mostaard Zaat		8.
Messel Steen	p° ton — p°	1.4.8
Mourilles	p° Catje	3.
Messelaars	p° dag — p°	8.
Matten ordinaire voor de schaepen		2
Mispels	p° Catje	1.5.
Mangos	p°	2.
Millioenen	p°	2

(13.4)

N.

	Unit	Price
Nooten Muscaat	p° Catje	1.6.
Naalden		
Nooten	p°	8.
Nieren		1.4.5.

O.

	Unit	Price
Oesters	p° Catje	5.
Verkens ooren		4.6.
Oranje Koekjes		7.

P.

	Unit	Price
Patryzen	p°	1.
Pompelmoesen		2.
Pompoenen		1.
Paling	p° Catje	7.
Pattates		1.
Pruymen		2.
d° Nankings		1.6
Peeren		3
persiken		1.
Pady		1.
d° Doppen		2.
Pisang		1.5
Peeper		1.4
Pampier		5.
proppen	p°	2
Potten ordinaire		6.
Paddy Stroo	p° Pekol	2.
pooten van Verken		4.
Pry Groene	p° Catje	2
d° gedroogde		3.
Peeper Lange		1.
Pampier witte 1ste zoort	1 vel	5
d° 2 d°		5.
Pooten van ossen		3.
Potten van aarde 1ste zoort	p°	8.
d° d° 2 d°		6.
d° d° 3e d°		2.
Porteleyn		2.

Q.

	Unit	Price
Quartels	p°	2.

R.

	Unit	Price
Reebock	p° Catje	[illegible]
Reusel gesmolten	p° Catje	1.2
d° ongesmolten		8.
Rosynen verse		8.
d° gedroogde	p° Catje	1.5.

(13.5)

R.	p. Pekel Catty Thl. M. C. C.
Raapen en Radys	2
Ryst witte	2.5
d°. Tweede Zoort	1
Risjes	3
Roode Ryst	8
S.	
Snippen	2
Slooten hang	8
Spuykers in Zoorten	8
Speck om te lardeeren	8
Schaap	7.4
Salpeeter	2.4
Swartsel	2
Sallade	3
Zout witte	2.2
d°. Grauw	2
Saucer	
Soya	13
Schilpaden	1.2
Seeft	1
Sago	8
Spinage	12
Suurdeeg	2.1
T.	
Talingen groote	1
d°. kleene	5
Tamarind	8
U.	
Uyen gedroogde	3
V.	
Vlees runde	1
Verkens d°.	8
Speen varken	6.5
Vis versche	5.5
gezoute d°.	1
d°. gemeene	4.5
W.	
Wortelen	2.5
Waater Lemoenen	5
Waater te drinken	1
Waayers van Bamboe	1

(13.6)

Y.	p. Pekel Catty Thl. M. C. C.
Yzer van alle Zoorten	8
d°. Draat	2.2
Z.	
Zeldery	2
Zeegelhaaren. 1st Zoort	2.4
d°. 2e. d°.	7
Zuyker Kandy	4.5
d°. Bruyne	

In de Neederlandse Factorij tot Canton in China den 7 august A°. 1760.

咪蘭伏食價錢單
買辦亞保、晚美

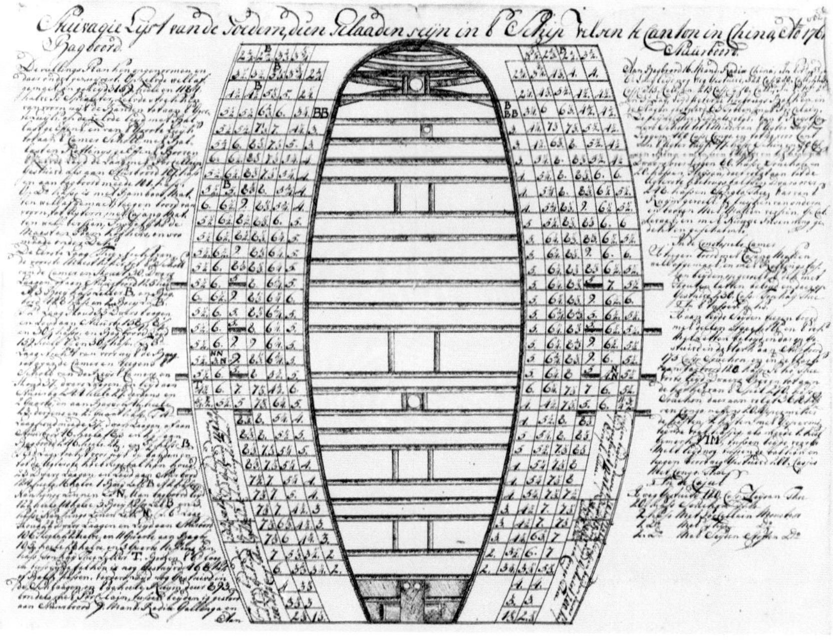

Plate 14 VOC stowing schematic (in Dutch) from 1761 for ship *Velsen*. Courtesy of National Archives, The Hague (NAH: VOC 4387).

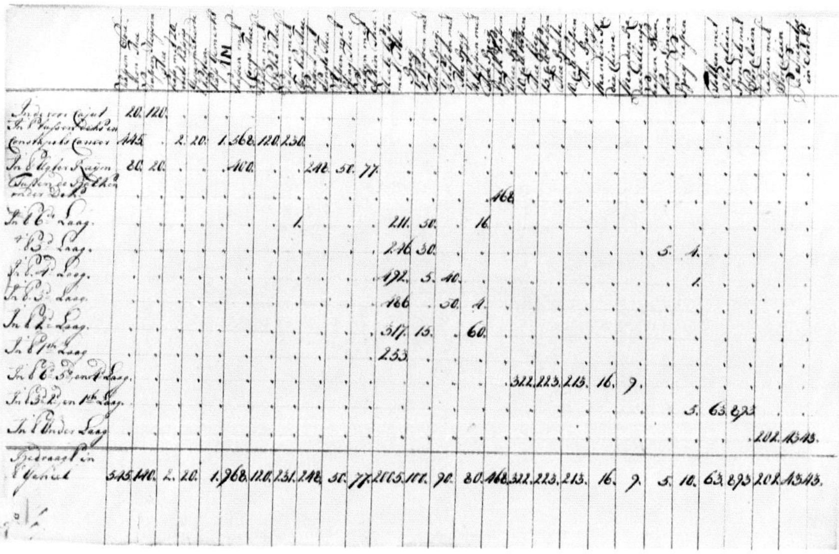

Plate 15 VOC stowing chart (in Dutch) from 1761 showing the chests placed in each layer of the ship. Courtesy of National Archives, The Hague (NAH: VOC 4387).

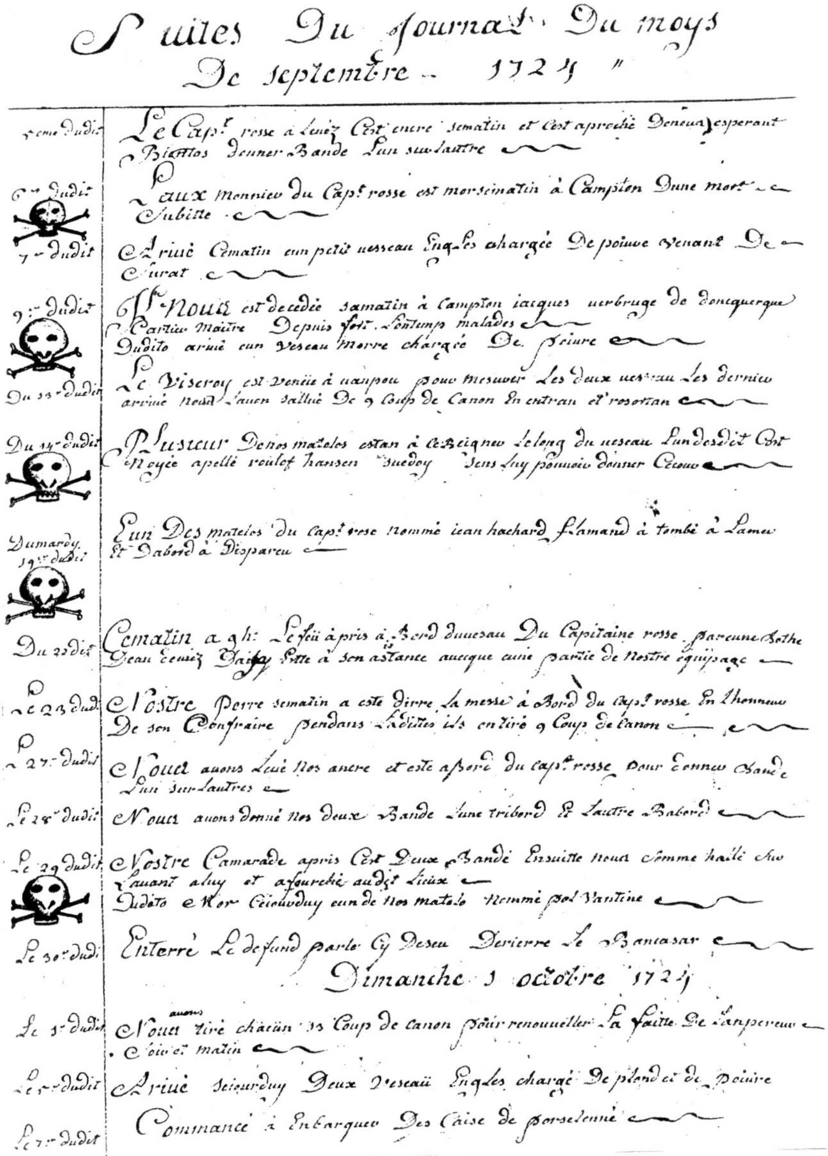
Suites Du Journal Du moys De septembre 1724

5eme Dudit — Le Capt. rosse a Leuez Cest encre Sematin et Cest apreché Deneuaz esperant Biettos Deuner Bande Lun sur Lautre

6e Dudit — Faux Monnieu du Capt. rosse est mor seimatin à Campton Dune mort subitte

7e Dudit — Ariué Cematin eun petit uesseau Engles chargée De poiuve venant De Surat

9e Dudit — Il nous est decedée samatin à Campton iacques uerbruge de doncquerque Cartier Maitre Depuis fort Lontemps malades
Dudito arriué eun veseau morre chargée De Peiure

Du 13e Dudit — Le Viseroy est venüe à uanpou pour mesuver Les deux uesseau Les dernieu arriué nous Lauen sallué De 9 Coup De Canon En entran et rosortan

Du 14e Dudit — Plusieur Denos matelos estan à se Beigneu Lelong du ueseau Lun desdit Cst noyée apellé reulef hansen suedoy Sens Luy pouuoir donner Secour

Dumardy 19e Dudit — Lun Des matelos du Capt. rose nommé iean hachard flamand à tombé à Lameu Et Dabord à Disparu

Du 22e Dudit — Cematin a 9 h: Le feu à pris à Bord du ueseau Du Capitaine rosse par eune Bothe Deau ... à son astance auecque eune partie de Nostre equipage

Le 23 Dudit — Nostre Perre Sematin a esté dirre La messe à Bord du Capt. rosse En Lhonneu De son Confraire pendans Ladittes ils en tiré 9 Coup De Canon

Le 27e Dudit — Nous auons Leué Nos ancre et esté a Bord du Capt. rosse pour donnée Bande Lun sur Lautres

Le 28e Dudit — Nous auons donné nos deux Bande Lune tribord Et Lautre Babord

Le 29 Dudit — Nostre Camarade apris Cest Deux Bande Ensuitte nous somme hallé Au auant alluy et afourché audit Lieux
Dudito e Mor Ceiourduy eun de nos matelo nommé Pol Vantine

Le 30e Dudit — Enterré Le defund parle Cy Desseu Derierre Le Bancasar

Dimanche 1 octobre 1724

Le 1e Dudit — Nous auons tiré chacün 11 Coup de canon pour renoueller La faitte De Lanpereu ce iour matin

Le 5 Dudit — Ariué Seiourduy Deux veseau Engles chargé De plond et de poiure

Le 7e Dudit — Commancé à Enbarqueu Des Caise de porselenne

Plate 16 Extract (in French) from a GIC journal for September 1724 showing a skull and crossbones each time someone died aboard the ship while anchored at Whampoa. Courtesy of Stadsarchief Antwerpen (City Archive, Antwerp) (SAA: IC 5688).

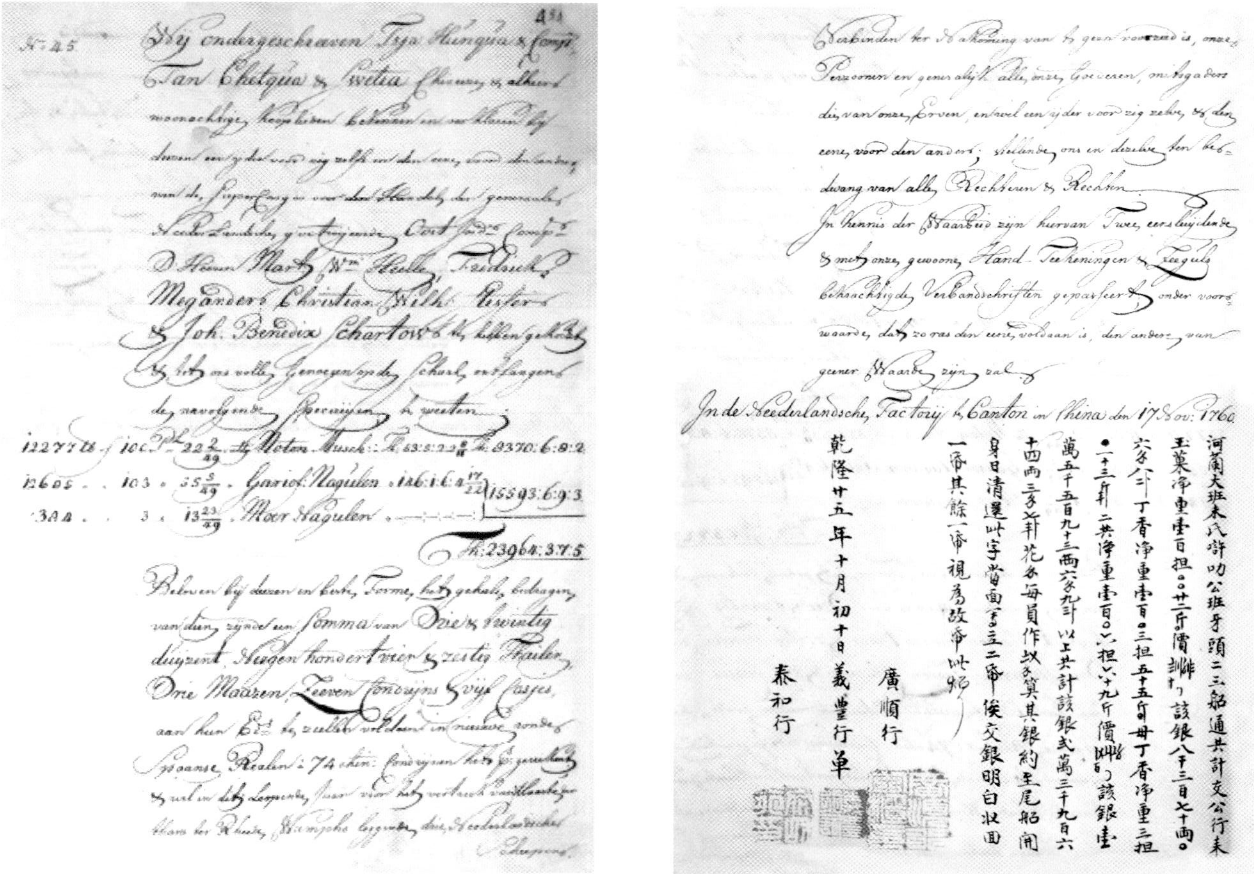

Plate 17 Contract (in Dutch) between the VOC and the merchants Tsja Hunqua, Tan Chetqua and Swetia for the Dutch imports of nutmeg and cloves, dated 17 November 1760. Courtesy of National Archives, The Hague (NAH: VOC 4384).

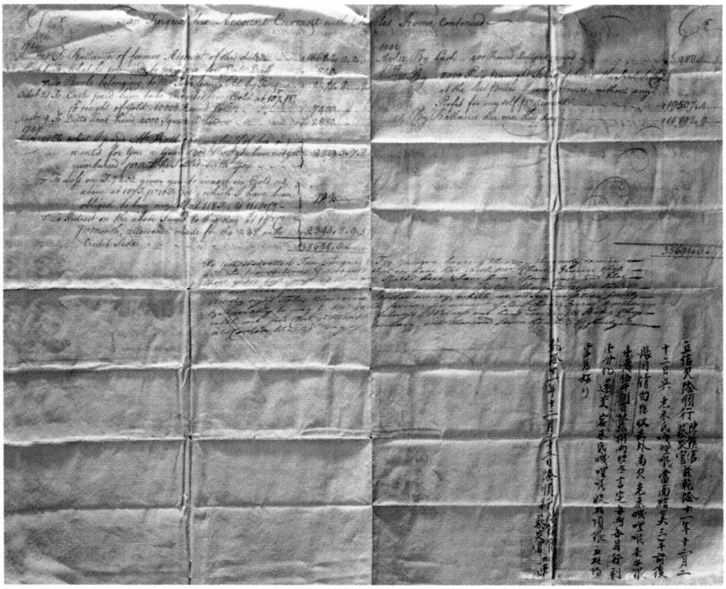

Plate 18 Contract from 1744/45 between the SOIC supercargo Charles Irvine and the merchants Tan Tinqua and Tzy Yamqua for an order of silk and gold, paid for mostly with silver. Courtesy of Nordic Museum Archive, Stockholm (NM: Godegårdsarkivet F17)

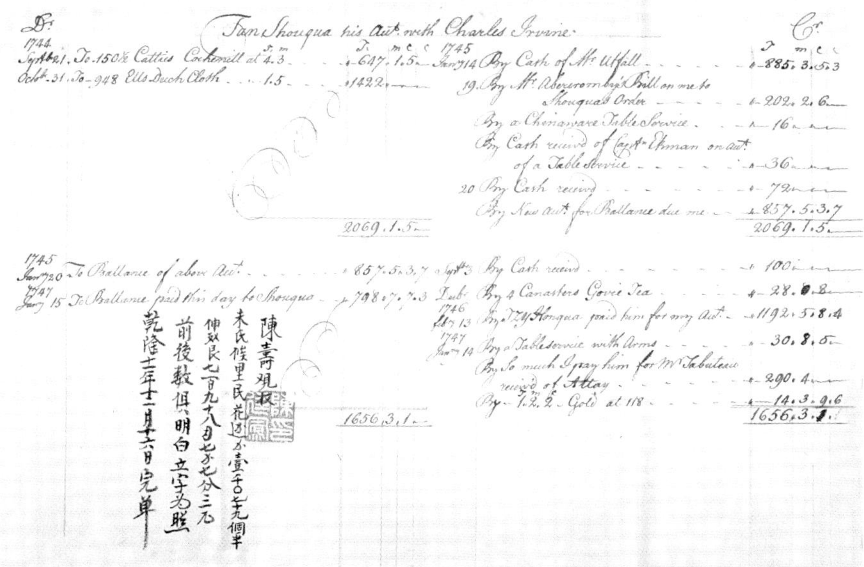

Dr. Tan Shouqua his Acct. with Charles Irvine Cr.

		T. m c c			T. m c c
1744 Septr. 21	To 150½ Catties Cochenill at 4.3	647.1.5	1745 Jany. 14	By Cash of Mr. Ulfall	885.3.5.3
Octr. 31	To 948 Ells Duch Cloth . . . 1.5	1422	19	By Mr. Abercromby's Bill on me to Shouqua's Order	202.2.6
				By a Chinaware Table Service	16
				By Cash receivd of Captn. Ekman on acct. of a Table Service	36
			20	By Cash receivd	72
				By New acct. for Ballance due me	857.5.3.7
		2069.1.5			2069.1.5
1745 Jany. 20	To Ballance of above Acct.	857.5.3.7	Septr. 3	By Cash receivd	100
1747 Jany. 15	To Ballance paid this day to Shouqua	798.7.7.3	Febr.	By 4 Canasters Govie Tea	28.0.8
			1746 Febr. 13	By Tzy Honqua paid him for my Acct.	1192.5.8.4
			1747 Jany. 14	By a Tableservice with Arms	30.8.5
				By So much I pay him for Mr. Tabuteau receivd of Attay	290.4
				By 1.2.2 Gold at 118	14.3.9.6
		1656.3.1			1656.3.1

陳壽観叔
前後數俱明白立字為照
乾隆十年十二月十六日完单

Plate 19 Contract from 1744/45 between the SOIC supercargo Charles Irvine and Tan Shouqua showing the practice of "truck", whereby imports of cochineal and cloth were applied to the purchase of chinaware. Courtesy of James Ford Bell Library, University of Minnesota (JFB: Charles Irvine Papers).

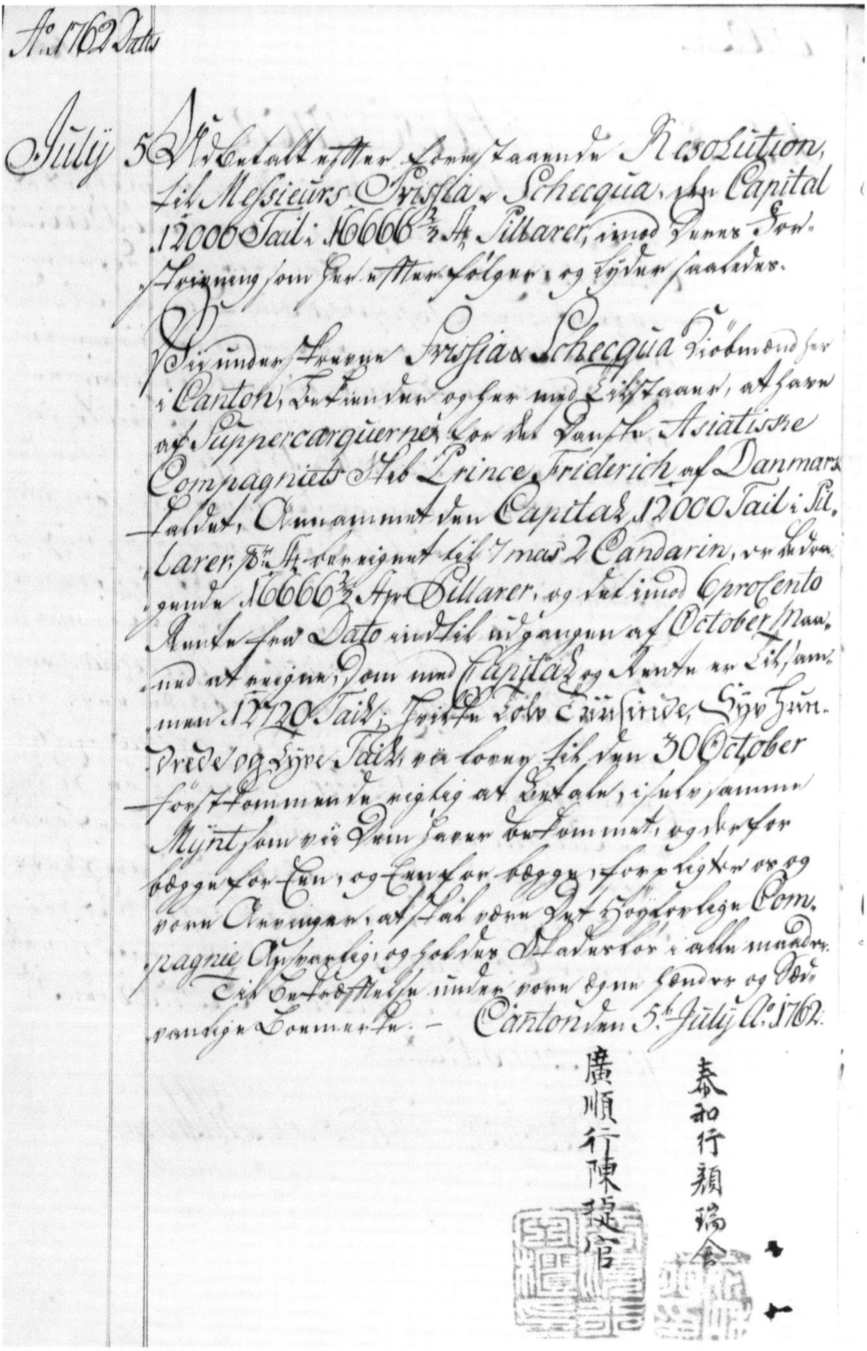

Plate 20 Contract (in Danish) between the DAC and the merchants Svissia and Schecqua for a loan of 12,000 taels for four months at 6 percent interest (1.5 percent per month), dated 5 July 1762. Courtesy of Rigsarkivet (National Archives), Copenhagen (RAC: Ask 1148a).

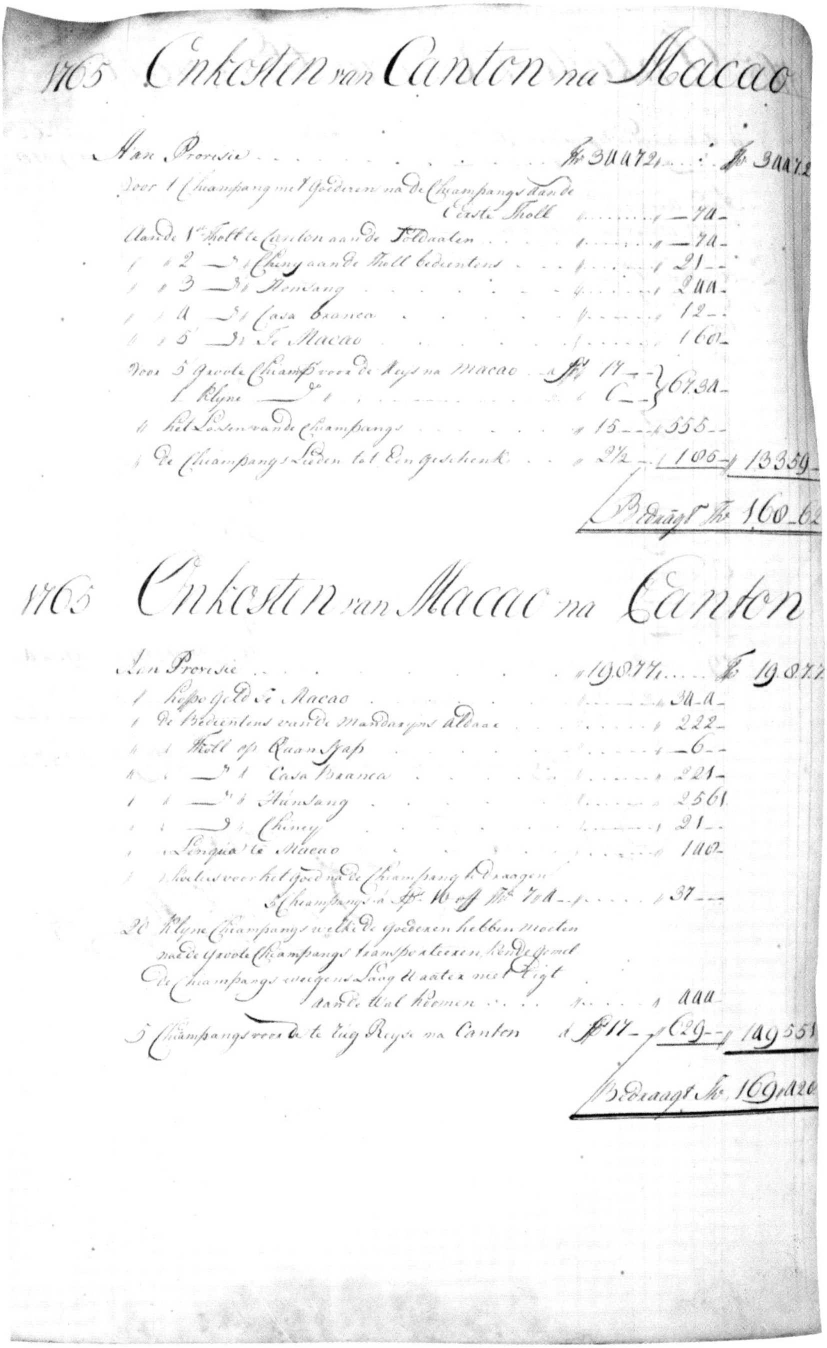
1765 Onkosten van Canton na Macao

Aan Provisie ... f 30472 ... f 30472
Voor 1 Champang met Goederen na de Champangs aan de Eerste Tholl ... 70
Aan de No. 1 Tholl te Canton aan de Toldaalen ... 70
" " 2 — Do. Ching aan de Tholl bedeientens ... 21
" " 3 — Do. Honsang ... 240
" " 4 — Do. Casa branca ... 12
" " 5 — Do. Te Macao ... 160
Voor 5 groote Champ voor de Reys na Macao a f 17 — } 6730
1 Klyne — Do. ... 6 —
" het Lossen van de Champangs ... 15 — 555
" De Champangs Lieden tot een geschenk ... 2½ — 105 — 13359
Bedraagt f 160.62

1765 Onkosten van Macao na Canton

Aan Provisie ... 19.877 ... f 19.877
" Hoppo geld te Macao ... 340
" De Bedientens van de Mandaryns aldaar ... 222
" " Tholl op Quanjap ... 6
" " — Do. Casa Branca ... 221
" " — Do. Honsang ... 2561
" " — Do. Chiney ... 21
" Lenquia te Macao ... 140
" Koelies voor het goed na de Champang te draagen 5 Champang a f 10 of f 700 ... 37
20 Klyne Champangs welke de goederen hebben moeten na de groote Champangs transporteeren, wijl de gemelde Champangs wegens laag water niet ligt aan de wal koomen ... 440
5 Champangs voor de te rug Reyse na Canton a f 17 — 629 — 14955
Bedraagt f 169.820

Plate 21 List (in Dutch) of the West River tolls and other costs the Dutch supercargoes were charged when travelling between Canton and Macao in 1765. Courtesy of National Archives, The Hague (NAH: VOC 4398).

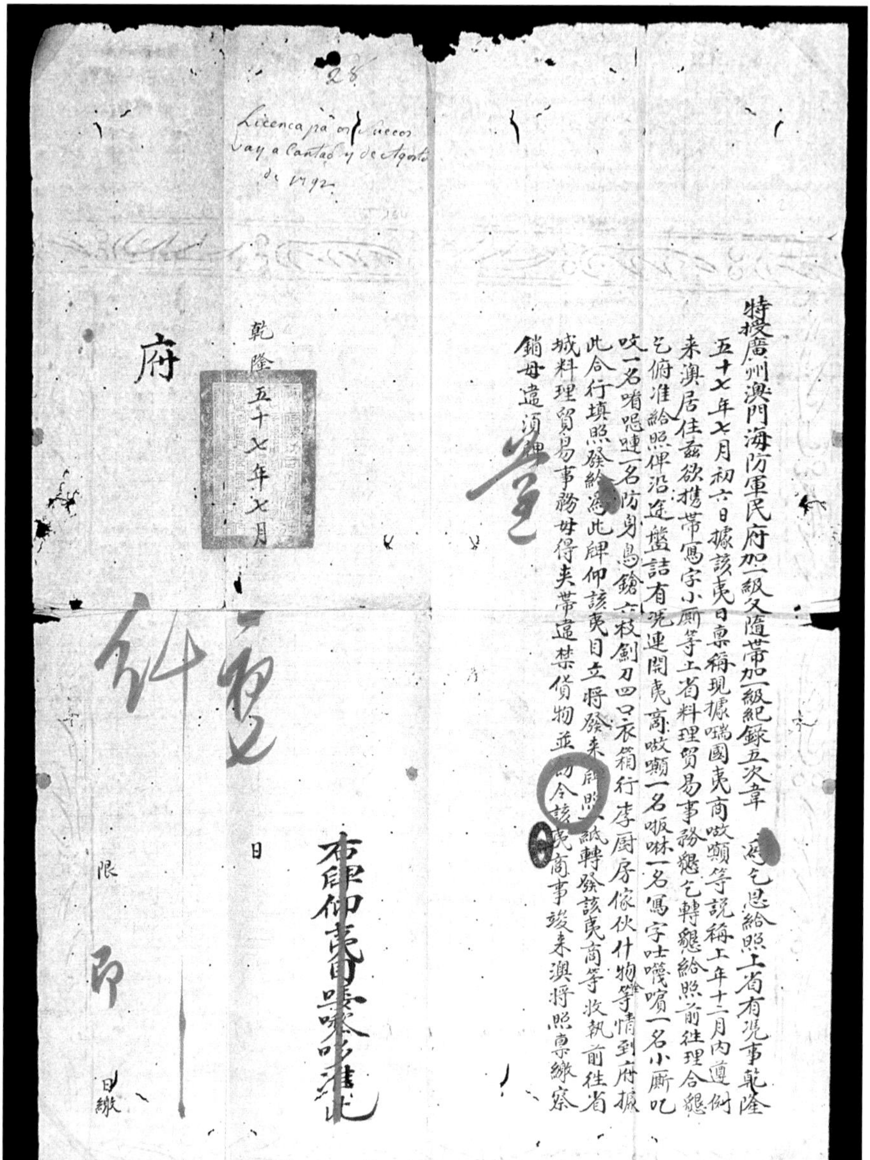

Plate 22 Licence known as the "small chop" to go to Canton via the West River issued to the SOIC supercargoes and their assistants in 1792. Courtesy of Instituto dos Arquivos Nacionais/Torre do Tombo, Lisbon, Portugal (Chapas Sínicas, T164).

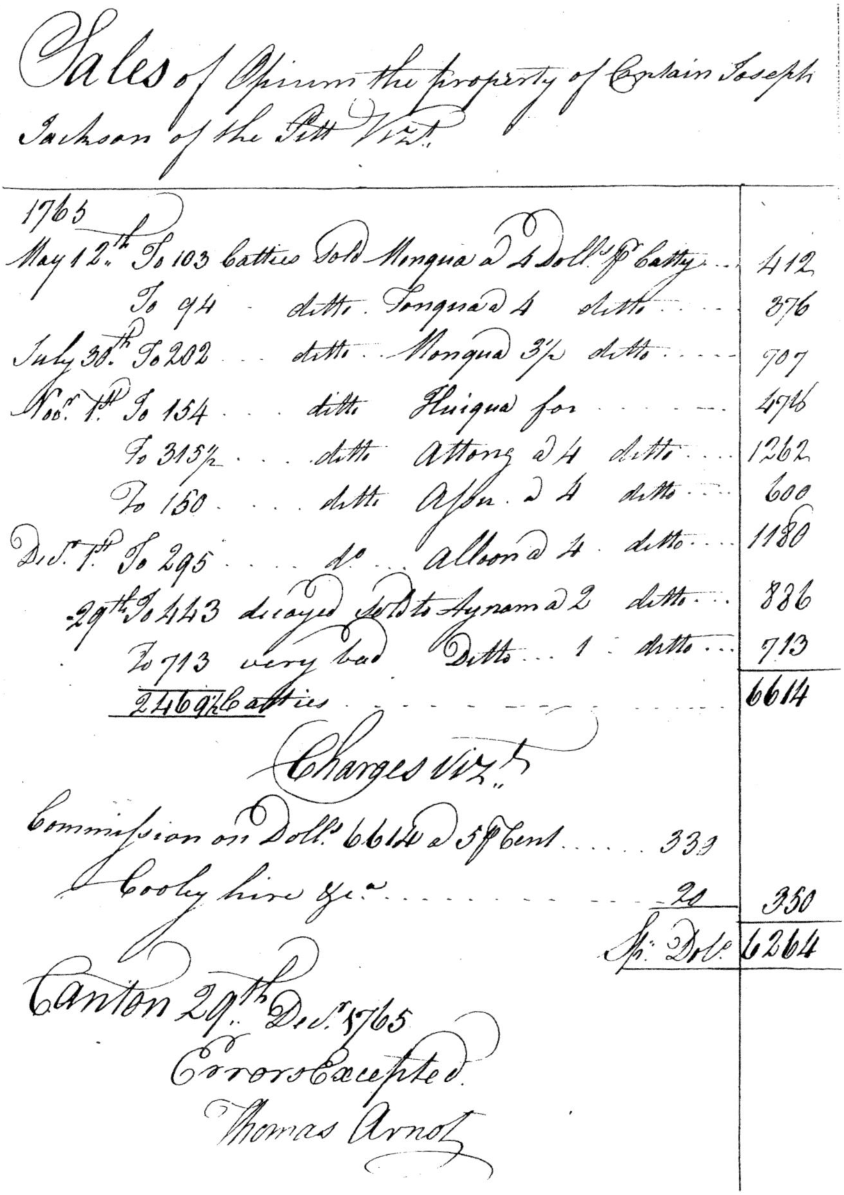

Sales of Opium the property of Captain Joseph Jackson of the Pitt Viz.t

1765		
May 12th To 103 Catties Sold Monqua @ 4 Doll.s p Catty		412
To 94 ditto Tonqua @ 4 ditto		376
July 30th To 202 ditto Monqua 3½ ditto		707
Nov.r 1st To 154 ditto Huiqua for		476
To 315½ ditto Attong @ 4 ditto		1262
To 150 ditto Afsu @ 4 ditto		600
Dec.r 1st To 295 d.o Alloon @ 4 ditto		1180
29th To 443 decayed Sold to Aynam @ 2 ditto		886
To 713 very bad Ditto 1 ditto		713
2469½ Catties		6614
Charges Viz.t		
Commission on Doll.s 6614 @ 5 p Cent	330	
Cooly hire &c.a	20	350
	Sp: Doll.s	6264

Canton 29th Dec.r 1765
Errors Excepted
Thomas Arnot

Plate 23 Captain Joseph Jackson's invoice for opium, sold in Canton in 1765, and the merchants who purchased it. Courtesy of Nordic Museum Archive, Stockholm (NM: Godegårdsarkivet F17).

PRYS COURANT.

CANTON in China den 3 January 1823.

INVOER.

ARTIKELEN.	Per	Thayl.	M.	C.	Piasters.
AREKE,	pikul				3
Assafœteda	..				—
Barnsteen,	catty				25
Benzoin,	pikul				30
Berlyns blauw,	..				—
Bezoar koe,	catty				30
Bind Rottingen,	pikul				4
Boomwol,	..	8	tot		Sp 10
Campher,	..				2600
Cochenille,	..				7 à 800
Ginsing,	..				24
Goud & Zilver draad,	catty				40
Grynen (Engelse),	stuk				26
Haaye Vinnen,	pikul				22
Kwik Zilver,	..				70
Lakenen,	ell				—
Lood,	pikul				6
Nagelen,	..				90
Nooten Muschaat,	..				75
Oliphants tanden,	..				65
Paerlamour,	..				45
Peeper,	..				12
Polemieten,	stuk				38
Ditto Breede,	..				40
Ryst,	pikul				2½

ARTIKELEN.	Per	Thayl.	M.	C.	Piasters.
Sago,	pikul				—
Sandul hout,	..	tot			16
Schilpad,	..				650
Snippers laken,	..				—
Staal,	..				4½
Swarthout,	..				1¾
Ditto (Mauritius)	..				5¼
Tin, Bankas,	..				22
Tripans,	..				25
Vis magen,	..				65
Vogelnestjes,	..				3600
Ditto, 2de soort,	..				2600
Ditto, 3de soort,	..				1600
Vellen, Bever,	stuk				4
Konijne,	..				55/100
Mater,	..				—
Otter (Zee),	..				38
Ditto (land),	..				—
Robbe,	..				1¾
Schaapen,	..				—
Tiger,	..				—
Vosse,	..				1¼
Wasch,	pikul				30
Wierook,	..				5

Opium Patna Sp 2420. Benares Sp 2320 p kist
Malwa " 1350 p pikul
Turkye " 1200 do. —

Plate 24 A Dutch *Prys Courant* (price courant) from January 1823, with the prices of different kinds of opium written in at the bottom. Courtesy of National Archives, The Hague (NAH: Canton 378).

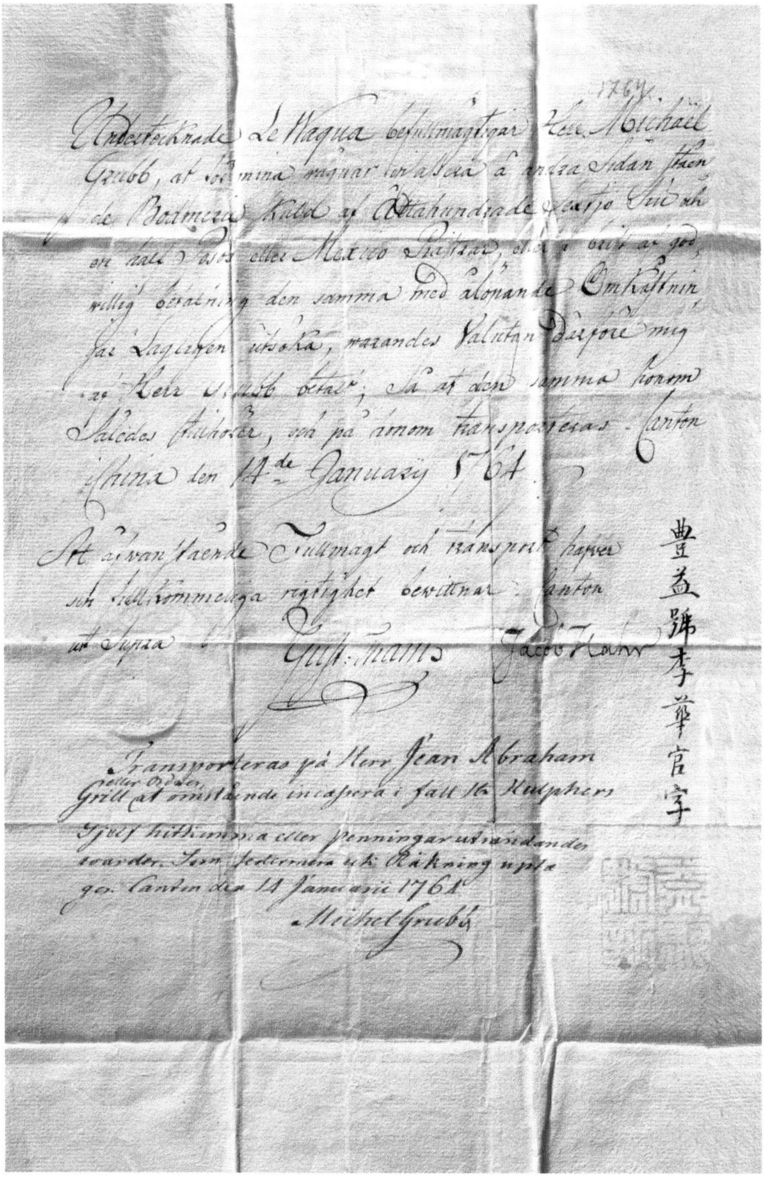

Plate 25 An invoice (in Swedish) dated 14 January 1764 showing the settlement of a bottomry contract from the merchant Le Waqua for the SOIC ship *Sophia Albertina*, which sailed from Canton to Sweden in 1761. Courtesy of Nordic Museum Archive, Stockholm (NM: Godegårdsarkivet F17).

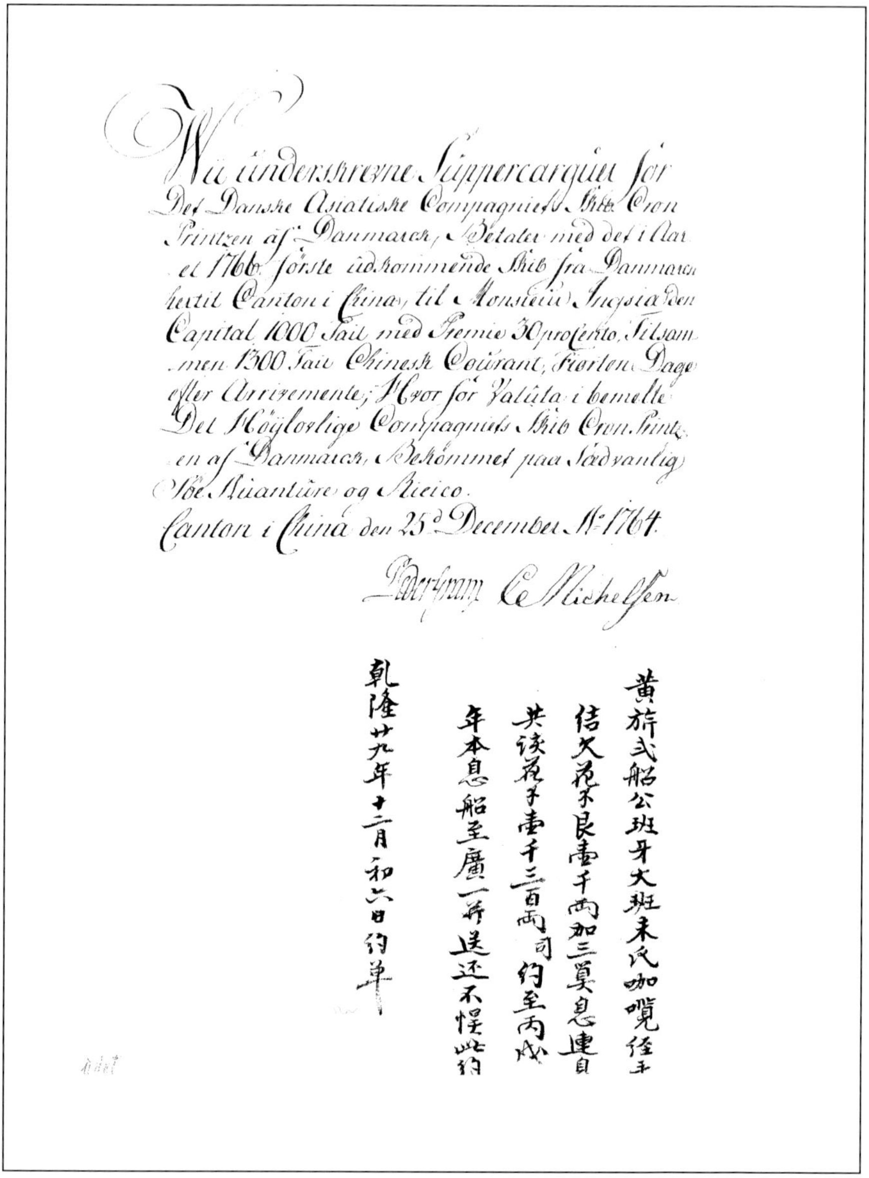

Wii underskrevne Suppercarguer for
Det Danske Asiatiske Compagnies Skib Cron
Printzen af Danmarck, Betaler med det i Aar
et 1766 første udkommende Skib fra Danmarck
hertil Canton i China, til Monsieur Ingsia den
Capital 1000 Tail med Premie 30 procento, Tilsam-
men 1300 Tail Chinesk Courant, Fiorten Dage
efter Arrivemente; Hvor for Valuta i bemelte
Det Høylovlige Compagnies Skib Cron Printz-
en af Danmarck, Bekommet paa Sædvanlig
Søe Avantüre og Risico.
Canton i China den 25d December Ao 1764.

[illegible] C. Michelsen

黄旂弍船公班牙大班未氏咖嚧侄手
信欠花不良壹千両加三算息連自
共該花子壹千三百両司 约至丙戌
年本息船至廣一併送还不悮此约
乾隆廿九年十二月初六日约单

Plate 26 A bottomry contract (in Danish) from the *Hong* merchant Ingsia, dated 25 December 1764, for the DAC ship *Cron Printzen af Danmarck*, to be repaid by the first DAC ship to arrive in China in 1766. Courtesy of Rigsarkivet (National Archives), Copenhagen (RAC: Ask 1156b).

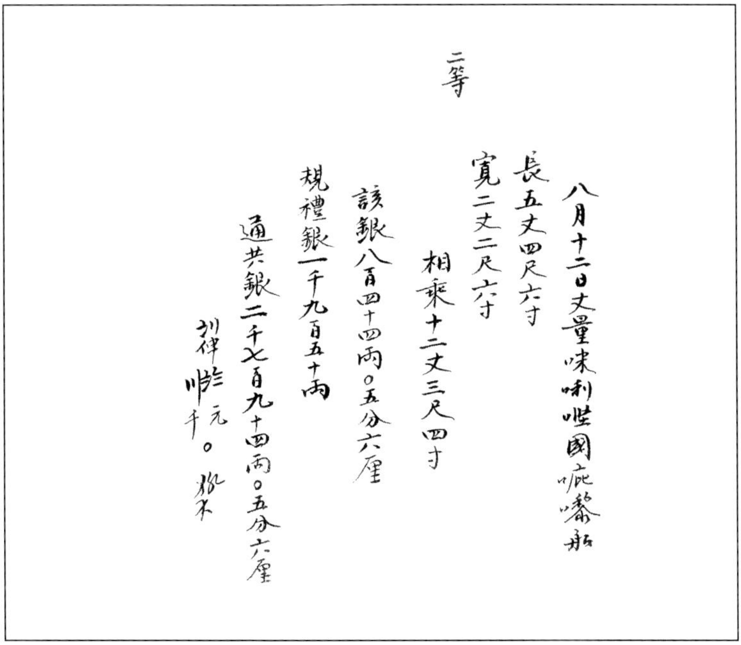

Plate 27 Chinese document showing the measurement figures and port-fee calculations for the American brig *Canton* in 1816. Courtesy of Phillips Library, Peabody Essex Museum, Salem (PEM: Shreve Papers).

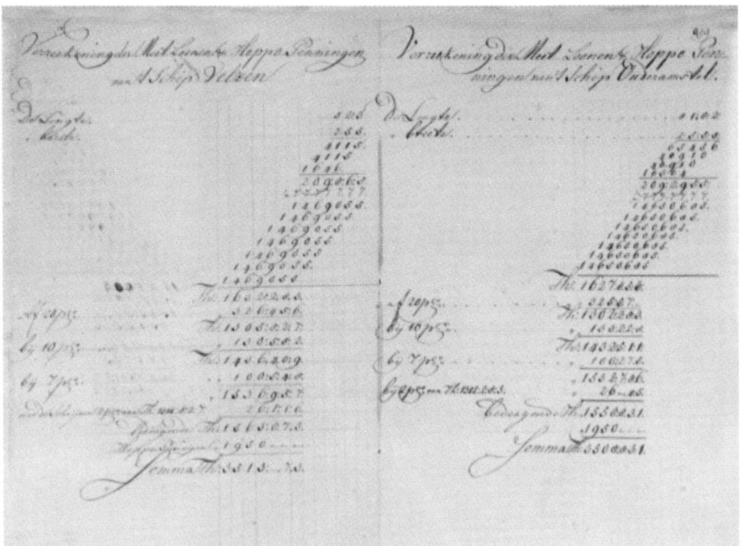

Plate 28 Dutch document showing the long-hand port-fee calculations for the VOC ships *Velsen* and *Ouderamstel* in 1761. Courtesy of National Archives, The Hague (NAH: VOC 4384).

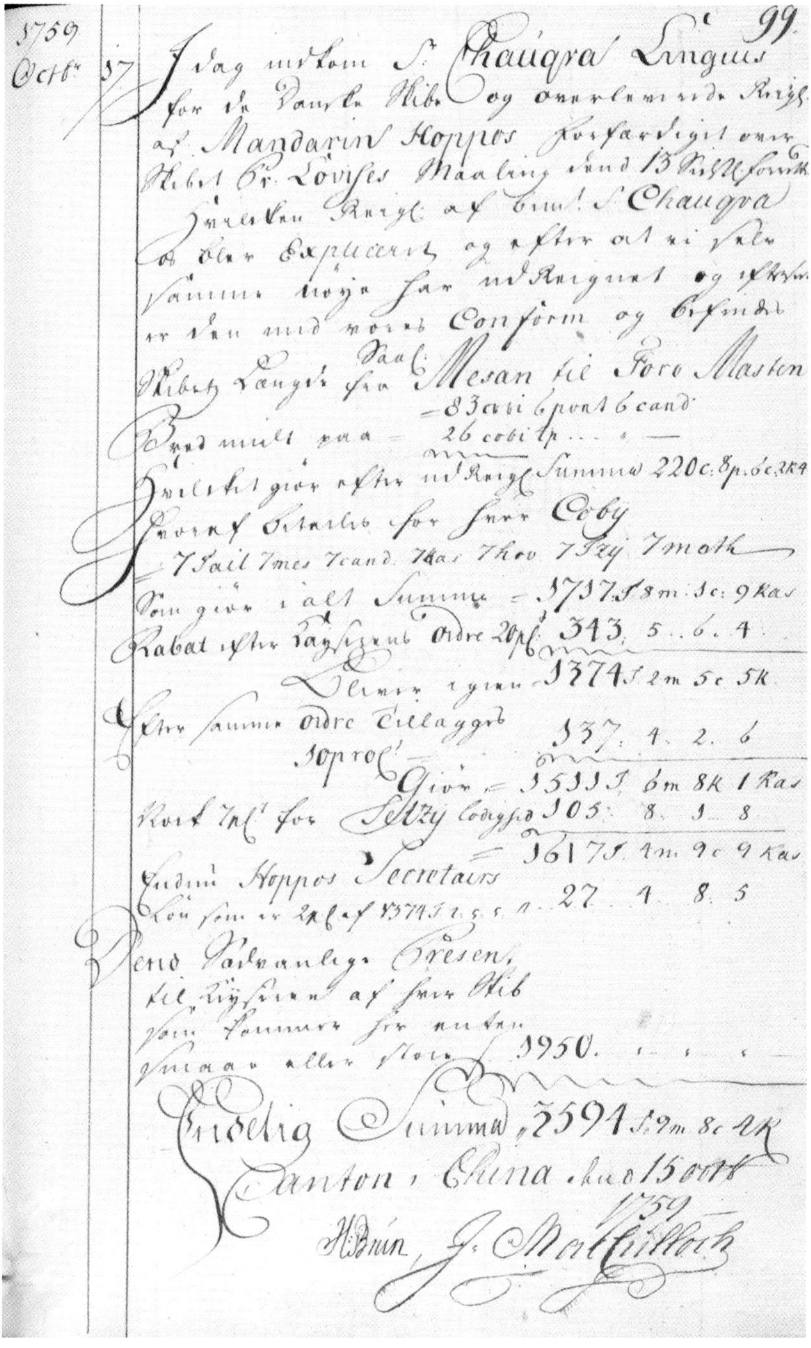
1759 Octbr 17 Idag medkom Sr. Chauqva Linguis for de Danske Skibe og overleverede Regning af Mandarin Hoppos Forfardigit over Skibet Pr. Lovises Maaling und 13 ... hvilken Regning af bem. Sr. Chauqva os blev Expliceret og efter at vi ... samme ... ud Regnet og efter er den med vores Conform og befindes

Skibets Længde fra Paal: Mesan til Foro Masten — 83 cobi 6 punt 6 cand

Bred midt paa — 26 cobi 1p ...

hvilket giør efter ud Regn. Summa 220 c. 8 p. 6 c. 2 K

Hvoraf betales for hver Coby 7 Tail 7 mes 7 cand. 7 kas 7 hov 7 szy 7 moth

Som giør i alt Summa — 1717 T. 8 m: 1 c: 9 kas

Rabat efter Keyserens Ordre 20 pC 343. 5. 6. 4

Bliver igien 1374 T. 2 m 5 c 5 K

Efter samme Ordre Tillagges 10 pro C 137. 4. 2. 6

Giør — 1511 T. 6 m 8 K 1 kas

Kort Tael for Sezy ... 105. 8. 1. 8

1617 T. 4 m. 9 c 9 kas

Endnu Hoppos Secretairs Løn som er 2 pC af 1374 T. 2. 5. 5. — 27. 4. 8. 5

Dend Sædvanlige Present til Keyseren af hver Skib som kommer fra enten smaa eller store — 1950.

Endelig Summa 3594 T. 9 m. 8 c 4 K

Canton i China den 15 Octb 1759

H. Bruun J. McCulloch

Plate 29 Extract from a Danish journal showing linguist Chauqva's report of the measurement and port-fee calculations for the DAC ship *Princesse Lowise* in 1759. Courtesy of Rigsarkivet (National Archives), Copenhagen (RAC: Ask 1144).

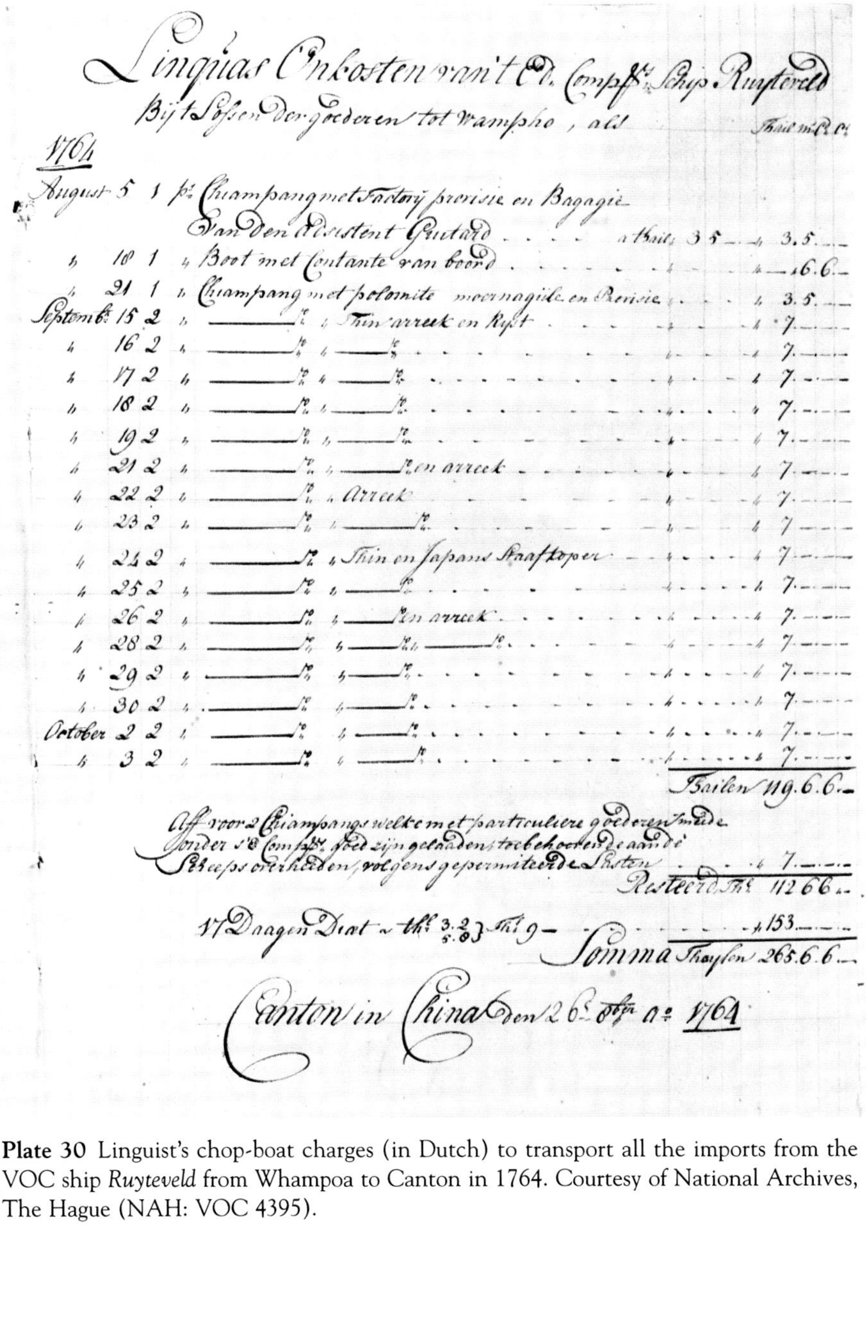

Lingùas Onkosten van't Ed. Comps. Schip Ruyteveld
Bij 't Lossen der goederen tot Wampho, als

				Thail m. C. C.
1764				
August	5	1	p: Champang met Factorij provisie en Bagagie van den Assistent Guitard … à Thail 3.5	3.5
"	18	1	" Boot met Contante van boord …	16.6
"	21	1	" Champang met polomite moernagiile en Provisie …	3.5
Septemb.	15	2	" ——— " Thin arreek en Rijst …	7
"	16	2	" ——— " ——— " …	7
"	17	2	" ——— " ——— " …	7
"	18	2	" ——— " ——— " …	7
"	19	2	" ——— " ——— " …	7
"	21	2	" ——— " ——— " en arreek …	7
"	22	2	" ——— " Arreek …	7
"	23	2	" ——— " ——— " …	7
"	24	2	" ——— " Thin en Japans Kaaftoper …	7
"	25	2	" ——— " ——— " …	7
"	26	2	" ——— " ——— " en arreek …	7
"	28	2	" ——— " ——— " ——— " …	7
"	29	2	" ——— " ——— " …	7
"	30	2	" ——— " ——— " …	7
October	2	2	" ——— " ——— " …	7
"	3	2	" ——— " ——— " …	7
			Tailen	119.6.6

Aff voor 2 Champangs welke met particuliere goederen mede onder s'E Comps. goed zijn geladen, toebehoorende aan de Scheeps overheeden, volgens gepermiteerde Lasten … 7
Resteerd Th: 112.6.6
17 Daagen Diet à th: 3.2 / 5.03 Th: 9 … 153
Somma Thaylen 265.6.6

Canton in China den 26 Octb. Ao. 1764

Plate 30 Linguist's chop-boat charges (in Dutch) to transport all the imports from the VOC ship *Ruyteveld* from Whampoa to Canton in 1764. Courtesy of National Archives, The Hague (NAH: VOC 4395).

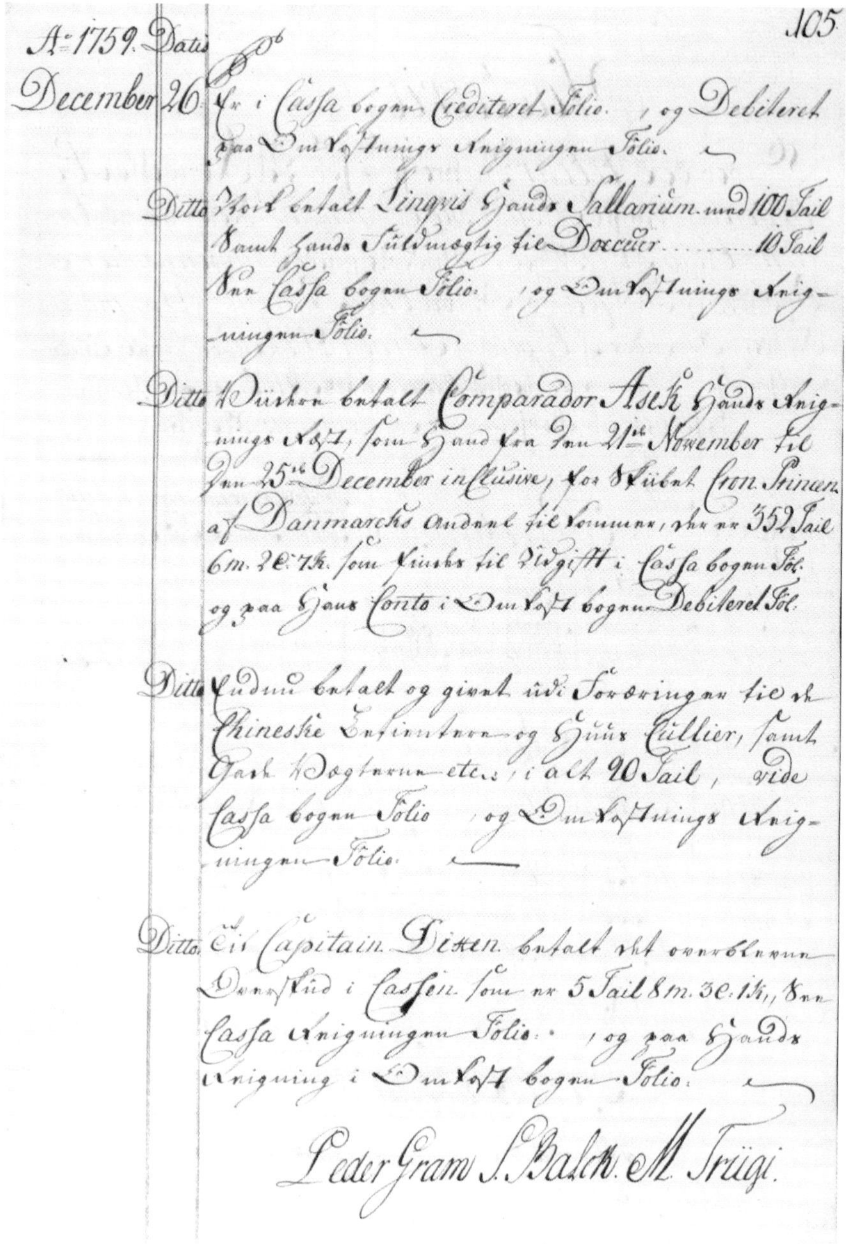

A° 1759. Datis | 106 | 105

December 26 | Er i Cassa bogen Crediteret Folio , og Debiteret paa Omkostnings Regningen Folio.

Ditto | Hvilket betalt Linguis Hands Sallarium med 100 Tail
samt Hands Fuldmægtig til Doceuer .... 10 Tail
Vid Cassa bogen Folio , og Omkostnings Regningen Folio.

Ditto | Udbetalt Comprador Asek Hands Regnings Bekost, som Hand fra den 21te November til den 25te December inclusive, for Skibet Cron Prinsen af Danmarcks andeel til sammen, der er 352 Tail 6 m. 2 C. 7 K. som findes til Udgifft i Cassa bogen Fol. og paa Hans Conto i Omkost bogen Debiteret Fol.

Ditto | Endnu betalt og givet udi Foræringer til de Chineske Enfinntere og Huus Cullier, samt Gade Vægterne etc., i alt 20 Tail, vide Cassa bogen Folio , og Omkostnings Regningen Folio.

Ditto | Til Capitain Dixen betalt det overblevne Overskud i Cassen som er 5 Tail 8 m. 3 C. 1 K., Vid Cassa Regningen Folio. , og paa Hands Regning i Omkost bogen Folio.

Peder Gram S. Balck. M. Trügi.

Plate 31 Extract from a Danish journal showing the linguist and his writer's salary for servicing one of the DAC ships in 1759, and another entry showing comprador Asek turning in his monthly expenses for reimbursement. Courtesy of Rigsarkivet (National Archives), Copenhagen (RAC: Ask 1142).

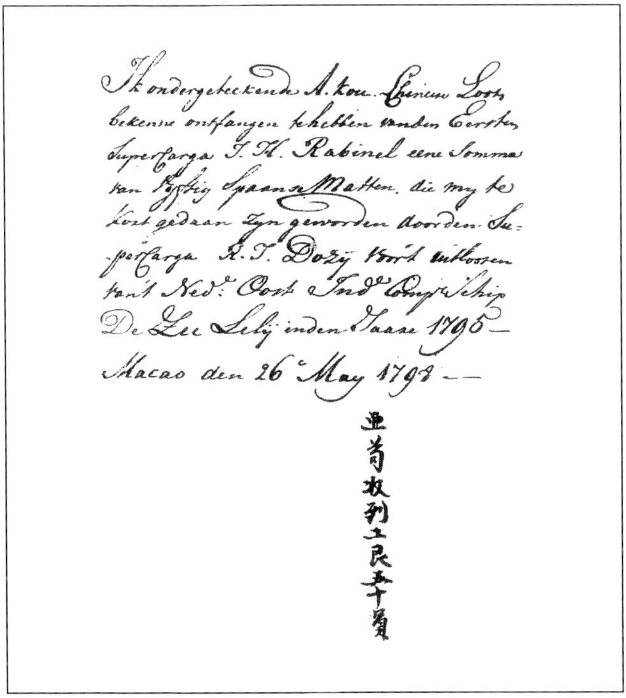

Ik ondergeteekende A.kou. Chinees Loots
bekenne ontfangen t'hebben vanden Eersten
Supercarga J. H. Rabinel eene Somma
van Vyftig Spaansche Matten. die my te
kort gedaan zyn geworden doorden Su-
-percarga R. T. Dozy voort uitloosen
van't Nedl. Oost Indl. Compe. Schip
De Zee Lely inden Jaare 1795—
Macao den 26e May 1798 ——

亞苟收到工艮五十員

Plate 32 A Dutch receipt from Macao pilot A-kou for payment of piloting the ship *Zee Lily* in 1795. Courtesy of National Archives, The Hague (NAH: Canton 60).

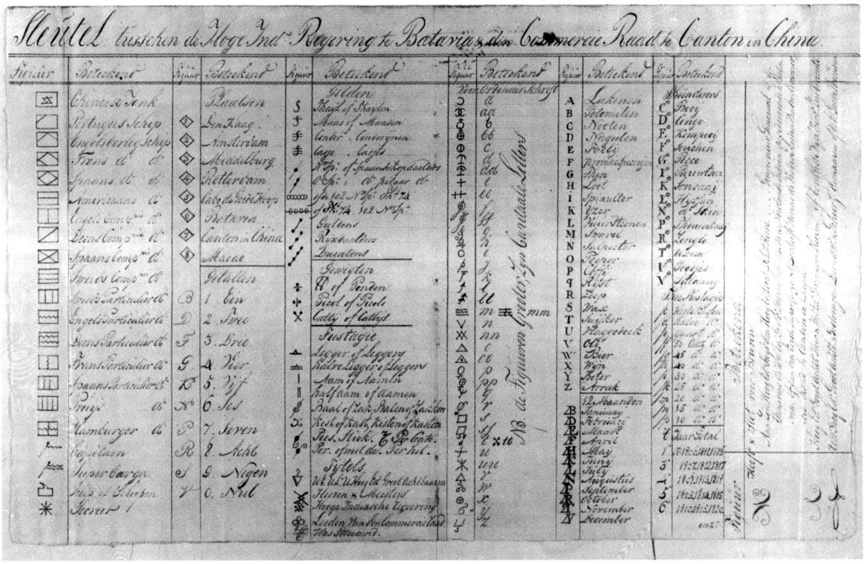

Plate 33 Secret code (in Dutch) devised by the Dutch in Batavia during the Napoleonic wars in the early nineteenth century to protect the China trade. Courtesy of National Archives, The Hague (NAH: HRVB 131).

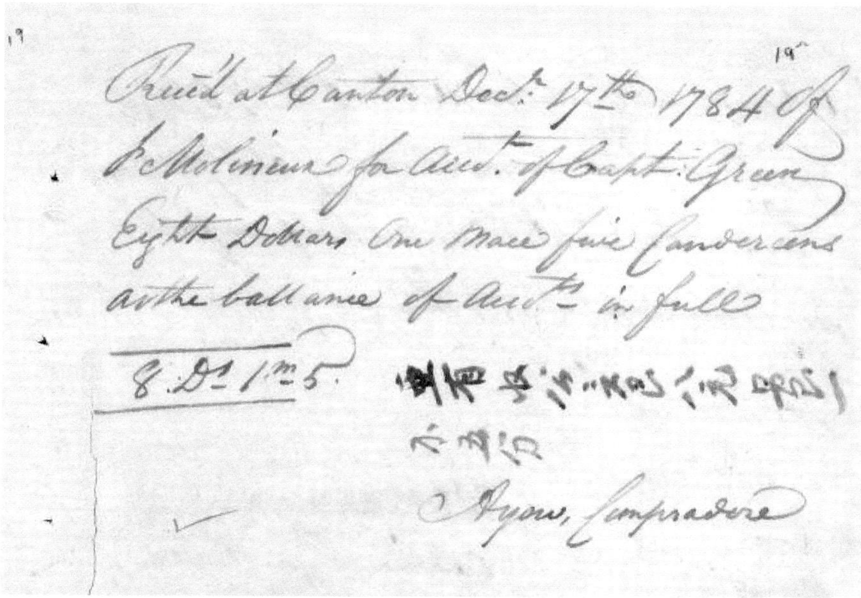

Recd at Canton Decr 17th 1784 Of
P. Molineux for Acct of Capt. Green
Eight Dollars One mace five Candereens
as the ballance of Acct in full
8 Ds 1m 5
Ayou, Compradore

Plate 34 A receipt from the American ship *Empress of China* in 1784 showing comprador Ayou's handwriting. Courtesy of Rare Book and Manuscript Library, University of Pennsylvania (UPL: John Green, Receits, 19r).

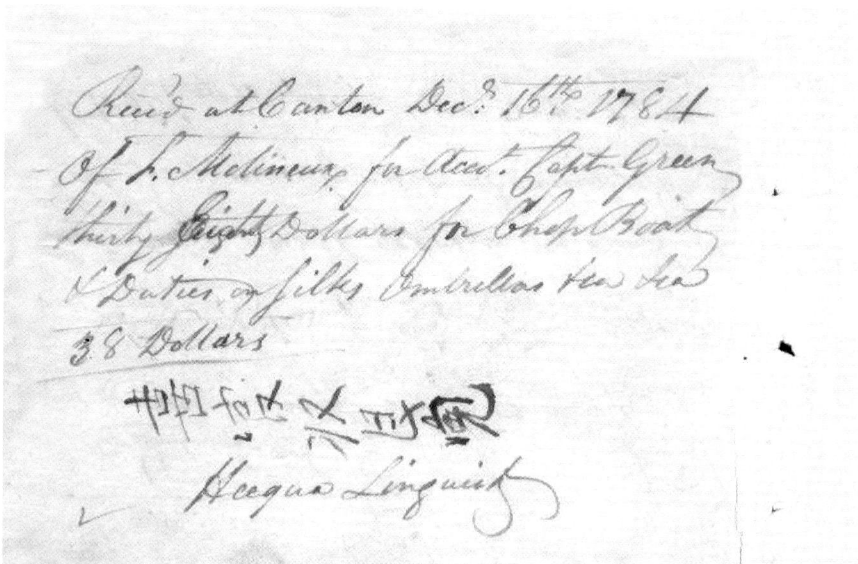

Recd at Canton Decr 16th 1784
Of P. Molineux for Acct Capt Green
thirty Eight Dollars for Chop Boat
& Duties on Silks Umbrellas fans tea
38 Dollars
Heequa Linguist

Plate 35 A receipt from the American ship *Empress of China* in 1784 showing linguist Heequa's handwriting. Courtesy of Rare Book and Manuscript Library, University of Pennsylvania (UPL: John Green, Receits, 18v).

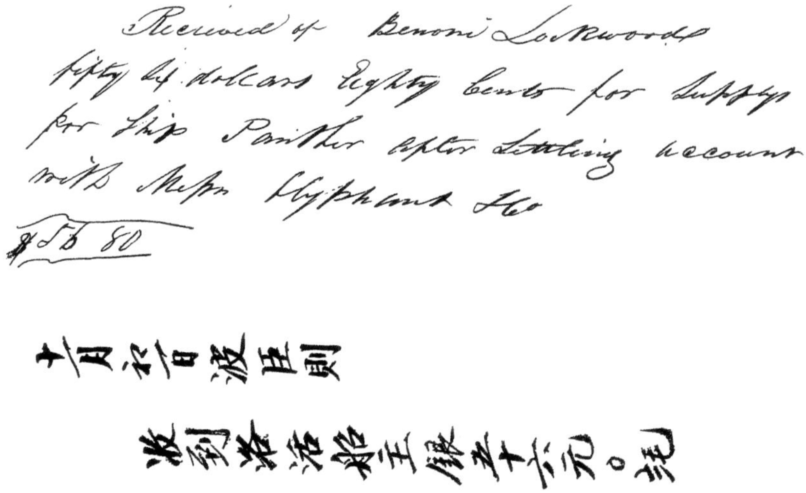

Received of Benoni Lockwood
fifty six dollars Eighty cents for supplys
for Ship Panther after settling account
with Messrs Olyphant & Co
$56 80

Plate 36 RHi X4 243 Comprador [Boston Jack]. Bill to Edward Carrington & Co., 1830, in the Carrington Papers (MSS 333), Sub-Group I, Series 7, Sub-series 14, Ship Panther, Voyages to South America & East Indies, 1828–1830. Courtesy the Rhode Island Historical Society.

Plate 37 Drawing of one of the many "fast crabs" that serviced the opium smugglers at Lintin Island in the early nineteenth century (by Haghe. London, Smith, Elder & Co., Cornhill).

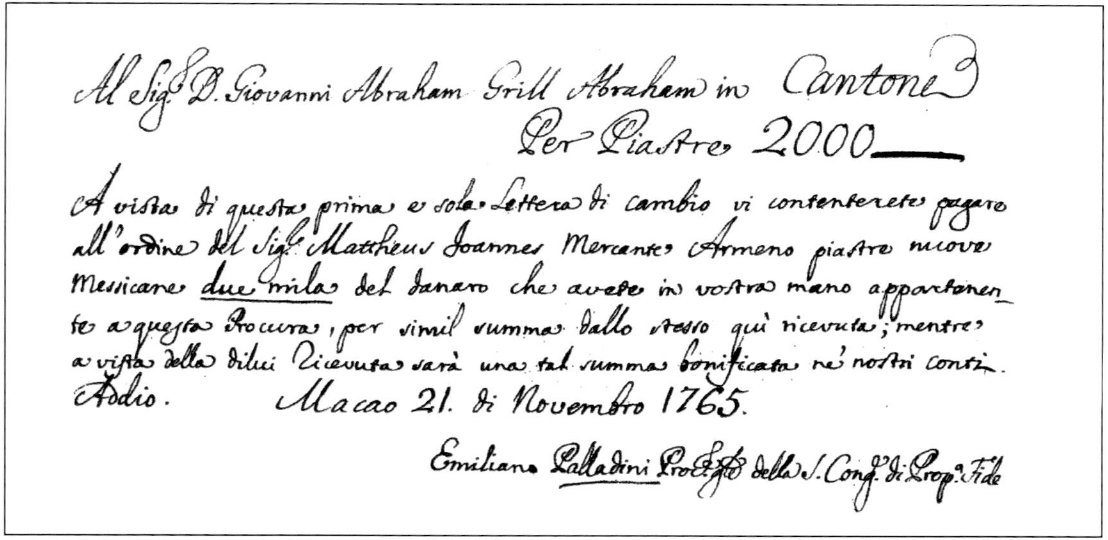

Al Sig.r D. Giovanni Abraham Grill Abraham in Cantone

Per Piastre 2000

A vista di questa prima e sola Lettera di cambio vi contenterete pagare all'ordine del Sig.r Mattheus Joannes Mercante Armeno piastre nuove Messicane due mila del danaro che avete in vostra mano appartenente a questa Procura, per simil summa dallo stesso qui ricevuta; mentre a vista della dilui Ricevuta sarà una tal summa bonificata ne' nostri conti. Addio.

Macao 21. di Novembro 1765.

Emiliano Palladini Proc.re Gen.le della S. Cong.e di Prop.a Fide

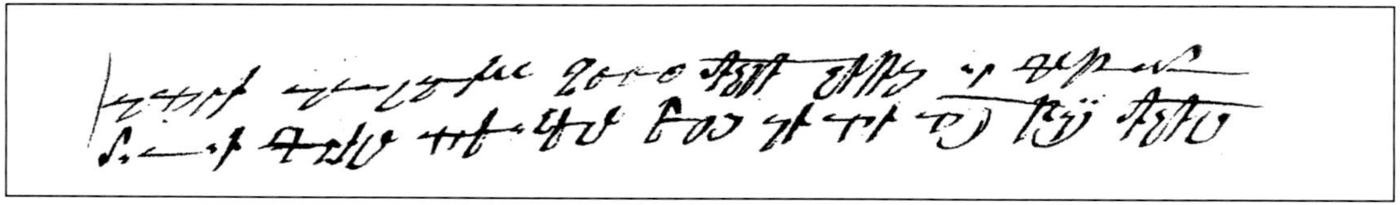

Plate 38 Letter of exchange (in Italian) dated 21 November 1765 concerning a payment of 2,000 piastres (in this case, new Mexican dollars) to Armenian Mattheus Joannes in Macao. The letter is addressed to Giovanni (Johan) Abraham Grill in Canton, and signed by Procurator of *Propaganda Fide* in Macao, Emiliano Palladini. The Armenian script appears on the reverse side. This is one of many examples of Joannes's vast dealings in the trade that not only involved traders, but ecclesiastics as well. Courtesy of Nordic Museum Archive, Stockholm (NM: Godegårdsarkivet F:17).

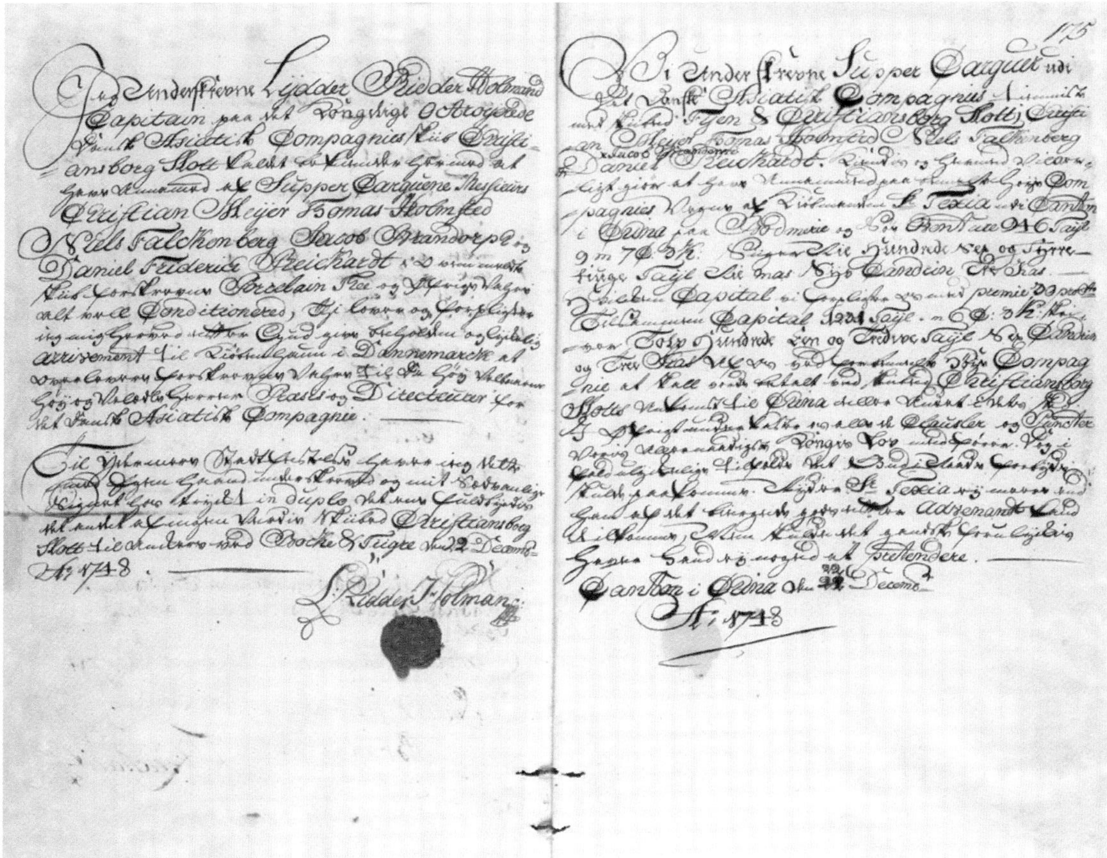

Plate 39 Two documents (in Danish) from a DAC journal both dated 22 December 1748. The left side is a declaration by Captain Lydder Ridder Holman of the *Christiansborg Slott* stating that the porcelain, tea and other wares are in good condition and properly stowed in the ship prior to leaving Bocca Tigris Roads. The right side is a bottomry contract for 946.973 taels at 30 percent interest from the *Hong* merchant Texia (Yan Deshe 顏德舍) to help finance the return passages of the ships *Fyen* and *Christiansborg Slott*. If the ships and cargos arrive safely at Copenhagen, then the principle and interest is to be repaid when the *Christiansborg Slott* returned to China. Courtesy of Rigsarkivet (National Archives), Copenhagen (RAC: Ask 1126).

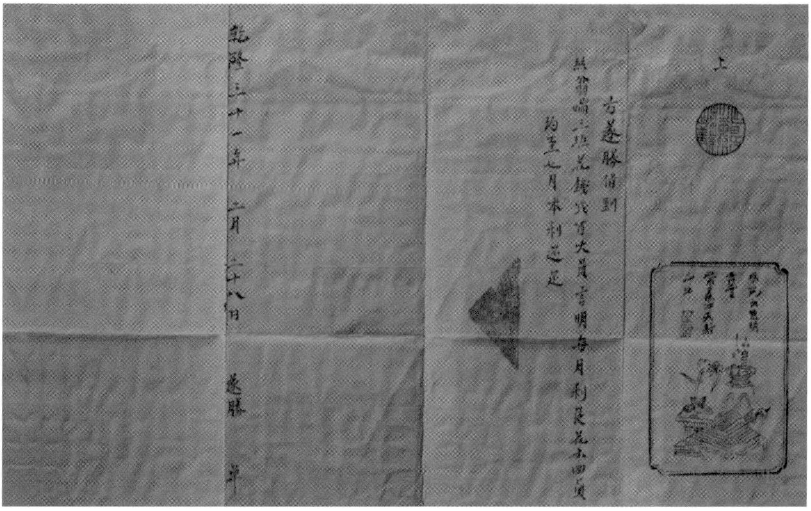

方遂勝借到
瑞國[illegible]三班花錢弍百大員言明每月利息花錢四員
約至七月本利送還
乾隆三十一年二月二十八日
遂勝 押

Plate 40 Short-term loan contract dated 7 April 1766 from the third Swedish supercargo to the embroiderer Soyching (Fang Suisheng 方遂勝) for 200 piastres at 2 percent interest per month (4 piastres each month). The loan is to be repaid in August/September (7th lunar month, when the ships arrive). Courtesy of Nordic Museum Archive, Stockholm (NM: Godegårdsarkivet F:17).

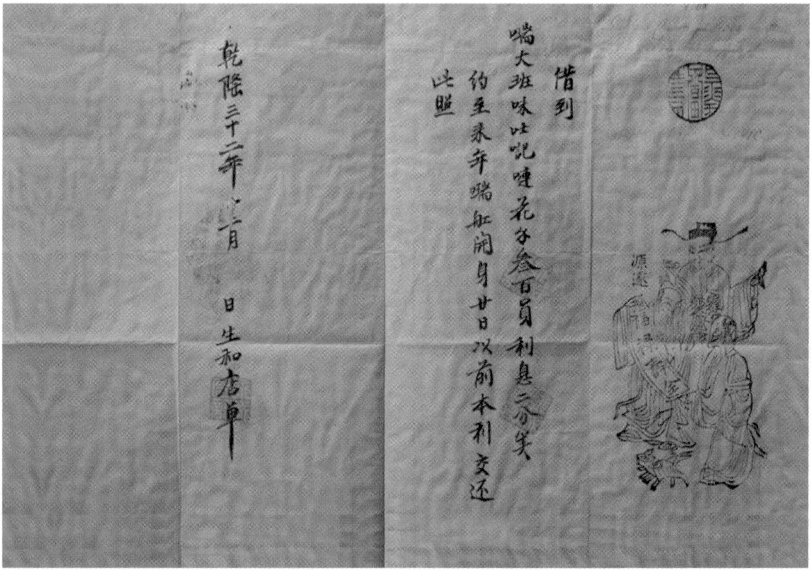

借到
瑞大班[illegible]花[illegible]叁百員利息二分[illegible]
約至来年瑞船開身廿日以前本利交还
此照
乾隆三十二年[illegible]月　日 生和店单

Plate 41 Short-term loan contract dated January/February 1768 from a Swedish supercargo to the merchant Suchin of the Shenghe Dian (生和店) for 300 piastres at 20 percent interest to be repaid 20 days before the SOIC ships leave China in the following season. The total duration of the loan is thus about one year. Courtesy of Nordic Museum Archive, Stockholm (NM: Godegårdsarkivet F:17).

CHAPTER SIX

ADMINISTRATIVE INITIATIVES AND SHORTCOMINGS

AFTER THEIR INCEPTION, MANY CHANGES were made to the customs procedures to help the Hoppos control and monitor smuggling and corruption. Moving the Junminfu to Qianshan in 1731 and licensing the pilots, compradors and linguists was part of this effort to tighten up the ranks. In 1744, the first vice-prefect (*tongzhi* 同知) was established in the village of Mongha near Macao.[1] These measures helped to bring Macao and the delta under closer administrative control, which, in turn, brought greater security to the regulation of commerce.

In later decades, the Hoppos and governors-general continued to experiment with other methods and policies to control trade better. Hoppos knew that, given the opportunity, some customs officers would be inclined to accept payments privately to let merchandise go unreported and 'duty free'. This was one of the ways in which foreigners could get around the silk quotas that limited the quantity and quality of certain types that could be exported. The Dutch, Swedes and English, among others, regularly exceeded their silk quotas by bribing customs officers.[2] The Chinese merchants who sold the textiles arranged the connivances.[3]

This subversion of the silk regulations became such a problem that by 1759 the tollhouse keepers made a bold initiative to charge all foreigners '[Spanish] $100 to every ship for the privilege of sending silk aboard', regardless of whether they were smuggling goods.[4] The English and Danish supercargoes complained to the new governor-general about this latest practice. The Danes were not smuggling silk this year, so they resented having to pay this connivance fee. Their complaints resulted in the arrest of all customs officers in the three tollhouses between Whampoa and Canton. Several of the officials managed to flee downriver, but were caught near Macao.[5] The crackdown was apparently effective because, a few months later, the English ships were inspected and found to have yellow and crimson silk on board: colours forbidden for export because they were reserved for the exclusive use of the emperor.[6]

The renewed interest in cracking down on corruption in 1759 encouraged the foreign supercargoes to send a long list of complaints to the Canton authorities. In addition to ending the connivance payments to tollhouse officers, their demands included the withdrawal of compradors' engagement fees, abolition of the emperor's present (the 1,950 taels charged to each ship) and settlement of all outstanding debts with Chinese merchants. Besides the arrest of all the tollhouse officers and the problem of how to settle Chinese debts, none of these other demands appear to have been acted upon because the fees were legitimate.

From the early years of trade, the Hoppos had been closely monitoring the chop boats hauling goods to Whampoa, and they continued to grow more stringent in regulating their movements. In the late 1750s and early 1760s the Danes and Dutch both tried to obtain permission to unload four sampans per day from each ship, but the Hoppos would allow only two.[7] Limiting the cargo sampans was a way to check smuggling.

In July 1766 the officers at the tollhouses caught a Danish and English captain trying to smuggle watches and other articles into Canton via one of the Chinese sampans from Macao. This led to more complaints from the foreigners, who sent protests to the governor-general reminding him of the long-established right of company officers to pass tollhouses unhindered and unmolested. In other words, never mind the smuggling, just remember our rights.[8]

In the late 1760s the Hoppos made it mandatory for every chop boat to have one of their most trusted deputies aboard. As expected, this new policy greatly hindered the smooth and timely conduct of trade. Foreigners often had to wait several days for a deputy to become available before they could ship their goods to Whampoa, which was cause for much complaint. It is not certain how long this new policy was in effect because it does not show up regularly as a problem in later records. It may have been only temporary because it did not accommodate efficiencies of time.

Other stipulations were introduced in the 1770s to ensure appropriate duties were paid on all imports and exports, and the collection of funds owed to the government by failed merchants. In 1772, the Hoppo abolished the old practice of allowing struggling merchants to pay the import and export duties before the beginning of the next season (five or six months after they were due), and demanded that all duties be paid before the Grand Chop was issued. This, of course, put great financial strain on the weak merchants, who were already suffering from reduced prices after the dissolution of their monopoly, the Co-hong. To pay the duties on time, some were forced to secure loans or advances from the foreigners at high interest rates, which put them even farther into debt.[9]

The *Hong* merchants did all they could to persuade the Hoppo to return to the old policy, but without success. This new initiative was in line with what the Hoppos had done in tightening up the collection of port fees in the 1740s, and made good sense for the timely collection of revenues. It also contributed, however, to more merchants failing and the accumulating of enormous debts in the late 1770s.[10]

Business was risky for the *Hong* merchants, even in the best of years, and the Hoppos never managed to come up with initiatives that could effectively minimize their failures. Merchants could anticipate certain costs in their day-to-day transactions, such as payment for the privilege of being a security merchant, import and export duties, and the ubiquitous 'rarity' contribution.

This latter expense, required merchants to purchase clocks and other luxury items at high prices from foreigners and then offer them to the Hoppos and Mandarins at reduced rates or as outright 'gifts'. The cost of these items could vary significantly from one year to the next, depending on what was available and whether the presiding Hoppo was about to make a trip to Beijing. The merchants knew they would have to buy these gifts so they could anticipate them to some extent, but the final amount was always a question.

One of the obvious disadvantages to the *Hong* merchants was the way the administration handled debts in Canton. Officially, Chinese were barred from borrowing money from foreigners, but because the trade could not grow without capital the Hoppos and governors-general tended to turn a blind eye to these transactions.[11] In the event a Chinese merchant failed, his individual debts were passed to his business partners, his family or the *hong* collective. A merchant's debt would not be forgiven or dismissed because that could have a negative effect on the growth of trade and, more importantly, on the revenues sent to Beijing. Foreigners who suffered a loss in China were not likely to return. As a result, if no other solution could be found to settle a debt, the *hong* collective became liable for it. Their priority was to pay government fees and duties first and then pay foreign debts.

Hoppos were much more lenient, tolerant and accommodating to foreigners than to Chinese when it came to the collection of debts. The ways debts were handled varied, and the Hoppos sometimes experimented with different approaches and different levels of tolerance. One bizarre example shows quite clearly that foreigners had much more leverage in China in forcing the collection of debts than the Chinese themselves.

In 1779 the private English trader Abraham Leslie was unable to collect the full amount he was owed by the failed merchant Coqua (Chen Keguan 陳科官). With loaded pistols in hand, the aid of several Moors (Lascars) from Bengal and three or four large dogs, he took possession of Coqua's factory and all the tea and porcelain it contained. He put his name above the door and hoisted a blue flag upon which was written in English and in Chinese, 'Leslie, an English merchant, has taken possession of this factory until he is paid'.[12]

Leslie stayed in Coqua's factory for two seasons until the debt was finally settled to his satisfaction, but he was holding debts of other merchants as well. In 1780 he and his gang took possession of the Taihe Hang (泰和行), which was owned by the failed merchant Ingsia (Yan Yingshe 顏瑛舍). Ingsia was banished to Ili to atone for the debts he had accumulated, and the government had taken possession of his factory.[13] Leslie broke the official seal forbidding entrance to the building and again hung placards, declaring his intention to occupy the factory until he was paid. He took down the lanterns in front, which had the characters Taihe (泰和) on them, and put up his own lanterns with his own name written in Chinese. A Chinese carpenter was later put in irons for helping him write the Chinese characters. Leslie then hung a placard in English advertising 'Rooms for Rent at a Reasonable Price' and declared that the remuneration from the rent would be applied to Ingsia's debt. An English captain from a private ship soon rented a room.[14]

Leslie was the senior surgeon with the English Company, but he did not have the full backing of the EIC in the collection of his debts. His earlier drastic action had forced the Hoppo to arrange for the repayment of Coqua's debts, and he hoped for the same outcome now. The English Company, however, did not approve of his insistence on being reimbursed 'on Claims that had been satisfied ten times more favourably than the rest of his fellow sufferers'. This time, his demands were more than the Chinese officials could tolerate. He was arrested and sent to Macao, where the Portuguese held him prisoner. Leslie was released a couple of years later and ignominiously despatched to Calcutta, where he complained to anyone who would listen about the treatment he had received in China.[15]

Leslie might have considered that he had been treated unfairly and harshly, but, if a Chinese merchant had taken such measures against a foreigner, the Hoppo and governor-general would have been merciless. They not only would have viewed such an action as an attempt to upset the harmony in Canton, but even as piracy or an attempt at treason. Such action would have certainly landed him in prison; he would have been severely punished and possibly executed or exiled to Ili.

The Hoppos also accommodated large companies in their efforts to collect from Chinese. In the debt crisis of the 1780s, the VOC granted credits to a number of merchants in Canton. Although the company folded in 1794 and sent no more ships to China, Dutch supercargoes continued to go to Canton every year to collect on their debts. They moved to Macao in the off-season, and returned to Canton the next year. The Dutch conducted some trade from 1795 to the 1820s, but the main reason they would go to Canton was to collect the interest and principal on their outstanding balances with the *Hong* merchants, and the Hoppos gave them permission to do so.[16]

The English Company was also fairly successful at recovering its debts by going through the traditional legal channels in Canton. Some companies, such as the EIC and VOC, refused to become involved in the collection of private debts, but other companies, such as those of the Swedish, Danish and French, regularly used the property of *Hong* merchants in their possessions 'to settle the private claims of their nationals'.[17] Sometimes private traders sold their debts to the companies, because the latter had more leverage to collect them.

Another shortcoming of the system was the periodic 'extractions' of local officials. If administrative coffers and budgets were insufficient to meet the needs at hand, the *Hong* merchant houses were among the first places the authorities went looking for money. The Hoppos had a window into the gross incomes of every merchant through the records of the import and export duties they paid. These figures gave them a rough idea of what each merchant might be capable of 'contributing'. When the emperor and top officials in Canton were in need of a special contribution — during times of famine or flood, the construction or repair of a fort along the river or the financing of a military campaign — the *Hong* merchants could expect to be summoned before the Hoppo and/or governor-general.

These contributions could be reduced through the normal process of political finesse and hard bargaining, but it was unrealistic for *Hong* merchants to think they could get away without giving something. The Hoppos had a good deal of leverage over the merchants, each of whom needed their approval to do business. If a Hoppo was dissatisfied with a merchant's performance, he might be denied the right to trade, or perhaps only be allowed to trade with small ships, thereby reducing his potential to make a profit and meet financial obligations. For the most part, merchants had no rights outside their local jurisdiction. They could try to appeal to the Imperial Court in Beijing, but such a move might cause them even more trouble when local administrators found out about it.[18]

Consequently, when officials came looking for a contribution, it was better to negotiate the best deal possible and keep the peace. If merchants managed to work out a deal that was more favourable to them than to the officials, they would probably be targeted for a greater contribution when the next crisis hit. Thus it was in the merchants' personal interests to submit to the authorities' demands, rather than leave themselves vulnerable to the spite of a discontented Hoppo or governor-general. It was not in officials' political interests to ruin merchants because that could bring condemnation to themselves if trade suffered so merchants had some leverage.

After the Co-hong monopoly was dissolved in 1771, the *Hong* merchants tried to solve the problem of covering the costs of unexpected gifts and extractions. They established a guild merchant association, and all merchants were required to contribute to an account called the '*consoo* fund'. A similar type of arrangement had already been in existence under the Co-hong, but now all merchants simply paid into the fund without having other aspects of their trade regulated as before. Official extractions and presents were then paid for from this *consoo* account. Sometimes past debts of failed merchants and port fees and duties that were in arrears were also settled out of this treasury. This policy helped to build some security and more predictability into the merchants' trade, because it was charged to all of them equally and was a fixed amount that could be calculated and worked into prices and budgets.

The problem with the *consoo* fund, however, was that the Hoppos became gradually more dependent on it. They came to see it as a source that could be tapped whenever funds were needed, which meant that it was not long before the demands outweighed the supply and there were not enough funds available. This forced the Hoppos and governors-general back to the old practice of looking for 'contributions'. By the late 1770s the Chinese merchants were again inheriting debts from failed merchants. This problem of assuming debts continued into the 1830s.[19]

One other means of reducing risk was to purchase civil degrees. Such degrees provided the *Hong* merchants with a level of respectability and some security. If a degree-holding merchant were charged with a fault, such as the accumulation of debt, he could appeal for leniency from the Hoppo, governor-general or emperor on the basis that he was a degree-holder. The degree itself could be surrendered as part of the punishment. If the merchant managed to recover from the financial penalties of failure and restore his reputation, he could try to purchase another degree to hedge against other unexpected reversals.[20]

Despite all these security and risk-reducing measures, *Hong* merchants still had much less protection for their capital than foreigners. Chinese were forbidden to go abroad, so it was not likely that they would be able to appeal effectively in a foreign debtors' court to collect on a foreign debt. In the early nineteenth century, for example, Conseequa (Pan Changyao 潘長耀) tried desperately to recover funds that some Americans owed him by going through the American courts. Despite hiring an American lawyer and even managing to send some Chinese (illegally) to the United States to represent him, he failed to retrieve any significant amount.[21]

Because of these disadvantages, it was very difficult to maintain a fortune in Canton, let alone provide for posterity. And *Hong* merchants could not quit the trade without permission, which, if granted, would cost them dearly in large payments to officials.[22] What was needed was a clear policy that arranged for the cancellation of debts and the regulation of extractions (including retirement fees) so merchants could protect their profits, anticipate their future earnings and set aside sufficient capital to finance their businesses. They had to be assured that any accumulated capital would not be tapped unexpectedly, but allowed to grow generation after generation, regardless of their ability to negotiate. Such a policy, however, was not conducive to the structure of the Canton System. The lack of any other effective measures to provide security meant that being a *Hong* merchant was always risky business.

Another stipulation initiated in 1774 made it mandatory for all import duties to balance against the export duties of each ship. This practice was already part of trading from the earlier years of the eighteenth century and a fairly effective way to monitor smuggling. The Hoppos were well aware that the amount of exports one could purchase was limited to the amount one had in imports (including silver). If the imports exceeded exports, it was a sign that some of the funds were used to purchase something that had not been recorded. If the exports exceeded imports, it was a sign that some of the imports (including silver) had been smuggled in and not recorded. The Chinese merchants were now made responsible for any differences in amounts that did not balance.[23]

The Hoppos paid very close attention to the silver that was being landed, even in the earliest years of trade. Permits to transfer silver from the ships to Canton listed the number of chests and, usually, their weight. The weighing of chests on the ships before they were unloaded, and again on the quay, ensured that no silver was stolen en route. A tally of how much silver had been unloaded was kept at the customhouse in Canton.[24]

For the first few years of this new policy, the security merchants wasted many days and weeks negotiating with the Hoppos about duties claimed to be in arrears. The merchants went so far as to have the Hoppos' secretary accompany them out to the ships to show them there was absolutely no space for a single additional chest, which they claimed was proof that nothing had gone unreported. Whether ships had any room left in their holds, however, had nothing to do with their cargos balancing. Although this measure was initiated to counteract smuggling, it also helped China to maintain an overall balance on foreign trade by ensuring imports did not exceed exports (with silver being considered an import commodity).[25]

There is probably no other policy in the Canton era that has been more widely misunderstood, misrepresented and misreported in the foreign records than that of balancing imports against exports. Most foreigners had no idea why the Hoppos were withholding their Grand Chops and demanding more money. They complained incessantly and often blamed the Hoppos for unjustly delaying them. The balancing of imports and exports, however, and the withholding of the Grand Chop until differences were paid, was a policy put into place to clean up corruption, not add to it.

In 1775 a procedure was added that required a pilot to take the depth of a foreign ship in the presence of a customs officer before it was allowed to remove downriver to Bocca Tigris. Apparently, some ships had been making the move when only half full, a circumstance viewed with much suspicion by the Hoppos.[26] If a ship passed the Hoppos' test, permission to move would be received a day or two later. This requirement was later changed to large ships that had already loaded at least 'six thousand pickles [piculs] of cargo'.[27] This made it easier for the Hoppos to figure out which ships were ready to make the move because they kept a running tally of the piculs being loaded into every ship.

In addition to these initiatives, there were other changes introduced in the controlling of Macao and foreigners in China. Edicts were issued periodically to crackdown on the spread of Christianity, and changes were made in how foreigners would be handled when accused of committing crimes against Chinese, and vice verse. Many of these issues had marginal connections to the day-to-day conduct of trade so we will not discuss them here, but refer the reader to the many studies that have been done about those matters.[28]

As more ships went to China it became increasingly difficult for the Hoppos to monitor all chop boats. A system was eventually worked out by which the issuing of chops and the dispatching of chop boats happened on certain days only. Import and export duties were also made payable at specific times of the month and year. By the 1820s, the duties on all imports were due on the 25th day of the 9th month (according to the lunar calendar). Export duties had to be paid in five-day intervals (on the 3rd, 8th, 13th, 18th, 23rd and 28th day of each month).

It is not clear when this policy was first adopted, but it was easy to regulate because every day that ended with 3 or 8 was a day to pay duties. On the 1st and 15th day of each month the Hoppos went to worship at the Tian Hou Temple, so this schedule worked out well with their other activities. Other responsibilities, such as issuing chops and weighing and inspecting merchandise, were also done on specific days and at regular intervals.[29] The Hoppos initiated all these policies to give them increased control of the lower echelons in the customs networks.

Another initiative was the requirement that all foreigners wanting to go to Macao had to go via the West River route. In the early decades of trade, foreigners who went to Macao to recover from illness or to escape the summer heat in Canton could take passage on any foreign ship leaving Whampoa Roads and ride downriver with it as part of the crew. By the mid-eighteenth century, however, the only legal way for foreigners to go downriver was to apply for a special permit to rent a transport sampan. Foreigners were no longer allowed to take sampans through Bocca Tigris, but had to use the West River route instead.[30]

The trip on the West River took a couple of days and the sampans were designed to accommodate foreign officers, with sleeping quarters, dining and cooking facilities, and places to store baggage. A limited number of these transport sampans were available and always based in Canton so the Hoppos could keep track of them. In addition, the Chinese navigators who operated these transports were closely monitored. If foreigners wanted to go to Canton from Macao, they had to request permission for a transport to be sent downriver to collect them. They could not legally hire any other Chinese vessels to carry them.

The Dutch have left us with the most complete record of the tolls and fees charged on the West River. Missing only a couple of years, the data cover 1763 to 1816. These figures offer a unique glimpse into this part of the customs operation that does not always appear in the records because the West River had nothing to do with the main traffic of goods and commodities going in and out of China. Table 4 lists the nine tolls that had to be paid. The fees were based on the number of sampans that passed along the river.

Table 4 List of Tolls Charged between Macao and Canton on the West River[31]

1.	Macao (Procurator)
2.	Guanzha (關閘, Quan Sjap, Porto Cerco or Barrier Gate)
3.	Qianshan (前山, also called Casa Branca or Chymie)
4 & 5.	Xiangshan (香山 Heongshan or 'fourth toll') and Hatschap
6.	Zini (紫泥, Che nae, Sinay, or 'third toll')
7.	Danes' toll (also called the 'second toll')
8.	Creek toll ('Porcelain Street' or 'Sijlap toll')
9.	Canton toll (also called the 'first toll')

Plate 21 lists the amounts the Dutch paid at each of the tollhouses in 1765. This document does not show all the tolls listed above because sometimes two tolls were combined into one such as Hatschap being included in the Xiangshan toll and Danes' toll being included in the Creek toll.[32] Apart from these tolls, there was also a 'baggage tax' that had to be paid at the customhouse in Canton or Macao. This was a simple calculation of so much per sampan, depending on the size of the vessel and the amount it could hold. Sometimes, however, the baggage was taxed according to its weight, which meant further delays because of time spent weighing the chests, as well as additional payments to the weigh-man and his servants.[33] This baggage tax was called the 'Mandarins' fee' in both Canton and Macao, but the Macao baggage tax sometimes also went by the name of the 'Mattow' fee.

The permit to go to Canton via the West River was called the 'licence to come to the province' (*shangsheng zhizhao* 上省執照). Plate 22 shows the license issued to the Swedish supercargoes and assistants to return to Canton in 1792. All names of the persons in their group are mentioned on the pass, which had to have the customs' stamp on it to be valid. After the foreigners had completed their trip, the document was surrendered and certain parts of the text were written over with red ink so it could not be used again.

The permit to go to Macao was called the 'licence to leave the province' (*xiasheng zhizhao* 下省執照). These licenses were often called the 'small chops' by the foreigners to distinguish them from the 'Grand Chops' (which were much larger). Hunter states that the officers recorded the date and time foreigners arrived at each tollhouse, which was probably written on one of the other three or four documents required for the trip.[34]

Occasionally, customs officers on the West River took advantage of their right to collect tolls and randomly inflated their fees. By 1765 the French were already complaining about the extortions, and by the 1770s, many foreigners had begun to complain. The Hoppos in Canton responded by sending a Mandarin with them to keep the tollhouses from charging too much. This action was somewhat successful. In 1780, for example, the foreigners had to pay an additional amount to cover the Mandarins' expenses, but the savings from the tolls were more than enough to offset those costs.[35] But for some unknown reason this measure was only used when stiff complaints were filed against the West River officers so when the Mandarins were not present the tolls rose again.

In March 1785 the Danes reported that the trip from Canton to Macao cost them Spanish \$600, an increase of \$128 over the preceding year.[36] In 1791 the English complained that the passage cost them nine times the amount they paid in 1772. In 1793 a Mandarin accompanied the British on their journey again, which saved them 40 percent on the previous year.[37] In August 1796, when the English were about to return to Canton again, the West River tollhouses were under strict orders from the Hoppo not to gouge them.[38] The Dutch records, however, show that tollhouse fees continued to rise, despite all efforts to curb them.[39]

Requiring foreigners to take the West River certainly gave the Hoppos more control over them than was the case with the old system, which allowed them to leave as they pleased. The new policy also gave customs posts on the West River a new source of income, which probably helped the overall budget of the Yuehaiguan. But the policy opened up new opportunities for extortion.

Another shortcoming of the Canton System was that it offered many advantages to large ships but prejudiced small ships. Companies generally had ships of at least 450 tons, and later dispatched much larger ones. By the 1770s many were more than 700 tons; by the 1790s more than 800 tons; and by the 1810s more than 1,100 tons. By the 1820s most company ships were from 1,200 to 1,600 tons. Until the 1740s company ships and private ships were about the same size, but by the 1780s most company ships were two, three or even four times as large as private vessels. Because large ships benefited from the Canton System more than small ships, a rift eventually developed between the common interests of the companies and those of the private traders.

By using the years 1799 to 1801 as an example, we see how significant the differences were between the companies and private traders. In those three years, the 66 private American ships that arrived at Canton averaged 305 tons.[40] Dermigny's estimate of the 42 private 'English' ships in Canton for these three years gives an average of 499 tons.[41] Between the Americans and the private 'English' traders, there were 108 ships, with a total capacity of 41,310 tons.[42]

There were only 54 EIC ships in Canton from 1799 to 1801, with a total capacity of 60,426 tons — one-third more than all the private ships put together.[43] The EIC's dominance over private traders continued in later years as well. Morse shows total American and British exports from Canton for the years 1818 to 1833 to be Spanish $103,255,875 for the Americans and $265,273,865 for the British. The total American trade was consistently only about one-third (39 percent) that of the British, which shows that the tonnage estimates are fairly consistent with cargo value estimates and, thus, a reliable way to assess the influence of each group in relation to the overall volume of trade in Canton.[44]

Only 15 other company ships were at Canton from 1799 to 1801, with a total capacity of 17,490 tons.[45] When we add this figure to the EIC number above, we get 77,916 tons compared with the total private capacity of 41,310 tons. Clearly, companies would be the dominant voice in having influence over the Chinese administration in Canton, and this was the case until company trade in China ended in 1834. We can see why private traders constantly fell under the umbrella of the companies.

After the Napoleonic Wars, the EIC's large ships dominated trade. The Dutch, Danes, Swedes and others continued to send the occasional private ship to Canton from 1806 to the 1820s, but these were usually small vessels (except for five DAC ships from 1820 to 1833).[46] The Dutch company known as the Nederlandsche Handel-Maatschappij (NHM) sent many ships to Canton from 1825 to 1849, but they were also mostly small vessels of less than 400 tons.[47] Other foreigners visiting Canton were primarily private traders from India and America, none of whom were united under a single body like the EIC, and the majority of their vessels were small. Even the NHM ships were represented in Canton by the Dutch consulate, rather than by company officers, which was a very different arrangement from that of the EIC or the old days of the VOC.

It was not in the EIC's interests to make changes in the port fees that would benefit small ships. Indeed, it was not until these conflicts of interests ended in 1834 that the private traders' gained the dominant force. The depth of these differences becomes more obvious when we analyse the data.

Table 5 shows the port fees from 1,470 foreign ships (company and private) in Canton from 1722 to 1842.

Table 5 Canton Port Fees Paid by 1,470 Foreign Ships, 1722 to 1842[48]

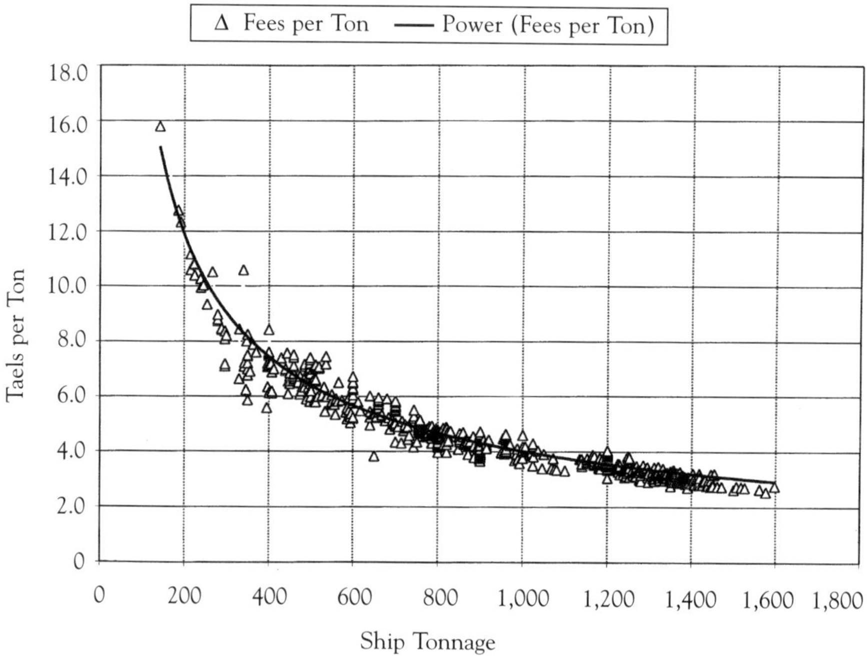

The figures from these ships show a dramatic difference between what small ships and large ships paid. Ships smaller than 250 tons were charged from 10 to 16 taels per ton; 400- to 500-ton ships, 6 to 7 taels per ton; 900- to 1,000-ton ships, about 4 taels per ton; and 1,400- to 1,600-ton vessels, about 2.5 to 3 taels per ton.

From these figures, we can estimate the percentage that the port fees made up of the value of the cargos. Cargo figures have been assembled from the records of 172 foreign ships in Canton from 1730 to 1833. Their total exports amount to 31,601,969 taels, and their total capacity was 147,449 tons. This gives us an average of 214 taels of cargo per ton of capacity.[49] If we apply that figure to the numbers above, then port fees for ships smaller than 250 tons were about 5 to 7 percent of the value of the export cargo; 400- to 500-ton ships, about 3 percent; 900- to 1,000-ton ships, about 2 percent; and 1,400- to 1,600-ton vessels, 1 to 1.5 percent.[50]

Obviously, it was in the companies' best interests to leave the port-fee structure the way it was. Reducing the emperor's present (the 1,950 taels explained in chapter 2) would benefit all parties equally because it was a fixed amount for each ship, but making the measuring fees correspond more equitably to ships' capacities would only help the private traders become more competitive with the companies. This is one reason why it was not until large company ships stopped going to China that foreign traders in Canton could finally agree on the changes needed in trade. In 1830 the EIC finally managed to negotiate a reduction in the emperor's present from 1,950 taels (Spanish $2,708) to 1,600.683 taels ($2,223).[51] This was a saving, but one that made little difference to the smaller ships because it came with an increase in rates.[52]

Up until the late-1820s, foreigners gained information about the trade in China by word of mouth, letters and reports, and by reading published journals of voyages to China. Companies were very protective of their trade data, but as chapter 5 pointed out, cargo data and some other factors could be attained from the Canton linguists. Price data of each *Hong* merchant was more difficult to ascertain because of the special private arrangements that affected the prices that were paid. The expenses that each ship was charged could vary widely and much of this detail was not openly shared so it was not always clear whether one ship or trader was paying more than another. Company ships knew among themselves what the costs were, but often did not have a clear idea of what other company ships were paying. This meant that everyone had different information about the trade and a different understanding of how the Chinese administration was operating as a whole.

The dissemination of information underwent a dramatic change in China in the early nineteenth century that brought more uniformity to the foreigner's understanding of how the trade was being managed. Translations of Chinese laws and edicts were done by Sir George Staunton and Robert Morrison and son, which brought more clarity to Chinese legal structures. In 1806, the EIC established a library in Macao, where published journals, memoirs and commercial guides about China, and pleasure readings, were made available to company employees. A few years later, the Morrison Library was established, which gave all subscribers access to that collection. By the early 1830s, the former library consisted of no less than 4,300 volumes and the latter, 2,000 volumes. The translations and books that were made available to the China traders in this period helped them to gain a deeper understanding of the political and commercial structures that were controlling the commerce. But access to the collections was restricted, so not everyone could use them.

In November 1827, the dissemination of knowledge made a giant step forward with the establishment of the first commercial newspaper on the China Coast, the *Canton Register*. Very quickly, other publications followed which made a wide range of information about China and the trade available to anyone who had the money to purchase them. This was the first time in the history of the China trade that the foreign traders, company and private alike, could all gain a fairly clear understanding of what everyone else was doing in the trade.[53]

The China Coast publications regularly monitored outside sources as well such as the *Bombay Gov. Gazette*, *Calcutta Govt. Gazette*, *Gibraltar Chronicle*, *Singapore Chronicle*, *Calcutta Courier*, *Madras Courier*, *Bengal Hurkaru*, *Javasche Courants*, *India Gazette*, *Liverpool General Advertiser*, *Lisbon Chronicle* and *Peking Gazettes*. Articles about Chinese customs, religion, society, politics and family values that appeared in French and British academic journals were republished in these Canton periodicals.[54]

In addition to these publications, the Dutch (and possibly English) kept copies of their China trade diaries in Canton for the benefit of the supercargoes. With these documents, the editors of the Canton periodicals could ask those persons to look up something that happen 50 or 100 years ago. Some of this detail about the particulars of trade in the past was translated and published for the benefit of everyone. With all of this new information now available, the Canton community became well grounded and informed of both the local scene in Canton, the central administration in Beijing, and the international environment in general.[55]

The media made clear that smuggling in the delta among private traders had developed partially as a means for them to avoid the heavy fees in Canton. Customs officials on all levels accommodated the traffickers in order to privately benefit from the prejudice that was built into the structure of the Canton fees. It was not difficult to conduct clandestine trade in the delta, because the means and methods of the connivances were very well established, and the newspapers kept the foreign community apprised of any change in the government's standing on smuggling. Large ships (which were mostly company ships), on the other hand, continued to go upriver to Whampoa, because they received preferential treatment and could afford to do so. The media laid all of these issues open for all to discuss, which contributed to the undermining of the EIC's control of the trade.

The last companies to trade in China were the EIC and the DAC, and both ceased sending ships there in 1834. All foreigners were then 'private', and were now also very well informed of the history of the trade, the way that Canton authorities had solved problems in the past and recent trends in international commerce. This opening of the information available quickly led to the formation of new ideas and means to bring change to the China trade.

China, on the other hand, was not paying attention to these changes in the environment, but continued to depend on the *status quo*, the Canton System. The Chinese Coast publications were freely available to everyone, even the *Hong* merchants subscribed to them. There was much talk in the foreign community about publishing Chinese versions of some of these volumes, but aside from the merchants, there was little interest in China of these matters.

In fact, the only detailed information that was being regularly and systematically collected about the foreigners and their ships were the entries noted on the Grand Chops, and the reports that were sent back and forth between customs posts. Much of the important information about the changing international environment was not included in these documents.

Table 6 below shows the 'fill in' sections on a 1742 Grand Chop issued to Captain Bengt Askbom of the SOIC ship *Götheborg* (the original can be seen in Plate 1).

Table 6 Inserted Portions of the Grand Chop of Ship *Götheborg* in 1742[56]

(yangchuanshang: Yashimeng) 洋船商亞氏夢 Ship's Captain: Askbom	(zhuangzai huowu qianwang: Ruiguo) 裝載貨物前往瑞國 Loaded with goods bound for: Sweden	
(fanshao: yibai ershi ming) 番稍壹百貳拾名 Foreign crew: 120	(jiandao: sanshi kou) 劍刀參拾口 Swords: 30	(dapao: sanshi men) 大砲參拾門 Cannons: 30
(niao qiang: sanshi zhi) 鳥鎗參拾枝 Fowling pieces: 30	(huoyao: shi dan) 火藥拾担 Gunpowder: 10 piculs	(danzi: sanbai ge) 彈子參百個 Cannon balls: 300
(Qianlong liu nian shi er yue shi yi ri) 乾隆陸年拾貳月十一日 6th year, 12th month, 11th day of the Emperor Qianlong: 17 January 1742		

Other information that we might think important seems to have been overlooked; for example, details of the size of the cannons and cannon balls, types of fowling pieces in the magazines, and any technological improvements in the firing and loading mechanisms were not recorded. Most of the foreign East Indiamen positioned their large (10- to 20-pound) cannons on the lower decks and the smaller (4- to 8-pound) cannons on the upper decks. Eighteen- to 20-pound cannons could level the walls of almost any Chinese fort in the Pearl River Delta, whereas 4- or 8-pounders would have little effect. Foreign rifles became steadily more accurate and lethal, with longer ranges and quicker and easier loading mechanisms. Having this information was certainly vital to maintaining effective defences, but it was not collected.

Reports of the present situation in each post in the delta were regularly forwarded to Canton, but many of these documents were not trustworthy. Important information was regularly and systematically omitted from the reports, and other information was doctored up in order to give a good report. When we cross-reference these documents with information in the foreign records, we begin to see the deep gaps in their content. They generally deal with problems and how they were handled and lack scope and depth. This underreporting by customs officers will be discussed more extensively in the next chapter. But the point to be made here is that much of the important information that would affect the trade was not being collected or reported.

One only needs to read a few of the many contemporary narratives written about the attacks during the opium wars to see how great the foreign military advantages were by the mid-nineteenth century. In many engagements, the foreigners were able to advance with relative ease and often defeated Chinese forces very quickly, despite their desperate efforts to manufacture duplicates of foreign armaments.[57] The important details of military advantages were not recorded, probably because there was no threat perceived.

The technological advances in the West gave foreigners the edge they needed. The invention of the chronometer in 1765 greatly aided maritime navigation by allowing the captains to determine their longitude. In addition to helping them avoid hazards at sea and find crucial watering and provisioning places, this instrument helped them to maintain their course. As a result, long-distance shipping became more timely, regular and predictable — all significant military advantages.[58]

New designs in sails and sleeker, copper-bottomed hulls made foreign ships faster and more manoeuvrable.[59] Improved steering mechanisms and the use (after 1815) of iron plating and iron anchor chains in place of hemp cables improved safety and manoeuvrability, especially in rough seas. In the 1830s, the clippers were introduced which could sail closer to the wind making it possible to undertake three voyages between India and China a year.[60] In the late eighteenth century the telescoping spyglass was invented, and it soon became standard equipment on China-bound vessels. It would prove a considerable advantage in carrying out reconnaissance operations in China and in the accurate aiming and firing of artillery during the opium wars.

One of the foreigners' most obvious advantages, the steamship, was also overlooked. This machine enabled foreigners to penetrate shallow rivers and streams that were inaccessible to large, wind-driven craft. In addition, because the steamer had its own source of power, it was not dependent on the winds, currents or tides, as were the foreign sail ships and the Chinese junks.

In 1835 the English tried to launch a steamer passenger service between Macao and Canton with the *Jardine*, but the Hoppos would not allow it to go into service. All the upper Chinese officers in Canton — *Hong* merchants, linguists, even pilots — launched a barrage of protests against this aggressive act. The *Jardine* was a small vessel of 85 feet in length and had a shallow six-foot draught, so it needed no assistance from the Macao pilots to traverse the river, nor did it have to wait on the wind or the tides.[61]

The *Jardine*'s arrival at Bocca Tigris created a strange scene. While it was being detained, about 100 curious Chinese officers, soldiers and attendants took the opportunity to go aboard and inspect the engine. The *Jardine*'s first attempt to go upriver was blocked by the Chinese; a second attempt was also foiled through the blocking of the passage with Chinese vessels and a barrage of cannon fire from the five forts at the mouth of the river. After several hours of bombardment, the *Jardine*, with its crew of thirteen, gave up.[62]

The Chinese government did not have a problem with the fact that the *Jardine* was a steamer, but that it intended to carry passengers through Bocca Tigris, which was forbidden. This incident, however, should have been a clear sign that the forts at Bocca Tigris were ineffective and that it would probably not be long before foreigners would have a war-steamer, such as the *Nemesis*, that could force its way upriver. Another obvious advantage of the steamer that seems to have been overlooked was that it could tow sail warships and position them quickly in strategic firing positions, which they could not do on their own power. With the aid of just one steamer, a fleet of sail ships became much more effective in coastal battles.[63] The Chinese coastal defence networks had no strategies in place to prevent foreigners making these manoeuvres.[64] After the *Nemesis* wreaked its havoc in the early 1840s, Commander Hú Cháu admitted that the reason they lost battles against the foreigners was 'because these rebels alone had steamers, cannon, and such sorts of things, by which they could overcome us'.[65]

The Qing government responded quickly to the opening salvoes of the First Opium War. Officials were sent scrambling to gain information about foreign steamships, and initiatives were launched to begin building ships and refitting junks with steam power so they could match their superior manoeuvrability and firepower. The Qing administrators were now well aware that their navy could not withstand such a foreign threat.[66]

All this information, however, had been available to officials in Canton long before the attack of the *Nemesis*, but no one took notice. It had been ten years since the arrival of the first steamer, *Forbes*, which was followed by numerous other steamers, but Chinese customs and coastal defence officials treated them no differently from their wind-driven counterparts. By the time these new 'catch-up' initiatives were launched in the early 1840s, foreigners had a fleet of steamers at their disposal. The Qing response was much too late to be effective, and, as a result, they suffered more losses.[67]

Many other large foreign steamships found their way to China too. The *Rattlesnake*, a ship of 503 tons and a draught of only ten feet, participated in the opium wars from 1839 to 1842. The steam paddle sloop *Vixen* plied Chinese waters from 1842 to 1846. It had a burthen of 1,054 tons and drew only eight feet of water. The first American steam schooner, *Midas*, arrived in Canton in 1845 and had a draught of only 9$^1/_2$ feet. The *Midas* made daily runs between Hong Kong and Canton in only sixteen hours — a fraction of the time it took a sailing ship.[68] The steam paddle sloop *Fury* was also in China about this time and had a burthen of 1,124 tons but drew only 8$^1/_2$ feet of water.[69]

As far as profits were concerned, it was more expensive to operate steamers because they needed fuel. However, they were less risky to sail, which meant lower insurance rates. Steamers carrying opium, for example, paid 1 percent of the value of their cargo for insurance, whereas sail ships were charged 2.5 percent. The lower insurance premiums more than made up for the higher operating costs. Consequently, steamers became popular with opium smugglers in China as well.[70] The Qing government was not keeping track of this factor either.

The steamers' shallow draughts enabled them to compete effectively (and illegally) in shallow ports all along the coast of China. In fact, during the Chinese blockade of Canton in 1857, one foreigner stated that 'since the blockade of the river, the whole trade with Canton has been carried along the passage at the back of Macao, known as the Broadway [another name for the West River]'.[71] This diversion of trade to the West River could only have been accomplished by shallow-bottomed steamers because the water was not deep enough for most sailing ships.

Over the next 20 years, steamers would gain control of much of the traffic in freight and passengers in the delta, completely transforming the traditional modes of lightering goods and transporting people up and down China's rivers.[72] Small steamers with draughts of no more than six feet explored many of the branches of the Pearl River and began servicing 'all the large towns in the provinces of Kwantung and Kwansi'.[73] Steamships also transformed the traditional Asian sea trade. The opium trade between India and China, which was sensitive to the product arriving in the market on time, was rapidly taken over by steamers.[74]

By the late nineteenth century there was a fleet of shallow-bottomed steamers carrying freight and passengers to Hong Kong, Macao and Canton, all drawing less than ten feet.[75] By 1914 steamers could make the passage between Macao and Canton in nine hours.[76] These machines could haul enormous volumes of merchandise up rivers where no deep-draughted junks could follow and no small wind- or oar-driven boats could compete with their speed or economies of scale. In a short time, steamers had revolutionised water transport in China. A long-time resident of Canton, Wells Williams, later commented that the old anchorage at Whampoa, which once harboured hundreds of the world's greatest sailing ships, had become 'nearly deserted since the river steamers began their trips'.[77]

The Canton System was based on deep-draughted sailing ships that had to navigate a long, shallow river. All that was needed to control them and the trade was to control the navigation of the river (the Macao pilots) and the entrance to the deep channels (Bocca Tigris). For 140 years, the natural constraints of the Pearl River had worked in favour of the Hoppos. With the arrival of the first steamship, however, the Hoppos' role as the fulcrum of harmony in Canton was suddenly and effectively turned on its head. The steamer was successful at tipping the balance of power in favour of the foreigners partially because it had not been given the attention it deserved. As a result, no counter-measures were initiated to neutralise its strategic advantages until war broke out, and then it was too late.

If one looks at the effectiveness of the Canton System from Beijing's point of view, it becomes more obvious why such minimal information was being collected. In many respects, the Canton System seemed to be operating smoothly until the mid-1830s. The volume of trade and revenues sent to Beijing continued to grow decade after decade. The duties collected on imports almost doubled from 1828 to 1832, rising from 780,000 taels to 1,257,000 taels.[78] Duties collected on exports and port fees also rose with the greater number of ships arriving each decade, so on paper the Canton System appeared to be operating as it was supposed to.

During the 1810s and 1820s, Beijing's concerns about the outflow of silver and increase in opium addiction among the Chinese also diverted attention from the potential of a 'foreign threat'. The thought of foreigners attacking China was still far from the minds of Chinese officials. The under-reporting of vital data continued to keep ministers in Beijing blind to the growing problems of trade.

To raise such concerns could also be looked upon as a lack of confidence in, or even criticism of, the emperor's policies, so it was safer for Hoppos, governors-general and other senior officials in the delta to let things lie. Even if they knew and understood the extent of the problems, they probably preferred to remain silent and hope that nothing drastic happened during their term of office. The problems themselves would eventually show the emperor that something was wrong, and then the court would be more willing to entertain a revision of its policies. The officials in charge at the time of the disturbance would, of course, be reprimanded for negligence and probably demoted, but even that was preferable to being accused of criticising the emperor's policies, which brought their loyalty into question and could end their careers, if not their lives.

SUMMARY

Contrary to what is often portrayed in the history books, the Canton authorities were quite serious about keeping a check on corruption and smuggling to compensate for the shortcomings in the procedures. Many initiatives were put forth throughout the era to give the Hoppos and governors-general better control of the foreigners and the lower echelons. The movement of the chop boats between Canton and Whampoa became more tightly regulated; there were periodic crackdowns on connivances in the customs networks that discouraged others; and the balancing of imports and exports gave officials a standard gauge by which they could ensure that all the duties were collected. Some of these initiatives were partially successful at curbing smuggling and protecting the emperor's revenues.

Hoppos accommodated the foreigners in helping them recover debts from Chinese. Companies had to be patient for repayment, but they were fairly successful at collecting them. Private foreign traders had less leverage than large companies, but they had other tools at their disposal to force collection of debts. In addition to appealing to Hoppos they could threaten the authorities with social disharmony by taking possession of a defaulter's factory and merchandise, which would bring immediate attention to their cases.

Chinese merchants, on the other hand, had much less leverage in collecting debts from foreigners. And each merchant's wealth depended largely on his negotiating skills, because there were many ways for the authorities to tap into private funds. The result was often a slow and constant whittling away of the merchants' fortunes. The administration was never able to find a formula that could adequately address the problems connected to the insecurity of the *Hong* merchants.

Other policies that were initiated had mixed results. Requiring all foreigners going to and from Macao to take the West River passage via the specially built and controlled sampans enabled the Hoppos to determine more clearly the number of foreigners and where they were. This measure undoubtedly helped to relieve the fears of administrators in Beijing as the numbers of foreigners going to China grew from hundreds to thousands to tens of thousands. The tolls charged on the West River were certain to have helped the Yuehaiguan's administrative coffers as well, but at the expense of advancing internal decay.

Other shortcomings were perhaps less obvious and went unnoticed until they had also weakened the system. The port fees discriminated against small ships throughout the Canton era. The calculations were not realistic representations of capacities, and the emperor's present was fixed, making it very expensive for small traders. After the private traders' interests became the dominant force in 1834, they were eager to end this discrimination and open up trade. If the government had addressed some of these prejudices earlier, it could have helped to pacify the private traders and perhaps turn the course of events in a different direction.

At the same time, surprisingly little attention was paid to the changing environment outside of China and to the increased military capability of the foreigners. There was an information revolution going on in Canton among the foreign community that was rapidly changing the structure of international trade, but China was not paying attention. The minimal information that was collected could not have allowed customs and coastal defence officers to project a potential threat with any degree of accuracy.

To see more clearly how and why the internal structures of customs administration began to decay, we need to look at the influences of smuggling. The next chapter turns to the expansion of the contraband trade in the delta to show the role it played in determining the course trade was to take.

CHAPTER SEVEN

FLAG BOATS, SILVER, CONTRABAND AND RICE

AS WOULD BE EXPECTED FOR any major maritime entrepôt, there was an active contraband trade in the Pearl River Delta. In the early decades of the eighteenth century, trade in metals, such as gold, iron and copper and regulated products like salt, saltpetre and certain silks were either forbidden or restricted as to the quantities and types that could be sold. But that did not prevent some of those commodities establishing a market in China. One of the ways contraband came in and out of China was in the bottoms of the foreign flag boats.

FLAG BOATS, SILVER AND CONTRABAND

As was noted earlier, foreign officers were granted freedom to go back and forth to Canton in service boats flying their flag. This was done as a privilege to the officers and it accommodated efficiencies of time, but it was also one of the channels through which the contraband trade developed. The smuggling went both ways in these flag boats: first, foreigners smuggled silver and luxury items into China so they could avoid paying duties and use those items to exchange for contraband; and second, contraband items were smuggled back to the ships at Whampoa so they could be exported duty-free.

In 1704 Charles Lockyer recommended that, as much as possible, the English Company make use of this opportunity to sneak in silver, and they continued to follow this advice in later years.[1] This practice led to fights developing with customs officers. The tollhouse keepers could see obvious contraband in the bottom of a boat, and they could also tell that there were no chief officers aboard. But, when approached by those officials, the foreigners often refused to stop.

In one case, an English boat fired on its Chinese pursuers to scare them off. Fist fights also occurred and could result in customs officers being thrown overboard or beaten to a pulp.[2] Another ploy was for foreigners to start a brawl among themselves when they saw customs officers approaching; the commotion discouraged the Chinese from coming closer.[3]

Despite these diversionary efforts, foreigners were sometimes caught with silver or merchandise, which, of course, caused much disruption in trade until matters were resolved.[4] In 1725 one of the GIC officers was caught trying to smuggle in two large tiger skins, which caused a temporary halt to trade.[5] Silk was regularly smuggled out of Canton in these boats by almost all companies.[6] Customs officers sometimes would allow flag boats to pass the tollhouses undisturbed, but then insist on following them to Canton to inspect them after everyone had disembarked.[7] This cat and mouse game between the tollhouse officers and the foreign flag boats continued throughout the Canton era.[8]

Silver was usually exempt from import duties and only required a small fee for a chop (0.66 taels, as compared to chops for trade goods, which were 10 taels each). Linguists charged a small fee for procuring the chop, but that was also minimal (5.92 taels). The money boat (also called 'specie' or 'bullion' boat) charge for American ships was even less, at three Spanish dollars (2.16 taels) per boat, which included both the fee for the chop and the linguist's services.[9]

Money boats were usually foreign-owned jollies or dinghies that were lowered down from the ships. Eight or more armed soldiers were often assigned to escort silver shipments to the factories in Canton. Foreigners did not usually allow Chinese aboard specie boats. For good reasons, some of the foreigners (especially the English) were wary of letting Chinese officials know exactly how much silver they had.

In the early decades of trade some Hoppos tried to tax silver, although they had promised it would be duty free. In 1726, for example, there was a rumour circulating in Canton that merchants were going to be charged 10 percent on all silver that was imported.[10] In 1728 and 1729, similar fears arose, which led Chinese merchants to request the English supercargoes to conceal their silver so the Hoppo would not be tempted to tax them more than they had agreed upon.[11] The English, who were already in the habit of sneaking in their silver, readily complied with the merchants' request.[12]

Another reason to conceal silver had to do with the smuggling of gold and other contraband out of China. Most companies were involved in the illicit export of gold, which usually required cash payment in silver. Of course, the foreigners ordered the gold from the *Hong* merchants, who also profited from the transactions, so both parties had an interest in concealing silver shipments. If Chinese customs knew exactly how much silver the companies brought into Canton each year, they could match that figure with the value of the exports to see how much silver was in surplus. As we saw in the last chapter, customs sometimes held foreigners (or Chinese merchants) accountable for the duties on the items that had apparently not been declared.

Despite the complaints of Chinese and foreign merchants that the taxing of silver was nothing but extortion, there was a logical rationale behind the policy. By treating silver as an import commodity rather than a currency, it could be monitored and controlled like all other trade goods. On the one hand, more revenues would be generated for the emperor (and the Hoppos) from silver duties. On the other hand, the taxing of all imports (including silver) gave the Hoppos an idea of what exports were likely to be, which, in turn, provided them with a gauge to help monitor smuggling. In a line of reasoning in which the value of the imports is the concern, there is no difference between a cargo of silver and a cargo of cotton; both are used to procure a return cargo based on their value. Why, then, should import duties suffer just because foreigners bring silver instead of cotton?

Foreigners, however, always stipulated that they would not tolerate the taxing of their import silver and often required this to be included in their articles of trade. Their threats were probably genuine because treating silver as a commodity would indeed make China different from the way trade was conducted in many other ports. Such a policy would undoubtedly discourage some traders from going to China and others from returning, which would not be good for the Hoppos' reputations or personal incomes. The idea of taxing silver continued to re-emerge throughout the Canton era, but, in daily practice, the Hoppos simply relied on keeping a tally of the silver and imports to estimate what the exports might be.

The permission chops allowing the transfer of silver coins from the ships to the factories recorded the number of chests that were sent each time. The chests were weighed and recorded by customs officers when they landed on the quay. By keeping track of the number and weight of the silver chests, and also recording all the imports, the Hoppos could figure out how much export cargo each ship was going to load.[13] This knowledge was something that the foreigners did not want Chinese customs to have because it could hinder their dealings in gold and other contraband.[14] Companies might have been opposed to their ships smuggling opium into Canton but they actively participated in all kinds of other illicit trade, as did the Portuguese in Macao.[15]

So far, we have only talked about the reasons for concealing the silver (to purchase contraband), but there were also reasons for exposing the amount of silver one brought. In 1763, for example, French supercargoes made a big display of bringing 100 chests of silver that were heavily guarded in three of their service boats from Whampoa to Canton. Everyone could clearly see the huge amount of money being landed, which resulted in the Chinese merchants immediately changing their strategies and demanding silver payments for their goods, rather than negotiating for foreign imports. This, of course, put the French supercargoes in a strategic position to negotiate the best price and purchase all the best merchandise on hand. Thus, it was not always the case that companies tried to conceal their silver.[16]

THE GOLD TRADE

To buy gold, a large amount of silver needed to be smuggled in. As early as 1704 the English traded illegally in gold with the connivance of the 'Mandarins' (customs officers).[17] The GIC exported gold from China in the 1720s, and the Dutch also dealt in the precious metal from the 1730s to the 1770s. The Portuguese in Macao were active in the gold trade as well throughout the eighteenth century.[18]

The supercargoes of the Swedish company bought gold regularly in Canton. Illustration 18 shows a contract between Tan Tinqua (Chen Zhenguan 陳鎮官) and Tzy Yamqua (Cai Yanguan 蔡炎官) and the SOIC supercargo Charles Irvine in 1746 and 1747. Irvine supplied the two merchants with 10,000 silver dollars to be invested in gold. Another gold contract that has survived from 1760 shows Tsja Hunqua (Cai 蔡 family), Semqua (Qiu Kun 邱崑), Chetqua (Chen Jieguan 陳捷官) and Swetia (Yan Ruishe 顏瑞舍) contracting with the VOC for 4,500 taels weight (450 ingots) of Nanking gold.[19]

Besides these men, other *Hong* merchants were also involved in this illegal commerce, including Tan Suqua (Chen Shouguan 陳壽官) and son Tinqua (Dengguan 登觀); Texia (Yan Deshe 顏德舍), his partner Simon (Huang Ximan 黃錫滿) and the writer in the Yan family factory, Zey Kinqua (Shi Mengjing 石夢鯨); Suiqua (Cai Ruiguan 蔡瑞官) and associates; Beaukeequa (Li Kaiguan 黎開觀) and associates; Poankeequa (Pan Qiguan 潘啟官), his brother and partner Sequa (Pan Seguan 潘瑟官) and their writer Namqua; and the porcelain dealer Lisjoncon (Li Xianggong 李相公). All the merchants show up in the foreign records from time to time trading in gold, so it was not difficult to arrange its export.[20]

THE OPIUM TRADE

By the mid-eighteenth century, opium had also established a firm market in Canton. In the early 1700s, opium was already being traded widely throughout

Asia, including Achin, Sumatra, Borneo and Java so its arrival to China is late in comparison.[21] It was now being smoked as an hallucinogen as well as being chewed for its medicinal qualities so its popularity expanded rapidly.[22] Opium was treated just like any other commodity in those ports. The studies that have been done about the opium trade in China generally do not show it establishing a firm market until the late-eighteenth or early-nineteenth centuries.[23] New information recorded below, however, will show that it carved out a market in China in the 1750s and was firmly established by the 1760s.

Anders Ljungstedt mentions that 'a few chests were imported (1720) from the coast of Coromandel' to Macao, and because the demand for the drug was 'growing yearly, the government of Goa strove to secure to Macao the exclusive market'.[24] By 1729 the Yongzheng Emperor had learned of the drug's destructive nature and banned its trade, but this did not stop it entering China via both land and sea.[25] By the early 1730s opium was a regular item of trade with English captains and supercargoes going from Fort St. George (in India) to China. The emperor's ban caused the EIC to forbid its importation aboard company ships because they feared, with good reason, that their trade in legitimate commodities would be adversely affected if they were caught smuggling opium.[26] Other East India companies also refrained from bringing the drug to China for the same reason, but private traders continued to smuggle it in small quantities. Ljungstedt states that the price of opium varied in China in the 1730s, ranging from about 70 taels per picul to as high as 225 taels, depending on the quality of the consignments.[27]

By the 1750s, the drug was making significant inroads into China. In 1747 Israel Reinius, of the SOIC ship *Cronprintzen Adolph Friedrich*, mentioned that private traders from Bengal were marketing opium in Canton.[28] It was known to be a forbidden article, but it could find a sale if a deal was struck with the 'Mandarins'.[29] In 1750, the Swede Christopher Braad listed opium among the articles that could be purchased in Surat and sold in Canton for 300 to 400 taels per chest.[30]

The Swedes, English, French, Dutch and Danes clearly acknowledge in their records that opium was a forbidden article in China. The companies' ban on the drug seems somewhat contradictory, given the fact that many of them traded regularly in other forms of contraband such as gold and illegal silk. Opium was a regular and legitimate item of trade for the English, Dutch and Danish companies in other Asian ports, but not China. For large companies, the tea trade was far too important to risk for the sake of a few chests of opium.

In 1750 security merchants for the EIC were perturbed to learn that a private English trader had tried to market the drug in Canton. Chinese merchants were also worried that they would incur the Hoppo's wrath if the attempted trade was reported. The supercargoes immediately inquired into the matter and issued instructions to all EIC officers to 'use the most effectual means to prevent its [opium] being landed here'.[31]

In 1752 the Danes worried about a small amount of opium that they had aboard one of their ships. Captain Lyder Holman of the *Kongen af Danmark* had died shortly after leaving Copenhagen. As was customary with most of the East India companies, Captain Holman's personal effects were auctioned off at sea to other members of the Danish crew. Some items did not sell, including a small stash of opium, which Captain Holman had kept for his private use. Opium was not illegal in many foreign countries and was considered to have valuable medicinal qualities so it was regularly consumed by many foreigners. The DAC officers decided to auction the remainder of Holman's possessions when they arrived in Canton, but after discussing the matter with some of the Chinese merchants they decided to hold back the opium.[32]

By 1757, however, opium had gained a firm footing in China. A Canton *Price Courant* from that year includes the following entry: 'Ophium 1st Sort, three dollars pr catty & rising' (about Spanish $300 per chest).[33] In 1762 the Dutch report 90 piculs (about 90 chests) of opium being sold in Macao for 400 taels per picul (about Spanish $540).[34] In 1763 opium does not appear in the list of Portuguese imports to Macao, but, in 1764 a 'Timor ship' (probably a Portuguese ship) was able to command Spanish $600 to $800 per picul in Macao for about 200 chests of opium.[35]

Swedish records for the same year show that the price for opium in Canton was Spanish $4 per catty (about $400 per picul for superior quality, see reference below), much less than what the Timor ship could command in Macao. This may be an indication of a greater demand in Macao, but could also be owing to varying risk factors, such as local Chinese or Portuguese officials in Macao profiting from the trade through increased bribes. Whatever the case may have been in 1764, the competition that would emerge in the Chinese market for the drug worked to keep prices and connivance fees fairly uniform.

The next chapter will show how war between the Europeans in the early 1760s was depleting silver supplies in China, which gave impetus to the opium trade. Dealing opium was a way for Chinese merchants to produce quick capital and much needed silver. They needed silver to purchase opium, but they sold it for silver as well so like tea, it could increase their capital reserves. With tea, they had to give silver payments in advance so it might be six months or more before they saw returns on their investments. But opium, in good years, could be sold within days of its purchase so silver supplies could be replenished very quickly.

A few quick sales of opium at the beginning of a season gave Chinese merchants more silver to buy tea and less need to take out high-interest loans from foreigners. Except for a few bribes to the Mandarins, no duties had to be paid to the government. Thus, opium had the unique characteristics of producing profits in its own sale, expanding tea sales and reducing usury costs both of which increased tea profits, and it did all of this without creating new debts (duties owed). The minimal risks involved in trading opium in China in the 1760s meant that there was much more to be gained in selling it than lost in avoiding it so the trade continued to expand.

The Swedish supercargo Jean Abraham Grill, together with his accomplices George Smith (a private English trader) and Thomas Arnot (surgeon for the EIC), speculated in opium in Canton in the 1760s. Two entries in Grill's account books for 23 March 1765 credit Smith with 488.400 taels and debit Grill by 545.750 taels for 'unsold opium'.[36] It is not mentioned why the opium did not sell; it may have been because of poor quality or spoilage.

In 1764 HMS frigate *Argo* and the sloop *Cuddalore* were suspected by the EIC of bringing opium to Whampoa.[37] In 1764 and 1765 Captain Joseph Jackson of the ship *Pitt* was marketing opium in China. Plate 23 shows his "Sales of Opium" in Canton in the latter year.[38] The Chinese merchants mentioned in this invoice cannot be identified conclusively. Such Romanised names as 'Monqua' and 'Tonqua' show up regularly in the foreign records of the 1760s as merchants. The suffix 'qua' suggests that they were either merchants or linguists.[39] Despite the ambiguities, the reference at least shows that foreigners had little trouble marketing opium in Canton in the mid-1760s.

In May 1767 Jacob Hahr reports 'a large quantity of opium' bound for China aboard the same English sloop *Cuddalore*, but this time it was under the command of Captain Richman. Hahr mentions that 'a great many chests of the drug were coming this year to China from all coasts and quarters'. Charles Adolph Heyberg was a passenger aboard the *Cuddalore*, and Hahr arranged for him to ship ten chests of opium for Grill. Hahr paid the freight plus ten pagodas per chest for bottomry insurance. The opium cost him 150 pagodas per chest, so the insurance amounted to 6.66 percent of the value. Heyberg had insured his cargo of Bengal and Madras wares for 20,000 pagodas. Hahr mentions in the same letter that Portuguese ships were carrying opium to Malacca and Macao under the security of bottomry contracts.[40]

In June 1767 Hahr states that he shipped nine chests of opium to Macao aboard the *Triton*, under the command of Captain Elphinstone, which would arrive ('shall trust in God') with '120 chests' of the drug.[41] In the same letter, Hahr also mentions that he had contracted with Andrew Rossi for twenty chests of Patna opium from Bengal to be shipped aboard the *Earl of Lincoln* under the care of Captain Hardwicke.[42] Hahr paid ten pagodas per chest for freight. The opium cost him 190 pagodas per chest, so the freight was only about 5 percent of its value. This was a reasonable rate for a contraband article and comparable to freight rates for legitimate goods. Hahr insured the cargo in a bottomry contract with Rossi for the sum of 2,000 pagodas. The premium on the loan was ten pagodas per chest, or about 5 percent of the value. The regularity of Hahr's transactions and the level of standardization for the fees suggest that there was probably much more smuggling going on than these records reveal.

On 13 June 1767, the Dutch report the arrival in Macao of the Portuguese ship *Bon Voyage* from Bengal, with a cargo of 'nothing but opium'.[43] This is the first clear reference we have to a ship being used exclusively to carry opium to China. The trade was obviously growing, and, in 1768, Mr Brunel lists Bengal opium as one of the popular import articles that could be sold at 'considerable profit' in China. Bengal opium was preferred above all others, and Brunel tells us that the best product should be soft, brownish in colour and have a 'strong fetid smell'. Opium that was 'dry, friable, burnt, and mixed with earth, is of a bad quality'. These statements suggest that the opium market in China was maturing rapidly and Chinese consumers were paying close attention to quality.[44]

On 13 June 1770, the Dutch report that the Portuguese ship *S. Antonio Novo*, owned by the procurator of the Macao Senate, Simão Vicente Roza, brought '31 chests of opium' to Macao.[45] The Canton *Hong* merchant Chetqua (Chen Jieguan) purchased some Portuguese opium for Spanish $430 (per chest/picul?), along with many other goods, such as pepper, kapok, sandalwood and benzoin.[46] In these early years, opium was generally traded as an item that was included with other legitimate articles. On 24 June 1770, for example, the *Boa Viagem*, owned by 'Emanuel Pereira', arrived in Macao with '11 chests of opium' as part of its cargo, and the *S. Cecilia*, owned by Vincente José de Campos and under the command of the English Captain Brown, arrived with '62 chests of opium' aboard.[47]

In 1772 the Dutch report that the 'Comptoir of Smith or Christen' in Macao was deeply involved in the opium trade and was shipping the article free of transport aboard Portuguese ships from Bengal, despite its being 'strictly forbidden' in China.[48] The 'Smith or Christen' was probably the private English trader George Smith. He had been trading in Canton since 1758, and one of his financial backers was the Governor of Bengal. Morse mentions that he 'remained, more or less continuously, through the next twenty years' in Canton and Macao.[49]

As these examples show, some senior government officials in Macao (and Bengal) were directly involved in the trading of opium, which helped the procedures to become standardised. In some cases, the Portuguese were bringing the drug to China on their own, and in other cases, they were joining together with other private traders from India. For all practical purposes, opium was now being traded in Macao as a legitimate commodity with a legitimate market. A detailed report of the Macao trade in 1771 shows 800 chests of opium being consumed in China, and, in that year, it sold for 260 to as much as 750 taels per chest.[50]

In 1772 the Dutch report the drug making rapid inroads. They record 600 to 800 chests of opium being imported into Macao annually. The demand for the drug was so strong in 1771 and 1772 that, if fewer than 600 chests arrived, prices skyrocketed to 1,200 to 1,400 piasters (same value as Spanish dollars) per chest.[51] The potential for huge profits quickly attracted more privateers to the trade.

Cargo lists of Macao imports that have survived show the Portuguese merchants treating the drug more as a speculative commodity than a major article of trade. In 1773 the Dutch report that out of thirteen Portuguese ships that arrived in Macao, a total of 715 chests of opium were aboard. In 1774, twelve Portuguese vessels brought a total of 313 chests of opium.[52] The units of measurement — sacks, bundles, piculs, pieces, and chests — of the products that were unloaded at Macao are listed differently in the Dutch documents and their values are not mentioned. Therefore, it is not possible to establish the exact proportion that opium represented of the ships' cargos, but for many of them it made up a small percentage of the volume.[53]

Some of these shipments may have been intended for personal consumption. The fact that all Portuguese ships were carrying opium in these years clearly shows the degree to which the trade had spread by the 1770s. Every vessel going to Macao had to pay duties and be closely scrutinised by the Chinese customs officials, who were undoubtedly aware of the contraband that was being landed. Such extensive transactions could not have proceeded so smoothly without the knowledge and connivance of these officers.[54]

In these early years, the opium brought in by the Portuguese appears to have come from both Bengal and Malabar.[55] The Malwa variety was from western and central India, but Patna came from Bengal. When the EIC gained control over Bengal, it also gained tighter control over opium in the region. The company offered incentives to improve the quality of the Patna variety and expand its trade in China via private traders. The EIC continued to ban opium on company ships going to China, but encouraged private traders to purchase the drug from the company in India and then smuggle it to the delta.

The EIC benefited from this commerce in two ways: from the profits on the sales in Bengal and from the silver that it received for the opium that was sold in China. Large quantities of silver were needed to purchase tea, and opium was about the only commodity that could be readily exchanged for that specie. The EIC sold its opium and such articles as Indian textiles to the country traders in exchange for silver, which it then used to buy tea.[56]

In 1776 the Danes report that the price of opium had stabilised again to Spanish $300 per chest. Danish records give us a glimpse at the structure of the opium trade in Macao, which now had well-established procedures and import 'duties'. Portuguese officials collected 16 taels (about Spanish $22) per chest as a 'toll'.[57] A chest of opium weighed 140 pounds (a little more than a picul).[58]

Thomé Francisco de Oliveira and José Xavier dos Santos quickly emerged as two of the major opium dealers in Macao.[59] Oliveira was a Portuguese citizen and Santos was a Chinese Christian who adopted a Portuguese name. Between the two of them, they could connect to both populations, and having a Portuguese name probably helped Santos shield his activities from the Chinese authorities. Santos traded the drug between Bengal and Macao fairly consistently year after year into the 1780s. The Danes also mention one António do Rosário, also a Chinese Christian who was knowledgeable about the particulars of the trade.[60]

The standardisation of the smuggling encouraged it to grow, and, by 1779, the supply of opium had clearly caught up with demand, which pushed prices down. A small English country ship brought opium to Whampoa that year and had to stay over the next season because the prices were too low to sell the drug. In June of 1780, the Dutch report a Portuguese ship in Macao with 200 chests of opium aboard that could not be sold because of low prices. The saturation of the market led to the practice of warehousing the product in China to give prices time to recover.[61]

In 1780 a reference describes the English anchoring a ship in Lark's Bay (also called 'Dirty Butter Bay') on the west side of Montanha Island (Hengqin Dao 横琴島) near Macao for the purpose of warehousing opium.[62] These floating brokering houses were called 'hulks' or 'depot ships' and, from this time forward, formed a permanent part of the contraband trade in China. Opium was stored in the hulks (for a fee) and kept there until prices recovered. It was then sold either on the China market, or to whoever wanted it (some opium was in fact exported from China). Lark's Bay was too shallow for anything except vessels of about 300 tons or less, so mostly small privateers operated there. This anchorage continued to be used by smugglers until the late 1790s.[63]

Many Chinese assisted the smugglers. Chinese fisherman piloted foreign ships into safe smuggling harbours, where Chinese compradors supplied them with provisions. Chinese fishermen, pilots and compradors were hired to transport contraband to Macao and upriver to Canton. The smuggling going on at Lark's Bay was common knowledge to everyone in the delta, including customs officers.

The Hoppos had express sampans that went up and down the river every day. Besides delivering soldiers and messages from post to post, the job of these customs officers was to inform the Hoppos of all activities and movements of foreigners and vessels in the area. The Hoppos would often share this information with the foreigners in Canton, which is how many of them knew one of their ships had arrived. On 28 August 1773, for example, the Hoppo sent word to the Dutch that his express 'Sappatin' (sampan) had arrived from Macao and reported that the Dutch ship *Holland* had arrived on the 26th at 8AM and that there was also an English ship from Surat in the delta.[64]

This monitoring of the movement of ships in the delta shows up regularly in both the foreign and Chinese records throughout the Canton era, which gives the impression that the Hoppos kept a tight rein on all maritime activities in the region.[65] The fact was, however, that many ships, such as those lying in Lark's Bay, went unreported or were only reported after they had successfully disposed of their contraband. The Mandarins would sometimes ask the foreign smugglers to temporarily move their operations to another location so they could give a report to the Hoppo in Canton that all was clear.[66] Customs officers regularly withheld information and/or doctored their reports to camouflage these connivances. In 1792 the Hoppo found out about the ships anchoring in Lark's Bay and issued a complaint to the EIC.[67] This trafficking, however, had been going on for twelve years.[68]

A detailed list that has survived from the Portuguese records of opium shipped into Macao covers the years 1784 to 1828 (although we know that the opium trade started much earlier). There were many up and down years, but figures show that, on the whole, opium trade increased fairly steadily in that port from 726 chests in 1784 to 4,602 chests in 1828.[69]

Major Samuel Shaw has left us with one of the best accounts of the contraband network in the early 1780s, which had by then expanded to 'two thousand chests' annually. The floating warehouse at Lark's Bay, which Major Shaw mentions, later became the foundation for the contraband trade at Lintin Island in the early 1800s. According to Shaw, 'twenty dollars' per chest was paid to the 'mandarins', who were undoubtedly the customs officers and/or naval patrols.[70]

A Portuguese document from 1803 also shows that when the compradors in Macao were involved in the smuggling, they received 'twenty patacas' (Spanish dollars) for each chest of opium as profit, but they had to forfeit fifteen of these to 'keep the mandarins quiet'.[71] John Robert Morrison wrote in 1834 that the opium connivance fee in the delta was still twenty dollars per chest, with additional transport charges.[72] In 1836, the connivance fee to smuggle opium into Amoy was also twenty dollars per chest.[73] We saw above that the Portuguese in Macao were charging twenty-two dollars per chest in 1776, and the regularity with which the drug was being brought to Macao and Canton by the 1760s shows that the procedures and rates were already well-established.[74] Thus, from the 1760s to the

1830s, smugglers could know in advance what they would be charged for each chest of opium to enter China.[75]

The development of the opium trade from 1800 to the 1840s has been well documented, so there is no need to retrace that here.[76] There are, however, a few references that have emerged recently which shed new light on the extent of the trafficking and the level of standardization. In August 1784 the DAC ship *Disco* arrived in Macao Roads with a quantity of opium on board. Despite the DAC's policy that forbade the drug being brought on company ships, the *Disco*'s captain was ordered not to unload the opium at Macao but to take it upriver. We have extracted entries below from the ship's journal showing opium being unloaded while at anchor in Whampoa Roads.

> September 14: Hoppo came on board to measure the ship and with his coming and going we saluted him with 9 [cannon] shots. The supercargoes and several English were aboard and saluted them with 3 shots. Several Chinese came aboard to sample the opium.
>
> September 20: Several Chinese came aboard to sample opium.
>
> October 17: Following orders from the factory, delivered 14 chests of opium.
>
> [In the mean time, there was a report from the ship that some of the opium was found to be of poor quality]
>
> November 11: Supercargoes came aboard to inspect the opium and sampled two cakes.
>
> November 14: Several foreigners, English and Swedes, came aboard. Gave them 2 salutes. After orders from the factory, delivered 12 chests of opium.
>
> November 16: Delivered 24 chests of opium.
>
> November 21: Following orders from the factory, delivered 3 chests of opium.
>
> November 23: Following orders from the factory, delivered 12 chests of opium.
>
> November 30: Following orders from the factory, delivered 3 chests of opium.
>
> December 3: Following orders from the Council in the factory, delivered 56 chests of opium.
>
> December 12: Following orders from Canton, delivered 3 chests of opium.
>
> December 18: Following orders, delivered 9 chests of opium.
>
> [The ship removed downriver to Bocca Tigris Roads on December 25.]
>
> December 29: Following orders from Canton, delivered the rest of the opium, being 25 chests.[77]

It must be remembered that every chest mentioned above was unloaded from the *Disco* under the watchful eyes of two Chinese tidewaiters stationed on each side of the stern. Opium chests weighed a little more than a picul, so they could not be tucked under the arm or hidden in an overcoat. They were probably lowered into the waiting lighters by the ship's yard arms, which was exactly what the tidewaiters were supposed to prevent. The example of the *Disco* is probably no different from what would have happened with the ships bringing opium to Whampoa in the 1760s as they also had no problem disposing of their cargo. Danish records are not explicit enough to determine how much the tidewaiters were paid to allow these chests to pass.

By 1798, the smuggling at Whampoa had become so regular that the captain of the private Danish ship *Fredriks Nagor* had the audacity to set up an opium warehouse business there. In August, however, the Hoppo heard of the connivance and ordered the ship to leave. This attempt was soon followed by the English ship *Nancy*, which operated as an opium warehouse at Whampoa until March 1804 when it was sold to the Portuguese in Macao. The ship was renamed *Nossa Senhora de Conceiçaõ*, and outfitted to cruise the coast for pirates (and smuggle opium, see below).[78]

Table 7 lists some of the connivance fees that were standard in the 1830s. The figures show that smuggling of other contraband also had fixed rates that could be anticipated in advance. These fees were probably not much different from those that would have been charged in earlier decades.

Table 7 Tidewaiters' Connivance Fees in Whampoa and Canton, 1834[79]

Silk, raw	per pecul	$4
Silk, wrought	per case	$2
Copper	per pecul	$5
Marble	per 100 slabs	$10
Cloth piece goods	per boat	$120
Cassia and Tea	per boat	$10

North American furs were also smuggled into China by British, French, Portuguese, Spanish, and American traders.[80] As the examples above show, smuggling had been part of the trade from the early eighteenth century, and by the middle of the century, there were well-established networks through which many products were illegally imported and exported. As long as the proper payments were put into the proper hands, there were ways of marketing almost anything in China.

All this bribing and diverting of funds from the Hoppos, however, put foreigners in a precarious position. To satisfy the customs officers, they had to ignore the port regulations and pay the tidewaiters their connivance fees. Obeying the port regulations ran the risk of offending these officials by denying them their 'privilege'. In both situations, foreigners risked disruptions to their trade, whether the Hoppos caught them cheating or whether the tidewaiters were not properly rewarded. The following excerpt from an American Consul report in Canton in 1838 gives a good picture of how ingrained this practice was at the time.

> The evasion of duties by collusion with the revenue officers goes on, at Whampoa, through the agency of the hoppo's boats, or tide waiters, appointed to guard each ship, and at Canton, by arrangements made between the linguists, hong clerks, and the custom-house examiners. In the former case, a hoppo-man agrees to land certain goods from on board the ship, at one half or one third of the provincial duty, or to buy them at a price so much above the market value. In this case the collusion does not probably extend beyond the very lowest grade of revenue officers employed on the river, and no money reaches the imperial treasury. . . . When the settlement of duties on the ship's cargo comes to be made, the smuggled goods are suppressed, and the duties on those really entered are paid to the Hong merchant directly, or sometimes, if the linguist be a responsible man, through the linguist.[81]

As can be seen, the bribes were fixed amounts that did not change from one year to the next, which reduced risks and made it easier to project profits and attract investors. Connivance procedures for products such as gold and illegal silks were already well established by the early decades of the eighteenth century. The normalisation of smuggling enabled contraband traders to anticipate their expenses and calculate their profits with as much clarity and reliability as legitimate traders.[82]

In fact, in some aspects, the contraband trade was less risky than the legitimate trade in tea. Unlike tea, which could lose 50 percent of its value if held over for a season,[83] opium was less prone to deterioration if properly stored. Moreover, the sales of Chinese exports were often tied to the purchase of foreign imports, such as cotton and textiles (a practice known as 'truck'). Plate 19, for example, shows the SOIC supercargo Charles Irvine exchanging cochineal and cloth in 1744 with the *Hong* merchant Tan Suqua (Chen Shouguan 陳壽觀) for chinaware.

After the Chinese merchants made the agreements, they took the import goods into their factories in September or October and sold the items before mid-November or December when the new tea arrived. Revenues from the sale of imports were used to purchase tea and porcelain, which meant that goods had to be sold at a time when the market was saturated and prices were at their lowest level. Merchants could not always afford to warehouse their import goods until prices had recovered, so this was a precarious situation for them.

Chinese merchants could not contract tea unless they agreed to buy a certain amount of textiles and other imports, and they could not pay for the tea until those products were sold. By the early nineteenth century import duties also had to be paid by late October or early November, so imports had to be sold immediately. There was no way of knowing how many ships would arrive each year or how much of one commodity would be dumped onto the market. Larger merchant houses in Canton tried to bring a little more security into these arrangements by buying up all the supply of a certain product to control its price. But this also required an enormous outlay of capital, which most merchants could not produce. Thus, for many of the Chinese merchants in Canton, the tea trade was risky business.[84]

If prices plummeted, all that merchants could do was to sell their import goods at a loss and hope to recoup their outlay with tea sales. The tea market, however, was also highly competitive, which meant that profit margins were extremely slim even in good years. Moreover, tea sales required huge advances, often with high interest rates. Thus, it was not likely that profits from tea would make up for losses from imports. Opium, on the other hand, was a cash-and-carry commodity. If the markets were saturated, opium could be stored until prices recovered because it was not tied to the sale of exports.

In the early nineteenth century there were many efforts made by the government to crack down on piracy in the delta, and some of those initiatives may have contributed to an increase in smuggling. In 1804 Portuguese patrol ships were commissioned by the Chinese government to help fight pirates. In July of that year, the Portuguese ship *Ouvidor Par* was sent out to capture pirates and, in the process, transhipped opium from the ship *Alexander* to Macao.[85] In August and September 1808, two other armed Portuguese patrols, the *Bellisarius* and the *Nossa Senhora de Conceiçaõ* (the previous ship *Nancy*), made a routine trip to 'Chin Chow' (Quanzhou) to quash piracy and took with them a shipment of opium to sell to the merchants there.[86] These voyages along the China Coast were often undertaken to protect Chinese junks that were going to those ports from pirate attacks, which was a great service to them. Portuguese patrols went out regularly in these years, guiding junks and small ships and scouring for pirates, and used that cover to advance the opium trade. Some of the junks they were escorting were certain to have been carrying opium as well that they purchased in Southeast Asia or from foreigners in the delta.[87]

In 1814, when the Jiaqing Emperor learned of the vast networks of opium smuggling around Macao, new initiatives were made to crack down on the trafficking. The Xiangshan magistrate arrested 18 opium dealers in Macao, and officials demanded rigorous inspections of all Portuguese vessels.[88] The studies that have been done on the opium trade of the nineteenth century have shown that these localised crackdowns had little effect because smugglers simply shifted their operations to other places in the delta. Because the opium trade in this period has been thoroughly researched, we will restrict our discussion to new information that sheds more light on the reasons for its rapid expansion.

By the 1810s and 1820s the smuggling procedures were so established, indeed, commonplace, it was no longer necessary to sell the goods aboard the ships at Whampoa. Foreigners could arrange for all contraband to be shipped direct to Canton, where they began warehousing such contraband items as opium and selling them directly out of their factories. Chinese buyers could go there and sample the goods instead of having to travel to Whampoa, as in the example of the *Disco*. The contraband trade was, by degrees, becoming almost as secure and stable as the legal trade. The legal trade was protected by Chinese imperial decrees and policies, and the contraband trade was protected by long-established local practice and procedures.[89]

Brokering houses were set up in Macao and Canton to arrange the sales and pay all the connivance fees, which will be discussed in the next chapter. These commission merchants dealt in legitimate items as well which is why they were allowed to stay in China. It is probably safe to assume that without the funds generated from the contraband trade, the legitimate trade would not have grown as fast, as extensively or as consistently as it did for 140 years. Thus, it was in the interests of the Hoppos to tolerate these illegal activities so that the tea trade would not be affected. Toleration was perhaps the easiest and most effective way to ensure that the flow of revenues sent to Beijing was uninterrupted. If no unnecessary ripples were made in the system, such as launching a campaign to wipe out corruption and opium, then the revenues from the legitimate trade might even increase during each of the three years that a Hoppo was in office. This was the optimum outcome.

By the 1820s there was so much collusion between the smugglers and Chinese officials that one foreigner stated: 'Complaints for smuggling are seldom carried into the city [Canton], untill the discoverers dispair of getting the hush money'.[90] As Morrison pointed out in 1823, the same could be said about Whampoa and Macao.

> At Macao and Whampoa, Opium has, heretofore, since its being prohibited, been smuggled into China by the connivance of local officers of government, some of whom have watched the delivery of every chest, and received a fee; whilst others, in the public offices, remote from the scene of smuggling, have received an annual bribe to acquiesce in a violation of the Imperial orders on the subject.[91]

Morrison mentions that many higher officials in Canton were themselves consumers of the drug. 'The Governor at no period could have been ignorant of what was going on in reference to Opium; for it is very commonly used by clerks, secretaries, military officers, and other persons in his own establishment'. The different varieties and qualities of opium meant there was a wide range of prices that made it affordable to persons on different income levels. Plate 24, for example, shows the different prices of goods in Canton in 1823, and the Dutch supercargoes wrote in at the bottom the prices for the different kinds of opium. Morrison explains that the government officials 'encouraged, and virtually protected the smuggling of Opium'.[92] Other evidence also suggests that opium smuggling extended to high levels within the customs networks. When the Hoppo died unexpectedly in 1829, for example, the transporting of his corpse to his home was also used as a cover to smuggle opium inland.[93]

A fleet of Chinese smuggling boats, known as 'centipedes', 'fast crabs' or 'scrambling dragons' (owing to their many oars and semblance to those creatures), provided lightering services for the illegal trade in the delta. Each boat had upwards of sixty oarsmen (twenty to thirty on each side), which gave them an advantage of speed. Despite the fact that these well-armed express boats had sails that could be spotted from a great distance during the day and many creaking oars, the noise of which echoed across the water at night, they carried contraband in and out of China with as much regularity as a postal service.

Plate 37 shows how large and obvious were these vessels. Crab boats made regular nightly runs upriver to Canton and other destinations. There were at least four thoroughfares and eight different river passages leading to the city so there were several avenues through which they could escape and evade customs officers.[94] They smuggled goods downriver as well and sold them to foreigners at Lintin. The contraband trade was so competitive that it was important to obtain a backhaul to cover costs. Foreigners could not afford to sail back to India without some type of saleable return cargo, and crab boats could not afford to run downriver empty because of the fierce competition.

By the early 1830s there were 35 to 40 of these specially outfitted boats servicing the smugglers in the delta, and they were shipping contraband into Canton at all times of the day and night.[95] The fast sailing clippers were also introduced into the opium China trade at this time, which enabled the product to arrive in a more regular and timely fashion.[96] There were now almost as many smuggling ships anchoring each year at Lintin Island and other harbours in the delta as there were legitimate ships going upriver to Whampoa.

Private traders also began sailing up the China Coast taking their contraband to other ports, and they found markets everywhere they went. Besides the Portuguese patrols mentioned above, private ships such as the *Merope*, *Eugenia* and *Glorioso* sailed up the coast in the 1820s selling opium and other contraband.[97] And in the early 1830s, Jardine and Dent began sending ships along the coast to find new markets.[98] The Chinese junks had been supplying those harbours with opium for decades so the connivance fees and procedures were just as normalized and competitive with those in the delta.[99] There were so many opportunities to sell the drug that the same connivance fees had to be charged everywhere otherwise the smugglers would move to other locations.

Chinese patrol boats could not out-sail the crab boats that were servicing the smugglers, but they occasionally ambushed one in order to 'keep up an appearance of vigilant honesty'.[100] The perpetrators, however, were more likely to be released than to be punished. It was in the personal interests of the customs officers to take their 'gratuity' and let the fast crabs go free because they could then tap them over and over again.[101]

The thriving contraband trade seems to have indirectly contributed to the impoverishment of Macao. Instead of keeping its connivance fees and trade terms competitive with other harbours, Macao continued to restrict commerce to protect its indigenous Portuguese citizens. The Mandarins and Portuguese officials had kept their fees higher in an attempt to generate more revenues, but with the reverse effect.[102] Even though we have shown above that Macao's opium imports had grown 600 percent from 1784 to 1828, the economy on the whole was severely pressed owing to loss of trade.

The crackdowns on opium in Macao in 1814 and 1815 had some effect on the loss of revenues. As a result of increased pressure and high fees some Portuguese diverted their operations to Lintin Island, and many of the remaining Portuguese in Macao became dependent on Chinese merchants and others to freight goods on their bottoms. The Macao Hoppo also complained that some of the ships were leaving port without paying the measuring fees.

With the arrival of a new governor and a new approach, Macao removed its restrictions and became a free port on 1 March 1836. Opium traders and others were encouraged to return, with the promise of favourable terms. But by then there was little hope of bringing the trade back to Macao because Canton was starting to crackdown on the smuggling and because other places still offered a freer environment. Macao's unfortunate outcome is an example of how competitive this illegal commerce was along the China coast.[103]

THE RICE TRADE

Besides opium, which was sold for silver and silver used to purchase tea, another commodity formed an important link between the legitimate trade and the contraband networks, and that was rice. As mentioned, it was important for opium ships to procure a backhaul for the return passage so they could remain competitive. Rice provided a means for smugglers to avoid the high fees at Whampoa.

In the eighth year of the Qianlong Emperor (ca. 1743), import duties on rice were reduced. Ships carrying 10,000 piculs or more received a discount of 50 percent on the duties, and ships carrying 5,000 to 10,000 piculs received a discount of 30 percent.[104] At some point thereafter, the minimum requirement was reduced to 4,500 piculs.

The policy, however, was relaxed in years of short supply. In 1833, for example, the minimum requirement was omitted for small ships, because they could not hold 4,500 piculs. As long as they came full of rice with no other cargo they were admitted as rice ships. Examples below will show that small ships were already being treated like this in the 1820s so the new 'official' policy may have just been a formality to put into writing what was already being done. Ships that could carry more than 4,500 piculs of rice, could also bring other merchandise and still qualify, as long as they had the minimum amount.[105]

Rice ships had to pay some nominal fees to the Mandarins so they were not entirely exempt. In fact, there was often much confusion as to how much they were supposed to pay, because it varied from one ship to the next. In 1837, the Canton General Chamber of Commerce (a foreign run organization) investigated the matter and determined that the acceptable amount a rice ship should pay to enter the port and to procure the necessary chops was Spanish $1,189.50. On average, it was found that a typical rice ship saved Spanish $2,566 on the normal port fees so it was a significant advantage.[106]

After secretly obtaining a load of rice in the delta, smugglers were granted permission to go upriver, where they unloaded the rice and purchased return cargos such as tea, silk and porcelain. Some private traders such as the American firms Edward Carrington & Co. out of Providence and Perkins & Co. from Boston made a regular business from the rice trade. After the rice was unloaded in Whampoa captains purchased export cargos. They could, in fact, purchase much more than their ship could normally carry because it was not necessary to put all the goods in the holds (depending on the weather). The decks, cabins and gangways could all be filled with merchandise because the excess would be transferred to the smuggling vessels at Lintin.

Smugglers needed just enough rice to fill a couple of the larger ships among them so those vessels could go upriver, procure the tea and other products for backhauls and unload the excess that they did not need onto the smaller vessels at Lintin. This explains why private traders who owned several ships, such as Perkins & Co., had some ships hauling rice and others smuggling contraband. The rice ships helped the others obtain their backhauls so they could compete effectively in the contraband trade.

Because the import cargos of the rice ships were not balanced with their export cargos, there was no fear of the Hoppos claiming that they were purchasing more than they had brought, and charging additional duties to make up the difference. After unloading the rice, the foreigners could pile as much as they could on the decks without its falling into the water or making the ship unstable. After the excess cargo was unloaded in the delta, the rice ships sailed back to Manila, Batavia or Singapore and exchanged their cargos for more rice. The opium ships then went back to India to exchange their cargos for more opium.

The following extracts from correspondence between the Perkins' house in Canton and Captain R. B. Forbes of the *Nile* shows more precisely how this trade was carried out.

> Canton, 9 April 1825
>
> Our object in sending the Brig over [to Manila from Lintin] is to obtain a cargo of rice & paddy, of the former article you will receive enough with what you have already on board to half load your vessel, & fill up with paddy; it will be necessary that the vessel should appear perfectly full of Rice & paddy when she comes to Whampoa, & you just manage to put the other goods that your brother may wish to send in the state rooms, sturage & Cabin, so that the whole of the vessel with the exception of the forecastle, sturage & Cabin shall when you reach Whampoa appear perfectly full of Rice & paddy.[107]
>
> Lintin, 21 December 1826
>
> . . . as soon as the [ship] Houqua arrives you will receive from her 1,000–1,200; peculs of Rice & Paddy, also the quantity that now remains on board the ####, & send for a pilot & proceed to Whampoa forthwith . . . before you start for Whampoa, You will recollect to stow the Rice & Paddy you may receive so as to make the vessel appear full at the main hatch.[108]

Forbes and Perkins continued shipping rice cargos into Canton in the 1830s, and Perkins used rice to cover up his opium dealings.[109]

The rice trade continued to form a link between the legitimate and contraband trades until the end of the Canton System. In reference to the 1830s, Downing writes: 'The importation of rice under the present regulations is the vehicle of many underhand transactions, by which the revenue from foreign commerce is materially lessened'.[110] All this activity was common knowledge among the foreigners in China and openly published in newspapers for everyone to read. Williams' states in 1863 that:

> The bonus of rice-laden ships led to the transhipment of merchandise into large vessels entering port from the anchorages at Lintin and Cumsing-moon, and taking in rice from stationary store-ships there, and going to Whampoa as rice ships.[111]

Despite all this illegal activity going on in the delta, we should not assume that, from time to time, the Hoppos and governors-general did not at least try to address the problems. As was shown in chapters 2 and 6, they did indeed launch many campaigns downriver to put a stop to the collusions between officials and smugglers. And governors-general occasionally arrested culprits and severely punished them as examples to others and as a sign to superiors that they were doing their jobs.

USING CORRUPTION TO CONTROL CORRUPTION

After the East India companies ceased their operations in Canton, the governor-general tried to withdraw the privilege of allowing foreign flag boats to sail between Whampoa and Canton without stopping at the tollhouses. He argued that this had been a privilege granted to the companies and not to private individuals.[112] The genius of this tolerance, of course, was that it provided a means by which the Hoppos could reach into the hearts and minds of the individual officers of the companies. By keeping the policy unofficial, it could be rescinded at any time as a tool of persuasion.

This privilege was not unlike the tolerance Hoppos and governors-general showed Chinese officers who were involved in connivances. Periodic crackdowns of corruption were effective ways to remove or punish recalcitrant officers and employing tolerance was an effective way to reward loyalty, obedience and diligence, albeit at the expense of internal decay. Despite his intensions, however, the governor-general found it very difficult to remove the flag boat privilege after its being in effect for 135 years.

One of the reasons why some of these remedial efforts failed was because the government was trying to use a corrupt system to eliminate corruption, which was not going to work. Local officials were much more likely to internalise the smuggling into their own networks so they could control it and continue to profit from it, which is exactly what happened. To solve the problem, the system itself had to change. Such fundamental initiatives, however, had to come from Beijing.

The Hoppos and governors-general could only refine the system here and there to make things operate more smoothly.[113] Some of their remedial efforts were well-intended, whereas others were half-hearted attempts that were merely done to give superiors the impression that everything was under control. Without exception, however, none of the policies that were initiated before 1835 (including those that were pointed out in chapter 6) had a scope broad enough to curb the advancement of smuggling.

BEIJING CONSIDERS LEGALIZING OPIUM

By the early 1830s, the outflow of silver was putting severe strain on administrative budgets to the point that Chinese officials in both Canton and Beijing began considering legalizing the opium trade as a means of curbing it, on the one hand, and taxing it on the other. The government could generate new revenues from its sale, and it was suggested that the trade could be controlled if the distribution and use of opium were tightly regulated. At the heart of these discussions, of course, was the silver problem. Many suggestions were put forth to limit the amount of opium purchases to one-third silver, or to only allow bartering where opium was exchange for other goods.[114]

In this new environment where officials in both Beijing and Canton were now more open in considering alternative measures of controlling the contraband, a very accurate and comprehensive report was handed to the emperor of the extent of smuggling and effects it was having on the empire.[115] After better understanding the situation, and after realizing the large number of officials who were involved in the smuggling, it was decided that controlling it was impossible. Legalization would only lead to more problems and would not solve the silver crisis. The emperor then began sending a series of edicts to Canton to put an end to the opium trade.[116]

THE CRACKDOWN BEGINS

In 1835, serious efforts were made by Beijing that for the first time begin to address the extensive problems connected to smuggling. Some of the orders that followed had been sent to Canton many times in the past with minimal effect. But now that Beijing was better informed of the situation and with the silver crisis providing a new catalyst for reform, the court was determined to rein in the abuses. The following extract is a translation from an edict that the Hoppo received from the governor-general and forwarded to the *Hong* merchants:

> Instructions also are given to the tungche of Macao, for him immediately to give strict orders to the pilots, the compradors, and so forth that they may obey, and act accordingly. Hereafter, they are imperatively required to adhere to the regulations established by memorial to the emperor: they are to be careful in piloting vessels; and they must not unlawfully combine (with foreigners) to smuggle; if the barbarian ships go out or come in contrary to the regulations, or if the barbarians clandestinely go about in small boats to places along the coast, rambling about the villages and farms, the said pilots are to be assuredly brought with strictness to an investigation: if there be any sale or purchase of contraband goods, or stealthy smuggling of goods liable to duty, and the compradors do not report according to the truth, they also are to be immediately punished with rigor; and are decidedly to have no indulgence shown to them.[117]

The events that followed this edict and that preceded the First Opium War have been given extensive coverage in studies in the past so there is no need to repeat them here. We will rather briefly point out a few important developments that changed the course of the trade.

Orders were given for the construction of boats that could outrun the fast crabs and by the end of 1836 the government had a number of them in service conducting raids all along the river capturing smugglers with contraband and silver. Foreigners with no ships in China were ordered to go to Macao, and foreign agents who had been providing the brokering services for the contraband trade were listed by name and ordered to leave Canton.[118] Edicts were issued forbidding foreigners from sailing their passage- or mail-boats between Macao and Canton (which were now a regular sight). The smuggling harbours in the delta were ordered closed, and all foreigners wanting to trade with China were ordered to either come upriver to Whampoa or leave. Foreigners conducting illegal commerce in other ports along China's coast were ordered to cease, and if the perpetrators continued they were to be captured, prosecuted and severely punished.

In response to the crackdowns, foreigners began looking for a safe harbour somewhere along China's coast where they could retreat if things became too intense. After investigating many locations, it was decided that Hong Kong would be a good place to move. This harbour was not new, of course, because it was already being used for clandestine trade and well known as a safe refuge against storm. The new surveys of the coast merely confirmed that a safer or more convenient place could not be found. In 1837, the Lintin Fleet began removing to Hong Kong when government patrols made it difficult to remain at Lintin or other depots like Cumsingmoon.[119]

These new initiatives and intensified focus on quashing foreign smuggling were probably great diversions for the junk traders to earn quick profits. The difficulties that foreign smugglers were now encountering in the delta would have given the junks a strategic advantage in the opium market in China. But owing to a lack of documentation, we have no way of knowing how they were affected. Perhaps a look at the opium leaving Singapore aboard Chinese junks might shed some light on this issue.

SUMMARY

There are many reasons why the contraband trade became so deeply embedded in the delta. First, many officials and individuals on all levels of society, in both Macao and Canton, were eager to become involved in such a lucrative trade. Portuguese officials were involved in opium smuggling in Macao, as were some of the Chinese Christians. It was relatively easy to find a Chinese buyer or seller for almost any type of contraband, and customs officers were easily bribed so merchandise passed 'undetected'. Because of the ease of marketing opium, it established a firm market in China in the mid-eighteenth century and standard fees and procedures encouraged it to grow.

Portuguese in Macao used their special privileges to profit personally from the contraband trade, which gave it another channel along which to expand. Competition between Portuguese and other private traders together with the preferential rates for opium in Macao and aboard Portuguese bottoms helped to keep prices down in the late-eighteenth century. As other smuggling depots were established at Lintin, Cumsingmoon and other places and with the crackdowns on opium in 1814, Macao lost its strategic advantage and trade was diverted to these harbours. Competition kept prices low, which encouraged greater consumption. If officials in Whampoa or Amoy wanted to benefit from the contraband trade, they had to offer fees and conditions that were competitive with those in the lower-delta.

The compradors, Macao pilots and fast crabs competed with each other for the privilege of hauling contraband between the delta and Whampoa, and the tidewaiters on the quay, and compradors and Hoppomen stationed next to the ships all competed among themselves. Competition normalised fees (bribes) and standard procedures gave the trafficking regularity, stability and security. The trade in contraband was almost as predictable as, and, in some ways, less risky than the legitimate trade in tea, which attracted more traders and investors.

The rampant rise of piracy in the delta in the late 1790s diverted attention from the smuggling problem. Under the guise of ridding the region of pirates, the Portuguese in Macao used their patrol boats and escorts to protect and advance their opium trade. Chinese merchants and officials in Macao and along the coast worked hand-in-hand with the Portuguese to carry this out.

On the other side of the equation, opium was not illegal in many ports in the eighteenth and early nineteenth centuries, which made it easy for smugglers to rationalise its trade, despite China's ban on it. It was well known that two sets of laws governed the commerce in China: one of official policy and the other of local practice. For the Chinese government to be serious about forbidding opium, those two laws needed to merge, and, for all practical purposes, that did not happen until 1835.

In the minds of company officials, the tea and porcelain trades were too important to be allowed to diminish or go to ruin for the sake of a lack of silver. There was not enough of a deterrent in Canton or the delta to discourage private traders or government officials from benefiting from the trafficking, so pressures of supply and demand for silver encouraged the continual expansion of the opium trade. In this way, the growth of opium trade went hand-in-hand with the growth of legitimate trade in tea.

The preferential treatment of rice shipments also contributed to the advancement of contraband. Smugglers in the delta could avoid the high fees at Whampoa by taking in rice at Lintin. After making a profit on the rice sales in Canton, they could then purchase backhaul goods to cover the cost of their return passages. All these factors helped to keep opium prices competitive.

This blending of legal and illegal trade, the willingness of Chinese on all levels to accommodate smugglers, the uniformity in connivance fees and practices, and the need for large quantities of silver to exchange for tea, all contributed to a flourishing opium trade. Because the illicit trade supported the legitimate trade, it was easy to justify or, at least, to tolerate. As a result, the efforts that the government made to stamp out smuggling before 1835 were always too little and too late, and often ill-matched to the situation.

We now turn to other important factors that were influencing the commerce, namely the Macao trade, junk trade, capital market and commission merchants.

C H A P T E R   E I G H T

MACAO TRADE, JUNK TRADE, CAPITAL MARKET AND COMMISSION MERCHANTS

IT HAS BEEN SHOWN IN past studies that Macao was in many ways an extension of the Canton market.[1] Chinese and Portuguese documents that have survived from the eighteenth century show how the two ports were operating closely with each other on administrative levels.[2] But owing to a lack of historical data, little has been said of market influences. With information that has recently emerged from European archives, we can now begin to show more clearly the relationship governing these cities. Because Macao was so closely connected with the junk trade, capital market and commission merchants, we will deal with all of these aspects in this chapter.

In many respects, the entire delta from Macao to Canton operated as one huge market with many variables within it. On one level, the Macao trade, junk trade and foreign trade were independent of each other with different sets of regulations governing them. But when we look at the capital market, commission merchants and inputs and outputs of each, the distinctions between them disappear and they become one. All parts were intricately dependent on each other and would cease to operate effectively without the inputs from the others.

THE MACAO TRADE

Macao had a significant impact on the environment in Canton, because much of the trade there was a direct extension of the market upriver.[3] When the Portuguese ships arrived in Macao, Chinese merchants from Canton came downriver to buy their goods. In the last chapter, we saw how Chetqua came to Macao to purchase Portuguese cargos and other *Hong* merchants were doing the same.

Merchants often assigned one of their sons or partners to take care of the Macao side of things, while other partners in the *hongs* were assigned to the junk trade or to the Chinese interior to order goods and make purchases. Other partners in the houses would then take care of the foreign trade. These were the four parts to all of the major *hongs*: Macao trade, junk trade, interior trade and foreign trade.

Macao maintained a separate set of standards that gave it an advantage in some products. Reduced duties, favourable exchange rates and the use of different units of measurement compensated for the cost of transporting the merchandise to and from Canton. In fact, if the city had not had these advantages, the trade would simply be diverted upriver. It was not until smuggling depots began to appear in the delta that other places could compete with the advantages in Macao.

The Dutch were constantly monitoring the price of coarse and fine goods going into Macao. The units of measurement for those products varied from 150 to 100 catties per picul, respectively, whereas the same products might all be measured at 100 catties per picul in Canton. The exchange rate for silver in Macao was also different from Canton, which gave money an advantage there. The different standards in Macao kept downward pressure on prices. In the mid-1760s, the Dutch found prices 'from all wares' to be 52 percent lower in Macao (but the different units need to be considered).[4]

Since the late-1680s, Macao had its own customhouse and Hoppo who supervised and taxed the trade.[5] In the 1760s, the duties charged to Portuguese ships were 6 percent less than those paid by ships that went to Whampoa. The preferential treatment gave them an advantage over their European competitors. The Canton junks and Spanish vessels from Manila also enjoyed the same preferential rate, so the Portuguese were not without competition.[6]

As a result of these benefits, the Dutch found it to be more advantageous to channel some of their tin and pepper through Macao. They hired Portuguese ships to carry the product from Batavia rather than send them on company ships. Pepper cost only 0.04 taels per picul to be secretly shipped upriver so there was much smuggling of that product through Macao.[7]

The Hoppos eventually became aware of some of the effects that Macao was having on Canton and tried to equalise the two markets. In the early 1780s, changes were legislated that aimed to put Macao ships on the same footing with those at Whampoa. By this time, there were also Armenian ships operating out of Macao and some Portuguese ships were freighted by Chinese so the trade was not all necessarily 'Portuguese'.[8] After the changes were made, foreigners in both places were to 'pay the same duties', which continued until Macao became a free port in 1836.

It is not certain how extensive the changes were or if the higher duties affected the flow of goods between the two cities. Some items were, in fact, already on an equal footing, so the changes did not affect all products. Macao continued to have a more favourable exchange rate on silver and different units of measurement, so these initiatives probably did not 'equalise' the two ports as was hoped.[9]

Portuguese supercargoes regularly went upriver to Canton while their ships were lying at Macao. They bought or consigned their export cargos with the Chinese merchants and had the goods shipped downriver.[10] Neither the imports nor the exports were double taxed in Macao or Canton, so the only additional fees were the transport costs up and downriver.

In 1772, for example, the Dutch bought the Portuguese ship *S. Simão* to replace the *Rynsburgh*, which sank off the South China coast.[11] The *S. Simão* was re-manned and re-outfitted according to VOC standards and then renamed the *Herstelder*. The fact that the ship was registered in Macao caused much confusion between the customhouses as to where the port fees and duties were to be paid. The Hoppo in Macao understandably did not want to lose the revenues from the ship. He complained to the Hoppo and governor-general in Canton that once the ship left the port there would be only ten Portuguese ships remaining, which he felt represented too great a reduction in duties.

Officials in Canton did not want to cause trouble with Macao, but neither did they want to arouse the suspicions of officials in Beijing. They were apprehensive that the court might view this transfer of the *Herstelder* from one port to another as an attempt to divert funds from the emperor into local hands. After several weeks of correspondence and much consternation between Macao and Canton, it was decided that the ship should go to Whampoa. Macao had lost out, and the *Herstelder*'s port fees and duties were paid at Canton.[12] As far as junks in the delta were concerned, they were allowed shelter in Macao's inner harbour, but operated out of Canton.

THE JUNK TRADE

The junk cargos made up a significant proportion of the overall volume of trade in Canton. There are 37 ocean-going junks listed in the foreign records as frequenting the port in the 1760s, but not all were based there. The Swedish and Dutch records show that in the 1760s and early 1770s, there were probably from 27 to 35 junks operating each year out of Canton.

Plate 12 shows the names of 28 of these junks, which the Swedes recorded in 1768. They operated out of five different factories, and we know from other sources that there were other junks and junk factories besides these.[13] The references are often vague, scattered and far from complete but nonetheless suggest that 30 or more junks were probably stationed there consistently until at least the 1840s, operating out of nine junk factories.[14]

Ocean-going junks were usually of at least 150 tons capacity, but some were as large as 1,000 tons. Most of the Canton junks appear to have been in the neighbourhood of 250 tons, with an average cargo capacity of 2,500 piculs. With this information, we can estimate what percentage they may have carried of the entire trade in the port.[15]

Tables 8 and 9 show estimates of the total exports from Canton for six years. Most of these figures were taken from the linguists' reports, which were extracted from the Hoppos' books and thus reflect the actual exports (excluding contraband). The numbers of junks and their cargos were estimated according to data collected from Dutch and Swedish records, and the numbers of Portuguese ships in Macao were taken from Do Vale. The Spanish vessels going to Manila were often small (sampans) and because their numbers and sizes are still unclear those cargos have not been included. The VOC cargos are estimates based on figures from 1763, but are fairly reliable because each of the VOC ships was loaded similarly according to detailed plans (Plates 14 and 15).

Table 8 Estimated Exports from Canton in 1763–1764, 1766–1769[16]

Bulk Goods by the Picul	*1763*	*1764*	*1766*	*1767*	*1768*	*1769*
EIC	58,297	79,959	101,598	48,243	77,329	100,568
English Country	6,493	–	–	21,507	21,129	31,305
CFI	20,432	19,031	23,488	21,222	23,897	22,331
French Country	–	–	–	–	1,336	–
DAC	28,487	23,815	12,562	25,091	12,456	11,903
SOIC	25,746	13,646	14,494	27,368	12,463	25,355
Estimated VOC	32,268	37,700	37,700	37,700	37,700	37,700
Est. Portuguese	25,000	32,500	30,000	27,500	27,500	25,000
Est. Canton Junks	75,000	75,000	70,000	75,000	75,000	67,500
Total Piculs	271,723	281,651	289,842	283,631	288,810	321,662
Comparison of Percentages between EIC and Junk Cargos Each Year						
Junks	0.28	0.27	0.24	0.26	0.26	0.21
EIC	0.21	0.28	0.35	0.17	0.27	0.31

Table 9 Distribution of Canton Exports in 1763–1764, 1766–1769[17]

Bulk Goods by the Picul	*Six-Year Total Piculs*	*Percent of Total Trade*	*Total Vessels*	*Average Piculs*
EIC	465,994	26.82	70	6,657
English Country	80,434	4.63	14	5,745
CFI	130,401	7.51	18	7,245
French Country	1,336	0.08	1	1,336
DAC	114,314	6.58	10	11,431
SOIC	119,072	6.85	10	11,907
Estimated VOC	220,768	12.71	23	9,599
Est. Portuguese	167,500	9.64	67	2,500
Est. Canton Junks	437,500	25.18	175	2,500
Total	1,737,319	100.00	388	4,478

The EIC made up about 27 percent of the total volume for the six years. For most of the Canton era the English dominated trade, but, in the 1760s, junk cargos were not far behind at 25 percent. Thus, in terms of volume, the junks were just as important as the EIC. The Swedish, Danish and French companies each made up about 7 percent, and the Dutch about 13 percent, making a total of 34 percent of exports. Each of these companies and the junks played a different role in the development of commerce that had an effect on the outcome. Macao trade also made up 10 percent, without including Spanish exports.

It is important to point out that most of what we have learned about the China trade from history books in the past comes from analyzing less than half of the factors influencing the commerce, with a strong emphasis on a quarter, the EIC. This outcome, of course, is the result of there being few Chinese records that have survived. We have no choice but to use foreign records to restructure the history, and the EIC archive is the only collection that covers the entire 140 years. But before we can arrive at a well-balanced history of what happened, we will need to consider all parts, especially the junks.

It was not until the Americans started going to Canton in 1784 that private trade began to rival junk trade. The figures that have been assembled of the total American cargos vary widely, but we can make a rough comparison with the junk cargos. If we use 75,000 piculs (about 10 million pounds) as a yearly standard for the junks, we see that their total volume surpassed the American exports from 1784 to 1805, and surpassed or rivalled the American trade each year from 1805 to 1833.[18]

Like the Portuguese ships in Macao, the junks consigned space in the holds to foreigners so the cargos were not all necessarily 'Chinese'. Foreigners paid all the import duties, lightering fees and labour costs themselves, but the duties in Canton were paid at the discounted Chinese junk rate. The preferential treatment gave the junks an advantage over their foreign competitors.[19]

In the 1760s, for example, the Swedish supercargoes arranged for sandalwood and mahogany to be shipped from Batavia to Canton on the junk *Sihing*. Plate 5 shows the fees and duties they were charged for arranging this service. The Chinese factory in Canton charged 5 percent commission on the value of the cargo, and Batavia charged another 5 percent. The freight rates for sandalwood were 0.72 taels (Spanish $1) per picul and for mahogany 0.6 taels per picul.

Plate 8 shows a Dutch consignment of porcelain aboard the Canton junk *Maansand* bound for Batavia, and Plate 9 shows a junk flying a Dutch flag. The VOC regularly commissioned Canton junks to haul Dutch cargos to and from Batavia. In fact, two or three of the junk cargos included in Tables 8 and 9 should rightfully be added to the VOC figures for each year, because they belonged to the Dutch. Unfortunately, we do not have figures to show the exact amounts.

In 1761, the Dutch found that the freight rates for goods shipped to Batavia aboard Canton junks amounted to an average of 12 percent of the value of the merchandise.[20] By 1769, they reported that it was cheaper to ship merchandise such as zinc to Batavia via junks or Macao (Portuguese) ships, rather than in European bottoms. In that year, however, the Dutch were forced to ship the merchandise on VOC bottoms owing to a lack of available cargo space for rent.[21] This shows that the junks were indeed loading to full capacity, as would be expected.

Some of the Canton junk imports from Southeast Asia were for the indigenous Chinese market, whereas other imports were used directly or indirectly for the export trade. Junks carried various types of wood and fragrances for the making of furniture and incense, different types of herbs and drugs, betel nuts, dried meats and fish, edible birds' nests, sharks' fins and skins, and trepans. Most of these items were for the Chinese market.

Other products, such as rattan, arrack and sago, were used in foreign trade. Foreigners in Canton purchased these items in huge quantities for the stowing of their cargos and consumption by their crews. Porcelain was often packed in sago that had been brought to Canton by the junks.[22] Tin and lead that junks imported were also used for packaging tea, giving rise to a huge demand for those two items in China. Inland wholesalers ordered tin every year as did the tinsmiths in Canton. Most of the tea that went abroad on foreign ships was packed into lead-lined wooden chests, which meant that huge quantities of sheet-lead were required every year as well. Tin was also used in the making of export items and in pewterware.

Junks imported wax and wax oils, which the foreigners used in huge quantities for candles and lanterns. Foreigners purchased animal hides that junks carried to repair their rigging. Dyes, paints and lacquers were imported to make export paintings, lacquerware and many different novelty items. These products were also used to repaint, repair and refurbish the foreign ships as they lay at anchor in Whampoa Roads. And import ivory from elephant tusks made novelty items for the export market.

The foreign export trade depended heavily on these junk imports. *Hong* merchants needed to make sure enough of each item arrived so they had sufficient quantities for packing the exports. In the eighteenth century, sago was widely used by all foreigners to pack porcelain, and a lack of that product could hold up porcelain sales. A lack of lead could limit the amount of tea that could be exported (wooden chests were durable and could be stacked in many layers but they needed to be lined with lead to prevent contamination); a lack of tin could affect the *Hong* merchants' dealings with the inland tea merchants, who needed that metal to make canisters to send the tea to Canton (tin canisters were light and protected the tea from contamination better than other containers); and a lack of rattan to place in between the layers of tea chests could affect tea sales as well (rattan was thin, flexible, strong, and had no aromatic qualities that could infect the tea).

It was important to have the precise dunnage materials. Rattan, for example, only took up half an inch of space in between each layer of chests. With a cargo of eight layers, such as is shown in Plate 15, the total space used by rattan dunnage was about four inches. If a thicker material was substituted that needed three-quarters of an inch, for example, then the dunnage would take up an additional two inches. If that happened, then the chests on the top layer in each ship would have to be shortened by that amount. If we multiply the two inch loss in volume by several hundred chests that were needed in the top layers of each ship, we see a significant reduction in the payload.

Rattan also produced a profit in its own sale after the ships were unloaded in Europe. If the merchants used dunnage that was the same thickness but less marketable, then this also reduced the value of the payload. The same was true with poor quality lead that had to be cut thicker to stay in one piece. It took up more space in each tea chest, which reduced payload, and it increased the duties that had to be paid according to the gross weight of the chests; the substituting of sago for a less suitable product such as chaff or straw increased the damage to porcelain and lowered foreign profits owing to those products being less saleable. If any substituting of dunnage resulted in a reduction in normal payload profits, then the foreigners would demand compensation from the merchants or threaten to switch to another house that could supply the materials they wanted.

This connection between Southeast Asian products and the Canton export trade made it essential for large merchant houses to maintain their own fleets of junks. It was also important for them to have agents in Southeast Asia buying up these materials so they could be assured of sufficient quantities when the junks arrived. Large houses had their own agents in China's interior ordering and purchasing the tea, porcelain and silk they needed, and those persons forwarded information back to Canton about the amount of tin that inland suppliers demanded each year.[23] Tin from Palembang was credited directly to inland tea purchases so those imports also affected export profits. Because of this connection, it was important for *Hong* merchants to keep close tabs on tin going to other Chinese ports as well. Many of those imports were also advanced to the inland dealers.[24]

The Canton junks were financed by many different persons, who were privately investing in the capital market in China.

THE CAPITAL MARKET

Canton had a lively private capital market that was limited only by customary practices and the supply and demand of the market. It was illegal for Chinese to borrow money from foreigners and some of the companies forbade their officers from giving loans to Chinese, but those restrictions did not prevent a market from developing. Financial transactions were often done privately, and the growth of the trade would have been greatly hindered without them.

Some directors feared that companies could encounter adverse effects on prices and terms if officers were allowed to privately invest in the trade. Chinese merchants might agree to lower prices or greater quantities if they were offered preferential private loans on the side. Although this might increase the companies' profits in the short term, the long-term disadvantages of such transactions far outweighed the advantages.

Chinese merchants could persuade foreign officers to accept a higher price on company exports or less desirable commodities by giving them better prices and superior products in their private trade; by privately extending them low-interest or interest-free credit; or by offering them a kickback on each picul of merchandise they contracted for the company. Directors in Europe were so concerned about the negative effects of such arrangements that officers were instructed to examine closely the private chests of captains, supercargoes and all crew members of ships before they left Whampoa. Private trade was allowed, but it was usually closely monitored and regulated so it would not harm the companies' interests.

As is often the case with regulations, there were ways round them. Private traders were eager to help anyone invest their capital in Canton or Macao. Plate 3, for example, shows the debts of the *Hong* merchant Monqua (Cai Wenguan 蔡文官) in 1797 and among the debtors are private English traders, Muslims, Parsees, Armenians, and others. Plate 6 shows a money transaction in 1798 between Armenians (in Java and Macao) and the Dutch in China. Many French, Spanish and Portuguese merchants carried on extensive private transactions in Canton and Macao.

It was impossible for companies to keep their employees from making these transactions if they had a mind to do so. In desperation, the directors of large companies often bound their officers to solemn oaths and then hoped their consciences would keep them focused on company interests.[25] Of course, this would only work with those who prided themselves on their integrity.

Not all foreign companies were against their officers participating in this capital market. In fact, the SOIC and the DAC used 'bottomry bonds' (*yangli* 洋利, also called 'respondentia') regularly to finance voyages. Those companies accepted bonds from anyone who wanted to invest, including officers of other companies, Portuguese in Macao, other private traders in China, and Chinese merchants (see Plate 39).

Bottomry was a means of credit widely used in the eighteenth century by all traders, including the Chinese. It was a combination of a simple insurance policy and business loan. The person advancing the funds (the insurer) assumed all risks at sea of the vessel and cargo they insured. Unlike an insurance policy, however, where the insured party pays a premium and only receives reimbursement if a claim is filed, in a bottomry bond the principle is advanced and nothing is paid if a claim is filed (providing the loss equaled or exceeded the amount insured).

The latter stipulation made bottomry different from a business loan, which had to be repaid regardless of any loss incurred. If the insured vessel arrived safely at its destination, both the principal on the bond and the interest came due within a specified period that varied widely according to the agreement. In a bond on a voyage where a vessel was insured from the time it left port to the time it returned, the bond usually came due within one to three months after it arrived. This delay gave the insured party time to sell some of the cargo to pay off the loan.

Bottomry rates for foreign ships (including Portuguese ships) bound for Southeast Asia or India ranged from as little as 16 percent per voyage to as much as 40 percent. These rates were already firmly established before the Canton trade began, and they varied according to the port of destination. This made good sense because some routes were more dangerous than others. Of course, the level of experience of the captain and crew and the seaworthiness of the vessels played a role in the safety of a voyage, but those factors were not taken into consideration in Canton. The type of cargo that was being shipped was also ignored.[26]

The Ostend Company, Portuguese traders in Macao and Spanish traders in Manila frequently depended on bottomry bonds to finance voyages.[27] The EIC also issued bonds to private traders going to China.[28] Thus, there were a lot of transactions going on each year that others in Canton had no knowledge of.

Unlike foreign ships, junk bottomry rates did not vary according to their destination (except for Manila). The bonds were usually set at 40 percent per voyage regardless of the destination which suggests junks were considered more hazardous than foreign ships. At least 24 of the 37 Canton junks mentioned in the foreign records in the 1760s took out bottomry bonds from foreigners.[29]

Because insurers could lose both principal and interest in a bottomry contract, they tended to spread their capital over several vessels. The Swedish supercargo Grill, for example, regularly issued bonds to a dozen or more junks each year during the 1760s, and his colleagues were doing the same. Spreading his risks helped Grill recoup the inevitable losses he incurred.

In 1766 the junk *Hing Tay* (*Hengtai* 恒泰) burned in Cochin China and the junk *Sihing* (*Ruixingzhou* 瑞興艚) was lost at sea. Grill had issued bonds on both vessels. Because these two junks did not return to port, the insured parties were not responsible for repayment, and as a result, these two contracts have survived in the Swedish archives (Plates 10 and 11).[30]

Both of these bottomry bonds carried an interest rate (premium) of 40 percent (*si suanxi* 肆算息) on the principal. The documents do not state the period they covered, but Grill's personal account books show that they were issued for a 'single voyage', which could last anywhere from eight to eleven months. The insured party had two months over and above this period in which to repay the principal with interest, so the total duration of the contracts ranged from about ten to thirteen months. Interest was due, regardless of whether the voyage took eight or eleven months, so this was not an 'annual', but rather a 'voyage' rate. If the junk was delayed longer than the eleven months, then the loan could be extended with more interest added accordingly.

Both contracts had a co-signer, Hongsia (Yan Xiangshe 顏享舍). Hongsia was one of the most prominent junk traders in Canton in the 1760s, and shows up regularly in the records sponsoring half of the Canton junk voyages to Southeast Asia. Hongsia took out bottomry bonds regularly with the Swedes (and probably others) and his Yan family relatives, who ran one of the large *hongs* in Canton, secured those loans. But a co-signer was only security against the insured party failing to pay after the junk returned safely to port.

Other *Hong* merchants were securing or taking out junk bottomry bonds in the 1760s as well, such as Poankeequa (Pan Qiguan), Semqua (Qiu Kun), Jauqua (Cai Yuguan 蔡玉官), Monqua (Cai Wenguan), Chetqua (Chen Jieguan) and Giqua (Ye Yiguan 葉義官). And sometimes the contracts were made without co-signers. Plate 7 is a bottomry agreement between Grill and Ma Guohu (馬國護) for junk *Samkonghing* (*Sanguangxing* 三廣興) sailing to Vietnam in 1763, and Ma is the only one who signed.[31]

It was common for foreigners to pool their funds and write one contract with a Chinese merchant for several junks. Individuals in Europe were also investing in these transactions, via correspondents in China. The amounts going to each junk had to be clearly spelled out so there was no confusion if a claim was later filed.

The frequency with which these loans were arranged with the foreigners in the 1760s (the years for which we have data) shows that there was clearly a lack of indigenous capital to finance the junks. Considering that the *Hong* merchants were the owners and operators of most of the Canton junks and that most of those houses were continually in need of investment capital, this outcome is understandable. But that did not prevent Chinese merchants from giving loans to foreigners to finance their return passages to Europe. Even though this practice may have strained the capital reserves of the *hongs*, aiding the foreigners in financing their trade helped maintain loyalties and patronage.[32]

Bottomry bonds for a single passage (rather than a complete voyage) were structured differently. Plate 25 shows the settling of a bottomry contract between the SOIC and the merchant Le Waqua (Li Huaguan 李華官). In January 1761, Waqua gave the Swedes 695 Mexican piasters at 25 percent interest to help finance the voyage of the ship *Sophia Albertina*. It arrived safely at its destination in Gothenburg so when the next SOIC ship showed up in China with news of the safe arrival of the *Sophia Albertina*, Waqua was repaid (January 1764) the principle plus interest (total: 867$^1/_2$ piasters). He made 8$^1/_3$ percent annual interest on his money so this was clearly a preferential loan he had given to earn the favour of the Swedes. He could have made two to four times that amount had he loaned the money to someone in Canton.[33]

Waqua's role in the trade is not well understood, but he shows up in the Swedish records trading in silk and porcelain. We know he was not a *Hong* merchant, and we know that all trade and transactions with foreigners were supposed to go through the Co-hong, at this time, so this transaction had to be done privately. These are the types of arrangements that make it difficult to do meaningful commodity price comparisons in Canton, because high prices that were paid were often off-set by preferential agreements like this one.[34]

Plate 26 shows a bottomry contract between the DAC and the *Hong* merchant Ingsia (Yan Yingshe). The Danes borrowed money regularly from the Yan family to help finance voyages, in this case the ship *Cron Printzen af Danmarck*. In December 1764, Ingsia gave the Danes 1,000 taels at 30 percent interest. He was repaid the principle plus interest (total 1,300 taels) when the next DAC ship arrived in China (August 1766) with news of the *Cron Printzen af Danmarck's* safe arrival in Copenhagen. Ingsia made about 18 percent annual interest on his money (20 months). These types of loans were usually done secretly so that other foreigners and Chinese would not learn of them (see also Plate 39).[35]

In addition to bottomry bonds, there were many private business loans given in Canton and Macao as well. Plate 4 shows the DAC receiving money from Portuguese in 1765 and 1766 to finance company trade. The Danes borrowed 4,000 piasters each from Joachem Joseph and Mr. Miranda in Macao at 13 percent interest per annum and 16,000 piasters from Louis Martin at 15 percent interest. The total amount of 17,280 piasters was then given to Ingsia (Yan Yingshe), Schecqua (Chen Jieguan) and Samqua (Qiu Kun) in Canton. These were advances on the purchase of 800 chest of new Bohea tea in the next season. These types of transactions were very frequent in China and numerous individuals were involved in them, which was one of the important roles Macao played in the trade. All of the companies and many private traders were getting money in Macao from time to time to finance trade (see also Plate 38).

For long-term loans of one or more years, foreigners could usually obtain capital from other foreigners in China at about 10 to 12 percent annual interest, but sometimes it was a little higher (as in Plate 4). Some foreigners took out loans and then re-loaned those funds to Chinese merchants at 18 to 36 percent interest per annum, or issued a junk bottomry bond for 40 percent interest per voyage.[36] The continual strong demand for foreign capital kept interest rates high for Chinese (Plates 40 and 41).

Table 10 shows a private balance sheet of business loans (not bottomry) that two Swedish officers arranged in 1768 and 1769. The 'Debit' section shows the source of the funds. Most of the money was obtained from other foreigners (Portuguese or English) at 10 to 12 percent per year. The Swedish supercargoes Grill and Hahr's personal contributions (entries dated 1769.12.31) only amount to about 7.5 percent of the total. Portuguese in Macau provided most of the funds, with the Englishman Robert Gordon and the Chinese comprador Ava supplying the remainder. The 'Credit' section shows the Chinese merchants to whom the funds were distributed, which were all loaned at 20 percent interest per year. These figures represent a fraction of the total number of private transactions being conducted in Canton each year so one can imagine the enormous amount of money that was secretly changing hands.[37]

Table 10 Jean Abraham Grill and Jacob Hahr's Balance of Accounts, 1768–1769[38]

Debit

Date	*Name*	*Principal*	*Rate*	*Interest*	*Piasters*	*Taels*
1768.09.30	Ant. Joze da Costa	1,452.000	10%	14,520.000	15,972.000	11,819.280
1768.12.01*	Jernad Salgado	3,008.666	12%	361.050	3,369.716	2,493.776
1768.12.01*	Miranda da Sousa	4,029.576	12%	483.424	4,513.260	3,339.880
1768.12.08	Ava (comprador)	2,000.000	12%	240.000	2,240.000	1,657.600
1768.12.21	Ant. de Liger Correa	2,500.000	12%	300.000	2,800.000	2,072.000
1769.01.21*	Robert Gordon	5,226.480	12%	627.144	5,853.624	4,331.844
Subtotal*					34,749.120	25,714.380
1769.12.31*	Grill				1,396.454	1,033.494
1769.12.31*	Hahr				1,396.454	1,033.494
Total*					37,542.288	27,781.368
1769.09.30	Ant. Joze da Costa		10%		15,972.000	11,819.280
1769.12.01*	Jernad Salgado		12%		3,369.716	2,493.776
1769.12.01*	Miranda da Sousa		12%		4,513.260	3,339.880
1769.12.21	Ant. de Liger Correa		12%		2,800.000	2,072.000
Total Repaid*					26,655.236	19,724.936

Credit

Date	*Name*	*Principal*	*Rate*	*Interest*	*Piasters*	*Taels*
1768.12.08	Zey Hunqua	3,000.000	20%	600.000	3,600.000	2,664.000
1768.12.08	Zey Jauqua	3,000.000	20%	600.000	3,600.000	2,664.000
1768.12.11	[Tan] Konqua	1,000.000	20%	200.000	1,200.000	888.000
1768.12.13	Ngan Hingsia	5,000.000	20%	1,000.000	6,000.000	4,440.000
1768.12.15	Tan Tietqua	4,000.000	20%	800.000	4,800.000	3,552.000
1768.12.17	Zey Munqua	2,000.000	20%	400.000	2,400.000	1,776.000
1768.12.17	Lisanchong	2,000.000	20%	400.000	2,400.000	1,776.000
1768.12.18	Samqua	2,000.000	20%	400.000	2,400.000	1,776.000
1768.12.18*	Poankeyqua	9,285.240	20%	1,857.048	11,142.288	8,245.368
Total					37,542.288	27,781.368

(Continued on next page)

(Table 10 — *continued*)

Date	*Name*	*Principal*	*Rate*	*Interest*	*Piasters*	*Taels*
1769.12.08	Zey Hunqua		20%		3,600.000	2,664.000
1769.12.08	Zey Jauqua		20%		3,600.000	2,664.000
1769.12.13	Ngan Hingsia		20%		6,000.000	4,440.000
1769.12.15	Tan Tietqua		20%		4,800.000	3,552.000
1769.12.17	Zey Munqua		20%		2,400.000	1,776.000
1769.12.18*	Poankeyqua		20%		6,255.236	4,628.936
Total Received					26,655.236	19,724.936

*These numbers do not calculate exactly either because different exchange rates were used (0.72 or 0.74 taels per piaster) or because the interest rate was applied to the tael rather than to the piaster.

Key: Zey Hunqua (蔡), Zey Jauqua (蔡玉官), Tan Konqua (陳), Ngan Hingsia (顏英舍), Tan Tietqua (陳捷官), Zey Monqua (蔡文官), Lisanchong (李相公), Samqua (邱崑), Poankeyqua (潘啟官).

There are many references to interest rates being 1.5 to 3 percent per month (to the Chinese) for short-term business loans, or 18 to 36 percent per annum for long-term loans.[39] Plate 20 shows the DAC giving a four-month loan in 1762 of 12,000 taels at 6 percent interest (1.5 percent per month) to the two *Hong* merchants Svissia (Yan Ruishe) and Schecqua (Chen Jieguan, same as Tietqua in Table 10; see also Plates 40 and 41).

In the same year, the three security merchants for the Dutch admitted that Europeans had more protection for their money than the Chinese, which was why the Dutch could borrow funds for less interest. The merchants used this argument in their efforts to persuade the Dutch to loan them 150,000 taels at 1.5 percent interest per month rather than the 2 percent the Dutch wanted. But the demand of the market prevailed and they had to succumb to 2 percent per month or go without.[40] Later in the 1830s, the *Hong* merchants again admitted that they were dependent on foreign capital to finance the trade.[41]

As the trade continued to expand, there was a parallel growing need for all types of financial and brokering services, which led to the establishment of agents or commission merchants in China.

COMMISSION MERCHANTS

In order to provide some of these financial services, a group of private individuals set themselves up in Macao and Canton as brokers and agents. Some of these commission merchants developed vast networks of associates throughout Asia. They channelled a great deal of private money into the trade from investors throughout Asia, the Americas and Europe, and became the best source of quick capital in China.[42]

Commission merchants could arrange for the shipment of merchandise to China aboard junks, Portuguese ships from Macao, Spanish ships from Manila, East India companies' ships, and the myriad private vessels heading for China, including those of the French, English, Belgians, Prussians, Danes, Swedes, Muslims, Parsees, Armenians and Americans. Agents rented space in the holds, arranged for the purchase of goods and then contracted their sale with Chinese merchants in Canton. If there were insufficient funds to complete the transactions, they could also arrange a loan or bottomry contract. There was a well-established set of commission fees for all these services.[43]

Some of these commission merchants rented their own factories and houses in Canton and Macao, and traded with their own ships. Others simply rented rooms from other traders and paid for passage for themselves and their silver and cargo aboard other vessels. Until the late-eighteenth century, all brokers had to conduct some trade in order to be allowed to stay in China. They often charged 2 to 5 percent of the value of the cargo depending on the length of the contract, the services they were asked to perform and the amount of the investments.[44]

During years in which fewer ships arrived than expected, commission merchants helped to fill the gap in capital. Foreign trading companies went through major restructures, which affected the number of ships they sent to China; typhoons and contrary winds were more frequent in some years than others, which caused ships to founder or to layover a season in a different port. In 1745, for example, the two SOIC ships *Stockholm* and *Swerige* foundered on their way to China, and their non-appearance strained the finances of several *hongs*. These ships were large and could carry as much as four English or French ships so this was a great loss to the trade.

To add insult to injury the Europeans were at war with each other in this year ambushing and attacking ships throughout Asia, and hindering them from going to China. Then in September 1745 a typhoon devastated South China flooding all of the *hongs* and factories in Canton and causing many shipwrecks along the coast. When the Swedes returned to China, they found only one house, Suqua's (Chen Shouguan), to be on a firm footing.[45] Commission merchants filled in the gaps in difficult years, like 1744 and 1745, in order to keep merchants from failing.

Wars between Europeans brought many difficulties to the China trade, but provided new opportunities for these agents and brokers. In dangerous times, information about merchant vessels had to be tightly controlled to prevent their location being discovered. This led some foreigners to establish elaborate secret codes, which shows how serious the threats were to vessels sailing to China (Plate 33). The increased risks, however, were a boost to private financiers, who could command higher interest on their money.

When ships did not show up, Chinese were left with bulging inventories and no funds to meet obligations. And because war consumed silver reserves, ships that arrived in China during war years were often lacking sufficient capital to purchase return cargos. Some of these private commission merchants such as the Armenians, Muslims, Parsees and Americans operated outside the nationalistic companies and colonies so they were not usually embroiled in these conflicts. Because of their 'neutrality', they were often sought by everyone in China who needed a loan.

The Seven Years' War (1756–63) provides a good example of how war affected the China trade. In these years, Suiqua's (Cai Ruiguan) house accumulated large debts when the French ships did not arrive. Poankeequa's (Pan Qiguan) Manila trade was interrupted when the English attacked the Spanish there and occupied the place from 1762 to 1764. Hunqua, Monqua and Chetqua were forced to pay higher interest on their loans because of a lack of silver coin arriving in China.[46]

The war drained the EIC of silver making it difficult for supercargoes in the early 1760s to get enough money for the advances needed for tea orders. The depleted silver supplies from English and French ships in China gave the Dutch, Swedish and Danish companies a strategic advantage in negotiating loans and trade with their merchants.[47] By January 1764, the EIC had become so drained of funds from financing the war that supercargoes had to run to private financiers in Macao for an emergency loan of 72,000 Spanish dollars.[48] As we saw in the last chapter, this was the same time that the opium trade became more competitive and widespread.

Other war years were no different. In the early 1780s, Tsjonqua's (Cai Xiangguan 蔡相官) house, which was already in a poor state, was forced into bankruptcy when the VOC ships were lost to enemy attack and did not arrive in China.[49] As Plates 3 and 6 reveal, private commission merchants were often the only source of funding for *Hong* merchants and foreign companies during years when capital was short. An emergency loan could help them through difficult times, but resulted in some Chinese becoming deeply indebted to these financiers.

A few of these men became immensely wealthy, and important to the commerce. One prominent example is the Armenian Matheus Johannes, who arrived in Macao from India in 1761 with three other Armenians. Matheus provided a wide range of financial and commercial services to East India companies, private traders and Portuguese and Chinese merchants (Plate 38). He went to Canton each year conducting his own trade, and then moved to Macao in the off-season.[50]

By the time of Matheus's death in 1794 (in Canton), his fortune had grown much larger than the annual budget in Macao (which in 1797 was 215,390 Spanish dollars). Various branches of the Portuguese government had become so dependent on his funds that the city fathers refused to allow his estate to leave out of fear the economy would collapse. His brother Lazaro continued to stay in Macao taking care of unfinished business and, of course, trying to collect on his inheritance (Plate 6). From the many private persons, Chinese merchants, companies and institutions mentioned in Matheus's estate papers we can see that the family had a huge influence in Macao and Canton. His business involvements were certain to have had far-reaching effects on commerce in Manila, places in India and ports throughout Southeast Asia as well. And the influence did not end with commerce.[51]

In 1802, Lazaro and his family moved to Calcutta. His son, Johannes Lazaro, was born in Macao and was raised by two Chinese Christians who instructed him in the Chinese language. In Calcutta, Johannes had become so skilled in the language that the English government hired him as a translator. A few years later, Reverend Brown at the college at Fort William learned of his ability and hired Johannes to translate the New Testament into Chinese, which he laboured in for years. All of this happened because his enterprising uncle had ventured to Macao forty years earlier as an independent entrepreneur anxious to try his luck in the China trade.[52]

Other commission merchants were less successful, but also very important to the commerce. By the early nineteenth century, there were several *ghaut serangs*, who had set themselves up in Macao to service the trade. These men acted as labour brokers for Muslim sailors. They provided room and board when sailors were out of employment, loaned them money, and arranged work for them aboard any ship that was in need of them. By this time, the Portuguese government had relaxed its residency requirements so many private persons (such as the painter George Chinnery) were able to stay in Macao without having to conduct trade or go to Canton each year. All of these private brokers and agents filled gaps in the financial, commercial and labour markets in the delta that kept the trade moving forward.[53]

SUMMARY

The Portuguese trade in Macao and the junk trade in Canton were critical to the foreign trade, and thus must be included in any historical discourse on Canton's commerce. The junk exports made up 25 percent of the overall volume in Canton in the 1760s, and the Macao trade made up another 10 percent. The other smaller East India companies made up another 34 percent of the trade, and like the junks and Macao trade have been given little coverage in the historical literature.

Many of the commodities shipped on the Canton junks were used to make and package exports. Many of the Macao imports and exports were, in fact, a direct extension of the Canton market. The advantages of shipping goods into Macao and then 'smuggling' or transhipping them upriver kept constant pressure on prices in Canton, which kept the trade competitive. After smuggling depots emerged, Macao found it increasingly difficult to compete and as a result, lost much trade to those places.

The considerable differences between the interest rates offered to the Chinese and those available to foreigners suggest that the capital market in Canton was controlled to a large degree by the foreigners. Private loans to both Chinese and Europeans could influence the final prices of commodities, which led some companies to forbid employees' involvement in the capital market. Private trade aboard junks and Portuguese ships also influenced the final prices. Even the most prominent merchants regularly took out loans from foreign creditors and paid their high rates, which is evidence that there was no cheaper money available. In the 1760s the *Hong* merchants admitted that foreigners had more protection for their capital, and in the 1830s they were still depending heavily on it to finance trade.

Chinese regularly borrowed money at 18 to 36 percent interest per year (or 1.5 to 3 percent per month), and took out junk bottomry bonds at 40 percent interest per voyage. The foreigners, on the other hand, could borrow those same funds from other foreigners at 10 to 15 percent interest per year (or about 1 to 1.25 percent per month), and then make a healthy profit by re-loaning the money to Chinese.

Now that we have laid out the main structures and factors controlling, influencing and guiding the commerce, we turn to an analysis of the trade as a whole. The next chapter will discuss more coherently how the different parts introduced in chapters 1 to 8, interacted with each other to determine the course that trade was to take.

CHAPTER NINE

THE CANTON TRADE IN RETROSPECT

THE CANTON TRADE WAS ONE of the most important contributors to the rise of modern 'global' economies. From 1700 to 1842, the foreign demand for tea and porcelain grew with each passing decade, and China continued to meet the demand with an ever-expanding supply. As the tea trade developed, world markets became more integrated; as investment capital continued to flow into China in ever increasing quantities, international financial structures became more sophisticated; as the global movements of silver and commodities became more structured, global commerce became more regular. Greater consistency, in turn, helped to reduce risks, which increased profits and made costs easier to assess. As costs stabilised and profits grew, international commerce attracted more investors.

As the hitherto discrete commercial networks became more integrated, private traders found increasingly inventive ways to fill the gaps between supply and demand in international markets (in both licit and illicit trade). At the same time, they learned how to operate effectively under the limitations placed on them by the large trading monopolies. The big companies, for their part, found ways to control and exploit the private traders to benefit their own businesses. Private traders were encouraged to smuggle contraband into China because it helped the EIC to expand its tea trade. As international commerce became more regular, prices were advertised for each port, procedures set, and regulations clearly defined. Free trade became more of a possibility, and, eventually, private traders replaced the large monopolies. This long historical process of reducing risks in global commerce was directly connected to the growth of the China tea trade.

As we have seen, the tea trade depended so heavily on silver that there was a huge incentive for the opium trade to grow in unison. Opium was the only commodity that could be easily exchanged for that metal in China. As trade became more dependent on opium revenues to finance the tea expansion, it was in the Hoppos' interests to tolerate the smuggling rather than to stop it. As corruption within Chinese administrative structures became the standard, rather than the exception, Hoppos' control over trade became increasingly threatened. Funds and power were siphoned away from the central administration, which weakened it.

In order to keep the huge trade machine running smoothly, the Hoppos, governors-general and ministers in Beijing altered the system here and there by adding another stipulation, another restriction or another monitoring device. As far as the expansion of trade was concerned, we would have to say that the Canton System was highly successful. Even the strict physical limitations of the Pearl River posed no real obstacle because the Macao pilots found ways to manoeuvre larger ships up a shallow river. The foreigners' dependence on the expertise of the Macao pilots allowed the Hoppos more control over them. In many respects, as late as the 1820s the Hoppos still appeared to be the iron-fisted masters of their universe, with a firm grip on trade and foreigners.

This illusion of increased control, together with the immense expansion of commerce, camouflaged the serious weaknesses that were gradually tearing the system apart. As long as the Hoppos maintained harmony and revenues continued to flow to Beijing, there seemed to be no reason to make any fundamental changes in the way trade was run. It was not until the outflow of silver had reached crisis proportions in the mid-1830s that a serious investigation was launched to find out what was causing the financial shortcomings.

The lack of efficient internal checks and balances to shore up the cracks within the Canton System led to its eventual collapse. The officers who were called on to eliminate corruption were themselves corrupt. What was needed was a change in the basic structure, but such an initiative had to come from Beijing. Fundamental changes, however, could reduce state revenues so, in the short term, it was more convenient to tolerate, hide, dismiss or ignore the problems. Moreover, the Imperial Court was so ill-informed of the situation in the delta that it was unlikely effective reforms would or could come from Beijing.

The inability to initiate sweeping changes, combined with the lack of understanding of the extent of the problems, worked together to undermine the long-term security of the trade. The Canton System was incapable of cleaning up its own house, let alone dealing with the threat that was building outside its boundaries. The intense inward focus on keeping the bureaucratic machine well-oiled and running smoothly enabled important changes outside China to go unnoticed until they became real threats. The lack of an administrative structure that could collect information about foreigners and international markets, analyse those data to determine their significance and then respond appropriately eventually let to China's downfall.

Because most histories about the Canton trade have been predominantly 'top-down' studies that depend heavily on correspondences, reports, letters, official decrees and other such documents, they have looked only at policies to the exclusion of practices. This has resulted in the trade being defined by its policies, which in turn has led to the creation of different eras. One of the divisions most commonly made is to call the period from 1757 to 1842 — when the trade was 'officially' restricted to Canton — the 'Canton System'.

This historical marker loses significance when we focus on the day-to-day practices. The daily routines of the trade and administrative networks within customs continued after 1757 as they had before; the conduct of business went on as usual with no change in the structure, and there were no major changes in the way that foreigners and trade were controlled. The new policy did not change the fact that Canton had already established itself as the most favoured port in China, nor that the foreigners had decided that themselves. If we continue to say that the 1757 decree changed the course of history by making Canton the centre of the trade, do we then also say that the 1729 decree ended the opium trade in China by outlawing its sale? Both statements are equally erroneous.

The structure of the trade and its dependence on the geographical and hydrographical qualities of the delta and proximity of Macao were unique to Canton. Because this system could not be duplicated in any other port, it is more appropriate to refer to the entire period as the 'Canton System'.

STRUCTURE AND PRACTICES

Trade in Canton was always restricted to a small number of Chinese merchants, from just a couple in the early decades to about a dozen in later years. By the 1720s the Hoppos and/or governors-general controlled all merchants who were in direct contact with foreigners. Although access was restricted, some level of competition was usually maintained, which helped to keep prices down. The same was true with pilots, compradors and linguists.

From the beginning of the trade, the Macao pilots were the gatekeepers the Hoppos used to decide who came to trade and who did not. In the 1760s there were eight Macao pilots to service all foreign ships, but their numbers increased to twenty-two by the early 1840s. As many of the company ships grew larger, the number of persons employed to assist in guiding ships upriver also increased. By the 1750s it was common for pilots to employ 15 to 20 tow and buoy sampans, but by the late 1760s that number had risen to 40 or 50. By the early 1800s, pilots were hiring as many as 60 or 70 sampans to assist them with the largest ships. They employed several junior pilots, as well as a dozen or more Chinese helpers to handle the lines going out to the sampans.

The compradors were also selected and controlled by the Hoppos. There were many more compradors than pilots, simply because their businesses involved perishable goods that had to be purchased from many suppliers in many locations. It was impossible to store some of these goods in a warehouse in an age before widespread use of preservatives and refrigerators, so many provisions had to be consumed within hours or days of being purchased. To obtain all the goods and deliver them in a timely manner, the compradors needed many assistants and sampans.

The Hoppos also appointed a small team of linguists to service the trade, three to five operating in Canton in any year. From the early eighteenth century, linguists were controlled by the governors-general and/or the Hoppos. The number of linguists that were licensed did not increase in proportion to the number of ships going to China; they coped with the increase in their responsibilities by hiring more secretaries, writers and runners. They also subcontracted some of their duties to their head secretaries. This meant that when a linguist died or was removed or reassigned by a Hoppo, their well-trained secretary could be appointed in their place, a move that would ensure the continued smooth running of trade.

Merchants and their households were under the direct control of the Hoppos. Linguists, compradors and pilots, together with their retinues and workers, were under the supervision of the *Hong* merchants. This management structure formed the backbone of the Canton System. It was firmly in place by the mid-1720s and remained intact until 1842.

One word from a Hoppo to the merchants could end all contact with the foreigners. This could result in the immediate end of all trade or even the talk of trade; the instant removal of all Chinese from factories and ships; the stoppage of all goods and provisions to and from the foreigners; the withdrawal of all Chinese pilots to guide the ships up and down the river; and the end of all travel to the factories, Whampoa and Macao. Controlling all key individuals who were in regular contact with the foreigners was the means the Hoppos used to keep harmony.

The policy that Hoppos and governors-general developed was to keep persons who were licensed to interact with foreigners to a minimum, and to allow those select individuals to subcontract part of their workloads to others. All professionals had to compete for the right to service foreign ships and factories. This pyramidal type of hierarchical administration, in which the pyramids grew larger over time and competed with each other, created constant downward pressure on prices and fees. It also shifted much of the increase in administrative responsibility to the lower ranks of the pyramids, which enabled the Hoppos to minimise the number of persons needed in the customs networks to control trade. The downward shift of responsibilities, however, also meant a downward shift of power from the Hoppos to the lower echelons.

Besides the merchants, linguists, compradors and pilots, there were thousands of other Chinese involved in the trade. They included tollhouse keepers; sentries and soldiers stationed in posts along the river; tidewaiters, who accompanied ships to and from Bocca Tigris; runners, scribes, secretaries, sailors, and petty officers who worked the customs posts and sampan networks in the delta; junk traders and their crews; up-country merchants and their retinues of workers; artisans, craftsmen and their couriers; porters; growers, producers and providers; tea packers, pickers and processors; spinners, weavers and potters; and scribes, secretaries and coolies, to name some.

The Canton System was like a huge machine, with thousands of little parts that worked independent of, but in concert with, each other to move trade forward. The Hoppos, and to some extent the governors-general, were responsible for keeping the machine running smoothly. An interruption in the output could quickly ruin their careers, but a successful Hoppo could walk away from his three-year stint with a shining reputation and a small fortune in his pocket.

The basic practices and principles on which the Canton System operated daily were not necessarily based on written instructions, nor did they necessarily originate from official edicts or decrees. They were simply the way things were done in Canton, regardless of whether they were supposed to be done that way. The description below is a summary of how the huge machine operated daily, from the time it was established in the early eighteenth century to the end of the system in 1842.

Every Chinese was held responsible for the conduct of the foreigners with whom they did business. The establishment of a 'security merchant' system in the 1730s was merely the formalisation of a practice already in existence. The official policy was that no persons other than those who had been licensed were supposed to have direct contact with foreigners above Bocca Tigris. In day-to-day practice, however, barbers, washwomen, prostitutes and others were allowed to engage the seamen on a regular basis. This was tolerated because they provided services that kept foreigners content, which helped to maintain harmony.

Every foreign ship was supposed to report to Macao before proceeding upriver or further into the delta. Every ship was also required to hire a Macao pilot to guide it past Bocca Tigris, regardless of whether it wanted or needed one. The Macao pilots were always monitored by customs and, in turn, were supposed to monitor the foreigners and ensure that they complied with the regulations, but many abused their freedom by engaging the foreigners in illegal activities. The Hoppos used the control they had over the Macao pilots to ensure that no foreigners went past Bocca Tigris or left Whampoa without obtaining permission.

All foreign ships were accompanied and guarded by two tidewaiters from the time they arrived at Bocca Tigris to the time they returned again on their way out to sea. All foreign ships had to be measured before they could carry on trade in Canton, and every ship had to be a trading vessel with trade goods aboard before it was allowed to go upriver. Except for the Russians and Japanese, who were under separate trade agreements, all other male foreigners were welcomed at Canton, regardless of race, skin colour, religion or country of origin — as long as all required duties were paid and regulations observed.

Every foreign ship that passed Bocca Tigris was required to anchor in Whampoa Roads. Foreigners had to pay small fees for chops and other services between Macao and Whampoa, but no tolls were charged in that section of the river. Service boats flying a foreign flag were exempt from stopping at the tollhouses between Whampoa and Canton. The policy dictated that a chief officer was supposed to be aboard and that no goods were to be carried, but the practice was that many flag boats had no chief officers aboard and many goods were smuggled in and out of China in the bottom of these boats. This freedom was more or less tolerated as a favour to officers, which could be rescinded at any time as a means of persuasion. In practice, there was not one year when this privilege was disallowed to everyone.

Every foreign ship had to settle all official accounts before the Grand Chop was issued. Although borrowing from foreigners was discouraged and 'officially' illegal, it allowed trade to grow. Foreigners were always allowed to advance money to Chinese merchants to place orders for the next season. Those private credit transactions had nothing to do with the Grand Chops being issued.

No Chinese, other than the pilots and their helpers, were allowed to pass Bocca Tigris aboard foreign ships. Chinese were not supposed to leave China to go abroad on foreign vessels, but many did. Chinese were 'officially' allowed to serve aboard licensed and regulated Chinese junks, but they were expected to return to China in those vessels. Leaving China for any other reason, such as becoming a sailor aboard a foreign ship or seeking employment in a foreign land, were 'officially' forbidden.

Foreigners were also forbidden to pass Bocca Tigris aboard Chinese vessels. In the early years, many traders were allowed to sail upriver to Canton in their own service boats to negotiate trade with the Hoppos. As trade became normalized, only merchant ships were supposed to use the main passage through Bocca Tigris. Passengers travelling between Canton and Macao were then supposed to use the West River passage, which required the permission of the Hoppo. No foreign merchant ships or any other type of foreign vessel (excluding the Chinese commissioned, but Portuguese owned and operated, patrol boats) were allowed in that passageway.

All foreigners residing in Macao were monitored and under the direct jurisdiction of the Portuguese governor, who usually intervened in matters concerning them. Foreigners needed permission from the Macao government to reside there. By the early nineteenth century, the residency requirements in Macao were relaxed and some foreigners such as the *ghaut serangs* began staying year round without going to Canton. In special cases, the Portuguese governor in Macao might be asked to intervene in problems concerning foreigners in Canton, but, as a rule, the authorities there took care of all matters after the foreigners passed Bocca Tigris.

These practices and principles formed the body of the Canton System. Like the backbone, the body was firmly in place by the 1720s and would remain in place until the downfall of the system in 1842. Although foreign trade was not officially restricted to the port of Canton until 1757, it was clearly the port of preference for Beijing long before then because it offered all the advantages above. No other Chinese port proved to be as good as Canton in simultaneously accommodating trade and addressing the concerns of Beijing.

STRENGTHS AND SUCCESSES

The administrative networks of Canton's maritime customs were extremely well organised. The procuring of chops, inspecting and measuring of ships, unloading and loading of cargo, coordinating of efforts to match the monsoons and the sophisticated licensing structures and monitoring devices all helped to facilitate the smooth and timely conduct of commerce. Special arrangements could be made to meet specific needs, such as organising emergency salvage operations. Some of those services had specific fees attached while others were negotiated on the spot. As far as the large company ships were concerned, Chinese officials in Canton were usually open to any arrangement as long as it did not affect the administrative apparatus controlling trade, upset the harmony of the port or arouse the suspicions of superiors. All other arrangements were open for discussion and consideration.

Foreigners were often not clear on these predetermined limitations, which led many of them to believe the Chinese were not interested in advancing commerce, but only restricting it. The examples presented in this study, however, demonstrate that Hoppos and governors-general could be very flexible within their set boundaries. They consistently encouraged and accommodated trade and only became inflexible when asked to go outside their limits. If we set aside all the complaints and look more closely at the broader evidence, it is clear from the increasing numbers of foreigners trading that the regularity of fees and procedures, combined with the accommodating attitude of the authorities, helped to nurture foreign trust.

In times of difficulty when the foreigners refused to comply, the Hoppos withdrew the merchants and pilots threatening the foreigners with a layover in port, which put profits at risk. Time was on the Hoppos' side because as the change in the monsoons grew nearer, the time to load cargoes grew shorter, which forced supercargoes to seek a compromise. The Hoppos had only to sit back and wait until the forces of time and money worked out a solution. The officials had to be careful not to be so inflexible that foreigners would refuse to return, but they could find that middle ground with the administrative tools at their disposal. In this sense, the Hoppos were the fulcrum that kept the trading universe in balance.

The giant bureaucratic machine's amazing ability to increase output to meet the growing demand for trade goods, packaging materials, services and provisions ensured that prices were not pushed up owing to deficiencies in supplies. Of course, inflation occurred in provision prices, but it was gradual, averaging about 3 percent per year from 1700 to the 1830s. The fact that many customs fees, import and export duties, service charges, linguists' fees and Macao pilots' fees (after 1809) did not increase with inflation meant that they became cheaper. Because the exchange rate between foreign silver (Spanish or Mexican dollars) and the Chinese tael was 'fixed', the purchasing power of the dollar decreased with inflation. This meant that foreigners preferred to continue paying the same old fixed fees.

The practice of advancing funds against future deliveries enabled Chinese merchants to expand the quantities they ordered from their up-country suppliers. Trade in packaging materials, such as wood and lead for the tea chests, tin for canisters, sago for porcelain chests, and bamboo and rattan for making containers and providing bracing for cargo, grew in unison with the tea trade. Up-country suppliers, Canton junks and private foreign ships all played a vital role in supplying those articles.

For the great expansion to occur, however, there had to be a good supply of investment capital. Private foreign investments made up a good part of the capital throughout the Canton era. The maintenance of high interest rates, combined with a fairly high level of protection provided by the Hoppos for the repayment of Chinese debts, ensured that there was a constant flow of foreign capital into Canton. Many private commission merchants set themselves up in Macao and Canton to provide financial and brokering services to whoever needed them. This lively money market helped to supplement shortcomings in short and long-term financing so Chinese merchants could meet obligations and all vessels left with hulls full.

If one looks only at the strengths and benefits of the Canton System, there seem to be no limit as to how far the trade could have grown. Foreign demands for Chinese wares seemed limitless; Chinese ability to meet those growing demands seemed boundless; and Canton's ability to attract capital seemed bottomless. While there were many Chinese merchants who failed miserably, and huge disruptions in trade in some years, on the whole, the Hoppos and governors-general managed to work things out. By applying a little pressure here, initiating a little punishment there, or making a little change in policy or procedure somewhere else, they kept the vast machine running. As far as the Hoppos' careers and future well-being were concerned, the best possible scenario was for them to walk away from their three-year stint with the machine pumping out more products and sending more revenues to Beijing than it had under previous Hoppos. And, of course, they had to do that without upsetting the rhythm (harmony) of that machine so their successors could do the same.

For the most part, it did not really matter or make any difference to the Hoppos that the machine was also pumping out more pollution (corruption and smuggling) as it grew. Most of that illegal activity was invisible from Beijing; as long as everything else fell into place there was no need to draw attention to it. Those factors would reveal themselves in time — during the next Hoppo's administration it was hoped, rather than their own.

When that crucial moment arrived, however, Beijing would have to initiate the changes necessary to stamp out the 'pollution'. Hoppos or governors-general did not have the power or incentive to come up with sweeping initiatives. Moreover, the smuggling and corruption contributed to the expansion of legitimate trade, so it was better to leave it alone. The top officials in Canton were itinerant officers with loose connections to local populations. Many of the other players in trading, however, such as low-level customs officers, merchants, linguists, compradors and pilots, were life-long residents of the region. These lower echelons formed the backbone and body of the Canton System. The Hoppos, together with the governors-general, might have comprised the head, but they needed the body's cooperation to keep the machine operating in line with Beijing's desires. While Canton rarely followed Beijing's decrees to the letter, there needed to be at least the appearance of compliance.

In the late 1720s the 'emperor's present' became an official part of the port fees, despite the many protests of foreigners, and there was nothing the Hoppos or governors-general could do about it. It was not until 1830 that foreigners managed to negotiate a reduction in the 'present', but this was then offset by an increase in the three port-fee rates. In 1741 the emperor made it mandatory for all foreigners to remove to Macao in the off-season, which was enforced with more rigour after 1757. Other ports in China were officially banned from trading with foreigners, which preserved Canton's place as the centre of foreign commerce. Initiatives such as these that had sweeping and lasting effects could come from Beijing only.

Beijing also initiated many crackdowns on smuggling, but none of the campaigns before 1835 were effective at stopping the contraband trade, or even to slow it down. Solutions were not effective because causes had not been identified. The lack of understanding of the situation in the delta continued to dictate the initiation of ineffective policies.

WEAKNESSES AND COLLAPSE

The contraband trade was one of the major faults in the system. Individuals on all levels of society, in both Macao and Canton, engaged in smuggling. It was relatively easy to bribe customs officials so shipments would pass 'undetected'. Many government fees did not adjust with inflation, which contributed to the 'have-nots' of trade trying constantly to reach deeper into the pockets of the 'haves' however they could. It is probably not a coincidence that the rise of the tolls along the West River in the 1760s and 1770s paralleled the development of an opium network. The Hoppos were either unable or unwilling to initiate any effective means to curb the extortions, and, as a result, they continued to grow.

The Portuguese in Macao were crucial to the control, establishment and management of the Canton trade, but many used their special privileges to profit personally from contraband. If Chinese customs officers in the delta wanted to benefit from illegal trade they had to match the connivance fees that the Portuguese were charging. If officials in Whampoa or Amoy wanted to benefit from the opium trade, they had to match the connivance fees that were being charged in the lower-delta. If the Hoppomen in Whampoa or the customs officers on the quay wanted to benefit from the smuggling, they had to compete with the connivance fees that the compradors and pilots were charging, and the compradors and pilots, in turn, had to compete with what the Portuguese charged in Macao.

This competition evened out connivance fees and procedures, which enabled smugglers to predict their profits more accurately. This security and clarity helped the contraband trade to become almost as predictable as the legitimate trade, which, in turn, attracted more investors. At the same time, there were many varieties of and prices for opium, which resulted in its penetrating all levels of Chinese society. Rampant piracy in the late eighteenth and early nineteenth centuries also contributed to the expansion and greater sophistication of contraband networks.

Issuing of credit might have facilitated the smooth conduct of trade, but it strained working capital, because many officers had to operate the entire season without receiving any fees until the ships were ready to leave. This put financial pressure on some officials in the customs networks to consider participating in the contraband trade and the acceptance of bribes in exchange for re-classifying commodities from 'dutiable' to 'non-dutiable'. This practice undermined the revenues going to Beijing and the financial structures supporting the Hoppos' networks. But as long as the overall volume of trade continued to expand, the increase in imperial revenues camouflaged the diverting of funds.

In the late-eighteenth and early-nineteenth centuries, tidewaiters and linguists took control of the black market trade in provisions. This also diverted funds and power from the Hoppos. Pilots, compradors and linguists had to pay large sums for the privilege of their appointments, which kept them in a sort of bondage to the government. Many had to borrow money to pay for their licensing fees, and interest rates were so high that it probably took many years for them to repay their loans. While this may have kept them working diligently at their posts until their debts were settled, it also encouraged them to trade outside the system and earn extra income. For all these reasons, many tidewaiters, linguists, compradors and pilots were only too willing to accommodate smugglers.

The regular 'contributions' and 'donations' requested from the Chinese merchants by the Hoppos also helped advance contraband. The Hoppos had a window into the gross incomes of every Chinese merchant by requiring them, rather than the foreigners, to pay all import and export duties. Figures from the duties gave the Hoppos a record of who might be able to contribute the most. Illegal trade offered merchants a way to hedge against these ubiquitous requests because it gave them income out of the purview of the Hoppos. As a result, even in the best years, some of the most prominent merchants in Canton eagerly entered into illicit transactions.

As the contraband trade grew, other merchants were attracted to it. In the late 1790s, rampant piracy in the delta distracted officials from smuggling operations; Portuguese and Chinese in Macao used the suppression of piracy to cover the advancement of their opium trade. The great dependence on silver for the purchase of tea and the fact that opium was the only article that could be easily exchanged in China for silver cemented the relationship between those two commodities. Because opium was considered a legitimate article of commerce in other ports in Asia, it was easy for both foreigners and Chinese to rationalise its sale in China. In years when fewer ships arrived and in times of war, silver was in short supply, and trading in opium provided a means for both Chinese and foreigners to supplement depleted silver supplies. As a result, by the 1760s, a steady flow of opium was going to China, and it continued to expand with private traders and junks carrying it to ports all along the coast.

The structure of the capital market also brought disadvantages to the Canton System. The disparity in the interest rates between foreigners and Chinese kept needed capital flowing into Canton, but forced Chinese to pay high rates. There was not enough indigenous capital to fill the demands so throughout the Canton era merchants were continually depending on foreign loans.

Canton merchants tried to protect their profits by forming monopolies. In 1720 and again in the 1760s, merchants created cartels and made arrangements to control prices and limit access to supplies, but those efforts were only marginally successful. They were not allowed to maintain their monopolies because controlling prices ran contrary to the Hoppos' interests in encouraging trade to grow. Hoppos knew that if foreigners were faced with prices that were too low for their import goods and too high for their export goods, they would not return to China. If they did not return, there would be no revenues to send to Beijing, and that would affect Hoppos' careers.

Although officers of the East India companies upheld and promoted monopolies as the best means of reducing risks and protecting profits, they did not want any such combinations affecting Chinese markets. They put constant pressure on the Hoppos to disallow all such arrangements. Because the foreigners and the Hoppos' interests coincided on this point, Chinese merchants were never successful at controlling prices or access to supplies.

A more successful protection for *Hong* profits was the *consoo* fund, which taxed all the merchants alike and thus was able to push prices up enough to protect profit margins. Gifts, presents, port fees and arrears in duties were paid out of this general fund. The *consoo* fund was more successful than monopolies and combinations because it coincided with the Hoppos' interests. The fund was replenished each year, so it provided the Hoppos with a steady source of welcome revenue.

In the long-term, however, the demands on the fund were more than it could bear, and government officials who needed to supplement budgets had to resort again to an occasional 'contribution'. The *consoo* fund brought more short-term security to the merchants, but it was not an effective long-term solution. Because no other measures came forth that could protect *Hong* merchant profits, their occupations were always associated with high risk.

In the short term, merchants did what they could to outwit the system, and some of them, such as Poankeequa and Howqua, were highly successful. However, even successful traders were not immortal. Eventually, less skilled negotiators in the family would gain control of their fortunes and their wealth would be gradually whittled away by demanding officials. Some merchants managed to hang on to their riches for decades, but in the long-term the odds were against them.

Owing to a lack of overall control, the system was also weakened by the many problems that developed in the customs networks. In 1759, for example, the Hoppos launched counter measures to quash the problem of the silk connivances that were being charged indiscriminately to all foreigners, but these connivances had been going on for decades. The Danes and English had to bring the problem to light because the Hoppos were not keeping track of the fees that foreigners were paying to the tidewaiters and linguists.

In the early 1770s new policies were introduced requiring the payment of all duties before the Grand Chops were issued, which set the stage for the accumulation of enormous debts by the end of the decade. This debt problem was unforeseen because no one was keeping track of the effects the new policy was having on merchants. Information about the increase in loans that were being given to the Chinese was not collected because they were not supposed to be borrowing money from foreigners in the first place. In this case, policy clearly did not take practice into account. What was needed was an overhaul of the structure of the capital market in Canton to equalise foreign and Chinese interest rates.

By the early 1780s foreigners were constantly complaining about the rapid rise in tolls being charged on the West River. The Hoppos had to summon all the compradors to give an account of the amounts being paid because they had not been checking what the tollhouses downriver were charging. Those fees had been rising steadily for ten years, but no one had taken notice.

At the same time, opium networks were developing deep roots in the delta, and customs officers and licensed compradors were implicated. In 1780, a permanent receiving hulk was anchored in Lark's Bay, but it would be another twelve years before the Hoppo in Canton recognised this trafficking, and another eight years after that before any countermeasures were introduced to stop it. Knowledge of this network had not reached Beijing because there were no monitoring devices to confirm that the information the Hoppos were receiving from their express sampans in the delta was accurate. It was not until the silver crisis intensified the need for change that Beijing initiated a thorough investigation.

The lack of an administrative infrastructure that could monitor and control the outside pilots, discouraging them from guiding ships into the smuggling depots in the delta, made it easy for smugglers to carry on their work. Both the outside pilots and Macao pilots were directly involved with contraband, so they were not the effective gatekeepers they were intended to be; nonetheless, the administration in Canton continued to rely on them.

In the 1790s and early years of the nineteenth century, the linguists and Hoppomen began taking control of the illicit provisions trade. Although the Hoppos were probably aware of the connivance, they did nothing to stop it, despite its being contrary to state policy. Beijing implemented no policies to counter the connivances because no one had informed them of the extent of the problems. Besides, the revenues going to the capitol were steadily increasing with each decade and foreigners were still under tight control in Canton, so it was assumed that everything was operating as it was supposed to.

In 1814 and 1815, another campaign was begun to end the opium trade in Macao and to inspect all Portuguese ships arriving in China, a move that was fifty years overdue. In the 1820s the Lintin campaign was embarked on to end the opium trade, but, by then, foreigners had been carrying on illegal commerce there for twenty years. By this time, other smuggling depots were in the delta so simply smashing one of them had little effect on the overall volume. Again, Beijing's response was too little too late.

For their part, as we have seen, the Hoppos had no time to deal with anything except the most important matters at hand. By the 1820s, however, the Canton System was showing serious weaknesses and the harmony of the port was at risk. The preferential treatment of rice contributed to the increase in smuggling in the delta. Smugglers avoided the high fees in Canton by buying rice at Lintin Island and sailing upriver on a preferentially treated 'rice ship'. They used their reserves from opium and rice to purchase backhaul goods, which helped to cover the cost of their return passages. Having a backhaul meant they could afford to sell their opium for a more competitive price. Lower prices, in turn, encouraged greater consumption. Officials did not make the connection between rice and opium because no one reported it, despite the fact that it was common knowledge in the delta and openly published in the foreign newspapers.

In 1827, the first newspaper appeared in Canton, and other foreign publications soon followed. Besides giving accounts of trade in other Asian ports, these periodicals kept the foreigners apprised of events happening worldwide. Numerous articles about Chinese politics, laws, society and culture were published each month dealing with both contemporary and historical issues. For the first time in the history of the trade, all foreigners in China had equal access to the same body of information on China and on recent trends in global commerce. Within a few years, the foreign community in Canton and Macao had become very well informed on both local and international issues. This helped to unite their opinions about the changes that needed to be made in China to accommodate the changes that were happening in the wider world.

The foreign press started to shift the balance of power in favour of the foreigners, and the arrival of the large shallow-bottomed steamers in the 1830s completed the transition. In one sweep, steamers undermined the role of the Macao pilots, made the forts at Bocca Tigris ineffective as they proceeded up the West River, and ended the Hoppos' control over those who came to trade and when they would be allowed to leave. This loss of power undermined the credit structures of the Canton System because the Hoppos could no longer guarantee that the foreigners would settle their accounts before leaving.

In the mid-1830s, the East India companies ceased their operations in Canton, and private traders began to unite with a common voice. The press gave them the medium to voice their opinions and express their ideas and the steamship gave them the power to follow through with their intentions. The foreigners openly discussed in the China Coast newspapers their intentions of going to war with China if changes were not forthcoming, and this information was available to anyone who purchased those publications.

Many other changes were taking place as well that were going to affect China's hegemony as the world's main source of tea. There was much talk in the press about the tea plantations that were being established in other areas. By the early 1830s, tea was being grown in Java, with the help of Chinese who were sent there to establish tea plantations.[1] The renewed crackdowns on smuggling in the mid-1830s gave rise to more talks of growing tea in other locations so there was not a need to purchase it in China.[2] By the 1840s tea was being grown in Sri Lanka and South America, and there were plans of introducing it to India. Tea had been flourishing in Japan, Korea, Tonkin, Cochin China and Burma all along, but the different preparation and processing methods used in those places rendered the final products less desirable than Chinese tea.[3] In the new centres that were established, however, the processing techniques were gradually perfected and China began to lose its comparative advantage of that product.

By this time, high quality porcelain was being made in almost every country in Western Europe and silk was also being produced and spun in France, the United States, and several other countries. In the 1850s Japan opened its doors to the West and became a source of high quality porcelain and silk as well. Korea would soon follow suit.

As a result of this new competition, from 1877 to the 1920s, China's foreign imports exceeded exports every year.[4] There were, of course, many other factors connected to this transformation, such as unequal treaties and foreign manipulation of Chinese trade and maritime customs. But we should not let those influences divert our attention from the fact that China lost its world monopoly on tea.

Thus, even without the Opium Wars that forcefully ended the Canton System, the China trade and its traditional methods of doing business were about to be seriously threatened by a more formidable opponent, competition. For more than 140 years, China had supplied the world with tea, porcelain and silk. By the end of the nineteenth century, China had turned into a consumer economy. Nothing was done to prepare the country for this new competitive environment, despite the fact that all these events, trends and problems had been clearly visible long before they became threatening. These ideas were openly discussed in the factories in Canton where the compradors could hear everything that was being said, in the Canton Chamber of Commerce of which the *Hong* merchants were members, and in the Canton periodicals.[5] In fact, foreigners openly declared that it was their intention to undermine China's monopolies.[6] And not knowing English was no excuse because the Canton junk traders were also exposed to all of these ideas and issues from their travels to Southeast Asia and could express them in Chinese to anyone who wanted to hear them.

Now that we have summarized the trade and shown how the different parts interacted to direct the course trade was to take, we conclude with the main reasons for the collapse.

CONCLUSION

THE ROOT OF THE PROBLEM

TODAY, FOREIGN ARCHIVES HOLD the best and most detailed accounts available about the *Hong* merchants, the Canton junk traders, the dozens of linguists, compradors and pilots, and the tens of thousands of other Chinese involved in trade. No records were kept or preserved about these matters because they were not important to the state. Some Chinese merchants became extremely wealthy and built large estates, but their fortunes did not last and the memories of many of their lives have vanished. This was not owing to deliberate or intentional efforts by the architects of the Canton System to undermine or prejudice local interests. Rather, it was a result of the intense focus on state matters that constantly overshadowed individual concerns.

The only records protected and preserved were those that concerned matters of state. All other Chinese records from the lower echelons have vanished. These documents numbered in the millions (and possibly billions). They included 140 years of daybooks from the local customhouses in the delta; thousands of chops issued to tranship merchandise between Whampoa and Canton; hundreds of Grand Chop inspection slips kept by customs to verify document authenticity (Plate 1); 140 years of Hoppos' ledgers recording the exports and imports of every foreign ship and junk; thousands of ship measuring calculations (Plate 27); dozens of articles drawn up for each foreign company spelling out the terms and stipulations of trade; hundreds of passes issued to foreigners for traversing the West River (Plate 22); thousands of reports from the express sampans in the delta informing the Hoppos of the maritime activities downriver; hundreds of letters, decrees and notices that were sent to foreign factories and ships; and hundreds of linguists, compradors and pilots' chops granting permission to service the foreigners.

We know that the *Hong* merchants kept detailed records, as well, because they were often asked to look up previous transactions that had transpired when questions arose of something that was still owed, miss-packed or undelivered. Occasionally, merchants also brought up past debts that the foreigners had failed to pay, which they could verify from their records. We also know that the merchants kept copies of the hundreds of contracts they signed with foreigners because sometimes they had to consult those documents to check the terms they had agreed on in past years. All these records show up in the foreign archives written in Chinese so we have physical proof that they existed (Plates 7, 8, 10, 11, 13, 17–20, 25–6, 40–1). But merchants did not dare to keep those records any longer than what they needed them probably out of fear that they could fall into the hands of greedy officials. This was another sign of the lack of protection to Chinese business.

Today, only a few hundred of these detailed Chinese records are known to exist and all are in foreign archives. The lack of attention to the restoration of historical records is another clear sign that local individual interests and the preservation of their local heritage (including the accumulation and long-term protection of local wealth) were not part of the basic mentality of the Canton System. The part of the history that has suffered most is the junk trade, which involved thousands of vessels and tens of thousands of people over hundreds of years, but there are now almost no documents to tell their stories.

The hundreds of detailed Chinese trade records used in this study, from the Swedish, Dutch, Danish, British, American and Portuguese archives, are also clear and indisputable evidence that such documents were regularly created in Canton. From information in the foreign records we have been able to describe the sophisticated and systematic record-keeping policies and practices of both the Yuehaiguan, in the control of trade, and the Chinese merchants, in the carrying out of trade. The only detailed Chinese records from any of the customhouses in the delta known to have survived, however, are those that were sent to Macao, and they exist today solely because they were important to the Portuguese.[1]

The only records that were systematically protected and preserved in China were official correspondences to and from the court in Beijing. Those documents, however, contain only information about individuals involved in trade whose actions in some way concerned the state. A short note might have been recorded about Chinese who amassed debts with foreigners, committed crimes, or created problems or disturbances that upset the harmony of the system or affected revenues going to Beijing, but, as soon as those matters were settled, their names disappeared. Those state documents tell us almost nothing about the lives of the hundreds and thousands of Chinese mentioned on the preceding pages. Almost all that detail is in foreign archives.

This lack of respect for its own history was one of the biggest flaws of the Canton System, because that information was vital for its efficient operation and preservation. Without a detailed account of all the particulars of trade and the changes in the environment, there was no way of accurately anticipating or determining when, what, where, why or how trade might have to change or fail. This is why some foreign companies (such as the Dutch) kept copies of their records in China so supercargoes could use them as reference to better understand the trade and their past dealings with the Chinese. That information, of course, was not enough in itself to ensure any of them would survive. If no action was taken, or unrealistic and impractical policies were initiated from the knowledge, no benefit was to be gained.

In a static world with constant demand, no changes in economic trends or attitudes and no great differences in technology or production, it was perhaps unimportant to keep close watch on all aspects of the trade and environment. But that was certainly not the position in eighteenth- or nineteenth-century Canton. By failing to preserve a detailed account of its track record, the Canton System guaranteed its own failure. The lack of accurate information forced the Hoppos, governors-general and ministers in Beijing constantly to treat the symptoms rather than cure the disease. Because administrators were not keeping on top of cracks that were developing in the lower echelons, counteractive measures were initiated many years after problems began, and it was usually a crisis that set them off.

Because of insufficient information collected about trade and the wider international environment, it was only a matter of time before the administrative structures would be so weakened that no one would be able to reverse the decline. Because of this lack of understanding of the depth and seriousness of the problems, the government's efforts to shore up the system failed. The foreigners were able to overcome the system because the system had already defeated itself.

There needed to be an administrative body that had the initiative, will, power and information necessary to analyze the weaknesses, review trade policies and procedures, and make the corrective changes needed. But without a detailed account of all the particulars of trade and changes in the environment, there was no way to arrive at an accurate or comprehensive understanding to formulate effective corrective policies. There needed to be checks and balances in the information flows so administrators could be assured that vital details were not being doctored or omitted, but the Canton System had no such mechanisms, at least none that were effective. As a result, the bureaucratic machine made decisions and formulated policies based on incomplete, inaccurate and misguided information.

Ironically, we can draw an analogy with the present day, which will hopefully enable us to learn from Beijing's mistake in Qing China. The new data presented on the preceding pages show clearly how important it is to have all of the vital details. Without them, we cannot understand how trade operates. In the past, histories of the trade have also depended on a fraction of the picture to tell the whole story. As was pointed out in the preface, this outcome has good reasons but has resulted in a situation like the court in Beijing. Because of a lack of data and knowledge of the junks and Macao trade in the EIC records, which have been mostly depended on to write the histories, those aspects have been omitted or ignored. The experience of the other small companies has also been largely overlooked in studies of the port, despite their importance to the development of the trade. And many of the immensely important commission merchants like the Armenian Matheus Johannes have received little attention.

As we have shown, these parts of the commerce made up about 70 percent of the total volume in the 1760s and made significant contributions that shaped and influenced history. They each played different roles that encouraged growth and filled gaps in the commerce that kept the trade machine running. To some extent, their omissions in the histories are the result of the intense focus on the collapse of trade, which was not concerned with reasons for growth, only reasons for its downfall. But how can we explain failure if we do not understand success? The difficulties in the past of accessing and using the many different historical records (in many places and languages) resulted in studies being based primarily on EIC documents.

As a result, up until now, our knowledge of the Canton trade has came primarily from 25 to 30 percent of the commerce (the EIC). Although the reasons and circumstances are different, the outcome of analyzing the trade without considering all of its parts is no different from what the Qing court was doing: making decisions about trade, defining the commerce and determining problems and solutions without knowing the full extent of what was happening. Writers and administrators have not understood the huge trade machine because they did not have information about all of its little parts.

We now have a new and more comprehensive picture to present because we have more complete data to analyse and explain better how the machine operated. In 1835, Beijing also began to collect and receive very detailed and accurate information about the trade, and then the court was finally able to see where changes needed to be made. For Beijing, however, it was too late to change the course of history, because it had been too long ignoring the problems. For historians, it is not too late to re-examine the evidence and revise the history books so we represent better the people. We hope with the new tools now available that researchers will write more detailed and comprehensive histories in the future to illuminate the areas this study has left dark.

NOTES

PREFACE

1. Here is a partial list of subjects and authors covering different aspects of the history during the Canton era. 1) American trade with China: Morison (1921), Dulles (1930), Dermigny (1964), Goldstein (1978), Christman (1984), Lee (1984), Grant (1988), Dudden (1992), Downs (1997); 2) Chinese *Hong* merchants: Cordier (1902), Liang (1932), White (1967), Ch'en (1990), Cheong (1997), Huang and Pang (2001), Van Dyke (2004); 3) Portuguese trade with China: Boxer (1948, 1959, 1969), Manguin (1984), Souza (1986), Guimarães (1996), Do Vale (1997), Ptak (2004); 4) Spanish trade with China: Chaunu (1960), Souza (1986), Lourido (2002), Legarda (1999); 5) Danish trade with China: Larsen (1932), Rasch and Sveistrup (1948), Bro-Jørgensen and Rasch (1969), Gøbel (1978), Diller (1999); 6) Dutch trade with China: Van der Kemp (1919), Mansvelt (1922), Du Hullu (1923), Glamann (1958), Jörg (1982), Bruijn and Gaastra (1987, 1993); 7) English trade with China: Eames (1909), Morse (1926), Pritchard (1936), Costin (1937), Greenberg (1951), Dermigny (1964), Chaudhuri (1978), Ch'en (1990), Cheong (1997), Le Pichon (1998); 8) French trade with China: Madrolle (1901), Sottas (1905), Cordier (1908), Conan (1942), Dermigny (1964), Manning (1996), Cheong (1997); 9) Belgian trade with China: Degryse (1974), Parmentier (1996); 10) Prussian trade with China: Cordier (1920); 11) Swedish trade with China: Hellstenius (1860), Nyström (1883), Olán (1920), Lind (1923), Kjellberg (1974), Koninckx (1980), Johansson, ed. (1992); 12) Armenian trade with China: Smith and Van Dyke (2003, 2004); 13) Muslim trade with China: Smith and Van Dyke (2004); 14) Parsee trade with China: Guo (2001, 2003), Smith (2004), Thampi (2004), Saksena (2004).
2. A workshop on the *Hong* merchants in October 2003 at the Harvard Fairbank Center also brought out many new aspects of their lives. Here are a few of the recent studies and collections of articles that have helped to expand the work: Steven Miles, 'Local Matters: Lineage, Scholarship and the Xuehaitang Academy in the Construction of

Regional Identities in South China, 1810–1880' (Ph.D. dissertation submitted to the University of Washington, 2000); Huang Qichen (黃启臣) and Pang Xinping (庞新平), *Ming-Qing Guangdong Shangren* (明清广東商人 Guangdong Merchants in the Ming and Ching Dynasty) (Guangzhou: Guangdong Jingji Chuban She, 2001); Huang Qichen, ed. *Guangdong Haishang Sichou zhi Lushi* (广東海上絲綢之路史 History of Guangdong's Maritime Silk Road) (Guangzhou: Guangdong Jingji Chubanshe, 2003); Zhang Wenqin, et al, eds. *Guangzhou Shisan Hang Cangsang* (广州十三行滄桑 The Thirteen Hongs in Guangzhou) (Guangzhou: Guangdong Ditu Chuban She, 2001).

3. Here is a partial list of subjects and authors. 1) Porcelain: Jörg (1982), Howard (1994); 2) Silk: Li (1981), So (1986); 3) Tea: Fortune (1857), Witham (1947), Hatano (1952), Whitbeck (1965), Chaudhuri (1978), Lin F. (1982), Lin Z. (1982), Mui and Mui (1984), Chen C. (1984), Hao (1986), Ch'en (1989), Gardella (1994); 4) All the above, plus lacquerware, export paintings, etc.: Bro-Jørgensen and Rasch (1969), Lee (1984), Wirgin (1998).
4. Here is a partial list of authors. Opium & Opium Wars: Collis (1946), Waley (1958), Dermigny (1964), Fay (1975), Beeching (1975), Wakeman (1978), Downs (1997), Trocki (1999).

CHAPTER ONE

1. For an account of the English and Dutch trying to open up the China trade, see Paul A. Van Dyke, 'The Anglo-Dutch Fleet of Defense (1620–1622): Prelude to the Dutch Occupation of Taiwan', in *Around and about Formosa : Essays in honor of professor Ts'ao Yung-ho*, ed. by Leonard Blussé (Taipei : Ts'ao Yung-ho Foundation for Culture and Education, [Dist. SMC Publishing Inc., Taipei], 2003), 61–81.
2. Leonard Blussé, *Strange Company* (Providence: Foris Publications, 1988); and John E. Wills, Jr., *Pepper, Guns, & Parleys. The Dutch East India Company and China, 1622–1681* (Cambridge: Harvard University Press, 1974). See also Jonathan D. Spence and John E. Wills, Jr., *From Ming to Ch'ing* (New Haven: Yale University Press, 1979); John E. Wills, Jr., *Embassies and Illusions, Dutch and Portuguese Envoys to K'ang-hsi, 1666–1687* (Cambridge: Harvard University Press, 1984); John E. Wills, Jr., 'China's Farther Shores: Continuities and Changes in the Destination Ports of China's Foreign Trade, 1680–1690', in Roderick Ptak and Dietmar Rothermund, eds., *Emporia, Commodities and Entrepreneurs in Asian Maritime Trade, c. 1400–1750* (Stuttgart: Franz Steiner, 1991), 53–77.
3. Wills, *Pepper, Guns, & Parleys*, 196.
4. K. C. Fok, 'The Macao Formula: A Study of Chinese Management of Westerners from the Mid-Sixteenth Century to the Opium War Period' (Ph.D. dissertation, Department of History, University of Hawaii, 1978).
5. Fei Chengkang, *Macao 400 Years* (Shanghai: The Publishing House of Shanghai Academy of Social Sciences, 1996), 133–4; Hosea Ballou Morse, *The Chronicles of the East India Company Trading to China, 1635–1834*. 5 vols. (Cambridge: Harvard University Press, 1926; reprint, Taipei: Ch'eng-wen Publishing Co., 1966), 1:198; and Tereza Sena, 'The Question of "Foreigners" Entering Macao in the 18th Century: Macao, a Metropolis of Equilibrium?', in *Culture of Metropolis in Macao* (Macao: Cultural Institute, 2001), 159–76.

6. Macao's inner harbour and the inner anchorage on Taipa Island were continually becoming shallower owing to silting. In the eighteenth century, vessels with draughts of eighteen feet could not enter those harbours. By 1835, American vessels with draughts of sixteen feet were also warned that the waters near Macao were too shallow for them. *Canton Register* (24 November 1835).
7. References from the early eighteenth century show the linguists speaking Portuguese, and by the early 1730s, switching to pidgin English. Paul A. Van Dyke, 'Port Canton and the Pearl River Delta, 1690–1845' (Ph.D. dissertation, Department of History, University of Southern California, 2002), 304–5; and Kingsley Bolton, *Chinese Englishes* (Cambridge: Cambridge University Press, 2003), 146–9.
8. Most histories of the China trade focus on policy rather than practice, and as a consequence they refer to the 'Canton System' as the period when the trade was 'officially' restricted to Canton (from the Flint Affair in 1757 to the end of the system in 1842). However, by the early eighteenth century, the trade was already centred in Canton. As far as the day-to-day transactions and the basic structure of the trade are concerned, there were no significant changes before or after 1757. Thus, as far as this study is concerned, the change in policy in this year is not a marker between two periods. The entire period from 1700 to 1842 will be referred to here as the 'Canton System'.
9. Carl T. Smith and Paul A. Van Dyke, 'Armenian Footprints in Macau', *Review of Culture*, International Edition, No. 8 (October 2003), 20–39; and Carl T. Smith and Paul A. Van Dyke, 'Muslims in the Pearl River Delta, 1700 to 1930', *Review of Culture*, International Edition, No. 10 (April 2004), 6–15.
10. There are very few detailed records from this early period. The best and most extensive account of the trade in 1704 is found in Lockyer, but Hamilton has also left us with some detail for 1703 and Barlow for 1702. Lockyer stated that the private Madras traders preferred Canton to Amoy because of the 'extravagant Demands, Charges, and Abuses of the Mandareens' in the latter port. Charles Lockyer, *An Account of the Trade in India* (London: S. Crouch, 1711), 98–9; Alexander Hamilton, *A New Account of the East-Indies ... from the year 1688–1723* (London: 1739; reprint, New Delhi: Asian Educational Services, 1995), 2:216–35; and Alfred Basil Lubbock, ed., *Barlow's Journal of his Life at Sea in King's Ships, East & West Indiamen & other Merchantmen from 1659 to 1703*, 2 vols. (London: Hurst & Blackett, 1934). The early French voyages to China can be found in C. Madrolle, *Les Premiers Voyages Français a la Chine. La Compagnie de la Chine 1698–1719* (Paris: Augustin Challamel, 1901); and E. A. Voretzsch, ed., *François Froger. Relation du Premier Voyage des François à la Chine fait en 1698, 1699 et 1700 sur le Vaisseau 'L'Amphitrite'* (Leipzig: Asia Major, 1926).
11. The port fees for the French ship *L'Amphitrite* in 1699 were determined with only the length and width measurements. Voretzsch, ed., *François Froger*, 103. There are many more records for the later years, and they clearly show that there was no change in the practice until 1842.
12. In 1702, for example, the Hoppo in Canton pressured each foreign ship to give him 'a present of 2,000 in moneys, besides several other gifts out of our goods and cargo' before he would allow any merchandise to be bought or sold. This could be an early

reference to what later became the 'emperor's present'. Lubbock, ed., *Barlow's Journal*, 2:538.

13. For a more thorough analysis of the calculation of the port fees, see Van Dyke, 'Port Canton', chapter 1.
14. Many lists have survived of the import and export duties and the way they were calculated. For a couple of early and later examples see Morse, *Chronicles*, 1:93–4; Oriental and India Office Library, London (OIO): Mss Eur D 0963 'Trade-Currency Book' (1757), 84–6; and Robert Morrison, *Notices Concerning China, and the Port of Canton* (Malacca: Mission Press, 1823), 39–49.
15. Merchants who used their connections to the imperial family to trade in Canton were called 'Mandarin's Merchants' or 'Emperor's Merchants'. Several examples can be seen in Morse, *Chronicles*, vol. 1.
16. Hamilton, *A New Account of the East-Indies*, 2:228–9.
17. Morse, *Chronicles*, vol. 1.
18. Paul A. Van Dyke, 'The Ye Merchants of Canton, 1720–1804', *Review of Culture*, International Edition, No. 13 (January 2005), 6–47, and Jan Parmentier, *Tea Time in Flanders* (Ghent: Lundion Press, 1996), 101. The GIC records that were consulted are listed in the Bibliography.
19. Stadsarchief (City Archive), Antwerp (SAA): IC 5757.
20. Morse, *Chronicles*, 1:173.
21. OIO: G/12/25–26. Morse mentions that the 'security merchant' system did not begin until 1736. Morse, *Chronicles*, 1:247. However, other references suggest that it began earlier. National Archives, The Hague (NAH): VOC 4374, 4375, 4376, 4377.
22. NAH: VOC 4374–4378.
23. Paul Hallberg and Christian Koninckx, eds., *A Passage to China*, by Colin Campbell (Gothenburg: Royal Society of Arts and Sciences, 1996), 90 n.170, 156.
24. There are no Danish trade figures available before 1734. Rigsarkivet (State Archives), Copenhagen (RAC): Ask 2190–2203.
25. Zhao Chunchen (趙春晨), ed. *Aomen Jilüe* (澳門記略 A Brief Record of Macau), by Yin Guangren (印光任) and Zhang Rulin (張汝霖) (1751; Macau: Aomen wenhua sidu 澳門文化司睹, 1992), 2–3.
26. Plate 2 is the Danish account of this declaration. On 5 February 1741, the linguists were ordered by the governor-general (Tsiun Touck), Nanhai County magistrate (Namheyhjen) and the Hoppo to inform all foreigners still in Canton they had to leave if they did not have a ship in China. From this time forward, all foreigners were required to leave Canton in the off-season. RAC: Ask 1120. It is not clear what triggered the February 1741 proclamation. We know it had nothing to do with Lord Anson and his flagship *Centurion*, because he did not arrive in China until November 1742. The edict may have had something to do with the Dutch massacre of Chinese in Batavia in October 1740. There was much concern about this tragedy among Canton Chinese when they heard of it, and word of the incident would have probably reached China by November or December. In July 1741, the Dutch were restricted to Macao because of the massacre, but were later allowed to go to Canton again. Fei, *Macao 400 Years*, 134–135; Blussé, *Strange Company*, 94–95; Morse, *Chronicles*, 1:274–281; William Remmelink, *The Chinese War and the Collapse of the Javanese State, 1725–*

1743 (Leiden: KITLV Press, 1994), 126–9; NAH: Canton 191; RAC: Ask 1120; and Roderich Ptak, 'Macau: Trade and Society, circa 1740–1760', in *Maritime China in Transition 1750–1850*, eds. Wang Gungwu and Ng Chin-keong (Wiesbaden: Harrassowitz Verlag, 2004), 193.

27. Ptak, 'Macau: Trade and Society, circa 1740–1760', 204–5.
28. These assumptions are the author's alone, but are based on many conversations with Carl T. Smith about why the foreigners do not show up in the Portuguese records. Many Portuguese records from the early eighteenth century no longer exist.
29. NAH: VOC 2410; and SAA: IC. 5757.
30. RAC: Ask 1120.
31. James Ford Bell Library, University of Minnesota (JFB): 1732 fIr. Charles Irvine (d. 1771). Archive of papers relating to the Swedish East India Company: 1732–1774.
32. Smith and Van Dyke, 'Armenian Footprints in Macao', 27.
33. Gothenburg Universitetsbibliotek (University Library) (GUB): H22.4a:1199 'Dagbok på Resan med Skieppet *Printz Carl* Ahr 1753–1756'.
34. Ptak, 'Macau: Trade and Society, circa 1740–1760', 204–5.
35. Smith and Van Dyke, 'Armenian Footprints in Macao', 27–36.
36. Ptak, 'Macau: Trade and Society, circa 1740–1760', 204–5.
37. JFB: B 1758 fNe. In 1759, James Flint, the interpreter for the EIC, was arrested for going to Ningbo contrary to the emperor's orders. He was imprisoned for three years as punishment.
38. There is some evidence to suggest that the Mandarins were using this requirement to extract money from foreigners. In 1763, for example, the linguists offered to arrange for the Dutch to stay in Canton the entire season for a payment of 1,500 Spanish reals. But such bribery became less effective after the Flint affair in 1759. The Dutch did not hand over the money. The English supercargoes' claim in 1759 that they knew nothing of the 'ancient Order for Foreigners to leave Canton' is misleading, and was probably a ploy to extend their stay. Morse, *Chronicles*, 5:76–90; and NAH: Canton 71–4.
39. The Spanish factory was located on the west end of the quay between the Danish and French factories. Hosea Ballou Morse, *The International Relations of the Chinese Empire. The Period of Subjection 1834–1911*, 3 vols. (London: Longmans, Green & Co., 1910; reprint, Taipei: Yung Mei Mei Publishing, 1966), 3:70–3; Morse, *Chronicles*, 2: 119, 122–3; NAH: Canton 91; Kuo-tung Anthony Ch'en, *The Insolvency of the Chinese Hong Merchants, 1760–1843*, 2 vols. (Taipei: Academia Sinica, 1990), 7, 268, 273n.7.
40. The Swedish and Dutch records provide some of the best detail about the Portuguese and Spanish officers and cargos moving regularly between Canton and Macao. Those records also show the *Hong* merchants going to Macao as soon as the ships arrived to examine and purchase the Portuguese and Spanish imports. The larger houses maintained agents in Macao to take care of transferring all the goods between the two cities. See Bibliography for references.
41. Lockyer, *An Account of the Trade*, 98–177; Hamilton, A *New Account of the East-Indies*, 2:216–35; and Royal Library, Stockholm (KBS): M295, 'Journal du Voyage du Perou en Chine', by Commander De Frondat in 1708–1710.

42. For an extract from the emperor's 1757 edict, see Chen Bojian (陈柏坚) and Huang Qichen (黄启臣), *Guangzhou Wai Mao Shi* (广州外贸史 The History of Guangzhou's Foreign Trade) 3 vols. (Guangzhou: Guangzhou Chubanshe 广州出版社, 1995), 1:238–9.
43. 'Yesterday arrived at Wampo a Dutch Sloop of about 70 Tons named the New: Mode Capt. Jacobus Van den Beake. She is said to be Freighted by the Chinese that live at Batavia, but it is thought she comes to try if the Chinese here will suffer the Dutch Bottoms to trade again into this Country'. OIO: G/12/26. Captain Jacobus van den Beake and his first mate were both Dutch officers from Batavia. SAA: IC 5704–5705; and Universiteits Bibliotheek, Ghent (UBG): Ms 1849, 1925.
44. Smith and Van Dyke, 'Armenian Footprints in Macau', 20–39; Carl T. Smith and Paul A. Van Dyke, 'Four Armenian Families', *Review of Culture*, International Edition, No. 8 (October 2003), 40–50; and Smith and Van Dyke, 'Muslims in the Pearl River Delta', 6–15.
45. Such statements as 'no Trade can support the heavy Impositions we labor under' are endemic in foreign records, yet those very same foreigners return year after year to trade, despite no changes being made in the fees that they say were 'intolerable'. Morse, *Chronicles*, 5:78.

CHAPTER TWO

1. Zhao, ed. *Aomen Jilüe*; and Fei, *Macao 400 Years*, 133–40.
2. The administrative hierarchy is more complicated than what is presented here. Macao was under the administration of the military brigade, which was itself under the Xiangshan County seat. Humen was also connected to a hierarchy of magistrates. But the entire delta was under the care of the Canton office, which had the final say on how things were to be administered.
3. NAH: Canton 73–8; Morse, *Chronicles*, 5:92–3; Paul A. Van Dyke and Cynthia Viallé, *The Canton-Macao Dagregisters*, 1762 (Macao: Cultural Institute, forthcoming); and Paul A. Van Dyke and Cynthia Viallé, *The Canton-Macao Dagregisters*, 1763 (Macao: Cultural Institute, forthcoming). Hereafter these translated and printed *Dagregisters* will be referred to as CMD 1762 and 1763, respectively.
4. NAH: Canton 73.
5. CMD 1762 and 1763; NAH: Canton 73–8; and Morse, *Chronicles*, 2:15, 18, 22, 33 and 5:92–3.
6. Morse, *Chronicles*, 5:77–9 and 2:19.
7. Morse, *Chronicles*, 2:21–2 and 5:105.
8. The Hoppo House was a short distance up Yat-tak-she Street, which ran east from the Yaoulan Gate. Many of the Chinese names and customs procedures in the preceding paragraphs were taken from Morrison, *Notices Concerning China*, passim.
9. For a summary of the requirements of all ships entering China, see Peabody Essex Museum, Phillips Library (PL): 'Logbook of Frigate Congress 1819–1820'; Morrison, *Notes Concerning China*, 29; John Robert Morrison, *A Chinese Commercial Guide. Consisting of a Collection of Details Respecting Foreign Trade in China* (Canton: Albion Press, 1834), 14; and Morse, *Chronicles*, 2:288.

10. It was also common in many western ports for tidewaiters to attend the ships upon arrival, to ensure that nothing was loaded or unloaded without duties being paid. Jean Gordon Lee, *Philadelphians and the China Trade 1784–1844* (Philadelphia: University of Philadelphia Press, 1984), 34; and George Dixon, *A Voyage Round the World* (London: Geo. Goulding, 1789; reprint, New York: Da Capo Press, 1968), 291.
11. Morrison, *Chinese Commercial Guide* (1834), 11–2; and Morse, *Chronicles*, 1:91.
12. Osbeck has left us with transliterated names (in Swedish) for the five tollhouses between Whampoa and Bocca Tigris. He numbers them 4 through 8. Moving downriver from Whampoa, they were: 4) Øtjy-funn, 5) Ø-tjång, 6) Bactsja-funn, 7) Tånn-tao, and 8) Pho-munn. Pehr Osbeck, *Dagbok öfver en Ostindisk Resa åren 1750, 1751, 1752* (Stockholm: 1757; reprint, Redviva Publishing House, 1969), 132. The English translation of Osbeck's *Dagbok* lists them as: 4) Oty, 5) O-tyoang, 6) Baxia-tunn, 7) Toann-tao, and 8) Pho-munn. John Reinhold Forster, trans., *A Voyage to China and the East Indies*, by Peter Osbeck (London: Benjamin White, 1771), 203.
13. 'By this time, the Compradore is on board, and Jack Hoppo has fastened his boat by a small chain to the stern, and thus hangs on and swings with the ship when the tide changes'. C. Toogood Downing, *The Fan-Qui in China*, 3 vols. (London: 1838; reprint, Shannon: Irish University Press, 1972), 1:85–6.
14. Morrison, *Notes Concerning China*, 14.
15. Many of the Chinese customs documents that have survived are now available in print. Lau Fong (劉芳) and Zhang Wenqin (章文欽), eds., *Qingdai Aomen Zhongwen Dang'an Hui bian* (清代澳門中文檔案匯編 A Collection of Qing Chinese Documents Concerning Macau) 2 vols. (Macau: Aomen Jijinhui 澳門基金會, 1999).
16. These names were taken from Morrison, *Notes Concerning China*, passim; and Liang Tingnan (梁廷楠), *Yuehaiguan Zhi* (粤海关志 Gazetteer of Guangdong Maritime Customs) (1839; reprint, Guangzhou: Guangzhou Renmin Chubanshe 广州人民出版社, 2001).
17. *Hanghou Guankou* literally means the customhouse at the back of the *hongs* (factories). From the Chinese perspective in Canton, this was at the back, but from the perspective of foreigners, who arrived on the river, this was the front of the *hongs*.
18. Osbeck, *Dagbok*, 129.
19. There were about fifty vessels in 1724 accompanying the Hoppo to Whampoa for the measuring ceremony and about forty vessels in 1726. SAA: IC 5689bis; and UBG: Ms 1837.
20. Hoppos were usually honoured with a salute of seven to thirteen cannons; the supercargoes, captains and Chinese merchants, five to nine cannons; other officers and important visitors, three to five cannons. Warships, naval flagships, or important Chinese officials from another province or from Beijing were honoured with nine to fifteen cannons, according to their rank. Hoppos, Chinese officials and merchants answered back with strikes on their gongs or with cannon fire. Van Dyke, 'Port Canton', chapter 4.
21. In 1838 Downing stated that 'formerly they [the Hoppos] used to be saluted with a round of artillery, but in consequence of a gun having burst on one of these occasions, and killed a Chinaman, the practice has been discontinued ever since'. Downing, *The Fan-Qui in China*, 3:236–7.

22. RAC: Ask 998; and Parmentier, *Tea Time in Flanders*, 94–5. For an interesting description of the Hoppo's band, which was said to resemble 'a low-gelder's horn and the cackling of geese', see Dixon, *A Voyage Round the World*, 313. John Nicol likened the Chinese instruments to 'bagpipes'. Tim Flannery, ed., *The Life and Adventures of John Nicol, Mariner* (New York: Atlantic Monthly Press, 1997), 160–1. Wathen was so disappointed by the Chinese musicians that he suggested the Chinese 'auditory nerves must have been very differently constructed from those which compose the European organs of hearing'. James Wathen, *Journal of a Voyage in 1811 and 1812 to Madras and China* (London: 1814), 208; and SAA: IC 5689[bis].
23. Parmentier, *Tea Time in Flanders*, 95; and RAC: Ask 1117.
24. The covid is a unit of measurement for length. The conversions used in the eighteenth century in Canton for the covid varied, but they usually fell within a range of one covid being equal to about 14.1 to 14.6 English inches. The covid itself was not a uniform measure within China, but could differ with each application and/or occupation, as well as location. Samuel Wells Williams, *The Chinese Commercial Guide* (Canton: Chinese Repository, 1856; 5th ed., Hong Kong: A. Shortrede & Co.; reprint, Taipei: Ch'eng-wen Publishing Co., 1966), 283–5. The following references show how the ships were measured at Whampoa: NAH: VOC 2410; SAA: IC 5704; JFB: Irvine Papers; John Carter Brown Library, Brown University, Providence (JCB): 'Journal of Benjamin C. Carter, Surgeon of the Ship *Ann and Hope* on her First Voyage from Providence to Canton'; Robert Peabody, *The Log of the Grand Turks* (Boston: Houghton Mifflin Company, 1926), 84; and Philip Chadwick Foster Smith, *The Empress of China* (Philadelphia: Philadelphia Maritime Museum, 1984), 153.
25. NAH: VOC 2410; and Smith, *The Empress of China*, 153.
26. For a breakdown of the measurements in Chinese, see Van Dyke, 'Port Canton', 82.
27. 'As soon as the tax [port fee] had been calculated, Pinqua [the security merchant] signed a bond for the Hoppo guaranteeing its payment'. Peabody, *The Log of the Grand Turk*, 85.
28. Josiah Quincy, ed., *The Journals of Major Samuel Shaw, the First American Consul at Canton. With a Life of the Author, by Josiah Quincy* (Boston: Wm. Crosby and H.P. Nichols, 1847; reprint, Documentary Publications, 1970), 176–7.
29. Parmentier, *Tea Time in Flanders*, 95; and RAC: Ask 1117. There are also English and Dutch references that show the Hoppos personally attending the ships in the early decades.
30. The acting Hoppo in July 1724 told the English they had to wait for another ship to arrive before he would make the trip to Whampoa. OIO: G/12/25. See also, Quincy, ed., *The Journals of Major Samuel Shaw*, 176. In 1770 the Swedish Captain Carl Gustav Ekeberg reported that the Hoppo measured 6 or 7 ships a day ('På detta såttet måter han ibland 6 til 7 skepp om dagen'). Carl Gustav Ekeberg, *Capitaine Carl Gustav Ekebergs Ostindiska Resa, åren 1770 och 1771* (Stockholm: Rediviva, 1970), 107.
31. Massachusetts Historical Society, Boston (MHS): 'William Elting Notebook 1799–1803'; Flannery, ed., *The Life and Adventures of John Nicol*, 161; Morse, *Chronicles*, 2: 14, 17; and Morrison, *Notes Concerning China*, 34.
32. There are many references in the foreign records to the difficulties these types of luxury goods caused for both the foreigners and the Chinese merchants. For a couple of examples, see Morse, *Chronicles*, 5:71, 79, 129, 154 and 2:15.

33. Smith and Van Dyke, 'Armenian Footprints in Macau', 20–39.
34. For some early accounts of the Hoppo's present, see Van Dyke, 'Port Canton', chapter 1; and C. Madrolle, ed., *Journal du Voyage de la Chine fait dans les Années 1701, 1702, & 1703*, in *Les Premiers Voyages*, by C. Madrolle, 109.
35. For several examples of these gifts and privileges given to foreigners, see Van Dyke, 'Port Canton', chapter 1.
36. Peter Dobell, *Travels in Kamtchatka and Siberia; with a Narrative of a Residence in China*, 2 vols. (London: Henry Colburn and Richard Bentley, 1830. Reprint, New York: Arno Press, 1970), 2:171.
37. For other examples of the poor quality of these gifts, see Van Dyke, 'Port Canton', chapter 1.
38. The Hoppo's measurements (dimensions) differed slightly each time the same ship was measured. Some ships measured three or four times in Whampoa had three or four different measurements. Captains and supercargoes squabbled about this inconsistency, but usually it was such a small difference it was not deemed worth the effort to correct it.
39. The port fees for the French Ship *L'Amphitrite* in 1699 were determined with only the length and width measurements. Voretzsch, ed., *François Froger*, 103. Records from later years confirm that the practice remained unchanged until 1842.
40. There may be exceptions, but this study has found that the foreigners never adapted to using the abacus despite the obvious advantages of doing so. With the abacus, the Chinese merchants could calculate complicated exchange rates, pricing structures and other relatively complex data with ease and without the use of pen and paper. The foreigners, on the other hand, continued to rely on their long-hand methods (as depicted in Plate 28) throughout the Canton era.
41. NAH: VOC 4375. The measurements of the first VOC ship in China in 1729, the *Coxhorn*, are also available. Those figures were not used for this example because of a couple minor mistakes in the calculations. The way the fees were calculated, however, is identical to the *Duifje*. NAH: VOC 4374.
42. The emperor's present was known by several different names, including the 'Hoppo's present', 'Hoppo's dues', 'Hoppo's money', 'Mandarin's present' and by the generic Chinese word '*cumshaw*' (meaning 'present' or 'gratuity'). The French paid 2,050 taels and the Moors 1,850 taels. William Milburn, *Oriental Commerce*, 2 vols. (London: Black, Parry, & Co., 1813; reprint, New Delhi: Munshiram Manoharlal Publishers, 1999), 2:492; SAA: IC 5696; and RAC: Ask 1141.
43. SAA: IC 5684, 5690, 5692, 5695, 5710.
44. For a more detailed discussion of the two different methods used to calculate the port fees and a list of the rates, see Van Dyke, 'Port Canton', chapter 1.
45. The reduction of the fees is mentioned in the *Canton Register* on 15 February and 29 March 1830. In the 31 May 1833 issue, an English translation of a Chinese proclamation clearly states that the emperor had granted the 1830 reduction of the port fees as a 'favor', and that this adjustment shows his 'compassion towards distant foreigners'. As a result of this benevolent act, the document goes on to say that the number of English ships increased to 26 in 1833 when there had only been 20 in 1830. For a simple breakdown of the emperor's present after the reduction, see Morrison, *Chinese Commercial Guide* (1834), 22–3. There are several records that give

a breakdown of the emperor's present before 1830, and they all disagree with each other. Two of them, along with an analysis of the figures, can be seen in Van Dyke, 'Port Canton', chapter 1. A third set of figures was found later in the GIC archives, SAA: IC 5740. A more basic breakdown of the emperor's present (called 'enter-port fee') can be seen in the *Canton Register* (26 December 1833). These figures were translated from the *Canton Custom-House Book* (published in 1725), which may have been the *Yuehaiguan Zhi*. Volume 9 of this series has a section governing the measuring of the ships and some identical information is shown there. There is also a breakdown of the emperor's present in a Chinese document from 1759 that was recently published in Xing Yongfu (邢永福) , et al., *Qing Gong Guangzhou Shisan Hang Dang'an Jingxuan* (清官广州十三行档案精选 A Selection of Qing Imperial Documents of the Guangzhou Shisan Hang) (Guangzhou: Guangdong Jingji Chubanshe 广东经济出版社, 2002), n. 41. There are such great differences, however, between all of these lists of figures, and a couple of them do not add up to 1,950 taels, so there is no way of knowing which breakdown is correct.

46. Hosea Ballou Morse, *The Gilds of China with an Account of the Gild Merchant or Co-hong of Canton* (London: Longmans, Green and Co., 1909), 66; and Morse, *Chronicles*, 1:81.
47. Morse shows clearly that the three-tiered rating system was already in place by 1699. The rates were not yet set to where they would remain for more than 100 years, but they were close. Morse, *Chronicles*, 1:88.
48. The 1699 reference is in Morse, *Chronicles*, 1:92.
49. Morse, *Chronicles*, 5:7–10, 105.
50. Morse mentions that 1727 was the first year the 1,950 taels appears in the English records. Morse, *Chronicles*, 1:185. The Ostend Company records, however, show that the present was a part of the port fees in earlier years. All three of the Belgian ships in 1726 paid 1,800 taels as the 'Mandarin's fee'. SAA: IC 5696. By 1730, the Ostend Company ships were paying the standard 1,950 taels. SAA: IC 5710.
51. MHS: 'William Elting Notebook 1799–1803'. I have found only one reference to the VOC officers being instructed to make use of this innovation. That statement, however, suggests it was indeed common practice. On 22 August 1764 the following is recorded: 'The Hoppo will come out to measure all four ships on the 29th of this month, which I inform Your Honours so that you can clear away and scrub the decks and also draw the fock- and mizzen-masts inwards as is the custom'. NAH: Canton 73.
52. JFB: Irvine Papers, Letter/Report dated 29 January 1733.
53. NAH: VOC 2410.
54. 'The first American sloop that came, she having only one mast, the Chinamen said, "Hey, yaw, what fashion? How can measure ship with one mast?"— they having been accustomed to measure ships with more masts than one'. Flannery, ed., *The Life and Adventures of John Nicol*, 161. This sloop may have been the *Grand Turk*, which arrived in Canton in 1786. 'The Hoppo's attendants first ran a measuring tape from the rudder-post to the foremast, and the length was carefully written down'. Peabody, *The Log of the Grand Turk*, 84. This, however, was not the first time that a sloop came to China. The Dutch also arrived in a sloop in 1727, and many private traders from India and Manila often had small vessels as well. OIO: G/12/26.
55. Smith, *The Empress of China*, 153.

56. SAA: IC 5704.
57. 'This morning I rec'd from the Linguist an account of the Ships measurement & their custom for measuring is from the Center of Foremast to Center of Mizen mast for length and from outside to outside on Deck for breadth, but they frequently extend the line beyond the side as they say to make up for a ships tumbling'. Rhode Island Historical Society, Providence (RIHS): Mss 828 'Logbook of Ship *Hope* 1802–1803', 10 September 1802.
58. On 25 July 1729, for example, the English reported: 'the Hoppo sending to us to desire we would advance him some mony on Account of the Measurage of the Ships'. OIO: G/12/28.
59. For a more detailed discussion of the payment of port fees, see Van Dyke, 'Port Canton', chapter 1.
60. Downs states that 'because nothing like Western commercial law existed in China, contracts were enforceable only at Macao'. He is correct in stating that much of the trade was done verbally, which was especially true with Americans who handled small volumes. The East India companies' orders with the *Hong* merchants, however, were usually put in writing and all parties signed them. The hundreds of Chinese commercial contracts in the foreign archives that were used for this study testify to this practice. The agreements were binding and enforceable. Jacques Downs, *The Golden Ghetto. The American Commercial Community at Canton and the Shaping of American China Policy, 1784–1844* (Bethlehem: Lehigh University Press, 1997), 95. See Plates 7–8, 10–1, 13, 17–20, 25–6. Other Chinese contracts from Canton can be seen in the following articles: Paul A. Van Dyke, 'A Reassessment of the China Trade: The Canton Junk Trade As Revealed in Dutch and Swedish Records of the 1750s to the 1770s', in *Maritime China in Transition 1750–1850*, eds. Wang Gungwu and Ng Chin-keong (Wiesbaden: Harrassowitz Verlag, 2004), 151–67; Van Dyke, 'The Ye Merchants of Canton', 6–47; Paul A. Van Dyke, 'Cai and Qiu Enterprises: Merchants of Canton 1730–1784', *Review of Culture*, International Edition, No 15 (July 2005), 60–101; and Paul A. Van Dyke, 'The Yan Family: Merchants of Canton 1734–1780s', *Review of Culture*, International Edition, No. 9 (January 2004), 30–85.
61. A few examples of foreigners selling goods to other foreigners can be found in RAC: Ask 896, 1130, 1131.
62. NAH: VOC 4556. Entries under 'Ballast' and 'Ballast (Steene)'; and George Bryan Souza, 'Country Trade and Chinese Alum: Raw Material Supply and Demand in Asia's Textile Production in the 17th and 18th Centuries', *Review of Culture*, International Edition, No. 11 (July 2004), 136–53.
63. For an explanation of the change in the *waiyang* in 1760 see Ann Bolbach White, 'The Hong Merchants of Canton' (Ph.D. dissertation, University of Pennsylvania, 1967), 54–5; and Ch'en, *Insolvency*, 7.
64. A couple of examples of this authenticity mark can be seen on the *jinshi* (進士) diplomas on display at the Imperial College (Guozijian 国子监) in Beijing.
65. *Chinese Repository* (Canton: The South China Mission, 1832–1852) 20 vols. (Jan 1845), 14:44–5 and (Mar 1846), 15:150–4. The latter reference has a list of the tonnages and port fees of several hundred British ships in Canton in 1846.
66. Morrison, *Chinese Commercial Guide* (1848), 185.
67. *Chinese Repository* (Mar 1846), 15:15–4 and (Apr 1846), 15:165.

CHAPTER THREE

1. I have converted fathoms to feet for the sake of clarity. Most of the contemporary charts and navigational guides use fathoms and the length of the fathom (an 'average' arm span) varied a little, but was usually 5½ to 6 feet. Lieutenant Commander Leland Lovette, *Naval Customs. Traditions and Usage* (Annapolis: US Naval Institute, 1934; reprint, 1936; reprint, 1939); and Peter Kemp, ed., *The Oxford Companion to Ships and the Sea* (Oxford: Oxford University Press, 1976; reprint, 1988).
2. John Robert Morrison, *A Chinese Commercial Guide. Consisting of A Collection of Details Respecting Foreign Trade in China* (Canton: Albion Press, 1834; 2nd ed., Macao: Wells Williams, 1844), 87. In 1832 an author in the *Chinese Register* stated that he thought the 'eddies and whirlpools' in the Pearl River were stronger than any other river he knew of. 'These eddies run so strong as to force a ship, even with a strong breeze, completely round; and to carry her along against her helm'. *Canton Register* (17 October 1832).
3. The Swedes record two sandbars above Lintin. One was called Lintin's bar and in 1791 the water over it was 4½ fathoms or 27 feet. The other was Longyt's bar and the water above it was 4 fathoms or 24 feet. Some of the contemporary maps list both of these bars as being one, Lintin's bar. GUB: Svenska Ostindiska Kompaniets Arkiv. Journal för Skeppet *Gustaf III* 1791–1792.
4. The numbers of ships were taken from Louis Dermigny, *La Chine et l'Occident. Le Commerce a Canton au XVIII Siècle 1719–1833*, 3 vols. and album (Paris: S.E.V.P.E. N., 1964), 2:521–5; and *Chinese Repository* (April 1846), 15:165.
5. 'On arriving on the coast [of China] you will get a Pilot firing a Gun, as soon as there will be occasion for one'. RIHS: 'Trader's Book'.
6. Glyndwr Williams, ed., *A Voyage Round the World in the Years MDCCXL, I, II, III, I, by George Anson* (London: Oxford University Press, 1974), 312; George Wilkinson, *Sketches of Chinese Customs & Manners, in 1811–12* (Bath: J. Browne, 1814), 107; Arva Colbert Floyd, ed., *The Diary of a Voyage to China 1859–1860*, by Rev. Young J. Allen (Atlanta: Emory University, 1943), 34; and Basil Hall, *Voyage to Loo-choo: and Other Places in the Eastern Seas, in the Year 1816, Including an Account of Captain Maxwell's Attack on the Batteries at Canton* (Edinburgh: A. Constable, 1826), 24.
7. Lau and Zhang, eds., *Qingdai Aomen*, 1: nos. 906, 907.
8. Ibid.
9. For a list of the outside pilots' fees from 137 foreign ships and a few examples of demanding pilots, see Van Dyke, 'Port Canton', 119–21 and appendix G. The fees they demanded could vary from a few Spanish dollars to as much as 300 dollars.
10. In 1742 Lord Anson communicated with his three outside pilots in broken Portuguese. Many outside pilots are recorded as not being able to speak a Western language. Leo Heaps, ed., *Log of the Centurion, by Captain Philip Saumarez* (New York: Macmillan Publishing Co., 1974), 188; and Williams, ed., *A Voyage Round the World*, 315. One example reads as follows: 'On concluding the bargain, he [the outside pilot] insisted on shaking hands with the captain, to ratify its conditions, or, as he expressed it, "so can secure". The next moment he assumed the direction, and, in barbarous English, aided by gesture, began to issue his orders. At half-past three o'clock P.M. we anchored about two miles from the town of Macao'. W. S. W. Ruschenberger, *Narrative of a*

Voyage Round the World, during the Years 1835, 36, and 37; including a Narrative of an Embassy to the Sultan of Muscat and the King of Siam, 2 vols. (London: 1838. Reprint, Dawsons of Pall Mall, 1970), 2:183.

11. August Frugé and Neal Harlow, trans. and eds., *A Voyage to California, the Sandwich Islands, & Around the World in the Years 1826–1829, by Auguste Duhaut-Cilly* (Berkeley: University of California Press, 1999), 231–2; Blanche Collet Wagner, *Voyage of the Héros around the World with Duhaut-Cilly in the Years 1826, 1827, 1828 & 1829*, by Lt. Edmond le Netrel (Los Angeles: Glen Dawson, 1951), 57; and Flannery, ed., *The Life and Adventures of John Nicol*, 99.
12. SAA: IC 5757; and CMD 1762, entry on September 6.
13. For other examples of pilots' receipts written in Chinese, see Van Dyke, 'Port Canton', 122.
14. One of these recommendations has survived in the Danish archives and reads as follows: 'The Pilot Asam has piloted this ship *Cron Printzen* from Ladrong [Island] to Macao well and without the least complaint on 21 September 1783'. Signed by Capt. Schifter. RAC: Ask 953. For other examples of pilots offering recommendations, see Van Dyke, 'Port Canton', 124–5; and UBG: Ms 1930.
15. In 1781 the officers on the ship *Printz Friderich* bought 4 cabbages, 8 catties of beef, 400 oranges, 200 onions and 150 bunches of radishes from their outside pilot. From their Macao pilot they purchased 160 eggs and 300 oranges. RAC: Ask 947. There are many other examples in the foreign records.
16. 'As soon as the Mandareens at Macao, are satisfied in all their enquires, he orders of a River Pilot, which never comes on board until you have laid 24 hours in the Road'. MHS: 'William Elting Notebook 1799–1803'. Milburn also mentions that it took about 24 hours. Milburn, *Oriental Commerce*, 1:462.
17. PL: Benjamin Shreve Papers, 'Ship *Minerva* Account book 1809'. One of Budwell's receipts dated November 1819 shows his charges to be one dollar for a room, half a dollar for breakfast and one and a half dollars for dinner. RIHS: Carrington Papers.
18. In the 1830s, ships were still stopping at the Macao Tavern to get their pilots. The editors of the *Canton Register* asked new arrivals to fill in forms while they were waiting, stating the number of passengers aboard, ports of call, cargos and any other important information. *Canton Register* (24 January 1833). This data was then published in the newspaper for all to read.
19. *Canton Register* (24 November 1835).
20. For an example of a ship plotting to run past the forts without permission, see PL: Waters Family Papers, 'Ship *Mariposa* 1835–1836'; and Van Dyke, 'Port Canton', 133 n. 229.
21. PL: 1819 C3, 'Log of Frigate *Congress* 1819'. This information about the small ships is based on several hundred ships' logs, journals and account books of vessels from Mystic, Providence, Boston and Salem. See Bibliography for details.
22. For examples of damaged ships arriving and being refused entry unless they conducted trade, see NAH: Canton 137 'Generaal Rapport'; and NAH: VOC 4556 under the heading 'Canton'. Pilots often reported ships that had no cargo aboard. Lau and Zhang, eds., *Qingdai Aomen*, 2: nos. 1313, 1314, 1343, 1405, 1464, 1467, 1484, 1492.
23. Lockyer, *An Account of the Trade*, 146 (see also 191); and UBG: Ms 1840 (ship journal from 1726).

24. In 1755, for example, the SOIC ship *Prinsessan Sophia Albertina* sailed upriver with the assistance of boats from Swedish, Prussian, Danish and French ships anchored at Whampoa. Johan Brelin, *Beskrifning öfver en Äfventyrlig Resa till och från Ost-Indien, Södra Amerika och en del af Europa af Johan Brelin 1758* (Uppsala, 1758; reprint, Stockholm: Tryckeri AB Björkmans, 1973), 16. In 1702, Edward Barlow also states that they waited at Bocca Tigris 'two days for a boat to come down to help us up the river'. The dependence on tow boats was a characteristic of the trade from the beginning. Lubbock, ed., *Barlow's Journal*, 2:538.
25. Milburn's trade manual suggests that 10 sampans were usually employed by the EIC ships in 1813, but some of his figures do not agree with many of the other companies' records. Because the EIC ships' expense books are not available in the company archive, we were not able to verify Milburn's numbers. It seems strange that the large EIC ships would only employ 10 sampans when the SOIC, DAC, CFI and VOC ships were consistently employing 40 to 80 sampans. Milburn, *Oriental Commerce*, 2:495. See Van Dyke, 'Port Canton', 138–48 passim.
26. For a list of sampans hired by 132 company ships from 1729 to 1833, see Van Dyke, 'Port Canton', appendix H. Charles de Constant also mentions pilots using 50 to 80 small boats to assist in the piloting. Louis Dermigny, ed., *Les Mémoires de Charles de Constant sur le Commerce a la Chine, par Charles de Constant* (Paris: S.E.V.P.E.N., 1964), 382–83.
27. The Dutch called this anchorage 'Zout Zout Ham' or its shortened version 'Zt. Zt. Ham'. This was probably a corruption of its Chinese name, *shiziyang* (Cantonese: *Sze-stze-yaong*) meaning 'Lion's reach'. Morrison, *Notices Concerning China*, 14. The English, French and Americans often referred to the place as 'downriver', the 'Second Bar', 'above the fort' or 'the bogue' anchorage. The Danes and Swedes called it 'Bocca Tigris Roads'. Van Dyke, 'Port Canton', chapter 2.
28. OIO: G/12/24–25, entries dated 12 January 1724 and 30 October 1724; UBG: Ms 1926 (ship journal from 1732); NAH: VOC 2410; and RAC: Ask 880. The Danish ship *Kongen af Dannemark* in January 1737 moved downriver after reaching a draught of 16½ feet, but 18 feet shows up more often. RAC: Ask 997. See also an entry from 1738 in Morse, *Chronicles*, 1:263.
29. For the size of the English ships at Canton in the early years see Morse, *Chronicles*, vol. 1. For the size of the Ostend Company ships at Canton in the 1710s and 1720s, see K. Degryse and Jan Parmentier, 'Maritime Aspects of the Ostend Trade to Mocha, India and China (1715–1732)' in *Ships, Sailors and Spices. East India Companies and Their Shipping in the 16th, 17th and 18th Centuries*, eds. Jaap R. Bruijn and Femme S. Gaastra (Amsterdam: NEHA, 1993), 165–75.
30. NAH: VOC 4388, 6346, 6364, 6375, 11269; JFB: B 1758 fNe; NAH: Canton 72; and Van Dyke, 'Port Canton', 141–2.
31. Van Dyke, 'Port Canton', appendices H and I.
32. 'Skibsprotocoler' from the 1760s, RAC: Ask 907–23. For the size of the Danish ships, see Van Dyke, 'Port Canton', appendices H and J.
33. NAH: Canton 72. For the size of the Swedish ships, see Van Dyke, 'Port Canton', appendices H and K.
34. Van Dyke, 'Port Canton', 142–3.

35. For a more detailed narrative of how the piloting procession moved, see Van Dyke, 'Port Canton', 143–9.
36. British Map Library, London (BML): MAR.VI.26, 'Map of the Pearl River', caption titled 'A Survey of the Tigris, from Canton to the Island of Lankeet', by J. Huddart, dated 10 October 1786.
37. By 1878 the river was reportedly seventeen feet deep over the shoals. If this reference is correct then the sandbars grew one foot in about 150 years. A. G. Findley, *A Directory for the Navigation of the Indian Archipelago, China, and Japan*, 2nd ed (London: Richard Holmes Laurie, 1878), 979.
38. The passenger sampans between Whampoa and Canton were also called 'dollar boats'. Howard Malcom, *Travels in South-Eastern Asia embracing Hindustan, Malaya, Siam, and China with Notices of Numerous Missionary Stations and a Full Account of the Burman Empire*, 2 vols. (London: Charles Tilt, 1839; facsimile reprint, New Delhi: Asian Educational Services, 2004), 2:169.
39. For a brief description of a two-week rescue operation to get the VOC ship *Slooten* afloat in 1763, see Van Dyke, 'Port Canton', 150.
40. The pilot responsible for running the VOC ship *Slooten* aground in 1763 was refused his pay for the passage. NAH: Canton 72.
41. Many of these examples were taken from the instructions for the piloting of naval squadrons in the delta in 1804, titled 'Piloting the fleet at the start of day' ('rijian kaichuan zuo jiachuan'). Lau and Zhang, eds., *Qingdai Aomen*, 1:no. 906. Foreign ships, of course, also had well-established procedures for sailing in fog and during times of limited visibility that were not dissimilar to the Chinese methods. Guns and bells were used instead of gongs and conch shells, but foreign ships also sounded out regular beats on their drums, hung a specific number of lanterns in the masts, or lit fires or torches on their decks to signal and warn others of their approach. Baker Library, Cambridge, Massachusetts (BL): Misc. Mss. 733, 'Instructions for the better keeping Company with His Majesty's Ship *Enterprize*', dated 16 August 1762. See also Williams, *Chinese Commercial Guide*, appendix 256–8. A reference from 1819 states that Chinese commanders used one cannon shot to signal their fleet to weigh anchor so the practice may have varied somewhat. Sir Richard Phillips, *Diary of a Journey Overland, through the Maritime Provinces of China, from Manchao, on the South Coast of Hainan, to Canton, in the Years 1819 and 1820* (London: Phillips, 1822), 51.
42. Carl Ekeberg mentioned in 1770 that Chinese vessels in the river gave commands with strikes on the gong. Ekeberg, *Ostindiska Resa*, 131. There are other examples in the foreign records.
43. William Shaler, *Journal of a Voyage between China and the North-Western Coast of America, made in 1804*. In *The American Register or General Repository of History, Politics, and Science*, Part 1 (Philadelphia: T. & G. Palmer, 1808; reprint, Claremont, California: Saunders Studio Press, 1935), 3:24; and Hall, *Voyage to Loo-choo*, 24.
44. Hall, *Voyage to Loo-choo*, 24.
45. James Johnson, *An Account of a Voyage to India, China, &c. in His Majesty's Ship Caroline, Performed in the Years 1803–4–5, Interspersed with Descriptive Sketches and Cursory Remarks* (London: J.G. Barnard, 1806), 59.
46. Lau and Zhang, eds., *Qingdai Aomen*, 1: no. 906.

47. Ibid.
48. These helpers show up in the records as 'fishermen pilots', 'under-pilots', 'river pilots' or, simply, 'assistant pilots'.
49. For a brief but colourful description of both the Macao pilots and the river pilots, see Dobell, *Travels in Kamtchatka*, 2:129; and Van Dyke, 'Port Canton', 155.
50. Zhao, ed., *Aomen Jilüe*, 79; *Chinese Repository* (Apr 1835), 582; Morrison, *Chinese Commercial Guide* (1834), 10; William Hunter, *The 'Fan Kwae' at Canton before Treaty Days 1825–1844*. (London: 1882. Reprint, London, 1885; London, 1911; Shanghai: Mercury Press, 1938; Taipei: 1966. Reprint, under the title *An American in Canton (1825–44)*, Hong Kong: Derwent Communications, Ltd., 1994), 17; and Yang Jibo (杨继波), Wu Zhiliang (吴志良), and Deng Kaisong (邓开颂), eds., *Ming-Qing Shiqi Aomen Wenti Dang'an Wenxian Huibian* (明清时期澳门问题档案文献汇编 Collection of Ming-Qing documents concerning Macau affairs) 6 vols. (Beijing: *Renmin Chubanshe* 人民出版社, 1999), 6:93, 148. There are English translations of some of these Chinese documents in the *Canton Register* (24 Mar 1835) and *Chinese Repository* (Apr 1835), 3:581.
51. Pilots were often accused of incompetence by foreigners. Morrison has few good words to say about pilots. Morrison, *Chinese Commercial Guide* (1834), 12. In the posthumous 1848 edition of this book, however, we find the following statement (probably added by Wells Williams): 'There is a good deal of difference however, among the pilots, and some of them are quite competent to carry a ship up the river; others know much less of the management of a ship, while still they are well acquainted with the channel; at times, whether skillful or ignorant, they are unreasonably blamed by the officers of the ship, and getting sulky, care but little where or how she goes'. John Robert Morrison, *A Chinese Commercial Guide. Consisting of A Collection of Details Respecting Foreign Trade in China* (Canton: Albion Press, 1834; 2nd ed., Macao: Wells Williams, 1844; 3rd. ed., Canton: *Chinese Repository*, 1848), 126.
52. Morrison, *Chinese Commercial Guide* (1848), 126.
53. This information was pieced together from several sources. KBS: M280; NAH: VOC 4387; SAA: IC 5697; and MHS: 'William Trotter Letter/Journal 1797'. For more details about the size of the Canton junks, see Van Dyke, 'Port Canton', 156–7, chapter 5 and appendix U; and Van Dyke, 'A Reassessment of the China Trade', 151–67.
54. RAC: Ask 1150.
55. Downing, *The Fan-Qui in China*, 1:113–4, 204–6, 232–4.
56. KBS: M280; NAH: VOC 4387; SAA: IC 5697; MHS: 'William Trotter Letter/Journal 1797'; and Van Dyke, 'Port Canton', 156–7, chapter 5 and appendix U.
57. Findley, *A Directory for the Navigation*, 979. The twenty-foot limitation is also mentioned in Williams, *Chinese Commercial Guide* (1863), appendix 34–9.
58. For a breakdown of pilots' fees charged in each decade, see Van Dyke, 'Port Canton', 160.
59. Milburn, *Oriental Commerce*, 1:495. See Van Dyke, 'Port Canton', 160 nn. 295 and 296.
60. Downing, *The Fan-Qui in China*, 1:85.
61. Morrison, *Chinese Commercial Guide* (1844), 88.
62. NAH: Canton 74; Morrison, *Chinese Commercial Guide* (1848), 123. One source from

1828 and a couple from 1835 show fourteen licensed Macao pilots in those years. *Canton Register* (23 August 1828); and Yang, et al., eds., *Ming-Qing Shiqi*, 6:93, 148, with English translations in *Canton Register* (24 March 1835) and *Chinese Repository* (Apr 1835), 3:581.

63. Morrison, *Notices Concerning China*, 30.
64. For a discussion of the pilots' incomes, see Van Dyke, 'Port Canton', 162–4.
65. Dobell mentioned in the early 1800s that the 'master' (presumably the Macao pilot) of the river pilot strutted about in 'silks' and lived like a 'gentleman'. Dobell, *Travels in Kamtchatka and Siberia*, 2:138–9.
66. NAH: VOC 4556; and NAH: Canton 72.
67. Lau and Zhang, eds., *Qingdai Aomen*, 1:nos. 906, 922, 934, 1003.
68. Paul A. Van Dyke, 'Pigs, Chickens, and Lemonade: The Provisions Trade in Canton, 1700–1840', *International Journal of Maritime History* (June 2000), 11–44; and Morse, *Chronicles*, 2:199–200, 259.
69. One of these popular smuggling anchorages was Cumsingmoon (Jinxing Men 金星門). Its location was between the present-day city of Zhuhai (珠海) and Qi'ao Island (淇澳島). This anchorage no longer exists because of recent landfill. Zhao, ed., *Aomen Jilüe*, 33–7; *Xiangshan Xian Zhi* ([新修]) 香山縣志 Xiangshan County Gazetteer) 2 vols. (1828; reprint, Taipei: Xuesheng Chubanshe 學生出版社, 1985), 1:641–50.
70. Even though Chinese records give the impression that everything was very tightly controlled in the delta the fact remains that smuggling was rampant. For examples of contemporary Chinese records, see Lau and Zhang, eds., *Qingdai Aomen*. The disagreement with the Dutch about towing charges in 1762 can be seen in CMD 1762, entry on October 18.
71. Morse, *Chronicles*, 2:344–6. Despite this discovery of pilots smuggling opium in 1799, they continued to be involved in that trafficking. *Canton Register* (24 March 1835).
72. As other chapters will show, customs officers were in fact part of the problem. 'Many of the government boats are also engaged in the smuggling trade . . . The fee on opium, of one dollar per chest, paid for connivance to the officers of the imperial preventive squadron, is left by the smugglers in charge of the commanding officer of the vessel, on whom the imperial officers call for what is due to them'. Morrison, *Chinese Commercial Guide* (1834), 29. There are many other references to officials smuggling opium into China in Morse, *Chronicles*, 4: passim.
73. Morse, *Chronicles*, 4:223; and OIO: Mss Eur Ph 377, 'Photocopy of the Ship *Forbes* Journal'. The English brig *Jamesina* was involved in opium smuggling from at least 1823 to the mid-1830s. It was also used as a floating 'hulk' for the warehousing of opium in Lintin harbour in the early 1830s. Morse, *Chronicles*, 4: passim. The *Forbes* towed the *Jamesina* from Calcutta to Singapore, then part of the way from Singapore to the Pearl River Delta. Hunt Janin, *The India-China Opium Trade in the Nineteenth Century* (London: McFarland & Co., 1999), 169–70.
74. In 1830 the ships *Dunira* and *Duchess of Atholl* left in the company of two other English ships that had received their Grand Chops and, presumably had their pilots and sampans to assist them. Morse, *Chronicles*, 4:24. There were, of course, other ships that threatened to leave without the Grand Chop, but if they did, they still had to deal with the shallows and the cannons at Bocca Tigris.

75. R. C. Hurley, *The Tourist's Guide to Canton, the West River and Macao* (Hong Kong: Noronha & Co., 1895), 59.
76. The Modao Fort was on the east and the Luozhou Fort on the west of the Luozhou entrance. Qing military maps show their locations. Zhao, ed., *Aomen Jilüe*, 202; Jin Guo Ping and Wu Zhiliang, 'Reformular as Origens de Macao', *Macao* (December 1999), 178–9; and *Xiangshan Xian Zhi* (1828; reprint, 1985), 641–43, 726 and (1880; reprint 1985), 1977, 1989.
77. William Dallas Bernard, *Narrative of the Voyages and Services of the Nemesis from 1840 to 1843*, 2 vols. (London: Henry Colburn, 1844), 1:7–9; Michael Levien, ed., *The Cree Journals. The Voyages of Edward H. Cree, Surgeon R.N., as Related in His Private Journals, 1837–1856* (Devon: Webb & Bower Ltd., 1981; Scarborough: Nelson Canada Ltd., 1981), 76; and *Chinese Repository* (Mar 1841), 10:180–1.
78. There were a number of other steamers in China at this time, including the *Columbine* and the *Queen*. The *Queen* towed the *Wellesley* behind it. Levien, *The Cree Journals*, 55, 72 and 75 n. 3. The steamers *Sesostris, Nemesis*, and *Phelgethon* were used to position the sail-driven warships into strategic firing positions during the First Opium War, and other steamers were engaged in other campaigns in China. Alexander Murray, *Doings in China. Being the Personal Narrative of an Officer Engaged in the Late Chinese Expedition, from the Recapture of Chusan in 1841, to the Peace of Nankin in 1842* (London: Richard Bentley, 1843), 85.
79. Morrison, *Chinese Commercial Guide* (1844), 86 and (1848), 123–4; and Gabriel Lafond de Lurcy, *Voyages Autour du Monde*, vol. 5 (Paris: Pourrat Frères, 1844), 113–4. See also R. B. Forbes, *Remarks on China and the China Trade* (Boston: Samuel N. Dickinson, 1844), 63.
80. 'The rates of pilotage are fixed at 5 cents per register ton, and the pilot receives his pay at Whampoa'. Morrison, *Chinese Commercial Guide* (1848), 124.

CHAPTER FOUR

1. The term 'comprador' refers to several different individuals or occupations in foreign records. The word is Portuguese and means 'buyer' or 'the one who buys' (*maiban* 買辦). The English and the Americans called both their chief clerks (foreign cashiers) in the factories in Canton, and the person who supplied provisions to the ships in Whampoa, 'compradors'. Morse, *Chronicles*, 1:179 n.1; and Downs, *The Golden Ghetto*, 24–5, 36–7 and 78. After the collapse of the Canton System and the rise of the treaty ports in 1842, the term 'comprador' referred predominantly to a Chinese merchant, manager, or agent in one of the foreign trading houses. Yen-p'ing Hao, *The Comprador in Nineteenth Century China* (Cambridge: Harvard University Press, 1970), 1. I use the term to refer only to the provision purveyors of the factories and the ships (the ships' chandlers) who were always Chinese.
2. Hunter, '*Fan Kwae*', 17; *Chinese Repository* (April 1835), 582; Morrison, *Chinese Commercial Guide* (1834), 10. Yang, et al., eds., *Ming-Qing Shiqi*, 6:93, 148, with English translations in the *Canton Register* (24 March 1835) and *Chinese Repository* (April 1835), 3:581.

3. Morse states that the compradors were licensed in 1731. An imperial decree spelling out their responsibilities was issued in 1755, and another decree mandated their licensing (along with the linguists) in 1760. A memorial from 1808 reiterated their mandatory registration with the Junminfu. Morse, *Chronicles*, 1:205; 3:355; and 5:40, 90, 96.
4. Hamilton does not appear to have purchased any provisions so it is not clear how accurate his information is. Hamilton, *A New Account of the East-Indies*, 2:224–5. There is also a contradiction in Lockyer's narrative because he first states that the compradors were supplying provisions, then says the English bought provisions directly from local suppliers. Lockyer, *An Account of the Trade*, 108.
5. Morse, *Chronicles*, 1:156; and OIO: G/12/21–28.
6. SAA: IC 5684, 5687, 5710, 5740.
7. NAH: VOC 4374-4376.
8. NAH: VOC 4375.
9. Translated from the Dutch. This reply from the Hoppo is dated the '20th day, 7th month, 8th year of the Yung Zheng Emperor: or 2 September 1730' and was 'sent to the foreign merchants in the factories' so it applied to everyone. NAH: VOC 4375.
10. The Hoppos present to each ship (explained in chapter 2) of two cows, eight sacks of wheat flour and eight crocks of Chinese wine was also a means of pacifying them.
11. RIHS: Mss 997, James Warner Papers. For a detailed description of the wash boats and the washwomen, see Downing, *The Fan-Qui in China*, 1:79–84. Foreigners were often welcomed to Whampoa by a swarm of small sampans offering all kinds of services and small items for sale. Some of the Chinese also offered their daughters for a fee. Noble, *A Voyage to the East Indies*, pp. 237–43, 279–80; Alfred Spencer, ed., *Memoirs of William Hickey (1749-1775)* (New York: Alfred A. Knopf, 1921), 198; Dobell, *Travels in Kamtchatka*, 2:140–1; and Downing, *The Fan-Qui in China*, 1:144–5, 224, 245–6.
12. RAC: Ask 1134; Morse, *Chronicles*, 5:40; RAC: Ask 1141; and *Canton Register* (13 December 1836).
13. Dermigny, *Le Commerce a Canton*, 2:521–5; and Morse, *Chronicles*, 1:212, 262.
14. Ruschenberger, *Narrative of a Voyage*, 2:221.
15. Hunter, '*Fan Kwae*', 50.
16. The factory owners were usually closely connected to the Chinese merchants. If not a merchant himself then the owner was often a partner or relative.
17. Atack died on 16 January 1798 at the age of 75, which would make him fifteen years old when he began work with the Dutch in 1737. NAH: Canton 97.
18. For a detailed account of other compradors who worked for the foreigners, see Van Dyke, 'Port Canton', chapter 3.
19. Van Dyke, 'Port Canton', chapter 3.
20. NAH: Canton 37, 46, 55, 58, 81, 84, 85, 88, 90, 91, 93—96; and Van Dyke, 'Port Canton', chapter 3.
21. NAH: Canton 97.
22. The day before he died, the Dutch recorded that Atack had been employed for 50 years. The VOC records clearly show, however, that he began in 1737 and was employed until his death. NAH: Canton 97. See also Jörg, *Porcelain and the Dutch China Trade*, 334 n.8.

23. Van Dyke, 'Port Canton', chapter 3.
24. Susan Fels, ed., *Before the Wind. The Memoir of an American Sea Captain, 1808–1833*, by Charles Tyng (New York: Viking Penguin, 1999), 29. For another description of the compradors' English, see Dobell's *Travels in Kamtchatka*, 2:129. For an extensive study of Canton pidgin English from a socio-linguistic point of view, see Bolton, *Chinese Englishes* (2003).
25. PL: 'Log of Ship *Logan* 1837–1838', typescript of Mrs. Follensbee's Memoirs.
26. For the return passage, the *Apollo* purchased fifty-six whole pigs to make into salt pork, twenty-one live pigs to be consumed as fresh meat, four live cows with a calf to provide milk and meat, and thousands of piculs of the other items. SAA: IC 5706.
27. GUB: H22.4A. Journal hållen på Swenska Ost Indiska Comp. Skepp *Adolph Fredrich* under Resan till och ifrån Canton Åren 1776 och 77. For other examples, see Paul A. Van Dyke, 'Pigs, Chickens, and Lemonade: The Provisions Trade in Canton, 1700–1840'. *International Journal of Maritime History* (June 2000), 111–44.
28. MHS: 'William Trotter Letter/Journal 1797'.
29. Some provisions in Canton (including animals) were grown or raised on the many sampans in the river. PL: 'Log of Ship *Logan* 1837–1838', typescript of Mrs Follensbee's Memoirs; and Noble, *A Voyage to the East Indies*, 279. Scurvy was a problem throughout the Canton era. Many ships that arrived in China had several seriously ill crewmen owing to vitamin-C deficiency. It was essential to give them fresh fruit as soon as possible. Heaps, ed., *Log of the Centurion*, 192; and PL: 'Log of Ship Packet 1824–1825'. Aside from humanitarian concerns for his crew's health, a captain would be conscious of the fact there was a constant shortage of able-bodied seamen among all the large trading companies for most of the Canton era. Thus, it was in his best economic interests to restore his crew's health quickly.
30. For a few examples of compradors offering recommendations, see Ellis, *An Authentic Narrative of a Voyage*, 2:330–1; RIHS: 'Trader's Book', 24–5; and Dobell, *Travels in Kamtchatka*, 2:129.
31. JFB: Irvine Papers, 'Price of Provisions Agreed with the Comprador' (1726).
32. For examples of the provision prices in Whampoa and Canton, see Van Dyke, 'Port Canton', chapter 3.
33. Many of these comprador contracts have survived and can be found in the Dutch, Danish, Swedish, English and American archives. See Bibliography for references and Plate 13.
34. Ruschenberger, *Narrative of a Voyage*, 2:221–2.
35. For an example of newcomers receiving instant credit from the compradors see Frederic W. Howay, ed., *Voyages of the Columbia to the Northwest Coast 1787–1790 & 1790–1793* (Boston: Massachusetts Historical Society, 1941. Reprint, Portland: Oregon Historical Society Press, 1990), 134; and John Leo Polich, 'John Kendrick and the Maritime Fur Trade on the Northwest Coast' (MA thesis, University of Southern California, 1964), 59.
36. Competition led many compradors to meet the foreigners downriver so they would be the first to engage them. Downing, *The Fan-Qui in China*, 1:88. See Van Dyke, 'Port Canton', chapter 3, for examples of foreigners pegging compradors' prices to those of previous years.

37. Foreigners often referred to these agents as compradors as well, but they were the compradors' assistants.
38. Downing, *The Fan-Qui in China*, 85–92.
39. Hunter, '*Fan Kwae*', 8.
40. Sometimes Chinese tried to sneak into the bankshalls at night to steal things. Noble, *A Voyage to the East Indies*, 294.
41. Many sailors could not swim. Even if they could they were often injured when falling from the ship and incapable of saving themselves.
42. In the early eighteenth century, the linguists arranged for foreigners (usually captains and supercargoes) to be buried at a site north of Canton. This gravesite was used until at least the 1750s, but the foreigners were later restricted to graveyards in the Whampoa region. The location of the Canton graveyard is noted on a couple of Swedish maps, and lies somewhere in the vicinity of present-day Yuexiu Park at the southern base of a hill (possibly Yuexiu shan 越秀山) that used to support a small pagoda. One of the foreign cemeteries on Danes Island has now been restored, and an old Parsee cemetery there has also survived. But the foreign graves on Whampoa and French Islands and the Catholic cemetery that was consecrated by a Catholic bishop and located 'one hour from Whampoa' have not been found. Two Catholic sailors from a GIC ship were interred in the latter site in 1727. The French sailors (many of whom were Catholics) would have also been buried in a consecrated graveyard, which suggests it may have been on French Island. *Chinese Repository* (October 1832), 1:219; SAA: IC 5704; and Van Dyke, 'Port Canton', chapter 3. The epitaphs on the gravestones in the old foreign cemetery north of Canton have been preserved in the following journal: Library of the Royal Academy of Sciences (Kungliga Vetenskaps-akademiens Bibliotek, Stockholm, KVB): Ms. Braad, C. H. 'Berättelse om Resan med Skeppet *Hoppet* under Capitaine Fr. Pettersons Commando från Götheborg till Canton i China 1748–1749'.
43. P. du Halde, *The General History of China. Containing a Geographical Historical, Chronological, Political and Physical Description of the Empire of China, Chinese-Tartary, Corea and Thibet*, 3rd ed. (London: 1741), 2:237–8.
44. Johnson, *An Account of a Voyage*, 53.
45. This price is from data assembled from numerous compradors' price lists in many foreign records. Wild ducks commonly sold for 0.01 or 0.02 taels per catty less than domestic ducks.
46. There are many accounts of this floating city in the foreign records. For one that mentions the floating shops, see Phillips, *Diary of a Journey Overland*, 85.
47. Johnson, *An Account of a Voyage*, 53.
48. Henry Charles Sirr, *China and the Chinese* (London: 1849; reprint, Taipei: Southern Materials Center, Inc., 1977), 1:71.
49. Dobell, *Travels in Kamtchatka*, 2:320–323; and Downing, *The Fan-Qui in China*, 1:70–1, 3:241. There are many other references to the duck boats in the delta.
50. Foreigners often fetched the water themselves. Sometimes several crew members were put on 'water duty', which would entail going back and forth from the ship to the islands on the river or to an upstream spring. At other times, the compradors were hired to provide this service.

51. 'In sailing up the river you may observe a very small boat, perhaps the smallest you ever saw, exposed on the water, being nothing more than a few planks fastened together. This is the barber's boat, who is going bout, or rather swimming about following his daily avocation of shaving the heads and tickling the ears and eyes of the Chinamen'. Robert Fortune, *Two Visits to the Tea Countries of China and the British Tea Plantations in the Himalaya*, vol. 1 (London: John Murray, 1853), 120.
52. *Chinese Repository* (Jan 1834), 2:432; and Ruschenberger, *Narrative of a Voyage*, 2:225.
53. 'Tommy Linn the barber was the agent we employed. He brought us any article we wanted from the city and, like his brethren in Europe, was a walking newspaper'. He was said to have paid seventy dollars to the Mandarins for the privilege of being a barber, and agreed to shave the entire crew for six months at the charge of half a dollar per man. Flannery, ed., *The Life and Adventures of John Nicol*, 103, 106, 108.
54. *Canton Register* (22 November 1836).
55. The flower boats provided services that helped to pacify the foreigners and the Mandarins received regular payments from them so in the interests of keeping harmony and benefiting oneself, the establishments were allowed to exist. They were, in fact, a regular part of the trading environment in China throughout the era of the Canton trade that rarely gets mentioned in the history books. Some of these ladies learned to speak a few words of several different languages in order to better entice their foreign customers so it was an aggressive and competitive business that went into action every day as soon as the sun went down. For a brief discussion about the sex trade in Whampoa and Canton, the unfortunate individuals who were forced into that industry, and the infanticide that resulted from it, see Van Dyke, 'Port Canton', 208–11. Sometimes prostitutes tried to escape when a fire or other catastrophe provided a distraction to their masters, but then they ran the risk of falling into the hands of an even worse oppressor. *Canton Register* (15 November 1836).
56. The foreign cooks were sent to the factories to give the supercargoes who had wintered in China a taste of home. Many ships hired Chinese cooks for the return voyages as well, but this had to be done covertly because Chinese were not allowed to pass Bocca Tigris aboard foreign vessels. Van Dyke, 'Port Canton', chapter 3.
57. Noble, *A Voyage to the East Indies*, 224.
58. Downing, *The Fan-Qui in China*, 1:76.
59. It is amazing how many leaks there were in some ships. Fifty strokes in a 24-hour period was common, but some ships pumped that number in four hours. In 1738 the crew of the *Kongen af Danmark* regularly pumped anywhere from 200 to 1,400 strokes in twenty-four hours and even put out to sea in that condition. It is no wonder so many Chinese caulkers were hired by ships to have those holes plugged before setting sail. RAC: Ask 999.
60. There are many examples of destitute persons resorting to crime because of a loss of their incomes. For one example in 1835 when eight silk weavers were displaced due to a decrease in foreign orders and went round pillaging several residences in Canton to support themselves, see *Canton Register* (2 June 1835).
61. There are many examples of punishments in the foreign records. For one example of the Mandarins attending a Dutch hanging of a murderer in Whampoa in 1762, see CMD 1762.

62. In volume 1 of Morse's *Chronicles*, page 179, it is mentioned that the fee in 1724 was 120 taels, but on page 181, 150 taels is stated. It is not clear whether this ambiguity came directly from the EIC documents or whether it is an error. Morse, *Chronicles*, 1: 179–81.
63. NAH: VOC 4376, 20 August 1731.
64. In 1732 supercargo Colin Campbell mentioned the Swedes paid inflated prices for their provisions because they had refused to pay the licensing fee. The other companies in Canton at the time, however, submitted to the additional charge. According to Campbell, the fees were temporarily rescinded the next year on account of trouble with the previous Hoppo. Hallberg and Koninckx, eds., *A Passage to China*, 96, 125.
65. RAC: Ask 1141. The difference between the Swedish 111 taels and the French 108 taels is because of their different exchange rates, which were 0.74 taels per Spanish dollar for the Swedes and 0.72 taels for the French.
66. For the sizes of ships and crews in Canton, see J. R. Bruijn and F. S. Gaastra, eds., *Ships, Sailors and Spices. East India Companies and Their Shipping in the 16th, 17th and 18th Centuries* (Amsterdam: NEHA, 1993); Christian Koninckx, *The First and Second Charters of the Swedish East India Company (1731–1766)* (Belgium: Van Gemmert Publishing Co., 1980); Gøbel, 'Asiatisk Kompagnis Kinafart'; and Van Dyke, 'Port Canton', appendices. Morse shows a comparison of the cargos of the European ships for the year 1764. Morse, *Chronicles*, 5:114.
67. Many of these fees are recorded in different sections of the *Yuehaiguan Zhi* (see Volume 9 for example). Some of these fees have been translated into English and can be seen in the *Canton Register* (26 December 1833) and various other English publications. See also Earl H. Pritchard, *The Crucial Years of Early Anglo-Chinese Relations 1750–1800* (1936; reprint, New York: Octagon Books, 1970), passim; Milburn, *Oriental Commerce*, 2:492–5; and Van Dyke, 'Port Canton', passim.
68. These prices were taken from the East India companies' compradors' price lists and contracts, where the cost of anything and everything is mentioned in precise detail. Many of the data are incomplete and foreigners sometimes paid different prices according to exchange rates agreed with their compradors, so only the more complete data containing ample references were used for these examples. Beef was popular with the foreigners. Because it was cheaper than pork it was usually the meat of choice for the crew, but some of the animals were beasts of burden and often butchered when old so their meat tended to be tough. Young bullocks, however, were also butchered regularly aboard the ships at Whampoa. Foreigners also bought pork in large quantities, but it was often reserved for the officers. Capons were usually priced a little higher than hens or other fowl, but occasionally they could be purchased at the same price as 'chicken'. Eggs were purchased by the 'each', in fives, by the dozen, by the hundred and by the thousand, but they were usually the same price regardless of quantity. It is difficult to ascertain fish prices because there were many types, such as 'best', 'common', 'dried' and 'salted', all commanding different prices. I have listed only the 'common' sort, because those prices are more consistent. Goat and mutton were also popular meats for the crews. The data for mutton are incomplete so are not included here. Note that pork is more expensive than beef, which is consistently the case throughout the 130 years of data. There is not one year where pork is cheaper than beef. Pork is

usually considered a better buy because of the better natural efficiency of the pig in putting on weight compared to that of the cow. Thus, it is not known why beef was cheaper. Chicken (hens), duck, geese and fowl were usually close to the same price each year, but duck and geese were sometimes cheaper. Fowl included large quantities of pigeon, quail and pheasant. Some of these birds commanded higher prices occasionally, but when listed under the category 'fowls' they were usually the same price as chicken.

69. PL: Benjamin Shreve Papers, 'Ship *Minerva* Account Book 1809'.
70. Morse, *Chronicles*, 2:129.
71. Blancard, *Manuel du Commerce*, 398.
72. Morse, *Chronicles*, 3:184.
73. Ibid., 3:235.
74. Ibid., 4:232. A Chinese document dated January 1831 that was translated and published in the *Canton Register* states that the reduction was granted in 1829, but the amounts of the compradors' fees vary a little from the ones mentioned here. Out of 35 ships in 1830, the average comprador's fee was Spanish $411. *Canton Register* (19 February 1831). An anonymous document from 1839 also states that 'the comprador's fees, like the cumsha, were considerably reduced in the beginning of 1830, but still amount to about $400'. Anonymous, *Descriptions of the City of Canton*, 110. In contrast, the American trader Nathan Dunn states in 1830 that 'the reductions . . . in the Compradores & Linguists fees exist only on paper, as these men resist any change'. G. W. Blunt White Library, Mystic Seaport, Connecticut (BW): Misc. Vol. 552. 'Nathan Dunn Letter book 1830'.
75. *Canton Register* (19 and 26 January 1836) 'List of Fees Paid by the Ship-Compradors at Whampoa'. The enormous amount to which the compradors fees had grown by this year led the author of the articles in the *Canton Register* to say: 'we do not see the necessity for the employment of a Chinese steward, or comprador, to cheat the owners, captains, and crews, whilst he is, in his turn, a *spunge* [sic] to the officers of the government'.
76. PL: Shreve Papers. Ship *Minerva* Account Book; and NAH: Canton 100.
77. Stanford and Marks ran weekly ads in the *Canton Register* of provisions for sale. For a good example of the varieties they handled, see the 4 October 1836 issue.
78. The first Swedish ship in China in 1732 supplied provisions to three different small private traders. Hallberg and Koninckx, eds., *A Passage to China*, 154.
79. For references to foreigners capitalising on the provisions trade in Canton, and to Hawaii's becoming a provisions depot, see Meares, *Voyages Made in the Years 1788 and 1789*, 10; Bancroft Library, University of California, Berkeley (BC): G161 P55 v. 6 x. Otto Von Kotzebue, *Voyage of Discovery in the South Sea, and to Behring's Straits, in Search of a Northeast Passage; Undertaken in the Years 1815, 16, 17, and 18, in the Ship Rurick*, part I (London: Bride Court, 1821). This journal is also contained in a larger selection entitled *New Voyages and Travels Consisting of Originals and Translations*, vol. 6 (London: Bride Court, 1821). See also, Dick A. Wilson, 'King George's Men: British Ships and Sailors in the Pacific Northwest-China Trade, 1785—1821' (Ph.D. dissertation, Department of History, University of Idaho, 2004), passim.
80. Downs, *Golden Ghetto*, 91.

81. John Rickman, *Journal of Captain Cook's Last Voyage to the Pacific Ocean* (London: printed for E. Newberry, 1781; reprint, New York: Da Capo Press, 1967), 387. In the late 1840s Henry Charles Sirr also found China (especially Hong Kong) to be expensive compared to other places he had visited. Sirr, *China and the Chinese*, 1:32–3.
82. In the early English language newspapers on the China Coast (the *Canton Register* and *Chinese Courier*), there are numerous entries advertising supplies and provisions for sale.
83. There are many examples of ships being able to obtain provisions in Macao, legally and illegally. For one reference, see Ellis, *An Authentic Narrative of a Voyage*, 333–4.
84. Morse, *Chronicles*, 5:79; RAC: Ask 879a; Downing, *The Fan-Qui in China*, 1:197–9, 2:214; Dobell, *Travels in Kamtchatka*, 2:132; Morse, *Chronicles*, 2:409–10; and *Chinese Repository* (January 1834), 2:423–4.
85. PL: Benjamin Shreve Papers, 'Ship *Minerva* account book 1809'.
86. This 'per catty' entry is clearly a mistake. It should read 'per day' because 0.30 taels was the going daily labour rate for coolies.
87. For a list of the fees linguists had to pay to various local officials in 1836, see *Canton Register* (12 January 1836).
88. Another example that shows high engagement fees is that of the ship *Derby* in 1805, which paid the comprador a 'comshaw' of $270. PL: Benjamin Pickman Papers, Mss 5, 'Ship *Derby* Papers 1805'. Many American captains could whittle the comprador down to $250 if they persisted, but some paid as much as $300.
89. RIHS: Carrington Papers.
90. For a list of these and other linguist's fees charged to 43 American ships, see Van Dyke, 'Port Canton', appendix L.
91. Michael Roe, ed., *The Journal and Letters of Captain Charles Bishop on the North-West Coast of America, in the Pacific and in New South Wales 1794–1799* (Cambridge: Cambridge University Press, 1967), 190.
92. Ibid., 191.
93. Ibid., 193–6.
94. There is a 'hoppoo Receipt' for providing provisions for the ship *Astrea* on 9 January 1796 in PL: MH-21, Dorr Family Papers. Another example can be found in the ship's papers of the snow *Pacific Trader* in 1801. MHS: 'Samuel B. Edes Papers 1799–1801'. For the collusion between the linguists and the Hoppomen in the 1830s, see *Chinese Repository* (March 1838), 6:511–3.
95. There are references in the Carrington archive of foreigners purchasing and selling provisions at Lintin. For one example, see RIHS: Carrington Papers, box 149.
96. Hunter, '*Fan Kwae*', 33–4.
97. Ibid., 55.
98. This is why the man-per-ton estimates often compiled for the East India companies' ships are not always reliable. The numbers of crew members are often taken from the muster rolls, which do not show the Chinese sailors (or perhaps other Asians) hired. Many of the American ships employed Chinese sailors as well. Wilson, 'King George's Men', 92.
99. Hunter, '*Fan Kwae*', 62–3.
100. 'Bohsan Jak' is the Cantonese pronunciation of the Chinese characters.

101. The most extensive study of the compradors in the era of the Treaty Ports (after 1842) is Hao, *The Comprador in Nineteenth Century China*. Downs also provides a brief glimpse of life in Canton before and after 1842. Downs, *Golden Ghetto* (1997).
102. Morrison, *Chinese Commercial Guide* (1844), 87 and (1848), 125. Samuel Wells Williams edited these editions.
103. Ibid.
104. One example is Chinese nails which did not have heads like the ones the foreigners used. Flannery, ed., *The Life and Adventures of John Nicol*, 159.
105. In the early nineteenth century, there were several Muslim *serangs* (labour brokers) established in Macao, who found employment for the many lascar seamen who were coming there. The Chinese sailors, however, were usually hired through the compradors. Smith and Van Dyke, 'Muslims in the Pearl River Delta, 1700 to 1930', 6–15.

CHAPTER FIVE

1. Morrison, *Notices Concerning China*, 65.
2. NAH: Canton 8.
3. Morrison, *Notices Concerning China*, 23, 65.
4. Morse, *Chronicles*, 2:343.
5. See Morse, *Chronicles*, for examples of foreign linguists in Canton.
6. By 1807, the DAC, SOIC, CFI and Prussians had all quit the China trade, and the VOC had collapsed in 1794. The DAC sent ships to China again from 1820 to 1833, but only five in thirteen years. Thus, beginning in 1807, the EIC was the only large company left in Canton.
7. Morrison, *Notices Concerning China*, 33.
8. A translation of Plate 27 is available in Van Dyke, 'Port Canton', chapter 1.
9. For several descriptions of these audiences with the Hoppos, see Van Dyke, 'Port Canton', chapter 4.
10. Hamilton, *A New Account of the East-Indies*, 2:224.
11. OIO: G/12/28, 21 June 1729.
12. Morse, *Chronicles*, 1:67.
13. SAA: IC 5757; and Parmentier, *Tea Time in Flanders*, 101. 'Suqua' is also spelled 'Chuqua'.
14. 'laat door den Tolk in 't Engels ons antwoorden', NAH: VOC 4377, 11 October 1732.
15. Morse, Chronicles, 1:217.
16. RAC: Ask 1118; and Williams, *A Voyage Round the World*, 355. These references to the linguists speaking English in the 1730s have pushed back the date of the earliest usage of 'English' in Canton. It was previously thought that Anson's 1743 reference was the earliest. Philip Baker and Peter Mühlhäusler, 'From Business to Pidgin', *Journal of Asian Pacific Communication*, 1:1 (1990), 87–115. Thanks to Kingsley Bolton for pointing this article out to me.
17. For a detailed analysis of Chinese pidgin Englishes and the reproduction of a Canton pidgin English dictionary used by the Chinese, see Bolton, *Chinese Englishes* (2003).

18. The GIC records are written in French, English and Dutch; many of the SOIC records are written in English, and some of the DAC journals are written in Dutch.
19. The private traders often originated from ports where English was spoken, such as Madras, Calcutta and Bombay. Some of them also came from the French colony Pondichéry. Carl T. Smith, 'An Eighteenth-Century Macao Armenian Merchant Prince', *Review of Culture*, No. 6 (April 2003), 120–9; Smith and Van Dyke, 'Armenian Footprints in Macau', 20–39; Smith and Van Dyke, 'Four Armenian Families', 40–50; and Smith and Van Dyke, 'Muslims in the Pearl River Delta', 6–15.
20. Lockyer, *An Account of the Trade*, 102.
21. Huang Guosheng (黄国盛), *Yapian Zhanzheng qian de Dongnan Sisheng Haiguan* (鸦片战争前的东南四省海关 The Customs in China's Four Southeastern Provinces before the Opium Wars) (Fujian: Fujian Renmin Chuban She, 福建人民出版社, 2000), 114–8; MHS: Ms.N–49.19, 'William Elting Notebook 1799–1803', 21–2; Morrison, *Notices Concerning China*, 23; *Canton Register* (2 February 1831); *Chinese Repository* (January 1837), 5:432; Morrison, *Chinese Commercial Guide* (1844), 161 and (1848), 200; and Downing, *The Fan-Qui in China*, 3:121. For a list of the linguists' names, see Van Dyke, 'Port Canton', chapter 4; and CMD 1762, nn. 50 and 82.
22. MHS: Ms.N–49.19, 'William Elting Notebook 1799–1803', 21–2.
23. For a more detailed description of how this subcontracting worked with the linguists, see Van Dyke 'Port Canton', chapter 4.
24. SAA: IC 5690, 5692, 5695. Because the GIC entries are inconsistent it is difficult to account for the different linguists' fees paid by each ship.
25. Dermigny, ed., *Les Mémoires de Charles de Constant*, 160–2.
26. Anonymous, *Descriptions of the City of Canton*, 1839; Morrison, *Notices Concerning China*, 37; and Morrison, *Chinese Commercial Guide* (1834), 22–3.
27. American linguists' fees were extracted from the original documents. See Bibliography for references. Because the exchange rates differed between foreigners from 0.72 taels per Spanish dollar to 0.74 taels, different rates were used in this section to calculate the fees in both currencies. Van Dyke, 'Port Canton', Appendix L: 'Linguists's Fees paid by 43 American Ships in Canton from 1789 to 1842'.
28. For the size of the companies' ships in China, see Jaap R. Bruijn and Femme S. Gaastra, eds., *Ships, Sailors and Spices. East India Companies and Their Shipping in the 16th, 17th and 18th Centuries* (Amsterdam: NEHA, 1993). For a more detailed discussion of the differences in the linguists' engagement fees, see Van Dyke, 'Port Canton', chapter 4.
29. Voretzsch, ed., *François Froger*, 86.
30. Lockyer, *An Account of the Trade*, 102; and Morse, *Chronicles*, 1:107, 143.
31. 'Tolck . . . haver eet vist Salarium af kiöbmændene af hver Picul stÿcke godz'. RAC: Ask 1118.
32. Milburn, *Oriental Commerce*, 1:495; and Morrison, *Chinese Commercial Guide* (1834), 18.
33. Morrison, *Notices Concerning China*, 37.
34. For a breakdown of the fees the linguists had to pay to tollhouses and officials, see *Canton Register* (12 Jan 1836).
35. For a more detailed analysis of the linguists' composite figures, see Van Dyke, 'Port Canton', chapter 4.

36. For more detailed coverage of the linguists' subversion of the compradors' businesses, see chapter 4 and Van Dyke, 'Port Canton', chapters 3 and 4.
37. NAH: VOC 4411, 4556. In 1761, the Swedes made a similar arrangement with the merchant Tayqua to salvage the ship *Prins Friederic Adolph*, which sank near the Prata Islands. He agreed to carry out the operation for 7½ percent of the recovered silver (he wanted 10 percent) and 40 percent of the cargo. Tayqua hired 40 Chinese (sailors and divers) from Macao and took them in 2 sampans to the site. Thirty Europeans were sent in another boat to accompany him. The expedition was arranged by Tayqua with the Mandarins, and approved by the Hoppo. Chops were issued to carry out the salvage, and when the boats returned they were allowed to pass Bocca Tigris and sail upriver. GUB: H21.1, 1149–50 'Bärgningen från Skeppet *Fredrik Adolphs Vrak* (1761–1762)' and 22.4a:1200 'Dagbok för Skept *Rijks Ständer* på Resan till Surrat och Canton 1760–1762'.
38. NAH: VOC 4411, 4556.
39. 'When a fire broke out near the Factories they [the linguists] were immediately in attendance'. Hunter, '*Fan Kwae*', 32.
40. This is a synopsis of English and Dutch reports of the fire. Morse, *Chronicles*, 5:173; and NAH: Canton 82, 7–8 February 1773.
41. NAH: Canton 86, 8 February 1777.
42. NAH: Canton 87, 18 December 1778.
43. NAH: Canton 87, 21–22 December 1778.
44. NAH: VOC 2438; and RAC: Ask 879a, 999, 1118.
45. The Danes were informed on 6 December and the Dutch the following day. RAC: Ask 879a; and NAH: VOC 2438.
46. A notation in the Dutch records suggests that the French were not in attendance ('alwaar meede alle de Cargas Excepto die de Franschen, zig meede Lieten vinden'). NAH: VOC 2438. The Danes, however, state that all were present including the 'Moorsche', RAC: Ask 1118.
47. This description of the meeting was pieced together from the following sources. NAH: VOC 2438, 'dagregisters'; and RAC: Ask 879a, 999, 1118. The Danes mentioned that the linguists translated everything into 'English'. RAC: Ask 1118.
48. NAH: VOC 2438, 'dagregisters'; and RAC: Ask 879a, 999, 1118. Such emotionally filled encounters were not uncommon. In 1811, Wilkinson attended a meeting with a viceroy and, at the end of the affair he mentioned that 'tears now interrupted the viceroy's endeavors to express his last words of parting, which we understood to be, that "The English people were great and good!"' Wilkinson, *Sketches of Chinese*, 161.
49. The Dutch also had several men desert this year, but this was a common occurrence and may not have been directly related to the participation in this ceremony. NAH: VOC 2438; and RAC: Ask 879a, 999, 1118.
50. NAH: VOC 2438, 'dagregisters', 2–4 February 1739.
51. CMD 1763; and NAH: Canton 73.
52. Williams, *Chinese Commercial Guide*, 161.
53. Information about the linguists after the collapse of the Canton System was taken primarily from Morrison, *Chinese Commercial Guide* (1848); and Williams, *Chinese Commercial Guide* (1863).

54. Williams, *Chinese Commercial Guide*, 169.
55. It would not have been difficult to arrange with any of the foreigners for language instructors to have been sent to Canton or to assign one of the company's employees to this task, but there was no demand. Some *Hong* merchants, such as Semqua (Qiu Kun 邱崑), who was active in the trade from 1729 to 1774 and ran one of the largest *hongs* (Yifeng Hang 義豐行), did not even bother to learn pidgin English, but depended on partners and secretaries to communicate for him. Van Dyke, 'Cai and Qiu Enterprises', 60–101.

CHAPTER SIX

1. Zhao, ed., *Aomen Jilüe*; and Ptak, 'Macau: Trade and Society, circa 1740–1760', 194–5.
2. Morse, *Chronicles*, 5:70; RAC: Ask 1141; NAH: Canton 25; and CMD 1762 and 1763.
3. For a couple of examples of how these connivances worked, see NAH: Canton 24–7, 73, 77–78.
4. Morse, *Chronicles*, 5:79; and RAC: Ask 1141.
5. RAC: Ask 1141.
6. The importation of yellow cloth was also prohibited. Morse, *Chronicles*, 5:70. See also Cheong, *Hong Merchants of Canton*, 163, nn. 141 and 142.
7. RAC: Ask 1141; and CMD 1762, see entries on September 22 and 30. In 1784, the Hoppo limited the chop boats to three a day per ship. Morse, *Chronicles*, 2:98. In 1811, the English were allowed a total of twelve chop boats per day to service all their ships. Morse, *Chronicles*, 3:168. In 1813, the Hoppo restricted the chop boats of several merchants. Morse, *Chronicles*, 3:200. In the 1820s, the ordering of chop boats continued to be very closely monitored. Morrison, *Notices Concerning China*, 31–3.
8. NAH: Canton 75.
9. NAH: Canton 81; and Pritchard, *The Crucial Years of Early Anglo-Chinese Relations*, 200–1.
10. NAH: Canton 81; and Morse, *Chronicles*, 5:171.
11. There are numerous references to it being illegal for Chinese to borrow money from foreigners. For a couple examples, see Dilip Kumar Basu, 'Asian Merchants and Western Trade: A Comparative Study of Calcutta and Canton 1800–1840' (Ph.D. dissertation, Department of History, University of California, Berkeley, 1975), 313–4; and Morse, *Chronicles*, 2:56–7 and 5:89–90.
12. The text is underlined in the original. NAH: Canton 89.
13. For a history of the Yan family business and the Taihe Hang, see Van Dyke, 'The Yan Family', 30–85.
14. NAH: Canton 89; and Morse, *Chronicles*, 2:33, 39–40, 46, 54, 66, 85.
15. Morse, *Chronicles*, 2:33, 39–40, 46, 54, 66, 85.
16. NAH: Canton 96–101, 378.
17. Cheong, *Hong Merchants of Canton*, 111. A VOC placard written in Dutch and Chinese declaring that the company would not be held responsible for private debts of employees, has survived in NAH: VOC 4385.
18. The Hoppos also had little power to change anything and no choice in their appointments. *Chinese Repository* (March 1834), 2:527.

19. For a summary of the *consoo* fund in the early nineteenth century, see *Chinese Repository* (January 1835), 3:424–5; and Morrison, *Chinese Commercial Guide* (1834), 42.
20. Ch'en, *Insolvency*, passim; and Van Dyke, 'The Ye Merchants of Canton', 6–47.
21. For Conseequa's experience in the American courts, see Frederic D. Grant, Jr., 'The Failure of the Li-ch'uan Hong: Litigation as a Hazard of Nineteenth Century Foreign Trade', *The American Neptune* 48, no. 4 (Fall 1988), 243–60; and Frederic D. Grant, Jr., 'Hong Merchant Litigation in the American Courts', in *Proceedings of the Massachusetts Historical Society*, Vol. XCIX (1987), (Boston: Massachusetts Historical Society, 1988), 44–62.
22. For examples of *Hong* merchants having to pay large sums to retire, see Ch'en, *Insolvency*, passim; Cheong, *Hong Merchants of Canton*, passim; and Van Dyke, 'The Ye Merchants of Canton', 6–47.
23. NAH: Canton 83. It is not clear how the duties would have been calculated without knowing what kind of merchandise went unreported. Nor is it clear how long this policy was in effect. It would have been much more difficult to carry out this cargo balancing with the companies that financed their voyages from a joint treasury in Canton, such as that of the EIC, which may account for Morse and Pritchard rarely mentioning this practice. Dutch records clearly show, however, that the Hoppos were applying this cargo balancing to the VOC ships and all other ships in Whampoa. See the 'dagregisters', passim and Morse, *Chronicles*, 2:62–3, 78–9 and 5:193–4.
24. Just having the number of chests could also give the Hoppos a rough idea, because they were often packed with the same number of coins. In the 1720s and 1730s, for example, the English usually packed 1,000 coins in a sack and put four sacks in each chest, making a total of 4,000 coins per chest. Morse, *Chronicles*, 1:186, 225 n. 1 and 2:280–1. The DAC, VOC and other companies also packed their silver chests fairly consistently, with a similar number of coins.
25. NAH: Canton 83.
26. NAH: Canton 84.
27. Morrison, *Notices Concerning China*, 34.
28. See, for example, books and articles listed in the Bibliography by Morse, Pritchard, Eames, Greenberg, Dermigny, Ptak, Fei, Huang Qichen, Do Vale, Jesus, Rubinstein, Fok, Fay and Guimarães. There are others.
29. Morrison, *Notices Concerning China*, 32–3.
30. This restriction making foreigners take the West River route was already in effect by 1699. Morse, *Chronicles*, 1:89. But it was enforced with much irregularity until the mid-1750s. By about 1756, references to foreigners sailing in their service boats through Bocca Tigris all but disappear until the 1810s and 1820s.
31. Van Dyke, 'Port Canton', 46. Sketches of several of these tollhouses and their locations on maps can be seen in Liang, *Yuehaiguan Zhi*, vol. 5 (1839); *Xiangshan Xian Zhi* (香山縣志 Xiangshan County Gazetteer) 2 vols. (1751; reprint, Taipei: Xuesheng Chubanshe 學生出版社, 1985); and Zhao, ed., *Aomen Jilüe*.
32. The Creek tollhouse was simply a boat with two men stationed in it. At some point in the early nineteenth century (perhaps after the 1822 fire) a shanty was built on this location to house these two men. As far as the trade was concerned, this post had no function other than keeping watch over the east end of the quay. By the early

1830s, the tollhouse had turned into a cover for a gambling operation that was run by these customs officers, and catered to the Chinese house servants in the foreign factories. In 1836, the building burned down, and the foreign community strongly protested its reconstruction. They complained that it was a source of much noise and commotion with gamblers coming and going day and night. And because it was located so close to the foreign factories, it was feared that another fire could spread to those buildings. As a response to their complaints, the governor ordered an investigation be made of illegal gambling operations. *Canton Register* (26 Janurary, 2 and 9 February 1836). Plans of the Canton factories which Morse reproduced show the location of the Creek tollhouse, but they do not show the Danes' tollhouse. Morse, *Chronicles*, 3: facing page 1; and Morse, *The International Relations of the Chinese Empire*, 1: facing page 70. One of the plans reproduced in Liang's book shows all three tollhouses on the quay as they should be (Danes', Canton and Creek tolls, locations G, H and J on the plan). Liang Jiabin (梁嘉彬), *Guangzhou Shisan Hang Kao* (广州十三行考 Study of the Thirteen Hongs of Canton) (1937; reprint, Taipei: 1960; reprint, Guangdong: Renmin Chubanshe 人民出版社, 1999), illustration 9.

33. NAH: Canton 74.
34. Hunter, 'Fan Kwae', 50–5. Several of these West River licenses have survived in Portugal, and have recently been published in Lau and Zhang, *Qingdai Aomen*.
35. NAH: Canton 74, 86, 89; and Morse, Chronicles, 2:29.
36. RAC: Ask 1197, 26 March 1785.
37. Morse states that the total cost was $9,000 in 1791 and only $1,000 in 1772. Morse, *Chronicles*, 2:208. The cost apparently rose to $10,000 in 1792 before dropping in 1793. Pritchard, *The Crucial Years*, 138.
38. Morse, *Chronicles*, 2:286–7.
39. Qianshan tolls rose from 0.142 taels per sampan to 8.856 (1763 to 1777). Zini tolls rose from 3.227 taels per sampan to 20.835 (1786 to 1792). A reduction in those tolls then shows up in the Dutch records, which was perhaps connected to the collapse of the VOC and restructuring of the Dutch trade. The Zini tolls then rose again from 4.440 taels to 17.390 (1796 to 1813). The Zini tollhouse was burned down by the Nemesis in 1841. *Chinese Repository* (Mar 1841) 10:180–1. For a detailed analysis and list of all the West River tolls the Dutch paid from 1763 to 1816, see Van Dyke, 'Port Canton', chapter 1 and appendix AH.
40. The figures for 1799 were taken from RIHS: Mss 828 'Logbook ship *Ann & Hope* to Canton 1799–1800'. The tonnages listed in this logbook were compared to many of the ships' papers and adjustments made accordingly. On the whole, however, the tonnages were fairly close. The figures for 1800 and 1801 were taken from Lawrence H. Leder, 'American Trade to China, 1800–1802', *The American Neptune* 23:3 (July 1963), 212–8. Some of these numbers were checked against the ships' papers. Tonnage figures, of course, vary widely in the historical records. The ones compiled for these three years are close to those assembled by Rhys Richards in 1994. Rhys Richards, 'United States Trade with China, 1784–1814', *The American Neptune* 54: Special Supplement (1994). Dermigny records a lower tonnage for the ships in Canton in these years, but he was using a simple estimate of 270 tons per ship. Dermigny, *Le Commerce a Canton*, 2:521–5. The American port registration papers that were

consulted for this study support a higher average. The tonnages of 594 American ships at Canton from 1818 to 1833, compiled by Morse, average 356 tons. His figures, however, were not taken from the American ship records and are often mere visual estimates that were recorded by EIC officers. Morse, *International Relations*, 1:89.

41. Dermigny, *Le Commerce a Canton*, 2:521–5.
42. For a more detailed breakdown and explanation of all these figures, see Van Dyke, 'Port Canton', chapter 1.
43. These figures were tabulated from Morse, *Chronicles*, 2: passim.
44. Morse, *International Relations*, 1:89–91.
45. These figures were tabulated from Dermigny, *Le Commerce a Canton*, vol. 2.
46. NAH: Canton 99–101.
47. W. M. F. Mansvelt, *Geschiedenis van de Nederlandsche Handel-Maatschappij* (Harlem: J. Enschedé and sons, 192?), Bijlage II. Mansvelt did not record the size of the NHM ships, but we know from other sources that they were usually small vessels. The total capacity of the 16 Dutch ships that frequented Canton in 1846, for example, amounted to 2,483 Dutch lasts. At 2.5 tons per last, the total capacity comes to 6,208 tons, or an average of 388 tons per ship. MHS: Bdses 1847 March 'Staat van den Handel in China onder Nederlandsche Vlag'. A list of the Dutch imports and exports at Canton from 1825 to 1847 is contained in the *Chinese Repository* (April 1848), 17:208.
48. The tonnages for the EIC ships before 1774 are less accurate. Prior to that year, the EIC regularly under-registered many ships at 499 tons or less even if they were much larger. This under-reporting was done because ships of 500 tons and over were required to carry a chaplain aboard. The cost and perhaps inconvenience of having a chaplain aboard led to this fudging of the tonnage figures. In 1772, the requirement was withdrawn and the EIC immediately listed the true tonnages of all ships. As a consequence, the capacity of some EIC ships grew 50 percent overnight. 1774 was the first year that the *actual* tonnages were listed in the EIC Canton records so from that year forward the figures are more accurate. Morse, *Chronicles*, 5:69 and 2:11; Koninckx, *The First and Second Charters*, 159 n. 26; and F. S. Gaastra and J. R. Bruijn, 'The Dutch East India Company's Shipping, 1602–1795, in a Comparative Perspective', in *Ships, Sailors and Spices*, eds., J. R. Bruijn and F. S. Gaastra (Amsterdam: NEHA, 1993), 183. The tons and port fees data from 1,450 ships were taken from Van Dyke, 'Port Canton', appendices. The figures for the remaining 20 ships (making a total of 1,470) were found later and taken from the GIC, VOC, DAC and US archives and various other references that are too numerous to list here (see Bibliography). The breakdown of the 1,470 ships is as follows: GIC 7, VOC 102, DAC 105, EIC 1,140, CFI 8, USA 48, SOIC 58, private 2.
49. All cargo data were taken from primary sources, usually the individual ships' documents (see Bibliography). Most of the tonnage figures came from the charts in Van Dyke, 'Port Canton', appendices. The 172 ships that loaded in Canton from 1730 to 1833 had capacities ranging from 239 to 1,350 tons. The breakdown of the 172 ships is as follows: DAC 109, SOIC 55, CFI 4, VOC 3 and USA 1. The values of the export cargos range from 97 to 316 taels per ton; the difference is owing to the different values of the cargo loaded rather than the size of the ship. The one American ship of 239 tons, for example, was the smallest vessel in the database but had a ratio of 206

taels per ton. The smallest ratio (97 taels) came from a 1,350-ton DAC ship and the largest (316 taels) from an 875-ton DAC ship. As a general rule, all ships loaded to full capacity with Chinese goods before they departed so these ratios are as accurate as the data will permit. The accuracy of tonnage and cargo figures from this period are always suspect because of the different ways they were tabulated and collected so we can only use these ratios as a rough guide.

50. These figures were obtained by dividing the numbers in the previous paragraph by the 214 taels average. As far as the foreigners were concerned, they usually attached all costs and expenses at Canton to the export cargos and not to the import cargos. The companies knew that small ships were disadvantage in Canton and preferred to send large ships. For an example of the EIC sending a couple of small vessels to China and then refusing to send them upriver to Canton because of the high fees, see Morse, *Chronicles*, 5:74–5.
51. There is some confusion in the final amount after the reduction in 1830. Morse states that it 'was lowered from Tls. 1,950 to Tls. 1,718.502 for the EIC ships. French, Prussian, and Austrian ships, paying normally 100 taels more, and Soola (possibly English country or Manila) ships paying normally 100 taels less'. Morse, Chronicles, 4:230–1. In contrast, Morrison states that it was reduced to 1,600.683 taels. *Morrison, Chinese Commercial Guide* (1834), 22. In reference to the negotiations to reduce the fees in 1829 and 1830, Auber also made an entry mistake. He mentioned that the English tried to reduce 'the enter-port fee of 2,780 dollars', when he meant 2,708 dollars. The standard amount charged to EIC ships was 1,950 taels. At the conversion rate of 0.72 taels to one Spanish dollar (which is what the English used), the amount comes to $2,708. Auber also mentions that the Hoppo informed the English that the enter-port fee was 'a fixed regulation and cannot be diminished'. All the quotes from the EIC records in Auber's book give us the impression that nothing was done about the request for a reduction. But as was shown in chapter 2, they were indeed reduced. Peter Auber, *China. An Outline of the Government, Laws, and Policy: and of the British and Foreign Embassies to, and Intercourse with, that Empire* (London: Parbury, Allen, and Co., 1834), 319–21.
52. For a more detailed analysis of this disparity between the companies and private traders, and private traders' responses to the changes to the port fees in the 1830s, see Van Dyke, 'Port Canton', chapter 1.
53. Some of the publications that followed the *Canton Register* were the *Chinese Courier* (1831), *Chinese Repository* (1832), *Evangelist* (1833), *Chronica de Macao* (1834), *Canton General Price Current* (1835), and *Canton Press* (1835).
54. Two academic journals that were being monitored by the Canton editors were the French *Journal Asiatique* and the English *Asiatic Journal. Canton Register* (16 August 1828).
55. For an example of the Canton editors translating and publishing extracts from the Dutch records from 1762 and 1803, see *Canton Register* (15 November 1830, 16 February 1833). Extracts of French records from 1754 which the Dutch consulate had were also translated and published in *Canton Register* (18 and 25 March 1834 and 10 March 1835). The information contained in these company records appears to have been fairly freely offered at this time, which was unthinkable in previous decades.

56. KBS: Kine. ms 14. The twenty or more Grand Chops that have survived span the years 1742 to 1837 and all list the same basic data.
57. There were many accounts written of the attacks during the opium wars. For a couple of detailed references that show how the Chinese were rapidly trying to duplicate foreign armaments, and the ease with which the foreigners could overcome them, see Murray, *Doings in China*; and Levien, ed., *The Cree Journals*.
58. By the 1780s, entries in the foreign records refer to ships having their chronometers calibrated in Canton or Macao prior to setting sail.
59. Morse, *Chronicles*, 2:145.
60. Carl A. Trocki, *Opium, Empire and the Global Political Economy. A Study of the Asian Opium Trade 1750–1950* (London: Routledge, 1999), 104–7.
61. *Chinese Repository* (January 1836), 4:436–8. By the 1820s there were so many foreigners in China that the Hoppos could no longer control their movements. Many of them went to Canton through Bocca Tigris as passengers on their own boats or on Chinese boats. Van Dyke, 'Port Canton', 44–5, 493–6; Suzanne Drinker Moran, ed., *A Private Journal of Events and Scenes at Sea and in India by Sandwith Drinker. Commencing April 26th, 1838* (Boston: 1990), 12–4; and MHS: Edward King Papers 1835–1842, letter dated 31 October 1835.
62. *Chinese Repository* (January 1836), 4:436–8.
63. There are some very detailed descriptions of how the steamers accomplished this in Murray, *Doings in China*, passim.
64. After the Nemesis's attack, some Chinese locals tried to capitalise on the event by drawing pictures of the steamer with a poem about the formidable machine. They made many copies and sold them in Canton. *Chinese Repository* (September 1841), 10:519–22.
65. *Chinese Repository* (August 1842), 11:454–5.
66. Murray, *Doings in China*, passim; Bernard, *Nemesis*, 1:215; and Jonathan Spence, *The Search for Modern China* (New York: W.W. Norton & Co., 1990), 157–8.
67. At the beginning of June 1842, for example, the foreign war fleet consisted of 27 vessels: 6 steamers, 8 men-o'-war, and 13 transports. By the end of June, there were 75 ships in the fleet: 10 steamers, 12 men-o'-war, and the rest were troop ships and transports. Murray, *Doings in China*, 152, 164–5.
68. MHS: '*Midas* (steam schooner) Papers 1844–1845'; and *Chinese Repository* (May 1845), 14:248.
69. Levien, ed., *The Cree Journals*, 268.
70. Janin, *The India-China Opium Trade*, 169–73. For insurance premiums in Canton in the 1830s, see Alain Le Pichon, *Aux Origines de Hong Kong. Aspects de la civilisation commerciale à Canton: le fonds de commerce de Jardine, Matheson & Co. 1827–1839* (Paris: L'Harmattan, 1998), 269–70.
71. Laurence Oliphant, *Narrative of the Earl of Elgin's Mission to China and Japan in the Years 1857, '58, '59* (New York: Harper & Brothers, 1860), 59.
72. The classic work on steamers in China is Kwang-Ching Liu, *Anglo-American Steamship Rivalry in China, 1862–1874* (Cambridge: Harvard University Press, 1962).
73. J. M. Tronson, *Personal Narrative of a Voyage to Japan, Kamtchatka, Siberia, Tartary, and Various Parts of Coast of China; in H.M.S. Barracouta* (London: Smith, Elcer, & Co., 1859), 75.

74. For a good example of sailing ships being replaced by steamers in the China-opium trade, see Thomas N. Layton, *The Voyage of the Frolic. New England Merchants and the Opium Trade* (Stanford: Stanford University Press, 1997).
75. For a list of the steamships servicing Canton from the 1890s to the 1910s, see Van Dyke, 'Port Canton', 179–80.
76. J. Arnold, *A Handbook to Canton, Macao and the West River, 9th ed.* (Hong Kong: Hong Kong, Canton and Macao Steamboat Co., Ltd., 1914), 41–3.
77. Wells Williams, *The Middle Kingdom*, 2 vols. (New York: Charles Scribner's Sons, 1907), 1:170.
78. Morrison, *Chinese Commercial Guide* (1834), 44.

CHAPTER SEVEN

1. Morse, *Chronicles*, 1:104; and Malachy Postlethwayt, *The Universal Dictionary of Trade and Commerce* (London: H. Woodfall, 1766), 1: no page numbers. See entry under 'CHI'. Lockyer, *An Account of the Trade in India*, 105–6.
2. Spencer, ed., *Memoirs of William Hickey*, 215–7; and CMD 1762, entry on December 13.
3. Flannery, ed., *The Life and Adventures of John Nicol*, 109, 162.
4. Morse, *Chronicles*, 1:212. There are other examples of foreigners getting caught smuggling that are not mentioned in Morse's *Chronicles*.
5. SAA: IC 5689[bis].
6. There are many references to smuggling silk in service boats in both the GIC and VOC records. But one needs to be very attentive to find them, because the writers do not usually call it 'smuggling' but state something like: 'service boat arrived today with silk aboard'. All legitimate goods were supposed to be shipped via the Chinese chop boats, but in practice, many things went to Whampoa in the bottom of the service boats. For a couple of more obvious references to smuggling silk between Canton and Whampoa, see NAH: Canton 25, 71.
7. In 1728, the Fooyen insisted on the English boats being followed and inspected after the officers disembarked at Canton. OIO: G/12/27.
8. Noble gives an account of one of these disputes between the English and customs officers in 1747. Noble, *A Voyage to the East Indies*, 286. These examples clearly show that statements made by the foreigners claiming that they would never think 'of defrauding the Chinese government of their rightful duties' need to be taken with a grain of salt. Morse, *Chronicles*, 5:78.
9. This lower fee was one of the few advantages private traders had. The journal of the American ship *Congress* lists the cost of a money boat at Spanish $3.60. It is not clear why this ship paid $3.60, when many other American ships paid only $3.00. PL: 'Log of Ship *Congress* 1819–1820'.
10. SAA: IC 5757.
11. For a few examples of the English smuggling silver into Canton, see Morse, *Chronicles*, 1:187, 192, 194.
12. Morse, *Chronicles*, 1:199.

13. Entries in the Dutch 'dagregisters' clearly show that the Hoppos were keeping close track of the movement of silver chests between Whampoa and Canton as early as 1729. NAH: VOC 4374. Other examples from the 1720s can be found in the GIC records.
14. OIO: G/12/23–25. 'Gold in great Quantities is Yearly carried out of this Port, yet the Exportation of it is absolutely prohibited by the Government, but for certain Reasons greatly connived at. On this Account Europeans generally run privately most of their Silver; not to avoid any Duties payable thereon, but to conceal the Amount of their Imports, that thereby no Conjectures may be made of the Gold they Export'. Anonymous, *An Authentick Account of the Weights, Measures, Exchanges, Customs, Duties, Port-Charges, &c, &c.* (London: C. Hendersen, 1763), 55.
15. CMD 1763, entry on 23 September 1763; and A. J. R. Russel-Wood, 'An Asian Presence in the Atlantic Bullion Carrying Trade, 1710–50's, *Portuguese Studies*, vol. 17 (2001), 148–67.
16. CMD 1763.
17. Lockyer, *An Account of the Trade in India*, 138.
18. For a few references of foreigners exporting gold, see CMD 1762; Jörg, *Porcelain and the Dutch China Trade*, 38; Russel-Wood, 'An Asian Presence in the Atlantic Bullion Carrying Trade, 148–67; SAA: IC 5753; and Nordic Museum Archive (NM), Stockholm. Godegårdsarkivet. Ostindiska Handling. F17 (hereafter referred to as NM: F17).
19. NAH: VOC 4387; and Van Dyke, 'Cai and Qiu Enterprises', 60–101.
20. The English estimated that the foreigners exported a total of 7,000 shoes of gold in 1731. Morse, *Chronicles*, 1:204. One example from the VOC is the shipment of 147 pieces (bars and shoes) of gold that was found in the wreck of the *Geldermalsen* in 1985. It sank in January 1752 on its return passage to the Netherlands. C. J. A. Jörg, *The Geldermalsen. History and Porcelain* (Groningen: 1986). The *Geldermalsen's* gold was one of many shipments that were leaving China each year via Canton and Macao. As late as the 1830s, gold was still being smuggled out of China. Morrison, *Chinese Commercial Guide* (1834), 68; Morse, *Chronicles*, 1:172, 176; SAA: IC 5753; NAH: VOC 4376, Canton 69; CMD 1762 and 1763; Van Dyke, 'Cai and Qiu Enterprises', 60–101; and Van Dyke, 'The Yan Family', 30–85; Cheong, Hong Merchants, 56–7.
21. Dermigny, *Le Commerce a Canton*, 3:1254–6; and Morse, *Chronicles*, 1:136, 215. There is a list of trade items including opium for many ports in Asia in the 1730s in the Uppsala University Library. UUB: L 181, 'Misc. papers of Chr. Henr. Braad 1732–1762 to East India'.
22. Trocki, *Opium, Empire and the Global Political Economy*, 34–5.
23. Almost without exception, histories of opium and the China trade show that market beginning in the late-eighteenth or early-nineteenth centuries, mainly because that is what appears in the EIC and American documents. For a few examples, see Amar Farooqui, *Smuggling as Subversion. Colonialism, Indian Merchants and the Politics of Opium* (New Delhi: New Age International, Ltd., 1998), 12–3; Morse, *Chronicles*, 2: 74–8; and D.E. Owen, *British Opium Policy in China and India* (New Haven: Yale University Press, 1934; reprint, Hamden: Archon Books, 1968), 63. Downs suggests that the smuggling networks became firmly established as a result of the War of 1812 calling

it a 'newly developed marketing system'. But by then, they had been in place for many decades. Downs, *The Golden Ghetto*, 125.

24. Ljungstedt, *An Historical Sketch*, 104.
25. For a couple recent studies on the Chinese domestic production of opium and the inland opium networks, see Timothy Brook and Bob Tadashi Wakabayashi, eds., *Opium Regimes. China, Britain, and Japan, 1839–1952* (Berkeley: University of California Press, 2000); and Trocki, *Opium, Empire and the Global Political Economy*, 118–25.
26. Morse, *Chronicles*, 1:215 and 2:326–7.
27. Ljungstedt, *An Historical Sketch*, 104.
28. Israel Reinius, *Journal hållen på resan till Canton i China* (Helsingfors: 1939), 223.
29. Ibid., 234.
30. GUB: Svenska Ostindiska Kompaniets Arkiv H22.3D 'Beskrifning på Skeppet *Götha Leyons* Resa till Surat och åtskillige andre Indianske Orter 1750–1752'. C. H. Braad.
31. Morse, *Chronicles*, 1:288–9.
32. RAC: Ask 896.
33. UUB: L 181, 'Misc. papers of Chr. Henr. Braad 1732–1762 to East India'.
34. CMD 1762.
35. The list of Portuguese imports in Macao can be seen in CMD 1763, entry on 10 December. For the Timor ship, see NAH: Canton 73, entry on 6 August 1764.
36. NM: F17; and Morse, *Chronicles*, 5:101.
37. Morse, *Chronicles*, 5:129.
38. Captain Jackson had come with the *Pitt* to China from Madras in 1761 as well. Anthony Farrington, *Catalogue of East India Company Ships' Journals and Logs 1600–1834* (London: British Library, 1999). There were several Captain Jacksons in China during the 1760s so it is not always clear which one is being referred to. The Swedes mention that one of the Captain Jacksons died in Macao in November 1772. NM: F17.
39. Other buyers names on the invoice had the prefix 'A' attached such as 'Attoong', 'Assu' and 'Alloon', which suggest they were probably small shopkeepers, compradors, or petty officers rather than *Hong* merchants. By the 1830s, all the Canton linguists were using the prefix 'A' rather than the suffix 'qua', but in the eighteenth century their names usually appear with a 'qua'. In the 1760s, there was both a linguist and a *Hong* merchant who went by the name 'Monqua'. Van Dyke, 'Port Canton', chapter 4; and *Chinese Repository* (January 1837), 5:432.
40. NM: F17, letter dated 7 May 1767.
41. NM: F17. Captain William Elphinstone went to China from Madras with the *Triton* in 1766 and again in 1769. Farrington, *Catalogue*.
42. Captain Peter Hardwicke went to China from Madras with the *Earl of Lincoln* in 1764, 1767 and again in 1769. Farrington, *Catalogue*.
43. NAH: Canton 76.
44. M. Brunel, 'A Memoir on the Chinese Trade', in *A Voyage to Madagascar, and the East Indies*, by Abbe Rochon, trans. from the French (London: Printed for G. G. J. and J. Robinson, Paternoster-Row, 1792), 470–3.
45. NAH: Canton 73, 79. Simão Vicente Rosa (1718–1773) was the procurator of the Macao Senate in 1745, 1759, 1761, 1764 and 1771. Manuel Teixeira, *Toponímia de Macao*, 2 vols. (Macao: Cultural Institute, 1997), 1:510.

46. Chetqua's youngest brother Quiqua arrived in Macao on 11 June, to inspect the Portuguese cargos. NAH: Canton 79.
47. Emanuel Pereira is possibly a reference to Manuel Pereira da Fonseca. Pires shows this man connected to the ship *Boa Viagem*, but he does not mention the year. Vincente José de Campos was investigated by the Macao Senate in 1770 for having a cargo belonging to the English. NAH: Canton 79; Ângela Guimarães, *Uma Relação Especial Macao e as Relações Luso-Chinesas 1780–1844* (Lisbon: Ediçao Cies, 1996), 292; and Benjamim Videira Pires, S. J., *A Vida Marítima de Macau no Século XVIII* (Macao: Cultural Institute, 1993), 63.
48. NAH: VOC 4556, entry under 'Amphioen'.
49. In 1764 Smith was the supercargo aboard the ship *Muxadavad*, which was sponsored by the Governor of Bengal. NAH: Canton 73, entry on 21 December 1764. See also Morse, *Chronicles*, 5:72, 103.
50. A. M. Martins do Vale, *Os Portugueses Em Macao (1750–1800)* (Macao: Institvto Portvgvês do Oriente, 1997), Anexo No. 20.
51. 'en wanneer den aanbreng slegts onder de 600 kisten beloopt, kan de prys tot 12 à 1400 piasters per kist monteeren'. NAH: VOC 4556, entry under 'Amphioen'. The Dutch text says 'piastres' but the English often referred to these as 'Spanish dollars'. Reals, piastres, patacas and Spanish dollars were usually exchanged at the same rate in China.
52. NAH: VOC 4411, 4412, 'Lyst van den Generaalen Aanbring te Macao'.
53. These lists of Portuguese imports to Macao in 1773 and 1774 are reproduced in Van Dyke, 'Port Canton', appendix Z.
54. A list of some of the magistrates who may have been involved in these connivances in Qianshan and Xiangshan can be seen in Deng Kaisong, Wu Zhiliang, and Lu Xiaomin, eds., *Yue Ao Guanxi Shi* (粤澳关系史 History of Guangdong-Macao Relations) (Beijing: Zhongguo Shudian, 1999), 637–42.
55. Do Vale, *Os Portugueses Em Macao (1750–1800)*, Anexo No. 20.
56. Wakeman has written one of the best summaries of the connection between opium and the tea trade. Frederic Wakeman Jr., 'The Canton Trade and the Opium War', in *The Cambridge History of China*, eds. Denis Twitchett and John K. Fairbank (Cambridge: Cambridge UP, 1978; reprint, Taipei: Caves Books, 1986), 10:163–212. For an example of opium revenues being deposited into the EIC treasury in Canton to purchase tea, see Morse, *Chronicles*, 2:189.
57. RAC: Ask 1175; and Do Vale, *Os Portugueses Em Macao (1750–1800)*, Anexo No. 20.
58. Owen, *British Opium Policy in China and India*, 101, 373.
59. 'Thome Francisco de Oliverya og Jose Xavier dos Santos, ere de sædvanlig Opium Handlere'. RAC: Ask 1175, entry on 19 August 1776.
60. Arquivo Histórico Ultramarino, Portugal (AHU): Macau cx. 6, no. 48 microfilm CO412; Carl T. Smith Collection in Macao; and RAC: Ask 1175.
61. NAH: Canton 89, VOC 4421; and Owen, *British Opium Policy in China and India*, 63. Owen mentions on this page that 1779 is 'the first mention of actual trading in opium at Canton', which shows why we cannot depend solely on the EIC records to explain the China trade. The opium trade is just one of the many issues that do not receive

full coverage or recognition in the EIC records, but are revealed in other East India companies' archives.

62. Owen, *British Opium Policy in China and India*, 63; and Dermigny, *Le Commerce a Canton*, 3:1269–70. Lark's Bay is noted on several maps, one being a 1912 map of Macao published by the Leal Senado. See also Williams, *Chinese Commercial Guide*, appendix 9.
63. NAH: Canton 96, entry on 13 March 1795; Morse, *Chronicles*, 2:188–9, 199–200, 258–60; Wilson, 'King George's Men', 241–4; *Canton Register* (19 January 1836); and Smith and Van Dyke, 'Armenian Footprints in Macau', 50 n. 39.
64. NAH: Canton 82.
65. For examples of this monitoring activity in the Chinese records, see Lau and Zhang, eds., *Qingdai Aomen*.
66. *Canton Register* (19 January 1836).
67. Morse, *Chronicles*, 2:199–200.
68. This is why the Chinese documents that have survived from the trade cannot be taken literally, but need always to be cross-referenced with other records to check their accuracy. Many of the Chinese records are now in print in Lau and Zhang, eds., *Qingdai Aomen*.
69. Do Vale, *Os Portugueses Em Macao (1750–1800)*, Anexo No. 11.
70. Quincy, ed., *The Journals of Major Samuel Shaw*, 238–9.
71. Guimarães, *Uma Relação Especial Macao e as Relações Luso-Chinesas 1780–1844*, 202. I am indebted to Dr John E. Wills Jr. for pointing out this reference to me.
72. Morrison, *Chinese Commercial Guide* (1834), 29–30.
73. *Canton Register* (12 January 1836).
74. The facts that the drug could be traded in Canton in 1747 by bribing the Mandarins, that it was known in Surat to be a common article of trade in Canton in 1750, that it is listed on a Canton *Price Courant* in 1757 as an article of trade, that several foreigners were bringing the drug to China in the 1760s, that hundreds of chests of opium were being unloaded in front of the two tidewaiters stationed next to the ships, that those hundreds of chests were then transported from Whampoa to Canton passed the three tollhouses without a problem, that several Chinese were buying the drug in Canton in the mid-1760s without a problem, and that a Portuguese captain was willing to risk binging an entire cargo of opium to China in 1767, all point to a safe market and high level of standardization by the 1760s.
75. Trocki has also shown that twenty dollars per chest was the standard commission Jardines charged on opium sales. Trocki, *Opium, Empire and the Global Political Economy*, 106.
76. For a few studies of the opium trade, see Owen, Downs, Eames, Greenberg, Fay, Farooqui, Trocki and Layton in the Bibliography.
77. RAC: Ask 956. Some of these entries are much longer, but only the parts mentioning opium are included here.
78. NAH: Canton 97–98; and Van Dyke, 'Port Canton', 455–6.
79. Morrison, *Chinese Commercial Guide* (1834), 30. Figures are in Spanish dollars.
80. The North American fur trade to China has now been fairly thoroughly researched. It was one of the important links that brought Hawaii into the trade, and it had close

connections to the smuggling networks in China. Samuel Eliot Morison, *The Maritime History of Massachusetts 1783–1860* (Cambridge: The Riverside Press, 1921, 1941, 1949, 1961); Howay, *Voyages of the Columbia to the Northwest Coast* (1941, 1990); Polich, 'John Kendrick and the Maritime Fur Trade on the Northwest Coast' (1964); James R. Gibson, *Otter Skins, Boston Ships, and China Goods. The Maritime Fur Trade of the Northwest Coast, 1785–1841* (Seattle: University of Washington Press, 1992); Downs, *The Golden Ghetto* (1997); Zhou Xiang (周湘), 'Qingdai Guangzhou yu Maopi Maoyi', (清代广州与毛皮贸易 Guangzhou and the Maritime Fur Trade in Qing Dynasty) (Ph.D. dissertation, Department of History, Zhongshan University, 1999); and Wilson, 'King George's Men: British Ships and Sailors in the Pacific Northwest-China Trade, 1785–1821' (2004).

81. *Chinese Repository* (March 1838), 6:511–2.
82. Ibid.
83. *Canton Register* (3 May 1833).
84. For one example of merchants trying to buy all the tin in Canton to control its price, see CMD 1763.
85. NAH: Canton 98. In 1804, Johnson also mentioned that the principle article of commerce in Macao was opium. Johnson, *An Account of a Voyage*, 85.
86. NAH: Canton 98.
87. Crawfurd and Gützlaff have references to Chinese junks smuggling opium. John Crawfurd, *Journal of an Embassy from the Governor-General of India to the Courts of Siam and Cochin China* (London: Henry Colburn, 1828; reprint, New Delhi: Asian Educational Services, 2000), 511–9; and Karl F. A. Gützlaff, *Journal of Three Voyages Along the Coast of China in 1831, 1832 and 1833 with Notices of Siam, Corea, and the Loo-Choo Islands* (London: Westley and Davis, 1834), 68, 74, 88–9, 113.
88. Lau and Zhang, eds., *Qingdai Aomen*, 1: nos. 242–7; Morse, *Chronicles*, 3:236–9; and NAH: Canton 101.
89. There are numerous references to the opium trade being even more secure than the legitimate trade. One of them quoted by Owen states that the contraband trade was 'the safest trade in China'. Owen, *British Opium Policy in China and India*, 117.
90. PL: 'Log of Frigate *Congress* 1819–1820'.
91. Morrison, *Notices Concerning China*, 67.
92. Ibid., 68.
93. *Canton Register* (3 October 1829).
94. *Canton Register* (4 April 1837).
95. *Canton Register* (20 December 1832).
96. Trocki, *Opium, Empire and the Global Political Economy*, 104–7; and Le Pichon, *Aux Origines de Hong Kong*, 73–4.
97. Morse, *Chronicles*, 4:62–3, 77. The logbook of the *Merope* was recently discovered at the Lowestoft Record Office (Halesworth Parish Collection) in Suffolk, and has much detail about the ports that were visited along the coast in the 1820s.
98. Trocki, *Opium, Empire and the Global Political Economy*, 102.
99. *Canton Register* (12 January 1836). For a few examples of the junks buying opium in Singapore and other Southeast Asian ports, or purchasing it from foreigners in the delta and then shipping it to other Chinese ports, see *Canton Register* (18 June, 2 September 1829; 3 February, 3 March 1830; 7 April, 3, 17 September, 17 October, 3

November 1832; 15 July, 5 August, 24 October 1833; 16 December 1834; and 19 January 1836).

100. Ruschenberger, *Narrative of a Voyage*, 2:210.
101. There are many accounts in the foreign records of the fast crabs. For a vivid account of one being ambushed, see Downing, *The Fan-Qui in China*, 1:121–32; and *Chinese Repository* (January 1837), 5:391.
102. In the early years of the 1800s, one of the reasons for higher fees in Macao was retaliation against the British for imposing a surcharge on Portuguese ships in Calcutta. Fei, *Macao 400 Years*, 168.
103. *Canton Register* (18 August 1832; 7 September, 13 April 1833; 6 October 1835; 15 March 1836); Morse, *Chronicles*, 4:107–8; and Guimarães, *Uma Relação Especial Macao e as Relações Luso-Chinesas 1780–1844*, chapter 5, 'Macau 1810–1820. Os Anos Tranquilos'.
104. Lau and Zhang, eds., *Qingdai Aomen*, 1: no. 382. The *Chinese Repository* has a translation of an edict concerning rice, which states that the tax exempt policy was in effect as early as the Qianlong (1736–1795) period and continued in Jiaqing (1795–1821) and Daoguang (1821–1851). *Chinese Repository* (January 1842), 11:17–20. According to official policy, ships had to be carrying at least 5,000 piculs to qualify for a discount, but documents contained in the *Qingdai Aomen* series and other references show that the stipulation was not followed to the letter.
105. *Chinese Courier* (3 August 1833); and *Canton Register* (5 August 1833).
106. *Canton Register* (15 September 1835, 7 November 1837).
107. MHS: Forbes Papers.
108. MHS: Forbes Papers.
109. Downs, *The Golden Ghetto*, 128; and *Chinese Repository* (December 1838), 7:439–41.
110. Downing states that 22,818 tons of rice were imported aboard British and American ships in 1834. The rice came from Manila, Batavia and Singapore. Downing, *The Fan-Qui in China*, 2:24. See also *Chinese Repository* (March 1838), 6:509–10.
111. Williams, *Chinese Commercial Guide*, 167.
112. *Canton Register* (29 December 1835).
113. There are many references in the foreign records to the Hoppos and governors-general being unable to make any changes to the basic structure supporting the trade. For one example, see Morse, *Chronicles*, 5:79.
114. *Canton Register* (17 September 1832, and 26 July, 2 August, 13 and 20 September 1836).
115. Many of the Chinese documents are now available in print in numerous collections and series (see Bibliography).
116. Besides the references mentioned in notes above about the opium problem in China, see also the volumes of the *Canton Register* and *Chinese Repository* for 1836 and 1837. Translated copies of the edicts and the foreigners' responses to them are available in these publications.
117. *Chinese Repository* (April 1835), 3:579.
118. All of these events are covered extensively in the 1836 and 1837 volumes of the *Canton Register*.
119. This discussion can be found in the *Canton Register*.

CHAPTER EIGHT

1. George Bryan Souza, *The Survival of Empire. Portuguese Trade and Society in China and the South China Sea, 1630–1754* (Cambridge: Cambridge University Press, 1986); Guimarães, *Uma Relação Especial Macao* (1996); and Do Vale, *Os Portugueses em Macao (1750–1800)* (1997).
2. Some of the Chinese and Portuguese records concerning the trade and the governing of Macao are now available in facsimile or print. Lau and Zhang, eds., *Qingdai Aomen* (1999); Yang, Wu and Deng, eds., *Ming-Qing Shiqi Aomen Wenti Dang'an Wenxian Huibian*; Jin Guo Ping (金國平) and Wu Zhiliang (吳志良), comps, *Correspondência Oficial Trocada Entre As Autoridades de Cantão e Os Procuradores do Senado. Fundo das Chapas Sínicas em Português (1749–1847)*, 8 vols. (Macao: Macao Foundation, 2000); and Xing, et al, eds., *Qing Gong Guangzhou Shisan Hang Dang'an Jingxuan.*
3. In 1986, Souza mentioned that 'Macao acted as an adjunct of the Canton market'. Souza, *The Survival of Empire*, 143.
4. NAH: VOC 4556, 'Gewigten', and 'Macao'.
5. Fei, *Macao 400 Years*, 116.
6. NAH: VOC 4556, 'Jonken', (13 October 1763) and 'Natien (Vreemde)', (18 October 1763); and Cheong, *Hong Merchants of Canton*, 28. For a more detailed analysis of the Canton junk trade to Southeast Asia, see Van Dyke, 'Port Canton', chapter 5.
7. NAH: VOC 4556, 'Gewigten', and 'Macao'.
8. Smith and Van Dyke, 'Four Armenian Families', 43.
9. Morse, *Chronicles*, 2:85–6; and Williams, *Chinese Commercial Guide*, 281.
10. The Dutch, Danish and Swedish records often mention the arrival and departure of the Portuguese in Canton.
11. The *S. Simão* was owned by Antonio Josè da Costa. NAH: Canton 35. He is also one of the merchants in Table 10 who loaned money to the Swedes.
12. NAH: Canton 81.
13. Some of the junk factories listed in Plate 12 are also mentioned in the *Yuehaiguan Zhi*, volume 25.
14. In 1764 and 1770, the Dutch in Canton mention 33 junks arriving, and in 1769 both the Dutch and the Swedes list no fewer than 27 junks. There were usually a couple that laid over in Southeast Asia each year so the actual number may have been larger. NAH: Canton 78, 127, VOC 3333; and NM: F17. In 1813, Milburn lists the imports of 32 junks in Canton so they seem to have maintained their numbers. Milburn, *Oriental Commerce*, 1:487–488. Crawfurd suggests that there were more than 50 junks plying between Siam and Canton in the early 1820s, but the source of his information is unclear. John Crawfurd, *Journal of an Embassy from the Governor-General of India to the Courts of Siam and Cochin China* (London: Henry Colburn, 1828; reprint, New Delhi: Asian Educational Services, 2000), 409–10, 512–13. It is not possible to give an accurate account of each decade, but there is ample evidence to suggest that there were probably at least 30 junks operating out of Canton consistently up to the first Opium War in 1840. See other references to the junks, in Downing, *The Fan-Qui in China*, 1:55, 108–14; Van Dyke, 'Port Canton', chapter 5 and appendices O, P and Q; Van Dyke, 'The Yan Family', 30–85; Van Dyke, 'The Ye Merchants of Canton', 6–47; and Van Dyke, 'A Reassessment of the China Trade', 153.

15. Downing, *The Fan-Qui in China*, 1:55, 108–14; and Crawfurd, *Journal of an Embassy*, 409–10, 512–13. For a more detailed analysis of the Canton junks and a comparison of the man-per-ton ratios with foreign ships, see Van Dyke, 'Port Canton', chapter 5; Van Dyke, 'A Reassessment of the China Trade', 151–67; and Paul A. Van Dyke (范岱克) 'Cong Helan he Ruidian de Dang'an kan Shiba Shiji 50 Niandai zhi 70 Niandai de Guangzhou Fanchuan Maoyi' (从荷兰和瑞典的档案看十八世紀50年代至70年代的广州帆船貿易 The Canton Junk Trade in the 1750s to 1770s as Revealed in the Dutch and Swedish Records), *Social Sciences in Guangdong* (广州社会科学), No. 4 (2002): 93–102.
16. Sources: NAH Canton 73, 74, 76, 77, 78, 79, VOC 4387, 4403, 4411, 4556; NM: F17; Do Vale, *Os Portugueses em Macau (1750–1800)*, Anexo No. 21; and Van Dyke, 'Port Canton', chapter 5 and appendices. Unfortunately, we have no complete data for 1765.
17. Sources: NAH Canton 73, 74, 76, 77, 78, 79, VOC 4387, 4403, 4411, 4556; NM: F17; Do Vale, *Os Portugueses em Macau (1750–1800)*, Anexo No. 21; and Van Dyke, 'Port Canton', chapter 5 and appendices.
18. This comparison with the American trade is based on the different sets of figures listed in Downs, *The Golden Ghetto*, appendix 2.
19. NAH: VOC 4556, 'Jonken', (13 Oct 1763) and 'Natien (Vreemde)', (18 Oct 1763); and Cheong, *Hong Merchants of Canton*, 28. The 6 percent advantage may have been put into place in 1699 when Macao's trade was brought in line with Zhejiang and Fujian standards. Fei, *Macao 400 Years*, 116.
20. NAH: VOC 4556, 'Goederen en Koopmanschappen'.
21. NAH: VOC 4556, 'Grynen'.
22. OIO: G/12/26.
23. For an example of the *Hong* merchants maintaining forward and backward linkages to markets abroad and within China, see Van Dyke, 'The Yan Family', 30–85.
24. Van Dyke, 'The Yan Family', 30–85; Van Dyke, 'Port Canton', chapter 5; Van Dyke, 'A Reassessment of the China Trade'; and Van Dyke, 'Guangzhou Fanchuan Maoyi', 93–102. One of the captains of the Canton junks, for example, had a brother, Tsey Pinqua, who was a tin agent in Palembang. NAH: Canton 73.
25. The supercargo Colin Campbell, for example, mentioned in 1732 that the first Dutch supercargo Schultz was secretly investing in the bottomry market. Hallberg and Koninckx, eds., *A Passage to China*, 166–7.
26. Numerous lists of bottomry rates in Asia in the eighteenth century have been compiled by contemporary authors. Lockyer, *An Account of the Trade*, 17–18; and UUB: L 181–182. See also NAH: Canton 80.
27. Jan Parmentier, *De holle compagnie. Smokkel en legale handel onder Zuidnederlandse vlag in Bengalen, ca. 1720–1744* (Hilversum: 1992), 53–5; Souza, *The Survival of Empire*, 60–3; and Ljungstedt, *An Historical Sketch*, 49.
28. A couple examples of the EIC issuing bottomry can be seen in Morse, *Chronicles*, 5: 73, 111, 149.
29. For a list of the bottomry bonds recorded in the Swedish records and other transactions connected to the junks, see Van Dyke, 'Port Canton', chapter 5.
30. For a more detailed explanation and breakdown of these two contracts, see Van Dyke, 'Port Canton', chapter 5.

31. NM: F17; Van Dyke, 'Port Canton', chapter 5 and appendices O, P and Q; Van Dyke, 'The Yan Family', 30–85; Van Dyke, 'The Ye Merchants of Canton', 6–47; and Van Dyke, 'Cai and Qiu Enterprises', 60–101.
32. Van Dyke, 'Port Canton', chapter 5 and appendices.
33. NM: F17.
34. The SOIC was using bottomry bonds 'as early as 1734'. Koninckx, *The First and Second Charters*, 295. The DAC was using bottomry bonds in the China trade at least by 1737, perhaps earlier. RAC: Ask 1116.
35. RAC: Ask 1156a; and Van Dyke, 'The Yan Family', 30–85.
36. Van Dyke, 'The Yan Family', 30–85. For other references to high interest in Canton, See Morse, *Chronicles*, passim; and Morse, *The International Relations of the Chinese Empire*, 1:68.
37. NM: F17; and Morse, *Chronicles*, 5:108. For interest rates of 2 percent per month paid by the Chinese in the 1720s, see SAA: IC 5695, 5740. And for later periods, see Van Dyke, 'Port Canton', chapter 5; Van Dyke, 'Cai and Qiu Enterprises', 60–101; and Van Dyke, 'The Yan Family', 30–85. For a more thorough analysis of the credit market and interest rates in the Canton era, see Van Dyke, 'Port Canton', chapter 5; and Ch'en's chapter on the 'Hong Merchants Financial Predicament' in Ch'en, *Insolvency*, 139–75.
38. NM: F17.
39. Morse states that he also found references to Chinese borrowing money at 5 percent interest per month, and that 2 and 3 percent per month were common. Morse, *The International Relations of the Chinese Empire*, 1:68.
40. CMD 1762. For a more detailed account of the Yan and Cai family trade and credit problems, see Van Dyke, 'The Yan Family', 30–85; and Van Dyke, 'Cai and Qiu Enterprises', 60–101.
41. *Chinese Repository* (Jan 1837), 5:385–90. Ch'en, in his extensive study on the indebtedness of the *Hong* merchants, also found a 'Dearth of Cash in the Canton Market'. Ch'en, *Insolvency*, 162; and Morse, *Chronicles*, 2:278–9.
42. For examples of foreign traders moving in and out of Canton and Macao with a few chests of goods and hiring passage on junks and foreign ships, see Smith and Van Dyke, 'Armenian Footprints in Macao', 20–39.
43. M. Greenberg, *British Trade and the Opening of China 1800–1842* (Cambridge: Cambridge University Press, 1951), 144–174; Wilson, 'King George's Men', chapter 6; Downs, *The Golden Ghetto*, passim; Guo Deyan (郭德焱), 'Qingdai Guangzhou de Basi Shangren' (清代广州巴斯商人 Parsee Merchants in Canton during the Qing Dynasty) (Ph.D. dissertation, Department of History, Zhongshan University, 2001); Guo Deyan, 'The Study of Parsee Merchants in Canton, Hong Kong and Macao', *Review of Culture*, International Edition, No. 8 (October 2003), 51–69; Shalini Saksena, 'Parsi Contributions to the Growth of Bombay and Hong Kong', *Review of Culture*, International Edition, No. 10 (April 2004), 26–35; Carl T. Smith, 'Parsee Merchants in the Pearl River Delta', *Review of Culture*, International Edition, No. 10 (April 2004), 36–49; and Madhavi Thampi, 'Parsis in the China Trade', *Review of Culture*, International Edition, No. 10 (April 2004), 16–25.

44. Brokerage fees of 5 percent were common, but the rate varied according to specific agreements. Le Pichon, *Aux Origines de Hong Kong*, 265–6; and Greenberg, *British Trade and the Opening of China 1800–1842*, 149.
45. Van Dyke, 'The Yan Family', 38; Fei, *Macao 400 Years*, 140–141; Ptak, 'Macau: Trade and Society, circa 1740–1760', 196; and JFB: Irvine Papers.
46. CMD 1762 and 1763; and NAH: Canton 73.
47. CMD 1762 and 1763; and NAH: Canton 73.
48. Morse, *Chronicles*, 5:108; and NAH: Canton 73.
49. Van Dyke, 'Cai and Qiu Enterprises', 60–101.
50. Armenians played a special role in the China trade that until recently has received little recognition. They were readily accepted by both Catholics and Protestants, because they were Christians. A branch of the Armenian Church had been reconciled with the Roman Catholic Church so Portuguese Catholics in Macao accepted them more openly than Protestants (who were considered outcasts). These religious connections enabled them to play a distinct role in the India–Manila–Macao–Canton trade, which they were involved with throughout the eighteenth century. Smith, 'Armenian Merchant Prince', 120–9; Smith and Van Dyke, 'Armenian Footprints in Macau', 20–39; and Smith and Van Dyke, 'Four Armenian Families', 40–50.
51. Smith and Van Dyke, 'Four Armenian Families', 40–50. A comparable nineteenth century example would be the Armenian Sir Paul Chater who also came from India and founded a few of Hong Kong's prominent financial institutions.
52. Smith, 'Armenian Merchant Prince', 120–9; Smith and Van Dyke, 'Armenian Footprints in Macau', 20–39; Smith and Van Dyke, 'Four Armenian Families', 40–50; and Van Dyke, 'Port Canton', chapter 5.
53. Smith and Van Dyke, 'Muslims in the Pearl River Delta', 6–15.

CHAPTER NINE

1. *Chinese Courier* (7 July 1832).
2. *Canton Register* (30 August 1836).
3. Ruschenberger, *Narrative of a Voyage*, 2:248–51; and *Chinese Repository* (July 1839), 8:155–63.
4. Julean Arnold, *Commercial Handbook of China*. 2 vols. (Washington: Government Printing Office, 1919), 1:47.
5. *Canton Register* (29 November 1836, 10 January 1837).
6. *Canton Register* (30 August 1836).

CONCLUSION

1. The Chinese records that have survived from the Yuehaiguan dealing with Macao reveal wonderful detail about local people. They survived because they fell into Portuguese hands and were shipped to Portugal. They were recently printed in Lau and Zhang, eds., *Qingdai Aomen*.

BIBLIOGRAPHY

UNPUBLISHED PRIMARY SOURCES

American China Trade Records

(Listed alphabetically by state/archive)

- ***California: Bancroft Library (BC), University of California, Berkeley***

Ms. C–E 54 Smith, William. Brig *Arab's* Logbook, 15 June 1821–5 January 1825.

Ms. P–C 23 Journal of the Hudson's Bay Company at Fort Simpson 1834–1837.

Ms. P–C 31 Phelps, William Dane. Solid men of Boston in the Northwest.

Ms. P–K 211 Logs of the Ships *Atahualpa*, *Behring*, and *Isabella* and the brig *Pedler*, 1811–1816.

- ***Connecticut: G. W. Blunt White Library (BW), Mystic Seaport***

Coll. 14 Stephen B. Chace Papers 1811–1822. Various documents concerning the China trade, including a Logbook and Account Book for the ship *Valentine* 1812.

Coll. 184 Isaac Hinckley Papers 1809–1818: Miscellaneous documents on China. Journal and Ship Papers for brig *Reaper* 1809–1810; Ship Papers for the ship *Tartar* 1812; and Ship Papers 1815 and Logbook 1816–1817 and 1817–1818 for ship *Canton*.

Coll. 238 William Goddard Papers 1800–1880. Trade document, papers, and logbooks from various ships.

HFM 176 Annual ledger of total American imports and exports in China 1804–1833.

Log 882 Ship *Lelia Byrd* Logbook 1803.

Log 947 Abstract Logs 1833–1838. The author is unknown but he traveled extensively aboard several ships. The text contains information about the following vessels: *Alexander Baring* 1838, *Asia* 1836–1837, *Delhi* 1839, *Horatio* 1837, and *John O Gaunt* 1838.

Log 951 Ship *Houqua* Logbook. 'Journal kept by Tho. Benedict. 1846'.

Misc. 487 Notebook on the China Trade 1842–1846.

Misc. 552 Nathan Dunn Letter-book 1830.

Misc. 556 George W. Lyman, Invoices 1812–1821. Invoices from several ships involved in the China trade.

VFM 969 Sketch Book of Canton.

- ***Massachusetts: Baker Library (BL), Harvard University, Cambridge***

Forbes Papers, H–1. *Canton Packet* (ship) Logbook 1817–1818; *Frederick* (ship) Logbook 1821–1825; *Levant* (ship) Logbook 1816–1817.

Heard Papers. Miscellaneous documents relating to the China Trade.

Miscellaneous Documents Un-catalogued. Folder Mss 733. 'Instructions for the better keeping Company with His Majesty's ship *Enterprize*, Captain John Houlton Commander'.

- ***Massachusetts: Houghton Library (HL), Harvard University, Cambridge***

MsAm 448.10 *Kamenele* (schooner) Logbook 1836–1838.

MsAm 448.10 *Walter Scott* (ship) Logbook 1836.

MsAm 454.2F Journal by Samuel Roundy aboard several ships from 1816 to 1818.

MsAm 457.1PF *Hancock* (ship) Logbook 1798–1800.

MsAm 459.1 *John Gilpin* (brig) Logbook 1832–1840.

MsAm 463.5F *Neponset* (ship) Logbook 1832–1833.

MsAm 465.5F *Perseverence* (ship) Logbook 1807–1809.

- ***Massachusetts: Massachusetts Historical Society (MHS), Boston***

Abbot, Thomas W. Journal 1845–1846.

Austin, Edward. Account Books 1826–1897.

Bdses 1847 March: List of 16 Dutch ships in Canton and Macao in 1846 with total exports.

Bowditch, Jonathan I. Papers 1836–1862: Miscellaneous documents on the China Trade.

Bullard Letterbook to Bryant & Sturgis 1821–1823.

Cabot, Samuel, Papers.

Cary, Samuel, Papers. Log of the ship *Levant* 1819–1821.

Child, John Richards, Papers 1731–1895. Log of the ship *Hunter* 1810–1815.

Dorr Family Papers 1683–1868.

Drew, Edward B. Papers 1882–1906.

Edes, Samuel B., Papers 1799–1801. Miscellaneous documents relating to the China Trade.

Elting, William P. 'Notebook on the China Trade 1799–1803'.

Faucon, Edward H. Papers 1850–1863.

Forbes Papers. Correspondences concerning the China Trade.
Forbes, James Murray, Papers 1868–1957.
Hooper-Sturgis Papers: Ship Accounts Bryant & Sturgis, 1815–1848.
Houqua Letterbook 1840–1843.
King, Edward, Papers 1835–1842. Log of the ship *Silas Richards* 1835. Correspondences.
Knox, Henry. Papers.
Lamb Family Papers. Miscellaneous documents relating to the China Trade.
Leonidas (ship) Logbooks 1825–1829.
Magee, Bernard. Logbooks 1790–1794.
Midas (steam schooner) Papers 1844–1845.
Miscellaneous 1792–1797. Documents concerning the China trade.
Morse Papers 1719–1843. Trade and Shipping Documents.
Perkins, Thomas H. Papers 1789–1892. Miscellaneous documents; Log of ship *Astrea* 1804.
Polly (snow) Logbook, 1800–1802.
Pulsifer, Robert Starkey. Papers 1765–1859.
Putnam, George. Journal of Voyage 1850–1851.
Sea Letters 1810–1881.
Story, Horace C., Papers 1842–1844. Log of ship *Probus* 1843.
Sturgis, William, Papers 1799–1804. Journals from China Voyages.
Sultan (ship) Account Book 1815–1819.
Surprise (ship) Logbook 1850–1861.
Suter, John, Papers. 1804–1848. Miscellaneous documents relating to the China Trade.
Thacher Family Papers. Correspondences Concerning the ship *Alliance*, to China in 1788.
Trotter, William. Letter/Journal 1797.
Wolcott, Bates and Company. China trade Cashbook 1851–1854 and Journal 1851–1855.
Woodard, Marcus L. Letters 1855–1862.

- ***Massachusetts: Phillips Library (PL), Peabody Essex Museum (PEM), Salem***

Aeolus (ship) Logbook 1805–1806.
Akbar (ship) Logbook 1839–1840.
Aleatus (ship) Logbook 1844–1845.
Alert (ship) Logbook 1819–1820.
Ann and Hope (ship) Logbook 1835.
Antelope (ship) Logbook 1864.
Andrews, John Hancock, Papers. Mss 2. Bark *Patriot* Papers 1811–1824.
Barton Family Papers. Mss 110. Ship Papers.
Barwell (ship) Logbook 1785–1786.
Bizar (ship) Logbook 1843–1844.
Brookline (ship) Logbook 1833–1834.
Caroline (ship) Logbook 1803–1805.
Charlotte (ship) Logbook 1841–1842.
China (ship) Logbook 1817.
Clarendon (ship) Logbook 1844.

Concord (ship) Logbook 1799–1802.
Congress (frigate) Logbooks (2) 1819–1820.
Cox, Bejamin. Papers. Mss 168. Ship Papers.
Derby Family Papers. Mss 37. Ship *Astrea* Papers 1789–1790, 1791–1794, 1799; Ship *Light Horse* Papers 1788–1795; Ship *Grand Turk* Papers 1780–1782, 1787–1791.
Derby (ship) Logbook 1804.
Diana (ship) Logbook 1799–1802.
Dorr Family Papers. MH–21. Miscellaneous documents relating to the China Trade.
Dromo (ship) Logbook 1807–1809.
Eclipse (ship) Logbook 1831–1832.
Eliza Ann (bark) Logbook 1845–1848.
Eugenia (ship) Logbook 1805–1806.
Follensbee, Mrs. (wife of Capt. Follensbee) Journal kept aboard the ship *Logan* 1837–1838.
Francis (ship) Logbook 1818–1820.
Friendship (ship) Logbook 1819–1820. Together with the Logbook of ship *Paragon*.
Governor Endicott (brig) Logbooks (2) 1819–1822.
Gustavous (snow) Diary written by John Bartlett aboard several ships from 1790 to 1793. It is incorrectly catalogued as the Logbook of ship *Massachusetts*.
Hale Family Papers. Mss 117. Ship *Geneva* Papers 1837–1847.
Hamilton (ship) Logbooks (2) 1809–1815, 1822.
Heber (ship) Logbooks (2) 1844–1846.
Heraclide (ship) Logbook 1835–1836.
Herald (ship) Logbook 1804–1805.
Hercules (ship) Logbook 1835–1836.
Hindoo (ship) Logbook 1838–1839.
Hunter (ship) Logbook 1809–1810.
Indus (ship) Logbook 1802–1803.
Inn (ship) Diary written by John Bartlett aboard several ships from 1790 to 1793. It is incorrectly catalogued as the Logbook of ship *Massachusetts*.
Joseph Peabody (brig) Logbook 1838–1840.
Kinsman, Nathaniel, Papers Mss 43: Ship *Zenobia* Papers 1839–1843.
Lady Washington (ship) Diary written by John Bartlett aboard several ships from 1790 to 1793. It is incorrectly catalogued as the Logbook of ship *Massachusetts*.
Leander (brig) Logbooks (2) 1827–1829.
Levant (bark) Logbook 1835–1838.
Logan (ship) Logbook 1837–1838.
London (ship) Logbook 1836–1837.
Louisa (ship) Logbook 1826–1829.
Lurat [This ship is incorrectly catalogued. It should be '*Surat*']
Mandarin (ship) Logbook 1809–1810.
Martain, William, Papers. Mss 123. Miscellaneous documents relating to the China Trade.
Martha (ship) Logbook 1831–1833.
Massachusetts (ship) Logbook 1790–1793.
Mentor (ship) Logbook 1824–1825 Together with the Logbook of ship *Nautilis* 1823. There is another Logbook for 1829–1830.

Merchant (ship) Logbook 1834.
Midas (ship) Logbook 1818–1819.
Misc. Journal Excerpts 1800–1803.
Monsoon (ship) Logbook 1834–1837.
Nautilus (ship) Logbook 1823. Together with the Logbook of ship *Mentor* 1824–1825.
New Hazard (ship) Logbook 1811–1812.
Packet (ship) Logbook 1824–1825.
Pallas (bark) Logbook 1800–1804. Together with the Logbook of ship *John* 1795–1798. There is another Logbook for 1832–1834.
Paragon (ship) Logbook. Together with the Logbook of ship *Leander*.
Peabody, Joseph, Papers. Mss 19. Ship *China* Papers & Account Books 1824–1828.
Pearl (ship) Logbook 1810.
Peele Family Papers. MH–5. Ship *Rachel* Papers 1802–1805.
Perseverance (ship) Logbook 1796–1801.
Phillips Family Papers 1636–1897. MH–4.
Pickman, Benjamin, Papers. Mss 5. Ship *Derby* Papers 1805–1807.
Potomac (ship) Logbook 1835–1837.
Roscoe (brig) Logbook 1827–1829.
St. Crouse (Portuguese ship) Diary written by John Bartlett aboard several ships from 1790 to 1793. It is incorrectly catalogued as the Logbook of ship *Massachusetts*.
Saphire (ship) Logbook 1834–1835.
Shreve, Benjamin, Papers. MH–20. Miscellaneous documents relating to the China Trade 1793–1848. This collection contains many journals, correspondences, logs, account books, and ship papers.
Silsbee Family Papers. Mss 74.
Sumatra (ship) Logbooks (3) 1830–1831, 1834–1835, 1835–1836.
Surat (ship) Logbook 1835 [incorrectly catalogued as ship '*Lurat*'].
Talent (brig) Logbook 1829–1831.
Theodore (ship) Logbook 1836.
Tremont (ship) Logbook 1833–1836.
Tucker Family Papers Mss 165: Ship *Concord* Papers 1802.
Union (ship/schooner) Logbook 1802–1803.
Ward Family Papers. Mss 46. Ship Papers.
Waters Family Papers MH–12 & Mss 92: Ship *Mariposa* Papers 1835–1837.
Wigglesworth, Thomas Jr. Papers. MH–6.
William & Henry (brig/ship) Logbook 1786–1790.
Zephyr (ship) Logbook 1829–1830.

- ***Minnesota: James Ford Bell Library (JFB), University of Minnesota, Minneapolis***

1732 flr. Charles Irvine (d. 1771). Archive of papers relating to the Swedish East India Company : 1732–1774. Collection contains some documents from the 1720s.
1801 sh. Journal of ship *Arat* bound for China 1801.
1801 sh. Logbook of ship *Ganges*, Boston to Canton 1801.

1801 fTr. Logbook of ship *Taunton Castle* of Deptford 1801–1802

B 1758 fNe. Dagregister in de Ned. Factory Canton 1758 en Onkost Reckening voor het Schippen *Velzen* en *Renswoude* 1758.

- ***Pennsylvania: University of Pennsylvania Library (UPL), Philadelphia***

Ms. Coll. 499 F. Molineux's Accounts of Purchases at Canton. 'Receits' for 1784–1786.

- ***Rhode Island: John Carter Brown Library (JCB), Brown University, Providence***

Brown Papers. The following files:

B126	Ship Papers 1797.
B655–657	Ship *Ann & Hope* Papers 1800–1821.
B658	Ship *Arthur* Papers 1803–1809.
B659–660	Ship *Asia* Papers 1822–1827.
B663	Ship *Isis* Papers 1805.
B664	Ship *John Jay* Papers 1800–1802.
B670	Ship *Rambler* Account Book (1818?).
B671	Ship *Washington* Papers 1820–1826.
B715–717	Ship *Ann & Hope* Logbook 1798–1806.
B720	Ship *Ann & Hope* Logbook 1816–1817, 1823–1826; Journal of Benjamin C. Carter, Surgeon aboard ship *Ann and Hope* 1798.
B721	Ship *Ann & Hope* Logbook 1823–1824.
B722	Ship *Arthur* Logbook 1803–1804.
B1131	Ship *John Jay* Papers 1797–1798; Account Book of supercargo John Bowers 1797

- ***Rhode Island: Rhode Island Historical Society (RIHS), Providence***

Carrington Papers. The following files:

B139	Ships *Trumbull*, *Baltic*, and *General Hamilton* Papers 1806–1811.
B149–150	Ship *Edwards* Papers 1831.
B151–152	Ship *Fame* Papers 1819–1825.
B153–156	Ship *Franklin* Papers 1823–1836.
B157–158	Ship *General Hamilton* Papers 1818–1824.
B159–160	Ship *George* Papers 1818–1827.
B161	Ship *John Brown* Papers 1819–1821.
B162–163	Ship *Grafton* Papers 1841–1847.
B164	Ship *Lion* Papers 1817–1820.
B165–166	Ship *Integrity* Papers 1817–1824.

B169–170, 172–174	Ship *Lion* Papers 1824–1844.
B175	Ship *Mary Ann* Papers 1815–1822.
B178–179	Ship *Nancy* Papers 1815–1824.
B181–187	Ship *Panther* Papers 1818–1843.
B190, 192–194	Ship *Providence* Papers 1825–1839.
B196–197	Ship *Trumbull* Papers 1816–1825.
B198–199	Brig *Viper* Papers 1815–1821.
B204	Ship *Zypher* Papers 1815–1820.

Other records consulted at RIHS:

Franklin (ship) Accounts, 1824–1825.
George (ship) Accounts, 1821–1823.
Grafton (ship) Disbursements, 1841–1844.
Journal A 1802–1804.
Journal B 1804–1806.
Journal C 1806–1811.
Mss 312. John Brown Papers 1770–1829. Ship *General Washington* Journal and Account Book 1788–1789.
Mss 776. Ward Family Papers. Ship *General Washington* Papers 1788–1789.
Mss 828. The following logbooks:
Ship *Ann & Hope* Logbooks 1798–1836.
Ship *Asia* Logbook 1804.
Ship *Canton* Logbook 1799.
Ship *Eleonora* Logbook 1804.
Ship *Essex* Logbook 1810–1812.
Ship *Fame* Logbook 1824.
Ship *General Washington* Logbook 1787–1789.
Ship *George Washington* Logbook 1794–1795.
Ship *Hope* Account Book 1802–1804.
Ship *Hope* Logbook 1802–1803.
Ship *Isis* Logbook 1804.
Ship *John Jay* Logbook 1804–1806.
Ship *Lion* Logbooks 1826–1833.
Ship *Panther* Logbooks 1819–1833.
Ship *Patterson* Logbook 1803–1804.
Ship *Resource* Logbook 1800–1802.
Ship *Superior* Logbook 1824–1826.
Ship *Susan* Logbook 1797–1798.
Mss 997. James Warner Papers. Ship *Ann & Hope* Logbooks 1797–1800.
Nightengale-Jenks papers.
'Trader's Book' for Canton, 1797–1808.

Danish Asiatic Company Records (DAC)

(Listed alphabetically by city/archive)

- ***Copenhagen: National Archives (RAC, Rigsarkivet)***

[Several ships in this series did not go to China and are incorrectly included in this section.]

Ask 879a–995	Skibsprotocoler for skibe til Kina 1738–1834.
Ask 996–1028	Skibsjournaler for skibe til Kina 1733–1758.
Ask 1112–1115	Skibsjournaler for skibe til Kina 1820–1829.
Ask 1116–1229	Negotieprotocoler for Kinafarere 1735–1833.
Ask 2190–2239	Kasse-og hovedbøger fra kinaskibene 1734–1772.
Ask 2240–2271	Hovedbøger for expeditioner til Kina 1782–1833.
Ask 2272–2273	Regnskabsjournaler for ekspeditioner til Kina 1782.
Ask 2295–2304	Regnskabsjournaler for ekspeditioner til Kina 1803–1833.
Lin 5893:1	Supercargo Lintrup Private Bog 1739–1741.
Soe 368B	Journal for Skibet *Cron Printz Christian* på rejsen til Kina 1730–1732.

- ***Copenhagen: Royal Library (KBC, Kungelige Bibliotek)***

Nye Kong. 512, 8°	Dag-Bog holden paa skibet Kron-Printzen paa Reysen til Canton i China Aarene 1802 & 1803. (Also covers 1804 and 1805).
Thottske 512	Extract of adskillige skibsjournaler 1677–1743.

Dutch East India Company (VOC) and Other Dutch China Trade Records

(Listed alphabetically by city/archive)

- ***The Hague: National Archives (NAH)***

AW 1.11.01.01	Aanwinsten: generaal rapport, missiven, bylagen en diverse stukken betreffende de China handel 1758–1779.
CANTON 1–390	Documenten van de Nederlandse Factorij te Canton 1742–1826.
COI 2.01.27.06	Comptabiliteit Betreffende Oost-Indische Bezittingen 1795–1813.
HD 2.01.27.05	Hollandse Divisie bij het Ministerie van Marine en Koloniën te Parijs 1810–1814.
HOPE 1.10.46	Hope familie archief 1630–1769.
HRB 1.04.17	Hoge Regering van Batavia: brieven, contracten, minuut, secrete brieven, papieren en bylagen betreffende de China handel 1790–1808.
MIN 2,6,11,25, 57,59,61	Ministerie van Koophandel en Koloniën: stukken betreffende de China handel 1798–1813.
MK 2.10.01	Ministerie van Koloniën: stukken betreffende de thee handel 1745–1851.
NED 1.10.59	Nederburgh familie archief 1790s.
NHM 2.20.01	Nederlandsche Handelsmaatschappij archief: brieven van Canton in China beginnende met 1830 tot 1838.

OIC 193–198	Comité Oost-Indische Handel en Bezettingen: Missive van Commissarissen, Generaal, Gouverneur-Generaal en Raden en Supercarga's en Commercie-raad te Canton, aan de Eerste Advocaat der compagnie en aan gecommitteer-den uit de Heren XVII en uit het Committé tot de directe vaart en handel op China, met bijlagen van 29 Nov. 1793 tot 31 Dec. 1798.
OIT 2.01.27.07	Oost-Indische Troepen 1799–1807.
OS 2.01.27.04	Commissarissen-Genereaal van Ned. Indie en Kaap ... Hoop 1791–1793.
RAB 140–142, 404–405	Raad der Aziatische Bezettingen en Etablissementen: eisch, scheeps papieren, ladingen, cognocsement, factuur, notitie, missiven, en diverse stukken betreffende de China handel 1801–1806.
RAD 1.10.69	Radermacher familie archief 1670–1796.
VDH 1.10.39	Van der Heim familie archief 1727–1793.
VELH 269–311	Kaarten van het zuide cust van China en de Canton rivier.
VG 1.10.31	Van Ghesel familie archief 1769–1771.
VHVR 1.10.45	Van Hoorn en Van Riebeek familien archieven.
VOC 4374–4444	Verenigde Oostindische Compagnie Archief: Overgekomen Brieven and Papieren uit China 1729–1790.
WIS 2.21.176	Collectie Wiselius: stukken betreffende de China handel 1769–1845.

- ***Leiden: Leiden University Library, Dept. of Western Ms. (DOOZA, universiteitsbibliotheek)***

BPL 617	stukken betreffende de Chinahandel en de China commissie 1750–1765.
BPL 621	register op de brieven naar China 1758–1778.
BPL 2177	verslag van Ambassade Titsingh naar China 1794–1795.

- ***Leiden: Royal Institute for Linguistics and Anthropology (KITLV)***

DA 8,1	Map of Hong Kong and territory.
DH 434	Chinese kaart van de Chinese zee.
DA 7,3	Kaart van cust te Macao.
DH 661	Inv. van het archief van de Ned. factorie te Canton.
DH 417	Groenevelt 'De Nederlanders in China'.
M 3c 92	'An Authentick Account of the Weights, Measures, Exchanges, Customs, Duties, Port-Charges, &c ...' (London: C. Hendersen, 1763).
Mo 319	Oost-Indies geldmiddelen: Japan en China handel van 1817 op 1818, door P.H. van der Kamp (Nyhoff, 1919).
Mww 247	John Francis Davis 'Sketches of China ... ' (London: Charles Knight & Co., 1841).
Mww 287	Anonymous. 'Description of the City of Canton ... Chinese weights and measures, and the imports and exports of Canton' (Canton, 1839).

Mww 413	'From Hong Kong to Canton by the Pearl River' (1902).
Mww 650	'The "Fan Kwae" at Canton'.
Ts 1720 k72d	*The Canton Miscellany*, vol. 1 (Canton, 1831).

- ***Rotterdam: Maritime Museum (MMR)***

C.H. Gietemaker "'t Vergulde Licht der Zeevaart ofte Const der Stuerlieden ... Negotie der Europeaane op China' 1731.

P 1711	Album te China.

English East India Company (EIC) Records

(Listed alphabetically by city/archive)

- ***London: British Map Library (BML)***

MAR vi 26	'A Survey of the Tigris, from Canton to the Island of Lankeet', by J. Huddart, 1786.
983g22 (1–7)	Dalrymple, Alexander. 'A Collection of Charts and Memoirs' (London: 1772).

- ***London: Oriental and India Office Library and Records (OIO, now in the British Library)***

E\3\101	China supercargoes' instructions copybook 1722.
E\3\109	China supercargoes' instructions copybook 1746.
G\12\1–17	Extracts from the China trade 1596–1759.
G\12\18–20	Miscellaneous documents relating to the China trade 1753–1815.
G\12\21–291	Diaries and Consultations from the Canton factory 1721–1840.
L\AG\1\5\11–12	The Accountant General's Cash Journals 1720–1728.
L\AG\1\6\8–10	The Accountant General's Commercial Journals 1714–1735.
L\MAR\A\138	Journal of ship *Trumbal* to China 1699–1702.
L\MAR\B\293nq	Ship *Walpole* ledgers and logs 1793.
L\MAR\B\599ah	Ship *Edgecote's* logs 1760.
L\MAR\B\699ad	Ship *Macclesfield's* logs for three trips to China 1721, 1724, and 1731.
L\MAR\B\703c	Ship *Addison* Log 1721.
Mss Eur B 0408	Letter book of Charles Millet, supercargo at Canton 1824–1827.
Mss Eur B 0420	Letter book of Captain Charles Besly Gribble 1815–1840.
Mss Eur C 0283	Letters of Lt. John Macdonald 1803–1808.
Mss Eur C 0425	Private trade book of Captain William Hambly to China 1780–1783.
Mss Eur C 0483	Papers of Patrick Begbie, merchant to China 1773–1775, 1782.
Mss Eur C 0555	Ship *Lowthan Castle* nautical log 1831–1832.
Mss Eur C 0606	Nautical Journal of ship *London* to China 1767–1769.
Mss Eur C 0619	Chinese calendar boards and list of ships arriving in Canton 1822–1829.

Mss Eur C 0721	Diary of ship's surgeon Edward Bucknell to China 1849–1851.
Mss Eur D 0675	Remarks in the *Brittania* bound for Madras and China 1757.
Mss Eur D 0963	Trade-Currency Book 1757.
Mss Eur D 1051	Robert Williams and Company Accounts of 5 East Indiamen 1782–1797.
Mss Eur D 1106	Plowden Papers, miscellaneous documents on the China trade 1805–1853.
Mss Eur D 1160	Prinsep Papers, memoirs, and miscellaneous documents 1794–1870.
Mss Eur D 1199	Journal of accounts of Capt. John Hamilton to Canton 1800–1801.
Mss Eur E 0286	Nautical Journal of ship *David Scott* to China 1810–1811.
Mss Eur E 0318	Account of the Wreck *Halsewell* 1786–1814.
Mss Eur F 0110	Paper of John Pybus concerning gold and silver standards in the Indies.
Mss Eur Ph 377	Photocopy of abridged journal of James Rodgers of the ship *Forbes*, first steam vessel in China 1830.

Ostend General India Company (GIC) and other China Trade Records in Belgium

(Listed alphabetically by city/archive)

- ***Antwerp: City Archive (SAA, Stadsarchief)***

IB 2562	Comptes du Comprador du hang à Canton. Expense Boek voor het Factorie en Imp. Schip *Prince de Kaunitz* 1779–1780.
IC 5682	*L'Aigle* et *S. Elisabeth*. Journal concernant le commerce fait par *l'Aigle* et la *Ste. Elisabeth* à Canton 1724.
IC 5684	Casse Boeck, Journael, Groot Boeck. Negotiatie van de laedinghe van den *Arent* en heylighe *Elisabeth* tot Canton anno 1724.
IC 5687	Copey boeck *Marquies de Prié* 1724 Dagboek op het Schip *Marquis de Prié* gehouden 1727. Daarna: de copie van brieven van Capt. Rijngoedt, Canton 1727.
IC 5688	Journal de Laville Pichard, lieutenant du vaisseau *L'Aigle* 1724. Journal pour le cervice du sieur de Laville Pichar ... d'Ostende à la Chine, sorti du port le 10 févr. 1724. (Microfilm: MF 002 K).
IC 5689bis	Scheepsjournaal, 'Particulier journaal van Gerard de Bock' 1724.
IC 5690–5692	Grand Livre et Journal du commerce du *Marquis de Prié* a Canton à la Chine 1725. Journal of affairs transacted by ... supercargoes.
IC 5695	Journael Groot- en Cas Boeck 1727 ... van de negotie ghederigeert tot Canton door de supercargoes van de *Leeuw*, den *Tiger* en den *Arent*.
IC 5696[2]	Chine. Journal de Waele 1726–1727. Journael van het schip 'den *Arent*'.
IC 5697–5701	Journaalen, Groot Boecken, en Resolutien van de scheepen *Tiger*, *Marquis de Prié*, *Concordia*, en *Leeuw* gedestineerd naer Canton 1726–1727.

IC 5704–5710	Journaalen, Grootboecken, Dagverhaal, Daegelyksche Aenteekeninghe, en Brieven van de scheepen *Concordia, Marquis de Prié, Apollo,* en *Duc de Lorraine* gedestined naer China 1727–1732.
IC 5710bis	Brieven uit Canton aan de directeurs, 1723–1729.
IC 5740–5741	Pakboeken en consumptieboeken — Canton 1724–1732.
IC 5744	Expensie Boeck in de factorie Canton. Anno 1727 ... van de twee K. I. C. schepen de *Concordia* en *Marquies de Prié.*
IC 5752–5753	Chine. Résolutions, Contats, et Journal par de *Lyon, Tiger, Eagle, Concorde,* et *Marquis de Prié* i Canton 1726–1727.
IC 5757	A Diary of Transactions by Robert Hewer in Canton 1726 (Microfilm: MF 002 K).
IC 5921bis	*St. Joseph* Canton 1723. Encaissage du thee. (Microfilm: MF 002 K).
IC 5922	Varia Documenten, Brieven, en Papieren van het Indische Compagnie 1720–1734.

- ***Antwerp: Plantin-Maretus Museum (PMA)***

1214–1215	Dossiers Commerciaux 1650–1787 (1–20).
1416	Grootboek van Schilder-Maretus 1730–1755.

- ***Ghent: University Library (UBG, Universiteits Bibliotheek)***

Ms 1837	Extrait du Journal du Capne Jacobus Larmes Commandant le Vaisseau le *Lion* 1726.
Ms 1839	*Tygers* Journall Ghehouden door my vierde Steerman Jacobus Laurence Cleere. Capn. Michiel Pronckaert 1726 en 1727.
Ms 1840	Journael Gehouden op het Schip genaemt den *Tyger* 1726.
Ms 1845–1846	Journaelen Gehouden op het Schip genaemt de *Marquis de Prié* 1727.
Ms 1847–1850	Journaelen Gehouden op het Schip genaemt de *Concordia* 1727.
Ms 1883	Resolutie en Contracten van het Scheepen *Leeuw, Tygher* en *Arent* 1726.
Ns 1920	Extract Journal van het Schip *Arent* 1724.
Ms 1923	Journael Gehouden op het Schip genaemt de *Marquis de Prié* 1725.
Ms 1925	Journael Gehouden op het Schip genaemt de *Concordia* 1727.
Ms 1926	Journael Gehouden op het Schip genaemt de *Le Duc de Loraine* 1732.
Ms 1927	Journael Gehouden op een Schip naer Canton in China 1733.
Ms 1928	Journael Gehouden op het (SOIC) Schip genaemt de *Coninck Frederick* 1738.
Ms 1930	Journael Gehouden op het (SOIC) Schip *Fredericus Rex Süesie* 1744.
Ms 1985	Dagregisters Gehouden in het (VOC) Factorie ter Canton in China 1791.
Ms 1987	Trieste Compagnie Documenten van vijf scheepen vaerende naer China 1771–1784.

Swedish East India Company (SOIC) Records

(Listed alphabetically by city/archive)

- ***Gothenburg: Gothenburg University Library (GUB, Universitetsbibliotek Göteborg)***

Svenska Ostindiska Kompaniets Arkiv

	Journal för Skeppet *Cron Prins Gustaf* 1781–1783.
	Journal för Skeppet *Gustaf III* 1791–1792.
	Journal för Skeppet *Gustaf Adolph* 1797–1800.

Svenska Ostindiska Kompaniets Arkiv H 22

3 D	Beskrifning på Skeppet *Götha Leyons* Resa till Surat och åtskillige andre Indianske Orter 1750–1752. C. H. Braad.
4a:1196	Journal Hållen uppå Respective Swånska Ost Indiska Compagniets Skiepp *Printz Carl* i från Giötheborg, destinerad till Canton üti China första Resan 1750–1752.
4a:1197	Rådplägnings Book på Skieppet *Giötha Leyon*. 1750–1752. Balance Sheet for Skeppet *Prins Carl* 1765.
4a:1199	Dagbok på Resan med Skieppet *Printz Carl* Ahr 1753, 1754, 1755 & 1756.
4a:1200	Dagbok för Skept *Rijks Ständer* på Resan till Surrat och Canton 1760–1762.
4a:1201	Journal hållen på Swenska Ost Indiska Comp. Skepp *Adolph Fredrich* under Resan till och ifrån Canton Åren 1776 och 77. Commenderadt af Capitaine Hr. Joh. Fr. Ekman.
4b	Journal Hållen om Borrd på Skeppett *Terra Nova* under Resan till och ifrån Canton uti China Åhren 1777–1779.
12	Avräkning med Superkargören i Kanton Gustaf Palm 1799–1801.
13	Inköps och försäljningsfakturor. SOIC Skeppet Factura 1768–1786 & 1800–1804.
15–16	Balansräkningar och andra bokslutspapper 1772–1814. Skeppspredikanten C.C. Ströms Papper 1121.
1	Diverse Documenter öfver Ostindie 1761–1804.

Skeppspredicanten C. C. Ströms papper. H 21:1

1148	Journal över Resan till *Fredrik Adolphs* Vrak (1761).
1149–50	Bärgningen från Skeppet *Fredrik Adolphs* Vrak (1761–1762).
1151	Kontrakt ang. Inköp av Te (1767).
1152	Promemoria med Råd om Te Inköp (1761).
1153	Kontrakt ang. Inköp av Te (1767).
1154	Inköpsräkning ang. 100 kistor Te (1767).
1155	Uträkning över Diverse Sålda Varor (1767).
1156–57	Uträkning över Sålt Bly (1767).
1158–59	Beräkningar till Skeppsritning (1771).
1160	Intyg ang. Skeppsbesiktning (1771).

1162	Skeppet *Gustaf III's* Last (1780).
1164–65	Anmärkningar ang. Rapport till Kejsaren av Kina (1780).
1166	Edikt av Mandarinen Fou Yune-Lhy (1781).
1167	Förteckning över Växlar (1781–1782).
1169	Journaler över resor med Skeppen *Gustaf Adolph* och *Sophia Magdalena* (1794–1796).
1170	Brev till Direktionen (1795).
1171	Anteckning om Kinesiska Mynt och Vikter (1796).
1173	Befattningshavare på Skeppet *Gustaf III* (1796).
1174	Skattsedel (1797).
1175	Proviant på Skeppet *Gustaf III* (1797–1798).
1176–77	Kontrakt ang. Inköp av Te mm. (1797).
1178	Proviantlistor (1797–1798).
1179	Omkostnader för Faktoriet (1797–1798).
1180–82	Utdrag ut Skeppet *Gustaf III's* Loggbok (1798).
1186	Omkostnader i Kinesisk Hamn (1797).
1187	Befattningshavare på Skeppen *Drottningen* och *Sophia Magdalena* (1800).
1190	Jämförelsetabell over Kinesiska och Svenska Längdmått och Vikter.
1191	Förhållningsregler Ombord på Kompaniets Skepp.
1192	Befattningshavares Löner.

- ***Gothenburg: Provincial Archive (LAG, Landsarkivet)***

Öijareds säteris arkiv A 406. Seriesignum F III.

1–5	Förteckning över Svenska Ostindiska Companiets skepp under gamla och nya octroyen, och en kort berättelse om göromålen i Canton med packningslista, kina prisbok u.å., 1720–1764.

Östadsarkiver Privatarkiv A 152

57	Räkenskaper för kompaniets affärer I Kanton 1743–1747. Handlingar rörande Ostindiska Kompanier och Chrijstian Tham.

- ***Gothenburg: Maritime Museum (SFG, Sjöfartsmuseum)***

Ms. No. 6131	Journal hållen under resan till Canthon uthi China 1748–1750.
Ms. No. 9571	Journal hållen på Resan till Canton i China 1745–1748.

- ***Gothenburg: City Museum (SMG, Stadsmuseet)***

Chinese Sea Pass. Yuehaiguan waiyang chuanpai

1815	Jiaqing ershi nian shi yue ershiwu ri. Issued to Captain Jianchen. Ruiguo (Sweden). 25 November 1815.
1860	Xianfeng shi nian jiu yue shiliu ri. Issued to Captain Dideshi. Muguo (probably short for Linguo = Sweden). 29 October 1860.

Göteborg Allmänt. Handel och Sjöfart.
I — Diverse Papier öfver Svenska Ostindiska Kompaniet.
Handel SOIC. 1–6 Sven Kjellberg's notes on the Svenska Ostindiska Kompaniet.

• *Kalmar: City Library (KSB, Stadsbibliotek)*

Ms 81 — Dagbok med Respective Ostindiska Compagniets Skepp *Adolph Fredrich* under Resan till och från Canton i China under 1768, 69, 70.

• *Lund: University Library (UBL, Universitetsbibliotek)*

Ostindiska kompaniet dokumenter, correspondence, breven, lijsten, pamphleter.

• *Stockholm: National Archives (RAS, Riksarkivet)*

UD Huvudarkivet E 2 FA.
13 — Skrivelse från konsuler 1809–80. Amoy, Canton, Chefoo, Newchwang, Ningpo. 1847–69.

Handel och Sjöfart: Ostindiska Kompagnier.
54 — Ostindiska Kompagnier Documenter 1740–1799.
55 — Ostindiska Kompagnier Documenter 1800–1813.

• *Stockholm: Royal Library (KBS, Kungliga Biblioteket)*

C.VI.1.24 — Wallenberg, Jacob. Min son på Galeian eller en Ostindisk Resa 1769–1771
Kine. ms14 — Yuehaiguan yangchuanpai (Chinese Customs Sea Pass). Qianlong liu nian shier yue shiyi ri. Issued to Captain Yashimeng (Askbom) of Ruiguo (Sweden). 11 January 1742.
M 270 — Dagbok anteckningar under en Resa till Ostindien 1767–1769.
M 278 — Journal hållen ombord på Skeppet *Gustaf III* till och från China 1799–1801.
M 280 — Dagbok hållen ombord på Skeppet *Götha Leÿon* af Carl Johan Gethe 1746–1749.
M 281a & b — Dagbok hållen på resan till China af Gustaf Fridrich Hjortberg 1748–1753.
M 285 — Lindahl, Olof. I Korthet war Handelsen 1784.
M 286 — Dagbok för Skeppet *Freden* på Resan till China 1746–1747.
M 287:1–2 — Osbeck, Pehr. Dagbok öfver en Ostindisk Resa åren 1750, 1751, 1752.
M 288 — Dagbok för Skeppet *Ricksens Stånder* på Resan till China 1760–1762.
M 289 — Journal ombord på Skeppet *Prins Carl* till China åren 1763–1764
M 292 — Dagbok ombord på Skeppet *Götha Leÿon* af Carl Fredrich von Schantz 1746–1749.

M 294	Ost. Indisk resa till Canton uthi China af Mag. Ternström 1745–1746.
M 295	De Frondat. Journal du Voyage du Perou en Chine 1708–1710. This Journal is published in Madrolle, *Les Premiers Voyages*, 1901 (see full citation below).
X 948:1–2	Angerstein, Reinhold R. Discourse over Trade.
X 988	Tabelier öfver Coopvardie Siömån och Fartyg för År 1783.

- ***Stockholm: Library of the Royal Academy of Sciences (KVB, Kungliga Vetenskaps-akademiens Bibliotek)***

RLF 50	Map of Canton River.
Ms. Braad, C. H.	Berättelse om Resan med Skeppet *Hoppet* under Capitaine Fr. Pettersons Commando från Götheborg till Canton i China 1748–1749.
Ms. Braad, C. H.	Beskrifning på Skeppet *Götha Leyons* Resa till Surat och åtskillige andre Indianske Orter 1750–1752.
Ms. Dalman, J. F.	Dagbok under resan från Giötheborg til Canton 1748–1749.
Ms. Ekeberg, C. G.	Dagbok under Resan till och ifrån Canton uti China 1746–1749.
Ms. Ekeberg, C. G.	Kort Dagbok ofver Resan med Skeppet *Hoppet* 1751–1754.
Ms. Elphinstone, G.	Dagbok öfver en Resa med Skeppet *Götha Leyon*.
Ms. Montan, B.	Resor til och ifrån Canton 1735 och 1737.

- ***Stockholm: Nordic Museum Archive (NM, Nordiska Museet Arkivet)***

Godegårdsarkivet. Ostindiska Handling.

F17:1–17	Ostindiska Kompagnier Documenter and Private Trade Documents 1744–1767. Skepps instruktioner, kassabokföring, protokollsutdrag, och inventarieförteckning. Bokföring med Compradoren 1762–1766.

- ***Stockholm: Sea History Museum (SHM, Sjöhistoriska Museet)***

S.B. 1212	Colored drawing of boats in Canton.
SMG 17987	Journal med Skeppet *Sophia Magdalena* åhren 1781 & 1782.
SMG 17993	Journal Skeppet *Finland* åhren 1777, 1778 och 1779.

Mathias Gustaf Homers arkiv H Nr. 511.

2	Annotaicions Book Annno 1747. Inventory and Provision List for ship *Göteborg* 1745 and ship *Printz Gustav* 1748.
511:8	Private China-trade papers. 1762–1763.
511:14	SOIC orders and instructions for Capt. Holmers on ship *Lovisa Ulrica* 1766.
511:24	Cassa Conto for Cadiz and Canton of private trade aboard ship *Stockholms Slot* 1762–1763. Some Bottomry info. Similar to 511:8.

- ***Uppsala: University Library (UUB, Uppsala Universitetsbibliotek)***

Handskriftsavdelningen.

Ihre 186	Christopher Järnström. Journaler förda under Resa till Ostindien.
L 133	Handlingar om Svenska Handeln. (1734 to end of century).
L 181–182	Ost Ind. Handl. Journaler, skeppsladdningar, kopierad, utdrag och anteckningar för diverse Ostindiska skeppen 1727–1762.
L 183	Journaler öfver flere Skepps Resor til och ifrån Ost Indien 1732–1765.
L 184	Journal öfver Resan med *Stockholms Slott* till och från Canton i China 1765–1767.
L 185	Handlingar Rorande Swenska Handelen til Ost Indien Häftad med Lösa Blad 1754–1756. C. H. Braad.
L 185a	Journal på Skeppet *Hoppet* under Resan till och från Canton 1748, Dagelige Anmärkningar öfwer Ost Indiske Handelen (1750s–1760s) och Rese Beskrifning till China 1748. C. H. Braad.
L 186	Diverse anteckningar om Svenska Ostindiska Kompagniets Handel, Räkningar 1759–1761. C. H. Braad.
L 190	Räkning för Skeppet 1760–1762.
Westen 163	Anteckningar och Bref af Assessor Christopher Henrik Braad under dess Resor till Ostindien åren 1748–1762.
X 388	Journal hållen på Resan till Canton i China 1745–1748 af Israel Reinius. [This journal is available in print].
X 389	Berättelse om resan med Skeppet *Hoppet* från Göteborg till Kanton 1748, 49. Med utsikter af passerade orter. Af C. H. Braad.
X 390	Berättelse om Resan med Skeppet *Hoppet* under Capitaine Fr. Pettersons Commando 1748–1749. C. H. Braad.
X 391	Annotationsbok under Resan. C. H. Braad.
X 392	Resebeskrifning ifrån Sverige till Chinesiska Staden Canton. C. H. Braad.
X 433	Journaler och Dagbok hållen om Bord på Engelska Skippet *Bolton* af Carl Leonard August Fries 1838–1839.

PUBLISHED PRIMARY SOURCES

(Listed alphabetically by author)

Abeel, David. *Journal of a Residence in China, and the Neighboring Countries from 1829 to 1833*. New York: 1834, and *The Missionary Fortified Against Trials*. Boston: Marvin and Company, 1835.

Anglo-Chinese Calendar (1847–1855).

An Official Guide to Eastern Asia Trans-Continental Connections between Europe and Asia. Vol. 4. 'China'. Tokyo: Imperial Japanese Government Railways, 1915.

Anonymous. *Descriptions of the City of Canton: With an Appendix, Containing an Account of the Population of the Chinese Empire, Chinese Weights and Measures, and the Imports and*

Exports of Canton. 2nd ed. Canton: 1839. Copy at Leiden University KITLV Library: M WW 287.

Anonymous. *Sketch of the Commercial Intercourse of the World with China*. New York: Hunt's Merchants' Magazine, 1845.

Anson, George, Esq. *A Voyage Round the World in the Years M, DCC, XL, I, II, III, IV.* (1740–1744) 3 vols. [London?]: John Wilson, 1790. Reprint, Philadelphia: D. N. Goodchild, 2002.

Arnold, J. *A Handbook to Canton, Macao and the West River*, 9th ed. Hong Kong: Hong Kong, Canton and Macao Steamboat Co., Ltd., 1914.

Arnold, Julean. *Commercial Handbook of China*. Washington: Government Printing Office, 1919.

Auber, Peter. *China. An Outline of the Government, Laws, and Policy: and of the British and Foreign Embassies to, and Intercourse with, that Empire*. London: Parbury, Allen, and Co., 1834.

Ball, J. Dyer. *Things Chinese*. 1903. Reprint, 5th ed. Singapore: Braham Brash, 1989.

Ball, Samuel. *An Account of the Cultivation and Manufacture of Tea in China: Derived from Personal Observation during an Official Residence in That Country from 1804 to 1826*. London: Longman, Brown, Green and Longmans, 1848.

Belcher, Captain Sir Edward. *Narrative of a Voyage Round the World, Performed in Her Majesty's Ship Sulphur, During the Years 1836–1842. Including Details of the Naval Operations in China, from Dec. 1840, to Nov. 1841*. 2 vols. London: Henry Colburn, 1843.

Bernard, William Dallas. *Narrative of the Voyage and Services of the Nemesis, from 1840 to 1843*. 2 vols. London: Henry Colburn, 1844.

Berncastle, Julius. *A Voyage to China: Including a Visit to the Bombay Presidency, the Mahratta Country, the Cave Temples of Western India, Singapore, the Straits of Malacca and Sundra, and the Cape of Good Hope*. London: Shoberl, 1851.

Bingham, John Elliot. *Narrative of the Expedition to China from the Commencement of the War to Its Termination in 1842*. 2 vols. 2nd ed. London: Henry Colburn, 1843.

Blancard, Pierre. *Manuel du Commerce des Indes Orientales et de la Chine*. Paris: Chez Bernard, 1806.

Boje, Jens. *Journal paa den anden Reyse til China med Skibet Dronningen af Danmark, indeholdende de Merkværdigste Ting, som fra Reysens Begyndelse Anno 1742, og til dens Ende 1744*. Copenhagen: Christoph Georg Glasing, 1745.

Brelin, Johan. *Beskrifning öfver en Äfventyrlig Resa til och ifrån Ost-Indien, Södro America, och en del af Europa, Åren 1755, 56, och 57*. Uppsala: Kongl. Acad. Tryckeriet, 1758; Reprint, Stockholm: Rediviva, 1973.

Bridgeman, Elijah C. *Glimpses of Canton: The Diary of Elijah C. Bridgman, 1834–1838*. Facsimilie. New Haven: Yale Divinity School Library, 1998.

Brunel, M. 'A Memoir on the Chinese Trade'. In *A Voyage to Madagascar, and the East Indies*, by Abbe Rochon. Translated from the French. London: Printed for G. G. J. and J. Robinson, Paternoster-Row, 1792: 415–75.

Campbell, Archibald. *A Voyage Round the World, from 1806 to 1812*. Facsimile of the 3rd American edition, 1822. Honolulu: University of Hawaii Press, 1967.

Canton Advertising & Commission Agency. *Canton. Its Port, Industries & Trade. With Maps, Drawings & Illustrations*. Compiled and Published by Canton Advertising & Commission Agency, 1932. Reprint, Taipei: Ch'eng Wen Publishing Company, 1971.

Canton General Price Current (1835–1844).

Canton Press (1835–1844).

Canton Register (1827–1843).

Careri, John Francis Gemelli. A *Voyage Round the World. Containing the most Remarkable Things he saw in China*. (in 1695). In A *Collection of Voyages and Travels*. By Messrs. Churchill. Vol. 4. London: Golden-Ball, 1745. pp. 274–396.

Chinese Courier and Canton Gazette (1831).

Chinese Courier (1831–1833).

Chinese Repository. 20 vols. Canton: The South China Mission, 1832–1852.

Churchill, Messrs. A *Collection of Voyages and Travels, some now first printed from Original Manuscripts, others now first published in English*. 6 vols. London: Golden-Ball, 1745.

Collins, Ferry McDonough. A *Voyage Down the Amoor: with a Land Journey Through Siberia, and Incidental Notices of Manchooria, Kamschatka, and Japan*. New York: D. Appleton and Co., 1860.

Coolhaas, W.Ph., ed. *Generale Missiven van Gouverneurs-Generaal en Raden aan Heren XVII der Verenigde Oostindische Compagnie*. 1725–1729. Vol. 8. The Hague: Instituut voor Nederlandse Geschiedenis, 1985.

Cordier, Henri. *Le Voyage a la Chine au XVIIIe Siècle. Extrait du Journal de M. Bouvet Commandant le Vaisseau de la Compagnie des Indes le <Villevault> (1765–1766)*. Extrait de la *Revue de L'Histoire des Colonies Françaises* (2e Trimestre 1913). Paris: Édouard Champion and Émile Larose, 1913.

Cossigny, C. Charpentier. *Voyage a Canton, Capitale de la Province de ce nom, a la China; Par Gorée, le Cap de Bonne-Espérance, et les Isles de France et de la Réunion; Suivi D'Observations sur le Voyage à la Chine, de Lord MaCartney et du Citoyen Van-Braam, et d'une Esquesse des arts des Indiens et des Chinois*. Paris: Chez André, 1803?.

Coxe, William. *An Account of the Russian discoveries between Asia and America*. London: J. Nichols, 1780.

Crawfurd, John. *Journal of an Embassy from the Governor-General of India to the Courts of Siam and Cochin China*. London: Henry Colburn, 1828. Reprint, New Delhi: Asian Educational Services, 2000.

Crow, Carl. *The Travelers' Handbook for China*. 3rd ed. Shanghai: Carl Crow, 1921.

Dalrymple, Alexander. *Memoir of the Chart of Part of the Coast of China, and the Adjacent Islands near the Entrance of Canton River. Containing Observations in the Schooner Cuddalore in 1759 and 1760. And in the Ship London, 1764. With Several Views of the Lands*. London: Alexander Dalrymple, Esq., 1771.

Dalrymple, Alexander. *Journal of the Schooner Cuddalore, Oct. 1759. On the Coast of China*. London: Alexander Dalrymple, Esq., 1771.

Dalrymple, Alexander. *Journal of the Schooner Cuddalore on the Coast of Hainan 1760*. London: Alexander Dalrymple, Esq., 1771.

Dalrymple, Alexander. *Memoir of the Chart of the West Coast of Palawan, or Paragua. Containing the Journal of the Schooner Cuddalore, in December, 1761*. London: Alexander Dalrymple, Esq., 1771.

Dalrymple, Alexander. *Essay on the most Commodious Methods of Marine Surveying*. London: Alexander Dalrymple, Esq., 1771.

Dalrymple, Alexander. *Memoir of a Chart of the China Sea*. London: Alexander Dalrymple, Esq., 1771.

Dalrymple, Alexander. *General Introduction to the Charts and Memoirs*. London: Alexander Dalrymple, Esq., 1772.

Dalrymple, Alexander. *Oriental Repertory*. Published at the charge of the East-India Company. London: George Biggs, 1793.

Dampier, William. *A New Voyage Round the World*. In *A Collection of Voyages*. 4 vols. London: Crown in St. Paul's Church-Yard, 1729.

Dann, John C., ed. *A Diary of the Life of Jacob Nagle, Sailor, from the Year 1775 to 1841*. New York: Wiedenfel & Nicolson, 1988.

Davis, John Francis. *Sketches of China; Partly during an Inland Journey of Four Months, between Peking, Nanking, and Canton; with Notices of Observations Relative to the Present War*. 2 vols. London: Charles Knight & Co., 1841.

Department of Overseas Trade. *Trade and Economic Conditions in China 1931–33*. No. 561. London: His Majesty's Stationery Office, 1933. Reprint, San Francisco: 1975.

Dermigny, Louis, ed. *Les Mémoires de Charles de Constant sur le Commerce a la Chine*, par Charles de Constant. Paris: S.E.V.P.E.N., 1964.

Diário da Navegação de Macau, 1759–1761. Códice No. 183. Do Arquivo Histórico do Ministio das Finanças. Lisboa: Agência-Geral do Ultramar, 1970.

Diplomatic and Consular Reports. *Report on the Trade of Central and Southern China*. Miscellaneous Series No. 458. London: Harrison and Sons, 1898. Reprint, San Francisco: Chinese Materials Center, Inc., 1975.

Dixon, George. *A Voyage Round the World; But More Particularly to the North-West Coast of America; Performed in 1785, 1786, 1787, 1788, and 1789*. London: Geo. Goulding, 1789. Reprint, New York: Da Capo Press, 1968.

Dobell, Peter. *Travels in Kamtchatka and Siberia; with a Narrative of a Residence in China*. 2 vols. London: Henry Colburn and Richard Bentley, 1830. Reprint, New York: Arno Press, 1970.

Downing, C. Toogood. *The Fan-Qui in China in 1836–7*. 3 vols. London: 1838. Reprint, Shannon, Ireland: Irish University Press, 1972.

Drinker, Sandwith. *A Private Journal of Events and Scenes at Sea and in India. Commencing April 26th, 1838*. Boston: Suzanne Drinker Moran, 1990.

Du Halde, P. *The General History of China. Containing a Geographical Historical, Chronological, Political and Physical Description of the Empire of China, Chinese-Tartary, Corea and Thibet*. 3rd ed. 4 vols. London: 1741.

Ekeberg, Carl Gustav. *Capitaine Carl Gustav Ekebergs Ostindiska Resa, Åren 1770 och 1771*. Stockholm: Henr. Fougt, 1773.

Ellis, William (assistant surgeon). *An Authentic Narrative of a Voyage Performed by Captain Cook and Captain Clerke in His Majesty's Ships Resolution and Discovery During the Years 1776 to 1780 in Search of a North-West Passage Between the Continents of Asia and America*. 2 vols. London, 1782. Reprint, New York: J. Da Capo Press, 1969.

Fels, Susan, ed. *Before the Wind. The Memoir of an American Sea Captain, 1808–1833*, by Charles Tyng. New York: Viking Penquin, 1999.

Fidlon, Paul G. and F. J. Ryan, eds. *The Journal of Arthur Bowes Smyth: Surgeon, Lady Penrhyn 1787–1789*. Sydney: Australian Documents Library, 1979.

Finlayson, George. *The Mission to Siam and Hué 1821–1822*. New York: Oxford University Press, 1988.

Flannery, Tim, ed. *The Life and Adventures of John Nicol, Mariner*. New York: Atlantic Monthly Press, 1997.

Fleurieu, C. P. Claret, trans. *A Voyage Round the World 1790–1791, and 1792*, by Étienne Marchand. London: 1801. Reprint, Amsterdam: N. Israel, 1969.

Floyd, Arva Colbert, ed. *The Diary of a Voyage to China 1859–1860*. By Rev. Young J. Allen. Atlanta: Emory University, 1943.

Forbes, Leut. F. E. *Five Years in China; from 1842 to 1847 with an Account of the Occupation of the Islands Labuan and Borneo by her Majesty's Forces*. London: Richard Bentley, 1848.

Forbes, R. B. *Remarks on China and the China Trade*. Boston: Samuel N. Dickinson, 1844.

Forbes, R. B. *Personal Reminiscences*. Boston: 1882; reprint 1970; London: Macdonald and Jane's, 1974.

Forster, John Reinhold, trans. *A Voyage to China and the East Indies, by Peter Osbeck. Together with a Voyage to Suratte, by Olof Torren, and An Account of Chinese Husbandry, by Captain Charles Gustavus Eckeberg*. Translated from the 1765 German ed. London: Benjamin White, 1771.

Fortune, Robert. *A Journey to the Tea Countries of China Including Sung-lo and the Bohea Hills; with a Short Notice of the East India Company's Tea Plantations in the Himalaya Mountains*. London: John Murray, 1852.

Fortune, Robert. *A Residence among the Chinese: Inland, on the Coast, and at Sea. Being a Narrative of Scenes and Adventures during a Third Visit to China, from 1853 to 1856. Including Notices of Many Natural Productions and Works of Art, the Culture of Silk, &c. with Suggestions on the Present War*. London: John Murray, 1857.

Fortune, Robert. *Two Visits to the Tea Countries of China and the British Tea Plantations in the Himalaya; with a Narrative of Adventures, and a Full Description of the Culture of the Tea Plant, the Agriculture, Horticulture, and Botany of China*. 2 vols. London: John Murray, 1853.

Franchere, Gabriel. *A Voyage to the Northwest Coast of America*. New York: The Citadel Press, 1968.

Frugé, August and Neal Harlow, trans. and eds. *A Voyage to California, the Sandwich Islands, & Around the World in the Years 1826–1829*, by Auguste Duhaut-Cilly. Berkeley: University of California Press, 1999.

Fu Lo-Shu, ed. *A Documentary Chronicle of Sino-Western Relations (1644–1820)*. Tucson: University of Arizona Press, 1966.

Gilbert, Thomas. *Voyage from New South Wales to Canton, in the Year 1788, with Views of the Islands Discovered*. Facsimile ed. New York: Da Capo Press, 1968.

Goor, J. van, ed. *Generale Missiven van Gouverneurs-Generaal en Raden aan Heren XVII der Verenigde Oostindische Compagnie*. 1729–1737. Vol. 9. The Hague: Instituut voor Nederlandse Geschiedenis, 1988.

Goor, J. van, ed. *Generale Missiven van Gouverneurs-Generaal en Raden aan Heren XVII der Verenigde Oostindische Compagnie*. 1737–1743. Vol. 10. The Hague: Instituut voor Nederlandse Geschiedenis, 2004.

Gordon, Charles Alexander. *China from a Medical Point of View in 1860 and 1861, to which is added a Chapter on Nagasaki as a Sanitarium*. London: John Churchill, 1863.

Gordon, G. J. *Address to the People of Great Britain, Explanatory of Our Commercial Relations with the Empire of China, and of the Course of Policy by which it may be Rendered an almost Unbounded Filed for British Commerce*. London: Smith, Elder and Co., 1836.

Gützlaff, Karl F. A. *Journal of Three Voyages Along the Coast of China in 1831, 1832 and 1833 with Notices of Siam, Corea, and the Loo-Choo Islands*. London: Westley and Davis, 1834.

Gützlaff, Karl F. A. 'Journal of a Residence in Siam, and of a Voyage along the Coast of China to Mantchou Tartary'. *Chinese Repository*, Vol. 1, July 1832.

Hall, Basil. *Voyage to Loo-choo: and Other Places in the Eastern Seas, in the Year 1816, Including an Account of Captain Maxwell's Attack on the Batteries at Canton*. Edinburgh: A. Constable, 1826.

Hallberg, Paul, and Christian Koninckx. A *Passage to China*, by Colin Campbell. Gothenburg: Royal Society of Arts and Sciences, 1996.

Hamilton, Alexander. A *New Account of the East-Indies being the Observations and Remarks of Capt. Alexander Hamilton from the year 1688–1723*. 2 vols. London: 1739. Reprint, New Delhi: Asian Educational Services, 1995.

Hanson, Reginald. A *Short Account of Tea and the Tea Trade*. London: Whitehead, Morris & Lowe, 1876.

Haussmann, Auguste. *Voyage en Chine Cochinchine inde et Malaisie. Délégué Commercial Attaché al le Légation de M. de Ladrené. Ministre plénipotentiaire de France pendant les années 1844–45–46*. 3 Vols. Paris: G. Olivier Librairie Française et Étrangère, 1847.

Hayes, Edmund, ed. *Log of the Union. John Boit's Remarkable Voyage to the Northwest Coast and Around the World 1794–1796*. Portland: Oregon Historical Society, 1981.

Heaps, Leo, ed. *Log of the Centurion*, by Captain Philip Saumarez. New York: Macmillan Publishing Co., 1974.

Hillard, Katharine, ed. My *Mother's Journal. A Young Lady's Diary of Five Years spent in Manila, Macao, and the Cape of Good Hope from 1829–1834*. Boston: George H. Ellis, 1900.

Hodges, Nan P. and Arthur W. Hummel, eds. *Lights and Shadows of a Macao Life. The Journal of Harriett Low, Travelling Spinster* (1829–1834). 2 vols. Woodinville, WA: The History Bank, 2002.

Hongkong Almanack (1846–1848).

Hong Kong, Canton & Macao Steam-boat Company, Limited and China Navigation Company Limited. *Information of General Interest to Travellers visiting Canton and Macao by the Steamers of the above Companies*. Hong Kong: Noronha & Co., 1893; 1894; 1897; 1898. All four editions were consulted.

Howay, Frederic W., ed. *Voyages of the Columbia to the Northwest Coast 1787–1790 & 1790–1793*. Boston: Massachusetts Historical Society, 1941. Reprint, Portland: Oregon Historical Society Press, 1990.

Huc, M. *The Chinese Empire: Forming a Sequel to the Work entitled 'Recollections of a Journey Through Tartary and Thibet'*. 2 vols. 2nd ed. London: Kennikat Press, 1855.

Hunter, William. *Bits of Old China*. London: Kegan Paul, Trench, & Co., 1855. Reprint, Taipei, 1966. Reprint, under the title *An American in Canton (1825–44)*, Hong Kong: Derwent Communications Ltd., 1994.

Hunter, William. *The 'Fan Kwae' at Canton before Treaty Days 1825–1844*. London: 1882. Reprint, London, 1885; London, 1911; Shanghai: Mercury Press, 1938; Taipei: 1966. Reprint, under the title *An American in Canton (1825–44)*. Hong Kong: Derwent Communications, Ltd., 1994.

Hurley, R. C. *The Tourist's Guide to Canton, the West River and Macao*. Hong Kong: Noronha & Co., 1895. Reprint, Hong Kong: Hong Kong Telegraph, 1898; Hong Kong: Hong Kong Printing Press, 1903 (all three editions were consulted).

Inglis, Robert. *The Chinese Security Merchants in Canton, and Their Debts*. London: J. M. Richardson, 1838.

Itier, M. Jules. *Journal d'un Voyage en Chine en 1843, 1844, 1845, 1846*. 3 vols. Paris: Chez Dauvin et Fontaine, 1848.

Jackman, S. W., ed. *The Journal of William Sturgis*. Victoria: Sono Nis Press, 1978.

Jenkins, Colonel Lawrence Waters, ed. *Bryant Parrott Tilden of Salem, at a Chinese Dinner Party. Canton: 1819*. Salem: Peabody Museum, 1944.

Jin Guo Ping (金國平) and Wu Zhiliang (吳志良), comps. *Correspondência Oficial Trocada Entre As Autoridades de Cantão e Os Procuradores do Senado. Fundo das Chapas Sínicas em Português (1749–1847)*. 8 vols. Macau: Macau Foundation, 2000.

Johnson, James. *An Account of a Voyage to India, China, &c. in His Majesty's Ship Caroline, performed in the Years 1803–4–5, interspersed with Descriptive Sketches and Cursory Remarks*. London: J.G. Barnard, 1806.

Jorge, Cecília and Rogério Beltrão Coelho. *Viagem por Macau. Comentários, Descrições e Relatos de Autores Estrangeiros (Séculos XVII a XIX)*. 2 vols. Macau: Livros de Oriente, 1997, 1999.

Kaplanoff, Mark D. *Joseph Ingraham's Journal of the Brigatine HOPE on a Voyage to the Northwest Coast of North America 1790–92*. Barre, Massachusetts: Imprint Society, 1971.

Kerr, Dr. *A Guide to the City and Suburbs of Canton*. Hong Kong: Kelly & Walsh, 1918.

Lau Fong (劉芳) and Zhang Wenqin (章文欽), eds. *Qingdai Aomen Zhongwen Dang'an Huibian* (清代澳門中文檔案匯編 A Collection of Qing Chinese Documents Concerning Macau). 2 vols. Macau: Aomen Jijin Hui (澳門基金會), 1999.

Lavollée, Charles. *Voyage en Chine*. Paris: Just Rouvier, 1853.

Leitch, Ritchie. *History of the Indian Empire and the East India Company, from the Earliest Times to the Present*. London: W. H. Allen and Co., 1848.

Levien, Michael, ed. *The Cree Journals. The Voyages of Edward H. Cree, Surgeon R.N., as Related in His Private Journals, 1837–1856*. Devon: Webb & Bower Ltd., 1981; Scarborough: Nelson Canada Ltd., 1981.

Li Guorong (李国荣) and Lin Weisen (林伟森), eds. *Qing Dai Guangzhou Shisan Hang Jilue* (清代广州十三行纪略 Chronicle of the Hong Merchants in Canton during the Qing Dynasty). Guangzhou: Guangdong Renmin Chubanshe (广东人民出版社), 2006.

Liang Tingnan (梁廷楠). *Yuehaiguan Zhi* (粤海关志 Gazetteer of Guangdong Maritime Customs) vol. 5 (1839). Reprint, Guangzhou: Guangzhou Renmin Chubanshe (广州人民出版社), 2001.

Lisiansky, Urey. *A Voyage Round the World in the years 1803, 4, 5, & 6*. London: S. Hamilton, 1814. Reprint, New York: Da Capo Press, 1968.

Ljungstedt, Anders (Andrew). *An Historical Sketch of the Portuguese Settlements in China*. 1832. Reprint, Boston: James Munroe & Co. eds., 1836; Hong Kong: Viking Hong Kong Publications, 1992.

Lockman, J. *Travels of the Jesuits in to Various Parts of the World Particularly China and East Indies Compiled from Their Letters Intermix'd with an Account of the Manners, Government, Religion, &c. of the Several Nations Visited by Those Fathers with Extracts from Other Travellers and Miscellaneous Notes*. 2 vols. London: John Noon, 1743; Reprint, New Delhi: Asian Educational Services, 1995.

Lockyer, Charles. *An Account of the Trade in India*. London: S. Crouch, 1711.

Loines, Elma. 'More Canton Letters of Abiel Abbot Low, William Henry Low, and Edward Allen Low (1837–1844)'. *The Essex Institute Historical Collections*. Vol. 85 (July 1949): 215–43.

Loines, Elma. 'Francis Low, a Salem Youth Dies on Board Ship in the China Sea'. *The Essex Institute Historical Collections*. Vol. 87 (July 1951): 261–305.

Lubbock, Alfred Basil, ed. *Barlow's Journal of his Life at Sea in King's Ships, East & West Indiamen & other Merchantmen from 1659 to 1703*. 2 vols. London: Hurst & Blackett, 1934.

Lurcy, Gabriel Lafond de. *Voyages Autour du Monde*. Vols. 5 and 7. Paris: Pourrat Frères, 1844.

Madrolle, C., ed. *Journal du Voyage de la Chine fait dans les Années 1701, 1702, & 1703*. In *Les Premiers Voyages Français a la Chine. La Compagnie de la Chine 1698–1719*. By Cl. Madrolle. Paris: Augustin Challamel, 1901.

Malcom, Howard. *Travels in South-Eastern Asia embracing Hindustan, Malaya, Siam, and China with Notices of Numerous Missionary Stations and a Full Account of the Burman Empire*. 2 vols. London: Charles Tilt, 1839. Facsimile reprint, New Delhi: Asian Educational Services, 2004.

Manwaring, G. E. *A Cruising Voyage Round the World*. By Captain Woodes Rogers. London: Cassel and Co., 1712. Reprint, Seafarers' Library, 1928.

Martin, R. Montgomery. *China. Political, Commercial and Social in an Official Report to Her Majesty's Government*. 2 vols. London: James Madden, 1847.

Mayers, William F. *The Chinese Government. A Manual of Chinese Titles, Categorically Arranged and Explained, with an Appendix*, 3rd ed. London: Kegan Paul, Trench, Trübner & Co., 1897

Meares, John. *Voyages made in the years 1788 and 1789, from China to the North West Coast of America. To which are prefixed, and Introductory Narrative of a Voyage performed in 1786, from Bengal, in the ship Nootka; Observations on the probable Existence of a North West Passage; and some account of the Trade Between the North West Coast of America and China; and the latter Country and Great Britain*. London: Logographic Press, 1790. Reprint, Amsterdam: Da Capo Press, 1967.

Milburn, William. *Oriental Commerce; containing a Geographical Description of the Principal Places in The East Indies, China, and Japan, with their Produce, Manufactures, and Trade, including the Coasting or Country Trade from Port to Port; also the Rise and Progress of the Trade of the various European Nations with the Eastern World, particularly that of the English East India Company, from the Discovery of the Passage round the Cape of Good Hope to the Present Period; with an account of the Company's Establishments, Revenues, Debts,*

Assets, &c. at Home and Abroad. 2 vols. London: Black, Parry, & Co., 1813. Reprint, New Delhi: Munshiram Manoharlal Publishers, 1999.

Milne, William Charles. *Life in China*. London: Routledge, Warnes & Routledge, 1861.

Ming Qing Shiliao Geng Bian (明清史料庚编 Collection of Ming-Qing Historical Materials). 2 vols. Taipei: Zhonghua Chuju (中华书局), 1987.

Money, Edward. *The Cultivation & Manufacture of Tea*. London: W. B. Whittingham & Co., 1873.

Moran, Suzanne Drinker, ed. *A Private Journal of Events and Scenes at Sea and in India by Sandwith Drinker. Commencing April 26th, 1838*. Boston: 1990.

Morrell, Abby Jane. *Narrative of a Voyage to the Ethiopic and South Atlantic Ocean, Indian Ocean, Chinese Sea, North and South Pacific Ocean, in the Years 1829, 1830, 1831, who accompanied her Husband, Capt. Benjamin Morrell, Jr., of the Schooner Antarctic*. New York: J. & J. Harper, 1833. Reprint, New Jersey: The Gregg Press, 1970.

Morrison, Robert. *A View of China for Philological Purposes; Containing a Sketch of Chinese Chronology, Geography, Government, Religion & Customs*. Macao: East India Company's Press, 1817.

Morrison, Robert. *Notices Concerning China, and the Port of Canton. Also a Narrative of the Affair of the English Frigate Topaze, 1821–22. With Remarks on Homicides, and an Account of the Fire of Canton*. Malacca: Mission Press, 1823.

Morrison, John Robert. *A Chinese Commercial Guide. Consisting of A Collection of Details Respecting Foreign Trade in China*, 1st ed., Canton: Albion Press, 1834; 2nd ed., Macao: Wells Williams, 1844; 3rd ed., Canton: *Chinese Repository*, 1848 (all three editions were consulted).

Mortimer, Lieut. George. *Observations and Remarks Made during a Voyage to the Islands of Neriffe, Amsterdam, Maria's Islands near Van Diemen's Land; Otaheite, Sandwich Islands; Owhyhee, the Fox Islands on the North West Coast of America, Inian, and from thence to Canton, in the Brig Mercury, commanded by John Henry Cox, Esq*. London: T. Cadell, 1791; reprint, Fairfield: Ye Galleon Press, 1988.

Munford, James K., ed. *John Ledyard's Journal of Captain Cook's Last Voyage*. Hartford: Nathaniel Patten, 1783. Reprint, Corvallis: Oregon State University Press, 1963. The journal was later identified as Lieutenant John Rickman's diary and not John Ledyard's: Rickman, John. *Journal of Captain Cook's Last Voyage to the Pacific Ocean*. London: printed for E. Newberry, 1781; New York: Da Capo Press, 1967.

Munroe, Frederick C. 'The Daily Life of Mrs. Nathaniel Kinsman in Macao, China. Excerpts from Letters of 1844'. *The Essex Institute Historical Collections*. Vol. 86 (July 1950): 257–84 and (October 1950): 311–30; Vol. 87 (April 1951): 114–49.

Munroe, Frederick C. 'The Daily Life of Mrs. Nathaniel Kinsman in China, 1846'. *The Essex Institute Historical Collections*. Vol. 87 (October 1951): 388–409.

Munroe, Mary Kinsman. 'Nathaniel Kinsman, Merchant of Salem, in the China Trade. From the Kinsman Family Manuscripts'. *The Essex Institute Historical Collections*. Vol. 85 (January 1949): 9–40 and (April 1949): 101–42.

Munroe, Rebecca Kinsman. 'Life in Macao in the 1840's. Letters of Rebecca Chase Kinsman to her Family in Salem'. *The Essex Institute Historical Collections*. Vol. 86 (January 1950): 15–40 and (April 1950): 106–43.

Munroe, Rebecca Kinsman. 'The Daily Life of Mrs. Nathaniel Kinsman in China, 1846'. *The Essex Institute Historical Collections*. Vol. 88 (January 1952): 48–99.

Murray, Alexander. *Doings in China. Being the Personal Narrative of an Officer Engaged in the Late Chinese Expedition, from the Recapture of Chusan in 1841, to the Peace of Nankin in 1842*. London: Richard Bentley, 1843.

Museum of the American China Trade. *Warner Varnham. A Visual Diary of China and the Philippines 1835 to 1843.Catalogue of an Exhibition of Drawings and Watercolors May through October 1973 with a Checklist of other known works*. Milton, Massachusetts: Museum of the American China Trade, 1973.

Noble, Charles Frederick. *A Voyage to the East Indies in 1747 and 1748*. London: T. Becket and P. A. Dehondt, 1762.

Oliphant, Laurence. *Narrative of the Earl of Elgin's Mission to China and Japan in the Years 1857, '58, '59*. New York: Harper & Brothers, 1860. Reprint, London: Praeger Publishers, 1970.

Oliver, Captain S. Pasfield. *Memoirs and Travels of Mauritius Augustus Count de Benyowsky*. London: Kegan Paul and Trench Trubner, 1904.

Osbeck, Pehr. *Dagbok öfver en Ostindisk Resa åren 1750, 1751, 1752*. Stockholm: 1757. Reprint, Redviva Publishing House, 1969.

Panyu Xian Zhi (番禺县志 Panyu County Gazetteer). Edited by Panyu Shi zhi Difang Bianzuan Weyuanhu (番禺市地方编纂委员会 Party Committee of Panyu City). Guangzhou: Guangdong Renmin Chubanshe 广东人民出版社, 1998.

Péron, Capitaine. *Mémoires du Capitaine Péron, sur ses Voyages aux Côtes D'Afrique, en Arabie, a L' Île D'Amsterdam, aux Îles D'Anjouan et de Mayotte, aux Côtes Nord-Ouest de L'Amerique, aux Îles Sandwich, al la Chine*. 2 Vols. Paris: Brissot-Thivars, Libraire, 1824.

Phillips, James Duncan, ed. 'The Canton Letters 1839–1841 of William Henry Low'. *The Essex Institute Historical Collections*. Vol. 84. (July 1948): 197–228 and (October 1948): 304–30.

Phillips, Sir Richard. *Diary of a Journey Overland, through the Maritime Provinces of China, from Manchao, on the South Coast of Hainan, to Canton, in the Years 1819 and 1820*. London: 1822.

Phipps, John. *A Practical Treatise on the China and Eastern Trade: Comprising the Commerce of Great Britain and India, Particularly Bengal and Singapore, with China and the Eastern Islands*. Calcutta: Baptist Mission Press, 1835.

Portlock, Nathaniel. *A Voyage Round the World; but more particularly to the North-West Coast of America: performed in 1785, 1786, 1787, and 1788, in the King George and Queen Charlotte, Captains Portlock and Dixon*. London: 1789. Reprint, Amsterdam: N. Israel, 1968.

Postlethwayt, Malachy. *The Universal Dictionary of Trade and Commerce*. 2 vols. London: H. Woodfall, 1766.

Power, Tyrone. *Recollections of a Three Years' Residence in China; including Peregrinations in Spain, Morocco, Egypt, India, Australia; and New Zealand*. London: Richard Bentley, 1853.

Prims, F. *De Reis van den St. Carolus, Kap. Cayphas 1724*. Antwerp: Leeslust, 1926.

Public Office Harbour Works Department. *Macao. A Handbook*. Macao: N.T. Fernandes e Filhos, 1926.

Publicity Office Port Works Department. *A Visitors' Handbook to Romantic Macao*. Macao: N. T. Fernandes e Filhos, 1928.

Qinggong Yue Gang Ao Shangmao Dang'an Quanji (清宫粤港澳商贸档案全集 Collection of Qing Dynasty Trade-related Documents Concerning Hong Kong and Macao). Edited by Zhongguo Diyi Lishi Danganguan, Zhongguo Guji Zhengli Yanjiuhui (中国第一历史档案馆中国古籍整理研究会). 10 vols. Beijing: Zhongguo Shudian (中国书店), 2002.

Qing Shilu Guangdong Shiliao (清实录广东史料 Veritable Records of the Qing Dynasty Concerning Guangdong Province). 6 vols. Guangzhou: Guangdong Sheng Chubanshe (广东省出版社), 1995.

Quaife, Milo Milton. *A Voyage to the Northwest Coast of America*. New York: The Citadel Press, 1968.

Quincy, Josiah, ed. *The Journals of Major Samuel Shaw, the First American Consul at Canton. With a Life of the Author*. By Josiah Quincy. Boston: Wm. Crosby and H. P. Nichols, 1847. Reprint, Documentary Publications, 1970.

Reinius, Israel. *Journal hållen på resan till Canton i China*. Helsingfors: 1939.

Rickman, John. *Journal of Captain Cook's Last Voyage to the Pacific Ocean*. London: printed for E. Newberry, 1781(?). Reprint, New York: Da Capo Press, 1967.

Robertson, Capt. *Wreck and Loss of the Ship Fanny, Capt. Robertson, on Her Passage from Bombay to China, November 29, 1803*. London: Thomas Tegg, 1808.

Rochon, Abbe. *A Voyage to Madagascar, and the East Indies*. Translated from the French. London: Printed for G. G. J. and J. Robinson, Paternoster-Row, 1792. Reprint, London: Johnson Reprint Corp., 1971.

Roe, Michael, ed. *The Journal and Letters of Captain Charles Bishop on the North-West Coast of America, in the Pacific and in New South Wales 1794–1799*. Cambridge: Cambridge University Press, 1967.

Ruschenberger, W. S. W. *Narrative of a Voyage Round the World, during the Years 1835, 36, and 37; including a Narrative of an Embassy to the Sultan of Muscat and the King of Siam*. 2 vols. London: 1838. Reprint, Dawsons of Pall Mall, 1970.

Sainte-Croix, Félix Renouard de. *Voyage Commercial et Politique aux Indes Orientales, aux Iles Philippines, a la Chine, avec des Notions dur la Cochinchine et le Tonquin, pendant les Années 1803, 1804, 1805, 1806 et 1807. Par M. Félix Renouard de Sainte-Croix, ancien Officier de Cavalerie au service de France, chargé par le Gouverneur des Iles Philippines de l'organisation des troupes pour la défense de ces iles*. 3 Vols. Paris: Archives du Droit Français, 1810.

Schooneveld-Oosterling, J. E., ed. *Generale Missiven van Gouverneurs-Generaal en Raden aan Heren XVII der Verenigde Oostindische Compagnie*. 1743–1750. Vol. 11. The Hague: Instituut voor Nederlandse Geschiedenis, 1997.

Schultz, Kaptajn J.H., ed. 'En Dagbog ført paa en Kinafarer 1730–32 af Kadet Tobias Wigandt'. In *Tidsskrift for Søvæsen*, by G. L. Grove. Copenhagen: Hovedkommissionær Vilhelm Tryde, Thieles Bogtrykkeri, 1900.

Seagraves, Eleanor Roosevelt. *Delano's Voyages of Commerce and Discovery. Amasa Delano in China, the Pacific Islands, Australia, and South America, 1789–1807*. Stockgridge, Massachusetts: Berkshire House Publishers, 1994.

Shaler, William. *Journal of a Voyage between China and the North-Western Coast of America, made in 1804*. In *The American Register or General Repository of History, Politics, and Science*. Part 1, Vol. 3. Philadelphia: T. & G. Palmer, 1808. Reprint, Claremont, California: Saunders Studio Press, 1935.

Sirr, Henry Charles, M.A. *China and the Chinese: Their Religion, Character, Customs, and Manufactures: The Evils Arising from the Opium Trade: With a Glance at our Religious, Moral, Political, and Commercial Intercourse with the Country*. 2 vols. London: 1849. Reprint, Taipei: Southern Materials Center, 1977.

Smith, Rev. George. *A Narrative of an Exploratory Visit to Each of the Consular Cities of China, and to the Islands of Hong Kong and Chusan, in Behalf of the Church Missionary Society, in the Years 1844, 1845, 1846*. 2nd ed. London: Seeley, Burnside, & Seeley, 1847.

Smith, Philip Chadwick Foster. *The Empress of China*. Philadelphia: Philadelphia Maritime Museum, 1984.

Spencer, Alfred, ed. *Memoirs of William Hickey (1749–1775)*. New York: Alfred A. Knopf, 1921.

Staunton, Sir George Thomas, Bart. *Miscellaneous Notices relating to China, and our Commercial Intercourse with that Country*. For private circulation only. 1822.

Taylor, Bayard. *A Visit to India, China, and Japan, in the Year 1853*. New York: G. P. Putnam & Co., 1855.

Taylor, Fitch W. *Voyage Round the World, and Visits to Various Foreign Countries, in the United States Frigate Columbia; Attended by Her Consort the Sloop of War John Adams, and Commanded by Commodore George C. Read* 2. vols. New Haven: H. Mansfield, 1848.

Ticknor, Benejah. *The Voyage of the Peacock*. Ann Arbor: University of Michigan Press, 1991.

Tiffany, Osmond, Jr. *The Canton Chinese, or the American's Sojourn in the Celestial Empire*. Boston: James Munroe and Company, 1849.

Torée, Olof. *Voyage de Mons. Olof Torée. Aumonier de la Compagnie Suedoise des Indes Orientales, fait à Surate, à la Chine &c. depuis le prémier avril 1750. jusqu' au 26. Juin 1752*. Traduit du Suedois par M. Dominique de Blackford. M. Linnaeus, Milan: Chez les Freres Reycends, Libraires sous les Arcades de Figini, 1771.

Tronson, J. M. *Personal Narrative of a Voyage to Japan, Kamtschatka, Siberia, Tartary, and Various Parts of Coast of China; in H.M.S. Barracouta*. London: Smith, Elcer, & Co., 1859.

Valentin, F., ed. and Julius S. Gassner, trans. *Voyages and Adventures of La Pérouse*. Honolulu: University of Hawaii Press, 1969.

Von Kotzebue, Otto. *Voyage of Discovery in the South Sea, and to Behring's Straits, in Search of a Northeast Passage; Undertaken in the Years 1815, 16, 17, and 18, in the Ship Rurick*. Part I. London: Bride Court, 1821. This journal is also contained in a larger selection of voyages under the title *New Voyages and Travels consisting of Originals and Translations*. Vol. 6. London: Bride Court, 1821.

Von Krusenstern, Adam J. *Voyage Round the World in the Years 1803, 1804, 1805, and 1806*. Vol. 2. London: T. Davidson, 1813. Reprint, New York: Da Capo Press, 1968.

Voretzsch, E. A., ed. *François Froger. Relation du Premier Voyage des François à la Chine fait en 1698, 1699 et 1700 sur le Vaisseau 'L'Amphitrite'*. Leipzig: Asia Major, 1926.

Wagner, Blanche Collet. *Voyage of the Héros around the World with Duhaut-Cilly in the Years 1826, 1827, 1828 & 1829*, by Lt. Edmond le Netrel. Los Angeles: Glen Dawson, 1951.

Wallenberg, Jacob. *Min Son på Galejan, eller en Ostindisk Resa, innehållande Ullahanda Blädhornskram, samlade på skeppet Finland, som usseglade ifrån Götheborg i Decemb. 1769, och återkom der sammastädes i Jun. 1771*. Stockholm: Joh. Christ. Holmberg, 1781.

Wathen, James. *Journal of a Voyage in 1811 and 1812 to Madras and China*. London: 1814.

Wilkinson, George. *Sketches of Chinese Customs & Manners, in 1811–12*. Bath: J. Browne, 1814.

Williams, Glyndwr, ed. *Documents Relating to Anson's Voyage Round The World 1740–1744*. Naval Records Society, 1967.

Williams, Glyndwr, ed. *A Voyage Round the World in the Years MDCCXL, I, II, III, I, by George Anson*. London: Oxford University Press, 1974.

Williams, Glyndwr. 'Anson at Canton, 1743: "A Little Secret History"'. In *The European Outthrust and Encounter. The First Phase c. 1400–c.1700: Essays in Tribute to David Beers Quinn on his 85th Birthday*. Eds. Cecil H. Clough and P. E. H. Hair. Liverpool: Liverpool University Press, 1994, pp. 271–90.

Williams, S. Wells. *The Chinese Commercial Guide, Containing Treaties, Tariffs, Regulations, Tables, etc., Useful in the Trade to China & Eastern Asia; with an Appendix of Sailing Directions for those Seas and Coasts*. Canton: Chinese Repository, 1856. 5th ed. Hong Kong: A. Shortreded & Co., 1863. Reprint, Taipei: Ch'eng-wen Publishing Co., 1966.

Williams, S. Wells. *The Middle Kingdom*. 2 vols. New York: Charles Scribner's Sons, 1907.

Xiangshan Xian Zhi (香山县志 Xiangshan County Gazetteer). 2 vols. 1751. Reprint, Taipei: Xuesheng Chubanshe (学生出版社), 1985.

Xiangshan Xian Zhi ([新修] 香山县志 Xiangshan County Gazetteer). 2 vols. 1828. Reprint, Taipei: Xuesheng Chubanshe (学生出版社), 1985.

Xiangshan Ming Qing Dang'an Jilu (香山明清档案辑录) Collection of Xiangshan Ming-Qing Documents). Shanghai: Shanghai Guji Chubanshe (上海古籍出版社), 2006.

Xiangshan Xian Zhi ([重修] 香山县志 Xiangshan County Gazetteer). 5 vols. 1880. Reprint, Taipei: Xuesheng Chubanshe (学生出版社), 1985.

Xing Yongfu (邢永福), et al, eds. *Qing Gong Guangzhou Shisan Hang Dang'an Jingxuan* (清官广州十三行档案精选 A Selection of Qing Imperial Documents of the Guangzhou Shisan Hang). Guangzhou: Guangdong Jingji Chubanshe (广东经济出版社), 2002.

Xu Dishan (许地山). *Da Zhong Ji: Yapian Zhan zheng qian Zhong Ying Jiaoshe Shiliao* (达衷集：鸦片战争前中英交涉史料 Collection of Historical Materials Concerning Sino-British Relations before the Opium War). 2 vols. Shanghai: Shang Wu Yinshuguan (商务印书馆), 1931.

Yang Jibo (杨继波), Wu Zhiliang (吴志良), and Deng Kaisong (邓开颂), eds. *Ming-Qing Shiqi Aomen Wenti Dang'an Wenxian Huibian* (明清时期澳门问题档案文献汇编 Collection of Ming-Qing documents concerning Macau affairs). 6 vols. Beijing: Renmin Chubanshe (人民出版社), 1999.

Zhao Chunchen (赵春晨), ed. *Aomen Jilüe* (澳门记略 A Brief Record of Macau), by Yin Guangren (印光任) and Zhang Rulin (张汝霖), 1751. Macau: Aomen wenhua sidu (澳门文化司睹), 1992.

PUBLISHED AND UNPUBLISHED SECONDARY SOURCES

(Listed alphabetically by author)

Alexander, William and George Henry Mason. *China. Beeld van het Dagelijks Leven in de 18de Eeuw*. Alphen: Atrium, 1988.

Antony, Robert. *Like Froth Floating on the Sea: The World of Pirates and Seafarers in Late Imperial South China*. Berkeley: Institute of East Asian Studies, 2003.

Baker, Philip and Peter Mühlhäusler. 'From Business to Pidgin'. *Journal of Asian Pacific Communication*. Vol. 1, No. 1, 1990, pp. 87–115.

Basu, Dilip Kumar. 'Asian Merchants and Western Trade: A Comparative Study of Calcutta and Canton 1800–1840'. Ph.D. dissertation, Department of History, University of California, Berkeley, 1975.

Bauer, R.W. *Handbog. Mont-, Maal- og Vægtforhold*. Copenhagen: P. G. Philipsens Forlag, 1882.

Bello, David. 'Opium in Xinjiang and Beyond'. In *Opium Regimes. China, Britain, and Japan, 1839–1952*, eds. Timothy Brook and Bob Tadashi Wakabayashi. Berkeley: University of California Press, 2000: 127–51.

Blussé, Leonard. *Strange Company*. Providence: Foris Publications, 1988.

Blussé, Leonard. 'Chinese Trade with Batavia in the Seventeenth and Eighteenth Centuries: A Preliminary Report'. In *Asian Trade Routes*, ed. Karl Reinhold Haellquist. London: Curzon Press, 1991: 231–45.

Bolton, Kingsley. *Chinese Englishes. A Sociolinguistic History*. Cambridge: Cambridge University Press, 2003.

Bonke, Hans. *De Zeven Reizen van de Jonge Lieve*. Nijmegen: SUN, 1999.

Bro-Jørgensen, J. O. and A. A. Rasch. *Asiatiske, vestindiske og guineiske handelskompagnier*. København: Rigsarkivet, 1969.

Broadbent, James, Suzanne Rickard and Margaret Steven. *India, China, Australia. Trade and Society 1788–1850*. Sydney: Historic Houses Trust of New South Wales, 2003.

Brook, Timothy and Bob Tadashi Wakabayashi, eds. *Opium Regimes. China, Britain, and Japan, 1839–1952*. Berkeley: University of California Press, 2000.

Brødsgaard, Kjeld Erik and Mads Kirkebæk, eds. *China and Denmark: Relations Since 1674*. [Copenhagen]: Nordic Institute of Asian Studies, 2001.

Bruijn, J. R., and F. S. Gaastra, eds. *Ships, Sailors and Spices. East India Companies and Their Shipping in the 16th, 17th and 18th Centuries*. Amsterdam: NEHA, 1993.

Bruijn, J. R., F. S. Gaastra, and I. Schoffer. *Dutch-Asiatic Shipping in the 17th and 18th Centuries*. The Hague: Martinus Nijhoff, 1987.

Buell, Robert Kingery and Charlotte Northcote Skladal. *Sea Otters and the China Trade*. New York: David McKay Co., 1968.

Bulley, Anne. *Free Mariner: John Adolphus Pope in the East Indies 1786–1821*. London: British Association for Cemeteries in South Asia (BACSA), 1992.

Bulley, Anne. *The Bombay Country Ships 1790–1833*. Richmond, Surrey: Curzon Press, 2000.

Cai Hongsheng (蔡鸿生), ed. *Guangzhou yu Haiyang Wenming* (广州与海洋文明 The Maritime Culture of Guangzhou). Guangzhou: Zhongshan Daxue Chuban She (中山大学出版社), 1997.

Cai Hongsheng, Leonard Blussé, et al. *Sailing the Pearl River. Dutch Enterprise in South China 1600–2000*. Guangzhou: Guangzhou Publishing House, 2004.

Chang T'ien-tsê (张天泽). *Sino-Portuguese Trade from 1514 to 1644. A Synthesis of Portuguese and Chinese Sources* (中葡通适研究). Leiden: E. J. Brill, 1934. Reprint, New York: AMS Press, 1973.

Chaudhuri, K. N. *The Trading World of Asia and the English East India Company 1660–1760*. Cambridge: Cambridge University Press, 1978. Reprint, New Delhi: S. Chand & Co. Ltd.

Chaunu, Pierre. *Les Philippines et le Pacifique des Ibériques (XVI*e*, XVII*e*, XVIII*e *siècles)*. Paris: S.E.V.P.E.N., 1960.

Chen Bojian (陈柏坚) and Huang Qichen (黄启臣). *Guangzhou Wai Mao Shi* (广州外贸史 The History of Guangzhou's Foreign Trade) 3 vols. Guangzhou: Guangzhou Chubanshe (广州出版社), 1995.

Ch'en Kuo-tung Anthony (陈国栋). 'Qingdai Qianqi de Yuehaiguan' (清代前期的粤海关 Maritime Customs of Early Qing Dynasty 1683–1842). M.A. thesis, Department of History, National University of Taiwan, 1979.

Ch'en Kuo-tung Anthony. *The Insolvency of the Chinese Hong Merchants, 1760–1843*. 2 vols. Taipei: Academia Sinica, 1990.

Ch'en Kuo-tung, Anthony. *Dongya Haiyu yi qian nian* (东亚海域一千年 One Thousand Years of Maritime East Asia). Taipei: Yuanliu Chuban Gongsi (远流出版公司), 2005.

Cheong, Weng Eang. *Mandarins and Merchants. Jardine Matheson & Co., a China Agency of the Early Nineteenth Century*. London, Curzon Press, 1979.

Cheong, Weng Eang. 'The Age of Suqua, 1720–1759'. In *Asian Trade Routes*, ed. Karl Reinhold Haellquist. London: Curzon Press, 1991: 217–30.

Cheong, Weng Eang. *The Hong Merchants of Canton*. Copenhagen: NIAS-Curzon Press, 1997.

Christman, Margaret C. S. *Adventurous Pursuits. Americans and the China Trade 1784–1844*. Washington D. C.: Smithsonian Institution Press, 1984.

Clemmensen, Tove and Mogens B. Mackeprang. *Kina og Danmark 1600–1950. Kinafart og Kinamode*. Copenhagen: National Museum, 1980.

Coates, W. H. *The Old 'Country Trade' of the East Indies*. London: Imray, Laurie, Norie & Wilson, Ltd, 1911. Reprint, London: Cornmarket Press, 1969.

Conan, J. *La Dernière Compagnie Française des Indes (1785–1875)*. Paris: Librairie des Sciences Politiques et Sociales, 1942.

Corning, Howard. 'List of Ships Arriving at the Port of Canton and Other Pacific Ports, 1799–1803'. *The Essex Institute Historical Collections*. Vol. 78. (October 1942): 329–47.

Costin, W. C. *Great Britain and China 1833–1860*. Oxford: Clarendon Press, 1937.

Cooke, Nola and Li Tana, eds. *Water Frontier. Commerce and the Chinese in the Lower Mekong Region, 1750–1880*. Singapore: Rowman & Littlefield Publishers, 2004.

Cordier, Henri. *La France en Chine au Dix-Huitième Siècle*. Paris: Libraire de la Sociètè Asiatique, 1883.

Cordier, Henri. 'Les Marchands Hanistes de Canton'. *T'oung Pao* 3 (1902): 281–315.

Cordier, Henri. 'Le Consulat de France a Canton au XVIIIe Siècle'. *T'oung Pao* 9 (1908): 47–96.

Cordier, Henri. 'La Compagnie Prussienne D'Embden au XVIIIe Siècle'. *T'oung Pao* 19 (1920): 127–243.

Crossman, Carl L. *The China Trade. Export Paintings, Furniture, Silver and Other Objects.* Princeton: The Pyne Press, 1972.

Crossman, Carl. L. *The Decorative Arts of the China Trade. Paintings, Furnishings and Exotic Curiosities.* Suffolk: Antique Collectors' Club, 1988.

Cushman, Jennifer Wayne. *Fields from the Sea: Chinese Junk Trade with Siam during the Late Eighteenth and Early Nineteenth Centuries.* Ithaca: Cornell Southeast Asia Publications, 1993. Reprint, 2000.

Degryse, K. and Jan Parmentier. 'Maritime Aspects of the Ostend Trade to Mocha, India and China (1715–1732)'. In *Ships, Sailors and Spices. East India Companies and Their Shipping in the 16th, 17th and 18th Centuries*, eds. Jaap R. Bruijn and Femme S. Gaastra, 139–175. Amsterdam: NEHA, 1993.

Deng Kaisong (邓开颂), Wu Zhiliang (吴志良), and Lu Xiaomin (陆晓敏), eds. *Yue Ao Guanxi Shi* (粤澳关系史 History of Guangdong-Macau relations). Beijing: Zhongguo Shudian (中国书店), 1999.

Dermigny, Louis. *La Chine et l'Occident. Le Commerce à Canton au XVIII Siècle 1719–1833.* 3 vols and album. Paris: S.E.V.P.E.N., 1964.

Dikötter, Frank, Lars Laamann and Zhou Xun. *Narcotic Culture: A History of Drugs in China.* Hong Kong: Hong Kong University Press, 2004.

Diller, Stephan. *Die Dänen in Indien, Südostasien und China (1620–1845).* Wiesbaden: Harrassowitz Verlag, 1999.

Dollar, Robert. *One Hundred Thirty Years of Steam Navigation.* San Francisco: Privately published for the author by Schwacher-Frey Co., 1931.

Dos Santos, Jorge Manuel et al., ed. *Estudos de História do Relacionamento Luso-Chinês. Séculos XVI–XIX.* Institvto Portvgvês do Oriente, 1996.

Do Vale, A. M. Martins. *Os Portugueses em Macau (1750–1800).* Institvto Portvgvês do Oriente, 1997.

Downs, Jacques M. *The Golden Ghetto. The American Commercial Community at Canton and the Shaping of American China Policy, 1784–1844.* Bethlehem: Lehigh University Press, 1997.

Dudden, A. P. *The American Pacific. From the Old China Trade to the Present.* New York: Oxford University Press, 1992.

Dulles, Foster Rhea. *The Old China Trade.* Boston: Houghton Mifflin Company, 1930.

Eames, James Bromley. *The English in China. Being an Account of the Intercourse and Relations between England and China from the year 1600 to the year 1843 and a Summary of later Developments.* London: Curzon Press, 1909. Reprint, 1974.

Emson, Hal. *Mapping of Hong Kong.* Hong Kong: The Government Printer, 1992.

Fairbank, John K. 'The Creation of the Treaty System'. In *The Cambridge History of China*, eds. Denis Twitchett and John K. Fairbank. Vol. 10., 213–63. Cambridge: Cambridge University Press, 1978. Reprint, Taipei: Caves Books, 1986.

Fan Fa-ti. *British Naturalist in Qing China. Science, Empire, and Cultural Encounter.* Cambridge: Harvard University Press, 2004.

Farmer, Edward. 'James Flint Versus the Canton Interest (1755–1760)'. *Papers on China.* Vol. 17. Cambridge: Harvard University, 1963: 38–66.

Farooqui, Amar. *Smuggling as Subversion. Colonialism, Indian Merchants and the Politics of Opium*. New Delhi: New Age International, Ltd., 1998.

Fay, Peter Ward. *The Opium War 1840–1842*. Chapel Hill: University of North Carolina Press, 1975.

Fei Chengkang. *Macao 400 Years*. Shanghai: The Publishing House of Shanghai Academy of Social Sciences, 1996.

Feldbæk, Ole. 'Den danske Asienhandel 1616–1807'. *Historisk Tidsskrift* 90:2 (1990): 320–52.

Fok K. C. 'The Macao Formula: A Study of Chinese Management of Westerners from the Mid-Sixteenth Century to the Opium War Period'. Ph.D. diss., University of Hawaii, 1978.

Fok K. C. 'The Ming Debate on how to Accommodate the Portuguese and the Emergence of the Macao Formula'. *Review of Culture* 13/14, January/June 1991, 328–44.

Forbes, Crosby, H. A. *Shopping in China. The Artisan Community at Canton, 1825–1830*. Baltimore: Garamond/Pridemark Press, 1979.

Gaastra, Femme. *The Dutch East India Company — Expansion and Decline*. Zutphen: Walburg Pers, 2003.

Gardella, Robert. *Harvesting Mountains: Fujian and the China Tea Trade, 1757–1937*. Berkeley, University of California Press, 1994.

Garrett, Valery M. *Heaven is High, the Emperor Far Away. Merchants and Mandarins in Old Canton*. Hong Kong: Oxford University Press, 2002.

Gibson, James R. *Otter Skins, Boston Ships, and China Goods. The Maritime Fur Trade of the Northwest Coast, 1785–1841*. Seattle: University of Washington Press, 1992.

Glamann, Kristoff. *Dutch-Asiatic Trade, 1620–1740*. The Hague: Martinus Nijhoff, 1958.

Glamann, Krsitoff. 'The Danish Asiatic Company, 1732–1772'. *Scandinavian Economic History Review* 8:2 (1960): 109–49.

Gøbel, Erik. 'Asiatisk Kompagnis Kinafart, 1732–1833. Besejling of Bemanding'. Ph.D. dissertation, University of Copenhagen, 1978.

Gøbel, Erik. 'The Danish Asiatic Company's Voyages to China, 1732–1833'. *Scandinavian Economic History Review* 27 (1979): 22–46.

Gøbel, Erik. 'Danish Companies' Shipping to Asia, 1616–1807'. In *Ships, Sailors and Spices. East India Companies and Their Shipping in the 16th, 17th and 18th Centuries*, eds. Jaap R. Bruijn and Femme S. Gaastra, 99–120. Amsterdam: NEHA, 1993.

Goldstein, Jonathan. *Philadelphia and the China Trade 1682–1846. Commercial, Cultural, and Attitudinal Effects*. University Park: The Pennsylvania State University Press, 1978.

Grant, Frederic D., Jr. 'Merchants, Lawyers, and the China Trade of Boston'. *Boston Bar Journal* 23:9 (September 1979): 5–16.

Grant, Frederic D., Jr. 'Hong Merchant Litigation in the American Courts'. In *Proceedings of the Massachusetts Historical Society*. Vol. XCIX (1987). Boston: Massachusetts Historical Society, 1988: 44–62.

Grant, Frederic D., Jr. 'The Failure of the Li-ch'uan Hong: Litigation as a Hazard of Nineteenth Century Foreign Trade'. *The American Neptune* 48:4 (Fall 1988): 243–60.

Greenberg, Michael. *British Trade and the Opening of China 1800–1842*. Cambridge: University Press, 1951.

Griffiths, Sir Percival. *A License to Trade. The History of English Chartered Companies*. London: Ernest Benn Ltd., 1974.

Guan Yadong (官亚东). 'Qingdai Qianqi Guangzhou Koan Zhongxi Maoyi de Hangwai Shangren' (清代前期广州口岸中西贸易的行外商人 The Outside Merchants of Sino-Western Trade in the Port of Canton during the Qing Dynasty). M.A. thesis, Department of History, Zhongshan University, 2001.

Guimarães, Ângela. *Uma Relação Especial Macau e as Relações Luso-Chinesas 1780–1844*. Lisbon: Edição Cies, 1996.

Guo Deyan (郭德焱). 'The Study of Parsee Merchants in Canton, Hong Kong and Macao'. *Review of Culture*. International Edition. No. 8 (October 2003): 51–69.

Guo Deyan. *Qingdai Guangzhou de Basi Shangren* (清代广州巴斯商人 Parsee Merchants in Canton During the Qing Period). Beijing: Zhonghua Shuju (中华书局), 2005.

Gütinger, Erich. *Die Geschichte der Chinesen in Deutschland. Ein Überblick über die ersten 100 Jahre seit 1822*. Munich: Waxmann Verlag, 2004.

Hammar, Hugo. *Fartygstyper i Swenska Ost-Indiska Compagniets flotta*. Gothenburg: 1931.

Hao Yen-p'ing. *The Comprador in Nineteenth Century China: Bridge between East and West*. Cambridge: Harvard University Press, 1970.

Hellberg, Harry. *Anders Ljungstedt och breven från Kina*. Askeby, Linghem: Stålgården Förlag, 1999.

Hellstenius, J. A. C. *Bidrag till Svenska Ost-Indiska Compagniets Historia 1731–1766*. Uppsala: Edquist & K., 1860.

Henningsen, J. *Kina under Forvandlingens Tegn*. Copenhagen: Gyldendalske Gogh. Bordisk Forl., 1913.

Howard, David S. *The Choice of the Private Trader. The Private Market in Chinese Export Porcelain illustrated from the Hodroff Collection*. London: Zwemmer, 1994.

Howard, David S. *A Tale of Three Cities: Canton, Shanghai & Hong Kong. Three Centuries of Sino-British Trade in the Decorative Arts*. London: Sotheby's, 1997.

Huang Guosheng. 'The Chinese Maritime Customs in Transition, 1750 to 1830'. In *Maritime China in Transition 1750–1850*. Eds. Wang Gungwu.and Ng Chin-keong. Wiesbaden: Harrassowitz Verlag, 2004: 169–89.

Huang Guosheng (黄国盛). *Yapian Zhanzheng qian de Dongnan Sisheng Haiguan* (鸦片战争前的东南四省海关 The Customs in China's Four Southeastern Provinces before the Opium Wars). Fujian: Fujian Renmin Chuban She (福建人民出版社), 2000.

Huang Qichen (黄启臣). *Aomen Tongshi* (澳门通史 General History of Macao). Guangzhou: Guangzhou Jiaoyu Chuban She (广州教育出版社), 1999.

Huang Qichen and Pang Xinping (庞新平). *Ming-Qing Guangdong Shangren* (明清广东商人 Guangdong Merchants in the Ming and Ching Dynasty). Guangzhou: Guangdong Jingji Chuban She (广东经济出版社), 2001.

Huang Qichen and Zheng Weiming (郑炜明). *Aomen Jingji Sibai Nian* (澳门经济四百年 400 years of Economic History in Macau). Macau: Macau Foundation, 1994.

Huang Qichen, ed. *Guangdong Haishang Sichou zhi Lu Shi* (广东海上丝绸之路史 History of Guangdong's Maritime Silk Road). Guangzhou: Guangdong Jingji Chubanshe (广东经济出版社), 2003.

Janin, Hunt. *The India-China Opium Trade in the Nineteenth Century*. London: McFarland & Co., 1999.

Jesus, C. A. Montalto de. *Macau Histórico*. Macau: Oriental Foundation, 1926. Reprint, 1990.

Jin Guo Ping and Wu Zhiliang. 'Reformular as Origens de Macau' (Reformulating the origins of Macau). *Macau* (magazine), December 1999, 175–90.

Joesting, Edward. *Kauai. The Separate Kingdom*. Kauai: University of Hawaii Press and Kauai Museum Association, Ltd., 1987.

Johansson, Bengt, ed. *The Golden Age of China Trade. Essays on the East India Companies' trade with China in the 18th Century and the Swedish East Indiaman Götheborg*. Hong Kong: Standard Press, Ltd., 1992.

Jörg, C. J. A. 'The China Trade of the V.O.C. in the 18th Century'. *Bulletin of the Institute of Oriental and Occidental Studies* 12. Kansai University, Osaka: December 1979, 1–17.

Jörg, C. J. A. *Porcelain and the Dutch China Trade*. The Hague: Martinus Nijhoff, 1982.

Jörg, C. J. A. *The Geldermalsen. History and Porcelain*. Groningen: 1986.

Kemp, Peter, ed. *The Oxford Companion to Ships and the Sea*. Oxford: Oxford University Press, 1976. Reprint, 1988.

Kerr, Phyllis Forbes, ed. *Letters from China. The Canton-Boston Correspondence of Robert Bennet Forbes, 1838–1840*. Mystic: Mystic Seaport Museum, 1996.

Kerr, Dr. *A Guide to the City and Suburbs of Canton*. Hong Kong: Kelly & Walsh, Ltd., 1918.

Kjellberg, Sven T. *Svenska Ostindiska Compagnierna 1731–1813*. Malmö: Allhems Förlag, 1974.

Koninckx, Christian. *The First and Second Charters of the Swedish East India Company (1731–1766)*. Belgium: Van Gemmert Publishing Co., 1980.

Kresse, Walter. *Materialien zur entwicklungsgeschichte der Hamburger Handelsflotte 1765–1823*. Hamburg: Museum für Hamburgische Geschichte, 1966.

Krieger, Martin. *Daufleute, seeräuber und Diplomaten. Der Dänische Handel auf dem Indischen Ozean (1620–1868)*. Köln, Weimar, Wien: Bohlau Verlag, 1998.

Kumar, J. *Indo-Chinese Trade 1793–1833*. Bombay: Orient Longman, 1974.

Lange, Ole. 'Denmark in China 1839–65: A Pawn in a British Game. An interim account of Danish economic and diplomatic activity'. *Scandinavian Economic History Review* 19:2 (1971): 71–117.

Larsen, Kay. *Den Danske Kinafart*. Copenhagen: G. E. C. Gads Forlag, 1932.

Larsen, Kay. *Guvernører*. Copenhagen: 1940.

Lauring, Kåre. 'Kinahandelen — et spørgsmål om finansiering'. In *Søfat, Politik, Identitet*, eds. Hans Jeppesen et al. Vol. 19. Søhistoriske Skrifter, 215–26. Copenhagen: Falcon, 1996.

Layton, Thomas N. *The Voyage of the Frolic. New England Merchants and the Opium Trade*. Stanford: Stanford University Press, 1997.

Le Pichon, Alain. *Aux Origines de Hong Kong. Aspects de la Civilisation Commerciale à Canton: le Fonds de Commerce de Jardine, Matheson & Co. 1827–1839*. Paris: L'Harmattan, 1998.

Le Pichon, Alain, ed. *China Trade and Empire. Jardine, Matheson & Co. and the Origins of British Rule in Hong Kong 1827–1843*. Oxford: Oxford University Press, 2006.

Leder, Lawrence H. 'American Trade to China, 1800–1802'. *The American Neptune* 23:3 (July 1963): 212–8.

Leder, Lawrence H. 'American Trade to China, 1800–1802'. *Proceedings of the Massachusetts Historical Society* 81 (1969): 104–19.

Lee, Jean Gordon. *Philadelphians and the China Trade 1784–1844*. Philadelphia: University of Philadelphia Press, 1984.

Legarda, Benito J., Jr., *After the Galleons*, Manila: Ateneo de Manila University Press, 1999.

Lessa, Almerindo. 'The Population of Macao. Genesis of a *Mestizo* Society'. *Review of Culture*, 1995, 56–86.

Lewis, Dianne. *Jan Compagnie in the Straits of Malacca 1641–1795*. Athens: Center for International Studies, Ohio University, 1995.

Li Tana and Paul A. Van Dyke. 'Canton, Cancao, Cochinchina: New Data and New Light on Eighteenth-Century Canton and the Nanyang'. *Chinese Southern Diaspora Studies*. Vol. 1 (2007): 10–28.

Liang Jiabin (梁嘉彬). *Guangdong Shisan Hang Kao* (广东十三行考 Study of the Thirteen Hongs of Canton) 1937. Reprint, Taipei: 1960. Reprint, Guangdong: Renmin Chubanshe (人民出版社), 1999.

Lind, Ivan. *Göteborgs Handel och Sjöfart 1637–1920. Historisk-Statistisk Översikt*. Gothenburg: Wald. Zachrissons Boktryckeri, 1923.

Liu, Kwang-Ching. *Anglo-American Steamship Rivalry in China, 1862–1874*. Cambridge: Harvard University Press, 1962.

Lovette, Lieutenant Commander Leland P. *Naval Customs. Traditions and Usage*. Annapolis: U.S. Naval Institute, 1934. Reprint, 2nd ed. 1936; 3rd ed. 1939.

Madrolle, Cl. *Les Premiers Voyages Français a la Chine. La Compagnie de la Chine 1698–1719*. Paris: Augustin Challamel, 1901.

Manning, Catherine. *Fortunes a Faire. The French in Asian Trade, 1719–48*. Aldershot, Hampshire: Ashgate, 1996.

Mansvelt, W. M. F. *Geschiedenis van de Nederlandsche Handel-Maatschappij*. Harlem: J. Enschedé and sons, 192?.

Middleton, Arthur Pierce. *Tobacco Coast. A Maritime History of Chesapeake Bay in the Colonial Era*. Newport News: The Mariners' Museum, 1953. Reprint, Baltimore: Maryland Paperback Bookshelf, 1994.

Morse, Hosea Ballou. *The Gilds of China with an Account of the Gild Merchant or Co-Hong of Canton*. London: Longmans, Green and Co., 1909.

Morse, Hosea Ballou. 'The Provision of Funds for the East India Company's Trade at Canton during the Eighteenth Century'. *Journal of the Royal Asiatic Society* (April 1922), 229–55.

Morse, Hosea Ballou. *Far Eastern International Relations*. Boston: Riverside Press Cambridge, 1931.

Morse, Hosea Ballou. *The International Relations of the Chinese Empire. The Period of Subjection 1834–1911*. 3 vols. London: Longmans, Green & Co., 1910. Reprint, Taipei: Yung Mei Mei Publishing, 1966.

Morse, Hosea Ballou. *The Chronicles of the East India Company Trading to China, 1635–1834*. 5 vols. Cambridge: Harvard University Press, 1926. Reprint, Taipei: Ch'eng-wen Publishing Co., 1966.

Morison, Samuel Eliot. *The Maritime History of Massachusetts 1783–1860. That magic era when America first became a world power and Salem boys were more at home in Canton than in New York*. Cambridge: The Riverside Press, 1921, 1941, 1949, 1961.

Mui, H. C., and Lorna H. Mui. *The Management of Monopoly. A Study of the East India Company's Conduct of its Tea Trade 1784–1833*. Vancouver: University of British Columbia Press, 1984.

Müller, Leos. 'Mellan Kanton och Göteborg. Jean Abraham Grill, en superkargörs karriär'. In *Historiska Etyder*, eds. Janne Becklund et al., 149–61. Uppsala: Idé Tryck Grafiska, 1997.

Murray, Dian. *Pirates of the South China Coast 1790–1810*. Stanford: Stanford University Press, 1987.

Nelson, Christina H. *Directly from China. Export Goods for the American Market, 1784–1930*. Salem: Peabody Museum, 1985.

Ng Chin-Keong. *Trade and Society. The Amoy Network on the China Coast 1683–1735*. Singapore: Singapore University Press, 1983.

Nyström, J. F. *De Svenska Ostindiska Kompanierna. Historisk-Statistisk Framställning*. Gothenburg: D. F. Bonniers Boktryckeri, 1883.

Olán, Eskil. *Ostindiska Compagniets Saga*. Gothenburg: Elanders Boktryckeri Aktiebolag, 1920.

Oliveira, Fernando. *Liuro da Fabrica das Naos*. Macau: Maritime Museum of Macau, 1995.

Orange, James. *The Chater Collection: Pictures relating to China, Hongkong, Macao, 1655–1860*. London: 1924.

Pan Gang'er (潘刚儿), Huang Qichen (黄启臣) and Ch'en Kuo-tung Anthony (陈国栋), eds. *Guangzhou Shisan Hang zhi Yi: PanTongwen (Fu) Hang* (广州十三行之一：潘同文[孚]行 One of the Thirteen-Hongs in Canton: Tung-Wan/Tung-Fu Hong Puankhequa I–III). Guangzhou: Huanan Ligong Daxue Chubanshe (华南理工大学出版社), 2006.

Parmentier, Jan. *De holle compagnie. Smokkel en legale handel onder Zuidnederlandse vlag in Bengalen, ca. 1720–1744*. Hilversum: 1992.

Parmentier, Jan. *Tea Time in Flanders. The Maritime Trade Between the Southern Netherlands and China in the 18th Century*. Ghent: Lundion Press, 1996.

Parmentier, Jan. *Oostende & Co. Het Verhaal van de Zuid-Nederlandse Oost-Indiëvaart 1715–1735*. Ghent: Ludion, 2002.

Parmentier, Jan. 'De Deense Investeringen van de Moretus-Familie Tijdens de 18de Eeuw'. In *De Gulden Passer. Ex Officina Plantiniana Moretorum. Studies over het Drukkersgeslacth Moretus*, eds. Marcus de Schepper and Francine de Nave, 203–14. Antwerp: Vereeniging der Antwerpsche Bibliophielen, 1996.

Peabody, Robert. *The Log of the Grand Turks*. Boston: Houghton Mifflin Company, 1926.

Phillips, James Duncan. 'East India Voyages of Salem Vessels Before 1800'. *The Essex Institute Historical Collections*. Vol. 79. (April 1943): 117–132, (July 1943): 222–45, and (October 1943): 331–65.

Phillips, James Duncan. 'American Vessels Laying at Whampoa 1789–1790'. *The Essex Institute Historical Collections*. Vol. 80. (April 1944): 177–9.

Phillpotts, Lieut-Col. 'Demolition of Forts on the Canton River in 1847'. *Royal Engineer Professional Papers*, (1852): 93–4.

Pickowicz, Paul G. 'William Wood in Canton: A Critique of the China Trade before the Opium War'. *Essex Institute Historical Collections*. Vol. 107 (January 1971): 3–34.

Pires, Benjamim Videira S. J. *A Viagem de Comércio Macau-Manila nos Séculos XVI a XIX*. Centro de Estudos Marítimos de Macau, 1987; Reprint, Museu Marítimo de Macau, 1994.

Pires, Benjamim Videira S. J. *A Vida Marítima de Macau no Século XVIII*. Macao: Cultural Institute, 1993.

Polich, John Leo. 'John Kendrick and the Maritime Fur Trade on the Northwest Coast'. M.A. thesis, Department of History, University of Southern California, 1964.

Pritchard, Earl H. *Anglo-Chinese Relations During the Seventeenth and Eighteenth Centuries*. New York: Octagon Books, 1970.

Pritchard, Earl H. *The Crucial Years of Early Anglo-Chinese Relations 1750–1800*. 1936. Reprint, New York: Octagon Books, 1970.

Ptak, Roderich. 'Macau: Trade and Society, circa 1740–1760'. In *Maritime China in Transition 1750–1850*. Eds. Wang Gungwu and Ng Chin-keong. Wiesbaden: Harrassowitz Verlag, 2004: 191–211.

Ptak, Roderich. *China, the Portuguese, and the Nanyang*. Burlington, VT: Ashgate, 2004.

Quiason, Serafin. *English 'Country Trade' with the Philippines, 1644–1765*. Quezon City: University of Philippines Press, 1966.

Rasch, A. A. and P. P. Sveistrup. *Asiatisk Kompagni i den florissante periode 1772–1792*. Copenhagen: Gyldendalske Boghandel, 1948.

Raquez, A. *Au Pays des Pagodes. Notes de Voyage Hongkong, Macao, Shanghai, Le Houpé, Le Hounan, Le Kouei-tcheou*. Shanghai: La Presse Orientale, 1900.

Remmelink, William. *The Chinese War and the Collapse of the Javanese State, 1725–1743*. Leiden: KITLV Press, 1994.

Richards, Rhys. 'United States Trade with China, 1784–1814'. *The American Neptune* 54: Special Supplement (1994).

Rubinstein, Murray A. *The Origins of the Anglo-American Missionary Enterprise in China, 1807–1840*. London: Scarecrow Press, 1996.

Russel-Wood, A. J. R. 'An Asian Presence in the Atlantic Bullion Carrying Trade, 1710–50'. In *Portuguese Studies*, vol. 17 (2001): 148–67.

Saksena, Shalini. 'Parsi Contributions to the Growth of Bombay and Hong Kong', *Review of Culture*. International Edition. No. 10 (April 2004): 26–35.

Santos, Isaú and Lau Fong (劉芳). *Chapas Sínicas*. Portuguese edition. 漢文文書. Chinese edition. Macau: Cultural Institute, 1997.

Sargent, William and Margaret Palmer, comps. *Views of the Pearl River Delta. Macau, Canton and Hong Kong*. Salem: Peabody Essex Museum, 1997.

Schulz, Günther T. *Unter Segeln rund Kap Hoorn*. Hamburg: Bei Hans Dulk, 1954.

Scofield, John. *Hail, Columbia. Robert Gray, John Kendrick and the Pacific Fur Trade*. Portland: Oregon Historical Society, 1993.

Sena, Tereza. 'The Question of "Foreigners" Entering Macau in the 18th Century: Macau, a Metroplis of Equilibrium?'. In *Culture of Metropolis in Macau*, 159–76. Macau: Cultural Institute, 2001.

Sheaf, Colin and Richard Kilburn. *The Hatcher Porcelain Cargoes*. Oxford: Christie's Limited, 1988.

Singh, S. B. *European Agency Houses in Bengal*. Calcutta: Firma K. L. Mukhopadhyay, 1966.

Smith, Carl T. 'Armenian Strands in the Tangled Web of the Opium Trade at Macau and Canton'. Unpublished paper presented at the Hong Kong Historical Museum Conference, December 18–20, 1998.

Smith, Carl T. 'An Eighteenth-Century Macao Armenian Merchant Prince', *Review of Culture*, International Edition. No. 6 (April 2003): 120–9.

Smith, Carl T. 'Parsee Merchants in the Pearl River Delta'. *Review of Culture*, International Edition. No. 10 (April 2004): 36–49.

Smith, Carl T. and Paul A. Van Dyke, 'Armenian Footprints in Macau', *Review of Culture*, International Edition. No. 8 (October 2003): 20–39.

Smith, Carl T. and Paul A. Van Dyke, 'Four Armenian Families', *Review of Culture*, International Edition. No. 8 (October 2003): 40–50.

Smith, Carl T. and Paul A. Van Dyke, 'Muslims in the Pearl River Delta, 1700 to 1930', *Review of Culture*, International Edition. No. 10 (April 2004): 6–15.

Snyder, James Wilbert, Jr. 'A Bibliography for the Early American China Trade, 1784–1815'. *Americana* 34, no. 2 (April 1940): 3–51.

Sokoloff, Valentin A. *Ships of China*. Macau: Maritime Museum, 1982.

Sottas, Jules. *Histoire de la Compagnie Royale des Indes Orientales 1661–1719*. Paris: Plon-Nourrit et Cie, 1905.

Souza, George Bryan. *The Survival of Empire. Portuguese Trade and Society in China and the South China Sea, 1630–1754*. Cambridge: Cambridge University Press, 1986.

Souza, George Bryan. 'Country Trade and Chinese Alum: Raw Material Supply and Demand in Asia's Textile Production in the 17th and 18th Centuries'. *Review of Culture*, International Edition. No. 11 (July 2004): 136–53.

Spence, Jonathan. *The Question of Hu*. Random House, 1989.

Spence, Jonathan. *The Search for Modern China*. New York: W.W. Norton & Co., 1990.

Teixeira, P. Manuel. *Toponímia de Macau*, 2 vols. Macau: Cultural Institute, 1997.

Terrell, John Upton. *Furs by Astor*. New York: William Morrow & Co., 1963.

Thampi, Madhavi. 'Parsis in the China Trade', *Review of Culture*, International Edition. No. 10 (April 2004): 16–25.

T'ien Ju-k'ang. 'Impact of American Maritime Trade Upon China 1784–1844'. In *Global Crossroads and the American Seas*, ed. Clark G. Reynolds, 155–62. Missoula: Pictorial Histories Publishing Co., 1988.

Trocki, Carl A. *Opium, Empire and the Global Political Economy. A Study of the Asian Opium Trade 1750–1950*. London: Routledge, 1999.

Van der Kemp, P. H. *Oost-Indië's Geldmiddelen Japansche en Chineesche Handel van 1817 op 1818*. The Hague: Martinus Nijhoff, 1919.

Van der Putten, Frans-Paul. *Corporate Behaviour and Political Risk. Dutch Companies in China 1903–1941*. Leiden: Research School of Asian, African, and Amerindian Studies, 2001.

Vande Walle, W. F. and Noël Golvers, eds. *The History of the Relations Between the Low Countries and China in the Qing Era (1644–1911)*. Leuven: Leuven University Press, 2003.

Van Dyke, Paul A. 'Pigs, Chickens, and Lemonade: The Provisions Trade in Canton, 1700–1840'. *International Journal of Maritime History* (June 2000), 111–44. This article also appears in Chinese under the titles 'Zhu, Ji he Limonshui: Guangzhou de Buji Pin Jiaoyi' *Xueshu Yanjiu* (Academic Research) (December 2000), 62–81; and '1700–1840

Nianjian Guangzhou de Buji Pin Maoyi'. In *Guangzhou Shisan Hang Cangsang* (广州十三行沧桑 The Thirteen Hongs in Guangzhou). Eds., Zhang Wenqin (章文钦), et al, Guangzhou: Guangdong Ditu Chuban She (广东地图出版社), 2001: 287–320.

Van Dyke, Paul A. 'Port Canton and the Pearl River Delta, 1690–1845'. Ph.D. dissertation, Department of History, University of Southern California, 2002.

Van Dyke, Paul A. (范岱克). 'Cong Helan he Ruidian de Dang'an Kan Shiba Shiji 50 Niandai zhi 70 Niandai de Guangzhou Fan chuan Maoyi' (从荷兰和瑞典的档案看十八世纪50年代至70年代的广州帆船贸易 The Canton Junk Trade in the 1750s to 1770s as Revealed in the Dutch and Swedish Records) *Social Sciences in Guangdong* (广东社会科学), No. 4 (2002): 93–102.

Van Dyke, Paul A. 'The Anglo-Dutch Fleet of Defense (1620–1622): Prelude to the Dutch Occupation of Taiwan'. In *Around and about Formosa: Essays in honor of professor Ts'ao Yung-ho*. Edited by Leonard Blussé. Taipei : Ts'ao Yung-ho Foundation for Culture and Education, [Dist. SMC Publishing Inc., Taipei], 2003: pp. 61–81.

Van Dyke, Paul A. 'The Structure of the Canton Trade'. In *Sailing to the Pearl River*. Ed. by Cai Hongsheng and Leonard Blussé. Guangzhou: Guangzhou Chubanshe, 2004: 45–54.

Van Dyke, Paul A. 'A Reassessment of the China Trade: The Canton Junk Trade As Revealed in Dutch and Swedish Records of the 1750s to the 1770s'. In *Maritime China in Transition 1750–1850*. Eds. Wang Gungwu and Ng Chin-keong. Wiesbaden: Harrassowitz Verlag, 2004: 151–67.

Van Dyke, Paul A. 'The Yan Family: Merchants of Canton 1734–1780s'. *Review of Culture*. International Edition. No. 9 (January 2004): 30–85.

Van Dyke, Paul A. 'The Ye Merchants of Canton, 1720–1804'. *Review of Culture*, International Edition. No. 13 (January 2005): 6–47.

Van Dyke, Paul A. 'Cai and Qiu Enterprises: Merchants of Canton 1730–1784'. *Review of Culture*, International Edition, No. 15 (July 2005): 60–101.

Van Dyke, Paul A. 'Manila, Macao and Canton: The Ties that Bind', *Review of Culture*, International Edition, No. 18 (April 2006), 125–34.

Van Dyke, Paul A. 'The Ca Mau Shipwreck and the Canton Junk Trade', in *Made in Imperial China*, Amsterdam: Sotheby's (January 2007), 14–5.

Van Dyke, Paul A. 'China Tea and the Southeast Asian Tin Trade in the 18th Century', forthcoming.

Van Dyke, Paul A. and Cynthia Viallé. *The Canton-Macao Dagregisters*. 1762. Macao: Cultural Institute, 2006.

Van Dyke, Paul A. and Cynthia Viallé. *The Canton-Macao Dagregisters*. 1763. Macao: Cultural Institute, forthcoming.

Vargas, Philippe de. 'William C. Hunter's Books on the Old Canton Factories'. *Yenching Journal of Social Studies* (Peking, 1939). Reprint, under the title *An American in Canton (1825–44)*, Hong Kong: Derwent Communications Ltd., 1994.

Viraphol, Sarasin. *Tribute and Profit: Sino-Siamese Trade, 1652–1853*. Cambridge: Harvard University Press, 1977.

Vollmer, John E., E. J. Keall, and E. Nagai-Berthrong. *Silk Roads, China Ships*. Toronto: Royal Ontario Museum, 1983.

Wakeman, Frederic, Jr. 'The Canton Trade and the Opium War'. In *The Cambridge History of China*, eds. Denis Twitchett and John K. Fairbank. Vol. 10: 163–212. Cambridge: Cambridge University Press, 1978. Reprint, Taipei: Caves Books, 1986.

Wang Gungwu and Ng Chin-keong, eds. *Maritime China in Transition 1750–1850*. Wiesbaden: Harrassowitz Verlag, 2004.

Wei, Betty Peh-T'i. *Ruan Yuan, 1764–1849. The Life and Work of a Major Scholar-Official in Nineteenth-Century China before the Opium War*. Hong Kong: Hong Kong University Press, 2006.

White, Ann Bolbach. 'The Hong Merchants of Canton'. Ph.D. dissertation, Department of History, University of Pennsylvania, 1967.

Williams, C. A. S. *Manual of Chinese Products*. Beijing: Kwang Yuen Press, 1933.

Williams, Glyn. *The Prize of All the Oceans. Commodore Anson's Daring Voyage and Triumphant Capture of the Spanish Treasure Galleon*. New York: Penquin Books, 1999.

Wills, John E., Jr. *Pepper, Guns and Parleys. The Dutch East India Company and China, 1622–1681*. Cambridge: Harvard University Press, 1974.

Wills, John E., Jr. *Embassies and Illusions, Dutch and Portuguese Envoys to K'ang-hsi, 1666–1687*. Cambridge: Harvard University Press, 1984.

Wills, John E., Jr. 'Maritime China from Wang Chih to Shih Lang. Themes in Peripheral History'. In *From Ming to Ch'ing*, eds. Jonathan D. Spence and John E. Wills, Jr., 201–38. New Haven and London: Yale University Press, 1979.

Wills, John E., Jr. 'China's Farther Shores: Continuities and Changes in the Destination Ports of China's Foreign Trade, 1680–1690'. In *Emporia, Commodities and Entrepreneurs in Asian Maritime Trade, c. 1400–1750*, eds. Roderick Ptak and Dietmar Rothermund, 53–77. Beitrage zur Sudasienforschung, Sudasien-Institut, Universitat Heidelberg, no. 141. Stuttgart: Franz Steiner, 1991.

Wills, John E., Jr. 'Maritime Asia, 1500–1800: The Interactive Emergence of European Domination'. *American Historical Review* 98, no. 1 (February, 1993): 83–105.

Wills, John E., Jr. 'Merchants, Brokers, Pioneers, Biculturals: Human Types in the Early Modern History of Maritime China, c. 1550–1850'. Paper for special regional seminar on 'Greater China', University of California, Berkeley, February, 1993.

Wills, John E., Jr. '"Very Unhandsome Chops": The Canton System Closes In, 1740–1771'. In *Tradition and Metamorphosis in Modern Chinese History. Essays in Honor of Professor Kwang-Ching Liu's Seventy-fifth Birthday*. Taipei: Academia Sinica, 1998.

Wilson, Dick A. 'King George's Men: British Ships and Sailors in the Pacific Northwest-China Trade, 1785–1821'. Ph.D. dissertation, Department of History, University of Idaho, 2004.

Wirgin, Jan. *Från Kina till Europa. Kinesiska konstföremål från ostindiska kompaniernas tid*. Stockholm: Östasiatiska Museet, 1998.

Woodhouse, Samuel W. 'The Voyage of the *Empress of China*'. *The Pennsylvania Magazine of History and Biography*. Vol. 63. Philadelphia: The Historical Society of Pennsylvania, 1939.

Yule, Henry and A. C. Burnell. *Hobson-Jobson. A Glossary of Colloquial Anglo Indian Words and Phrases, and of Kindred terms, Etymological, Historical, Geographical and Discursive*. 1886. Reprint, New Delhi: Rupa & Co., 1994.

Zhang Wenqin (章文钦) et al, eds. *Guangzhou Shisan Hang Cangsang* (广州十三行沧桑 The Thirteen Hongs in Guangzhou). Guangzhou: Guangdong Ditu Chuban She (广东地图出版社), 2001.

Zheng Yangwen. *The Social Life of Opium in China*. Cambridge: Cambridge University Press, 2005.

Zhou Xiang (周湘). 'Qingdai Guangzhou yu Maopi Maoyi' (清代广州与毛皮贸易 Guangzhou and the Maritime Fur Trade in Qing Dynasty). Ph.D. dissertation, Department of History, Zhongshan University, 1999.

Zhu Xiaodan (朱小丹). *Zhongguo Guangzhou Zhong Rui Haishang Maoyi de Menhu* (中国广州海上贸易的门户 Guangzhou China. Gateway of Sino-Sweden Marine Trade). Guangzhou: Guangzhou Chuban She (广州出版社), 2002.

Zhuang Guotu. *Tea, Silver, Opium and War: The International Tea Trade and Western Commercial Expansion into China in 1740–1840*. Xiamen: Xiamen Univeristy Press, 1993.

INDEX